The American Heart Association Cookbook

The American Heart

DAVID McKAY COMPANY, INC.

NEW AND EXPANDED EDITION

Association Cookbook

*Recipes selected, compiled, and tested
under the direction of Ruthe Eshleman
and Mary Winston, Nutritionists
of the American Heart Association*

Illustrations by Tonia Hampson

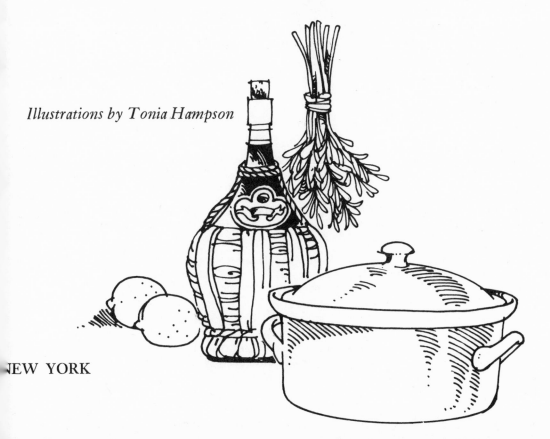

NEW YORK

Recipe numbers 23 and 24 in the Bread section are reprinted with the permission of Clive M. and Jeanette B. McCay.

Recipe numbers 6, 7, 8, 9, 11, 12, 13, in the Vegetarian section and recipe number 13 in the Breakfast section originally appeared in *Diet for a Small Planet* by Frances Moore Lappe. Copyright © 1971, A Friends of the Earth/Ballantine Book

Recipe numbers 9 and 10 in the Pork section and number 10 in the Veal section originally appeared in *Foods of the World, The Cooking of Italy* by Waverly Root and the Editors of Time-Life Books. Copyright © 1968, Time, Inc.

Recipe number 9 in the Lamb section originally appeared in *The New York Times Cookbook* by Craig Claiborne. Copyright © 1961 by Craig Claiborne. Reprinted by permission of Harper & Row Publishers, Inc.

10   9   8   7

ISBN: 0-679-50582-2
Library of Congress Catalog Card Number: 75-21859
Manufactured in the United States of America

Eating is one of life's great pleasures. And the wrong kinds of food can be as tasty as the right kinds. Although diets are drudgery, each of us, whether we like it or not, *is* on a diet. For better or worse, simply by eating the same things day after day, we maintain diet habits that affect our lives. This book is dedicated to the pleasures of eating well while eating right.

Medical research has shown that too many fatty foods can be damaging to the heart and blood vessel system. This is true for persons of ideal weight as well as for thin and fat persons, although overweight may bring a high risk of cardiovascular disease. When we speak of risk, we are really speaking in a group sense, since it is impossible to predict the individual's body response. Furthermore, dietary intake of fat is only one of the factors linked with the catastrophic rise in heart and blood vessel diseases. But it is one factor that we ourselves can do something about.

In these pages you will find some basic advice on how to plan daily menus for healthy living, and how to prepare fat-controlled meals, combining them for full nutritional benefit and abundant eating enjoyment. To aid those who need to watch their weight, the approximate caloric value per serving is included with each recipe.

This is not a diet book. It is a cookbook—a fun book for people who like to cook and to eat, whether they are young or old, living alone or in a family group, pursuing a career or busily involved in keeping a home. But the recipes contained herein and the recommendations for a prudent diet on page XVL will make it easier for you to follow the American Heart Association's eating plan.

We offer these recipes from personal files in kitchens across the country, wherever Heart Association Affiliates or Chapters are located. Volunteer workers and staff members, laymen and physicians, dietitians and nutritionists—all have contributed their favorites.

This is our way of demonstrating that eating well can be an adventure in healthy living, as much for the healthy person as for one who suffers from cardiovascular disease.

RICHARD E. HURLEY, M.D.
Deputy Vice-President
Office of Medical Programs
American Heart Association

The recipes for this cookbook have been selected from thousands submitted by friends, volunteers, and nutritionists of the American Heart Association and its Affiliates and Chapters across the country. The American Heart Association carries on programs through the fifty-five Affiliates listed below and their Chapters, divisions, and units.

Alabama Heart Association
Birmingham, Alabama

Alaska Heart Association
Anchorage, Alaska

American Heart Association
Arizona Affiliate
Phoenix, Arizona

Arkansas Heart Association
Little Rock, Arkansas

American Heart Association
California Affiliate
San Francisco, California

Chicago Heart Association
Chicago, Illinois

Colorado Heart Association
Denver, Colorado

Connecticut Heart Association
Hartford, Connecticut

American Heart Association
Dakota Affiliate
Jamestown, North Dakota

Delaware Heart Association
Wilmington, Delaware

Florida Heart Association
St. Petersburg, Florida

Georgia Heart Association
Atlanta, Georgia

American Heart Association
of Hawaii
Honolulu, Hawaii

Idaho Heart Association
Boise, Idaho

Illinois Heart Association
Springfield, Illinois

American Heart Association
Indiana Affiliate
Indianapolis, Indiana

Iowa Heart Association
Des Moines, Iowa

Kansas Heart Association
Topeka, Kansas

Kentucky Heart Association
Louisville, Kentucky

American Heart Association
Greater Los Angeles Affiliate
Los Angeles, California

American Heart Association
Louisiana , Inc.
New Orleans, Louisiana

Maine Heart Association
Augusta, Maine

American Heart Association
Maryland Affiliate
Baltimore, Maryland

American Heart Association
Massachusetts Affiliate
Boston, Massachusetts

Michigan Heart Association
Southfield, Michigan

Minnesota Heart Association
Minneapolis, Minnesota

Mississippi Heart Association
Jackson, Mississippi

Missouri Heart Association
Columbia, Missouri

Montana Heart Association
Great Falls, Montana

Nebraska Heart Association
Omaha, Nebraska

Nevada Heart Association
Reno, Nevada

New Hampshire Heart
Association
Concord, New Hampshire

American Heart Association
New Jersey Affiliate
Union, New Jersey

New Mexico Heart Association
Albuquerque, New Mexico

American Heart Association
New York State Affiliate
New York, N.Y.

New York Heart Association
New York, N.Y.

North Carolina Heart Association
Chapel Hill, North Carolina

American Heart Association
Northeast Ohio Affiliate
Cleveland, Ohio

American Heart Association
Ohio Affiliate
Columbus, Ohio

Oklahoma Heart Association
Oklahoma City, Oklahoma

Oregon Heart Association
Portland, Oregon

American Heart Association
Pennsylvania Affiliate
Harrisburg, Pennsylvania

Puerto Rico Heart Association
Santurce, Puerto Rico

Rhode Island Heart Association
Pawtucket, Rhode Island

South Carolina Heart Association
Columbia, South Carolina

Tennessee Heart Association
Nashville, Tennessee

American Heart Association
Texas Affiliate, Inc.
Austin, Texas

Utah Heart Association
Salt Lake City, Utah

Vermont Heart Association
Rutland, Vermont

American Heart Association
Virginia Affiliate
Richmond, Virginia

Washington, D.C. Heart
Association
Washington, D.C.

Washington State Heart
Association
Seattle, Washington

American Heart Association
West Virginia Affiliate
Charleston, West Virginia

Wisconsin Heart Association
Milwaukee, Wisconsin

Wyoming Heart Association
Cheyenne, Wyoming

Preface

This second edition of the American Heart Association Cookbook represents a response to the needs of individuals who are seeking not only to eliminate excess fat and sugar in their diets, but who also have a sincere desire to maintain their proper weight. As part of this increased emphasis on weight control, each recipe has been revised to include *approximate* caloric value per serving. And more than fifteen new recipes for meatless or vegetarian meals have been added. An all new section, "Lunch Box," has been included to offer tips on carrying food for eating away from home; and the section "When You Eat Out," for when you do not bring your own, has been enlarged.

In short, this revised edition of this important and valuable cookbook is even better than before, combining healthful cooking and shopping tips with new and expanded information on weight control. It offers a most palatable means of taking some of the fat and sugar out of your diet while leaving the spice intact.

Contents

> *Jack Sprat could eat no fat*
> *His wife could eat no lean*
> *And so betwixt the two of them*
> *They licked the platter clean.*

Favorite foods don't get to be favorites by accident. You like what you like for reasons of comfort, habit, convenience or because of memories that have stayed with you from childhood. What you eat is part of your way of living, and life-styles can differ as widely as those of Jack and his wife.

But your body knows nothing about life-styles. Your body's job is to keep you going by making use of certain elements in the foods you eat. Elements it does not need are processed too, but then they must be thrown off or stored somewhere.

Fats are necessary, but excessive amounts can cause problems. The body handles fat in several ways: by burning it to produce energy, by storing it in the tissues, or by silting it in the form of cholesterol along the walls of the arteries, the blood vessels that carry food and oxygen to all parts of the body. The silting of fats is part of the process called atherosclerosis, from the Greek "athero," meaning gruel or paste, and "sclerosis" (hardness). When atherosclerosis occurs, cholesterol is actually deposited in the artery walls.

Scientists have shown that when there is too much cholesterol in the blood, it is more likely to start piling up along the artery walls, in much the same way that silt being carried along by a river is dropped at certain points, causing the riverbed to build up and the channel to become narrower. Thus, people with high blood cholesterol levels are more likely to have heart attacks or strokes caused by blockages in arteries already narrowed by atherosclerosis.

Cholesterol is a waxy material that is actually essential to health. The body manufactures it for use in many chemical processes. But cholesterol is also present in foods of animal origin (egg yolks, meats and poultry), in foods made from animal products (whole milk, cream cheese, butter), and in fish. Atherosclerosis may be a sign that the body has been getting too much of a good thing.

Control of cholesterol and other fatty substances in the blood is not feasible when an individual is extremely overweight. In fact, it has been shown that life expectancy may be shorter for people who are markedly over their ideal weight. Middle-aged men who fall into this category, for example, have about three times the risk of a fatal heart attack compared with middle-aged men of ideal weight.

Most people reach their normal weight between the ages of twenty-one and twenty-five. With each added year, fewer calories are needed to maintain this normal weight. But people in their thirties and forties usually eat as much as they did in their early twenties, become physically less active, and store their excess calories as fat.

There is no quick, easy way to reduce your weight. Weight control requires a healthy balance between caloric intake (food consumption) and caloric expenditure (physical exertion). It is best to avoid extreme reducing diets, because they usually leave out foods essential to good health. Even when such diets are successful in bringing your weight down, they do not help you to develop a pattern of eating that will keep your weight under control.

Before embarking on a weight reduction program, ask your doctor or nutritionist to advise you. They are the best judges of how many calories you require each day to maintain good health while lowering your weight. The basic daily food pattern outlined on page xvi contains approximately 1200 calories, but may be altered to suit individual needs.

The caloric values of the majority of entrée recipes in this cookbook have been calculated on the basis of a 3-oz. serving of protein. There are some exceptions. In a few of the casserole dishes, the caloric values have been based on a 2-oz. serving of protein. To add variety and flavor and reduce caloric intake, vegetables may be seasoned with some of the daily margarine or oil allowance. For flavor enhancement, experiment with spices and herbs. Fresh or unsweetened fruit should also be used.

Some individuals may have high levels of "triglycerides" in their bloodstreams. Triglycerides are fatty substances found in foods and also manufactured by our bodies from excess sugar and alcohol. Sugar in both solid and liquid form is found in foods and beverages such as honey, syrup, jam and preserves, sweetened cereals and desserts, candy and pastries, and sweetened carbonated soft drinks. In some individuals, alcohol may or may not contribute to increased levels of triglycerides in the blood.

Increased amounts of triglycerides in the bloodstream can hasten the development of atherosclerosis. This disease process occurs more readily in overweight individuals. Consequently, a fat-modified, calorically controlled diet is frequently an effective treatment for this condition. Certain people of normal weight may also harbor high levels of blood triglycerides, and they are usually also advised to follow a diet plan restricted in sugar and fat.

Although the question of sodium consumption is important to many persons, we have not attempted to incorporate low-sodium dishes with fat-modified ones, since the dietary issues are separate and distinct. Thus, the sodium-restricted diet is not the subject of this book.*

Current scientific information suggests that it is prudent to avoid excess salt in the diet. For most people, this means simply not using salt at the table, minimizing intake of salty snacks and foods cured with salt or preserved in brine, and halving the amount of salt, MSG and soy sauce normally used in cooking. Although table salt and sodium are not the same thing, table salt is nearly 50 percent sodium. Individuals with established hypertension, congestive heart failure, or edema should consult their physician to determine their level of sodium restriction.

The problems of sodium restriction and high levels of blood triglycerides are better left to you and your physician. How to avoid the excess fats, maintain your proper weight, and, at the same time, enjoy a savory diet are the subjects of this cookbook.

* *For more information on the sodium-restricted diet, contact your local Heart Association.*

Today, in the United States, about 40 to 45 percent of the average daily caloric intake is fat. Think of it—nearly half the calories you eat. The aim of fat-control is to cut that percentage to 30 to 35 percent, about a 10 percent reduction for the normal person.

It is not surprising therefore that a fat-controlled cookbook differs very little from an ordinary cookbook. There are appetizers, interesting vegetarian dishes, stews, steaks, desserts, and delectable vegetable and salad combinations.

All of the recipes in this book have been carefully tested and standardized in their use of ingredients. Where a recipe calls for *"oil"* without specifying the kind, it means *polyunsaturated oil*. Where the term *"margarine"* appears, it specifically means a margarine *high in polyunsaturates*.

The dishes on the following pages all have nutritive value. This is an important point. Many of the calories absorbed by people today have little or no nutritive value, so a high-calorie diet is not necessarily a nutritious one. Not uncommonly, nutritional deficiencies are found in persons who eat large amounts of rich foods.

To understand something about nutrition, it is necessary to think of food in terms of average servings. None of us is average, but if we were, the following list would cover our nutritional needs, except perhaps for calories (caloric needs vary with the individual and with varied physical activity).

Average daily nutritional needs:

2 CUPS OF LOW-FAT MILK OR LOW-FAT MILK PRODUCTS

6 OUNCES OF LEAN MEAT (INCLUDING FISH, POULTRY, BEEF OR THE EQUIVALENT IN VEGETABLE PROTEIN SUCH AS BEANS)

2 CUPS OR MORE OF VEGETABLE AND FRUIT ITEMS (SOME DARK GREEN AND SOME BRIGHT YELLOW)

4 OR MORE SERVINGS OF WHOLE GRAIN OR ENRICHED BREADS OR CEREALS (ONE SERVING IS 1 SLICE OF BREAD, OR 1 CUP OF COLD CEREAL OR ½ CUP OF COOKED CEREAL)

2 TO 4 TABLESPOONS OF POLYUNSATURATED FATS OR OILS

The average person who eats these foods will get essential food elements: protein, carbohydrate, calories, minerals, vitamins, water and even fat.

But what an unappetizing list! Eating is more fun than that. Let's leave the drab Land of Average and translate this nutritional grocery list into food that tempts the appetite, delights the eye and helps make life interesting. There is a touch of elegance in this meal plan:

· · · · · · · · · · · · · · · *Breakfast*

FRESH STRAWBERRIES—1 CUP = 40 CALORIES

WHEAT GERM PANCAKES*—2 PANCAKES = 230

MAPLE SYRUP OR PRESERVES OR COTTAGE CHEESE—

   1 TABLESPOON SYRUP, PRESERVES = 60

   1 CUP UNCREAMED COTTAGE CHEESE = 85

LOW-FAT MILK—1 CUP = 90

COFFEE OR TEA

APPROX. CAL/SERV.: 420 OR 445 WITH COTTAGE CHEESE

· · · · · · · · · · · · · · · *Lunch*

NEW ENGLAND FISH CHOWDER*—1 CUP = 175 CALORIES

RAW VEGETABLE PLATTER*

CURRY-YOGURT DIP*—2 TABLESPOONS = 50

WHOLE WHEAT MUFFIN*—1 MUFFIN = 175

LEMON SHERBET*—½ CUP = 150

APPROX. CAL/SERV.: 550

· · · · · · · · · · · · · · · *Appetizers*

TUNA-DILL PÂTÉ*—2 TABLESPOONS = 20 CALORIES

GARLIC RYE TOASTIES*—2 TOASTIES = 70

YOUR FAVORITE BEVERAGE—115

APPROX. CAL/SERV.: 205

* *Recipes included in this book.*

. . . . *Dinner*

JULEP LAMB CHOP PLATTER*—325 CALORIES
PANNED BROCCOLI*—4 OUNCES = 95
BAKED GRATED CARROTS*—½ CUP = 65
SPINACH-AVOCADO-ORANGE TOSS*—1 CUP = 170
HERBED BISCUITS*—1 BISCUIT = 120
APPLE PIE*—⅛ = 345
APPROX. CAL/SERV.: 1120

For the young snacker whose flight pattern sends him by the family table at high speed, here is a daily piecemeal plan that is nutritious and low in fat:

. . . . *Breakfast*

CHILLED GRAPEFRUIT JUICE—¼ CUP = 40 CALORIES
COTTAGE CHEESE AND CINNAMON TOAST*—1 SLICE = 115
LOW-FAT MILK—1 CUP = 90
APPROX. CAL/SERV.: 245

. . . . *Snack (1)*

CRUNCHY CEREAL*—⅓ cup = 210 calories
LOW-FAT MILK—1 CUP = 90
BANANA—1 SMALL = 80
APPROX. CAL/SERV.: 380

. . . . *Lunch*

TUNA SALAD SANDWICH ON WHOLE WHEAT PITA BREAD*—295 CALORIES
RAW VEGETABLE PLATTER*
RAISIN OATMEAL COOKIES*—2 COOKIES = 140
LOW-FAT MILK—1 CUP = 90
APPROX. CAL/SERV.: 525

* Recipes included in this book.

. . . . *Supper*

COMPLEMENTARY PIZZA*—¼ PIZZA = 220 CALORIES
ANY BEAN SALAD*—½ CUP = 135
FRESH FRUIT BOWL—½ CUP = 40
APPROX. CAL/SERV.: 395

. . . . *Snack (2)*

PEANUT BUTTER ON WHOLE WHEAT BREAD—330 CALORIES
APPLE PIE*—⅛ SLICE = 345
LOW-FAT MILK—1 CUP = 90
APPROX. CAL/SERV.: 765

Each of these menus differs markedly from the other, but each is fat-controlled. This means that the foods are chosen for their fat content, then prepared in a way that tends to remove any remaining undesirable fats while using polyunsaturated fats in the cooking.

Polyunsaturated, monounsaturated, saturated—just so many words until their part in the total chemical plan is clear. Simply it is this.

Polyunsaturated fats are those that tend to help the body get rid of newly formed cholesterol and thereby keep the blood cholesterol level down and reduce cholesterol deposition in the arterial walls. Some of the world's great cooking oils—safflower, soybean, corn, cottonseed, and sesame seed—have this property. As liquid vegetable oils, they have the highest concentrations of polyunsaturated fatty acids and no cholesterol.

Olive and peanut oils are also liquid and of vegetable origin, but they contain largely monounsaturated fatty acids and not the beneficial polyunsaturated ones. They do not contain cholesterol, but neither do they have a cholesterol-lowering action.

On the other hand, foods high in saturated fats tend to elevate the cholesterol concentration in the blood and frequently contain cholesterol itself. These include meat, lard, and butter, all high in fats of animal origin.

The body can use all three types of fats, but the average person should control fat intake to constitute not more than 35 percent of total

* Recipes included in this book.

calories. Of that amount, less than 10 percent of the total calories should come from saturated fatty acids and up to 10 percent of total calories from polyunsaturated fatty acids to enhance the cholesterol-lowering process. When these proportions are achieved, the remainder of the ingested fat is derived from monounsaturated sources.

Although the major portion of the body's cholesterol is made in the body, dietary cholesterol is a substantial contributor. Therefore, it is recommended that the average daily intake of cholesterol be approximately 300 mg.

As you can see in the chart on page 436, one large egg yolk has 250 mg. of cholesterol. This is why the recipes in this book limit the use of egg yolk. We also speak of fat-controlled rather than fat-free eating. No one type of fat should be consumed in excess, but neither should any one type be entirely removed from the diet. For example, even if it were possible to remove all saturated fats, this would be neither necessary nor desirable. By lowering total fat intake and substituting polyunsaturated fat for a portion of the saturated kind, you are helping your body work to its own advantage.

How do you know that you are correctly controlling animal fat and cholesterol intake? Although there are some individuals with inherited metabolic patterns that require very special diets, these can be prescribed only after special studies of their body chemistry. For most of us, if we follow these suggestions, we'll be on the right track.

1. Maintain a body weight that is right for you by controlling total calories. Overweight usually results from eating too much food, which naturally means eating more fats as well.

2. Eat foods that will satisfy daily needs for protein, vitamins, minerals, and other nutrients.

3. Avoid eating excessive amounts of food containing saturated fat. For example, eat fish, chicken, turkey and veal more often than beef, lamb, pork and ham. Substitute vegetable protein combinations such as dried beans and rice for meat or combine them with chicken, fish or leftover meat.

4. Control your intake of cholesterol-rich food. Eat no more than three egg yolks a week, and don't forget to count the ones used

in bakery goods. Limit shrimp, which are moderately high, and organ meats, which are high in cholesterol.

5. Use 2 to 4 tablespoons a day of polyunsaturated oil or margarine.

These steps will help lower the amount of cholesterol and saturated fats entering your system. At the same time, the polyunsaturated fats will do you a favor by helping to lower serum cholesterol.

Enough of rules! Now that we know what they are, let's move on to the best part of food—cooking and eating it. On the following pages, you will find some savory dishes and a new life-style in fat-controlled cookery. If you thought eating had to be dull to be fat-controlled, there are surprises in such dishes as beef bourguignon, paupiettes de veau, tomatoes Rockefeller, and for dessert fresh strawberry pie, fresh fruit compote with kirsch or lemon fluff pudding. Bring variety to your table. Every meal will be filled with tasty dishes for a long and healthy life.

Acknowledgments

DEPUTY VICE-PRESIDENT,
OFFICE OF MEDICAL PROGRAMS   Richard E. Hurley, M.D.

EDITORS   Ruthe Eshlenian and Mary Winston, Nutritionists
of the American Heart Association

CONTRIBUTING EDITORS   Karen Soderquist
Diane Farmakis

RECIPE TESTING   Leona M. Weitz Test Kitchen

ARTIST   Tonia Hampson

This cookbook is the result of the devoted efforts of many people, including our Affiliates and friends who contributed the recipes and the members of the tasting panels—children and adults who evaluated them. The editors wish to express their appreciation to the members of AHA's Nutrition Committee and Subcommittee of Dietitians and Nutritionists for their consultation and continued support during the gestation period of this book. Our special thanks to AHA Executive Vice-President William W. Moore for his encouragement and support. Special thanks also to the chairmen of the committees: René Bine, Jr., M.D.; John Mueller,

M.D.; Robert Shank, M.D.; Eleanor Williams, Ph.D.; Virginia Stucky; and Marilyn Farrand.

Our gratitude to Campbell Moses, M.D., former medical director of AHA, for his leadership, guidance and sense of humor. Special thanks to Richard E. Hurley, M.D., Deputy Vice-President, Office of Medical Programs, and to Central Office staff members Ezra Lamdin, M.D., and Kenneth Lane, M.D., for their constructive criticism and assistance, to J. Keith Thwaites, John Gould, Placide Schriever, Margaret Reynolds and Sylvia Fung Chin, who were always there when needed, and to Sarah Kamp who was always helpful.

For their help in the development and testing of new recipes, we wish to acknowledge Teresa Shaffer, Gary Miller, Ph.D., and Hazel Fox, Ph.D., and the students at the University of Nebraska at Lincoln who assisted them in this project. Our thanks to UNL students Colleen Crone-Rohan and Marian Cast for calculating the caloric value per serving of each recipe.

Our deep appreciation goes to Raffaela Coppeto for her untiring efforts in assembling the original manuscript.

—R.E.
—M.W.

Table of Equivalents

Dash	=	2–4 drops		
3 teaspoons	=	1 tablespoon	=	½ fluid ounce
4 tablespoons	=	¼ cup	=	2 fluid ounces
16 tablespoons	=	1 cup (½ pint)	=	8 fluid ounces
2 cups	=	1 pint	=	16 fluid ounces
2 pints	=	1 quart	=	32 fluid ounces
4 quarts	=	1 gallon	=	128 fluid ounces
2 tablespoons	=	1 ounce	=	⅛ cup
4 tablespoons	=	2 ounces	=	¼ cup
16 tablespoons	=	8 ounces	=	1 cup
2 cups	=	16 ounces	=	1 pound

• • • • • • • • • • • • *Beans*

	DRIED			COOKED
Kidney	1 pound	(1½ cups)	=	9 cups
Lima beans	1 pound	(2⅓ cups)	=	6 cups
Navy	1 pound	(2⅓ cups)	=	6 cups
Soybeans	1 pound	(2 cups)	=	6 cups

Rice, Wheat and Pasta

		DRIED		COOKED
Rice	1 pound	(2 cups uncooked)	=	6 cups
Macaroni	1 pound	(4 cups uncooked)	=	8 cups
Spaghetti	1 pound	(5 cups uncooked)	=	9–10 cups
Bulgur	1 pound	(2 cups uncooked)	=	6 cups

Cheese for Grating

1 pound = 4 cups

Flour

Enriched white	1 pound	=	4 cups sifted
Enriched cake	1 pound	=	4½ cups sifted
Whole wheat	1 pound	=	3½ cups sifted
Whole wheat pastry	1 pound	=	4 cups sifted

1. Make a shopping list and plan meals for the week, using the nutritional guide on page xvi. This saves time at the store and cuts down on impulse buying. Take advantage of special sales only if you need that particular item. Shopping wisely can mean considerable savings.

2. Eat before shopping. If you go to the store hungry, you are likely to make unnecessary purchases.

3. Consider store brands. They are usually less costly than national brands.

4. Buy lean meats, fish, chicken, turkey and veal more often than beef, lamb, pork and ham, which contain more fat and consequently less meat per pound. Use chicken breasts in recipes that call for veal steaks or cutlets. Restrict your use of luncheon and variety meats such as sausage, salami, frankfurters and liverwurst, all of which have a high fat content.

5. Buy dried beans, peas, lentils and legumes and use these sources of vegetable protein in the many tasty recipes available in the Vegetarian section of this cookbook.

6. When choosing hamburger, look for the medium-to-deep color that signifies a low fat content (a light pink color is a warning that excess fat has been ground in with the meat). Or buy ground round, which is usually very lean. Better yet, select a well-trimmed piece of steak, lean stewing beef or lean chuck roast, a cut that is easier on the budget, and ask the butcher to grind it for you or grind it yourself at home.

7. Buy polyunsaturated vegetable oils and use them for cooking. Safflower oil is the most polyunsaturated with soybean, sunflower, corn, cottonseed and sesame oils following in descending order. Where a brand name does not specify the type of oil, read the fine print. Some oils now on the market are mixtures and you should know what you are buying. Olive oil and peanut oil are primarily monounsaturated. They may be used in small amounts for seasoning, but they do not have the cholesterol-lowering properties of the polyunsaturates.

8. Read the label before selecting a brand of margarine. The product that is high in polyunsaturates lists a recommended *liquid* vegetable oil (see Shopping Tip 7.) as the first ingredient, followed by one or more partially hydrogenated vegetable oils. If the first ingredient on the list is *liquid* oil, the margarine is preferred. Some hydrogenation reduces the polyunsaturated nature of the product, transforming it into a saturated one. Tub margarines tend to be more polyunsaturated than stick margarines, since they are not required to hold stick form. Diet margarines contain water and provide half the amount of fat found in recommended polyunsaturated margarines and, consequently, must be labeled "imita-

tion." They are usable for seasoning or as spreads but are not desirable for cooking because of their high water content.

9. Read labels on packaged foods. Do not be misled by obvious ambiguity. "Vegetable fat" or "vegetable oil" in a list of ingredients frequently means *saturated* vegetable fat, such as coconut oil or palm kernel, which are not high in polyunsaturated fat. Be particularly careful to read the label when shopping for nondairy coffee creamers since they often list "vegetable fat" or "vegetable oil" as an ingredient. Remember, when reading labels, that all food processors must list ingredients in the order in which they predominate—in other words, in decreasing order according to their weight present in the product. For example, a label that lists, "Gravy, beef, carrots, salt" contains more gravy than anything else. Nutrition information listed is per serving. The label gives the size of the serving, such as one cup or three ounces, and tells how many servings are in the container. Calories are then listed followed by the amounts in grams of protein, carbohydrate and fat. Protein is listed twice, in grams and as a percentage of the U.S. Recommended Daily Allowance. The U.S. Recommended Daily Allowances (U.S. RDA) are the amounts of protein, vitamins and minerals that an adult should eat every day to remain healthy. Seven vitamins and minerals must be shown, in the same order, on all nutrition labels. Other vitamins and minerals may also be listed. The listing of cholesterol, fatty acid and sodium content is optional.

10. Select fat-free or low-fat dairy products: skim milk, low-fat milk, evaporated skim milk, nonfat dry milk and buttermilk made from skim milk are all acceptable. Cheeses made from skim milk are low in fat and high in protein. These include dry cottage cheese, farmer's cheese and pot cheese. Parmesan cheese, ricotta, mozzarella, Port du Salut, or other cheeses made from partially skimmed milk may be used in small amounts.

11. Butter rolls, commercial biscuits, muffins, doughnuts, egg bread, cheese bread, sweet rolls, cakes or commercial mixes are unacceptable if they contain dried egg yolks or whole milk. Any

kind of packaged or prepared food that contains *no fat at all* and is otherwise allowed on your diet is all right for you to buy. Examples are vegetarian baked beans and angel food cake mix. (Regular cake mixes, on the other hand, are not allowed.)

12. Convenience foods—those premixed, packaged, frozen, dehydrated and crystallized "instant" edibles—may prove to be very inconvenient for fat-controlled eating. Read labels carefully to be certain you are not buying a product rich in saturated fat. The following pointers will be helpful as a general shopping guide to convenience foods. Packaged or prepared foods *with* fat may be used only if the fat is one allowed on your diet. (You may use sardines packed in cottonseed or soybean oil, for example.) Avoid items such as packaged popcorn, potato chips and French fried potatoes. Do not buy frozen dinners or other ready-to-eat canned or frozen food mixtures that contain fat, since you usually cannot tell what kind of fat was used or how much. Dehydrated foods, such as potatoes, and mixes to which you add the fat yourself, such as pancake mixes, are usually all right. Read the labels to be sure the product does not contain any fat. For true convenience, no commercial product can equal nature's own fresh fruits and raw vegetables—the potato that bakes in its own jacket, the apple that needs only washing.

Beef

ROUND STEAK

- look for round (leg) bone
- a less tender cut—cook with moist heat
- *very lean* beef

RUMP ROAST

- look for split surface of the pelvic bone—may often contain the tail bone (often sold as a boneless, rolled roast)
- a less tender cut—cook with moist heat
- *lean* beef

FLANK STEAK

- a boneless cut, muscles run lengthwise, usually scored to increase tenderness
- a less tender cut—cook with moist heat
- *very lean* beef

SIRLOIN TIP ROAST

- a boneless roast from the section adjoining the flank area
- a less tender cut—cook with moist heat
- *very lean* beef

BEEF LOIN
and
CHUCK SECTIONS

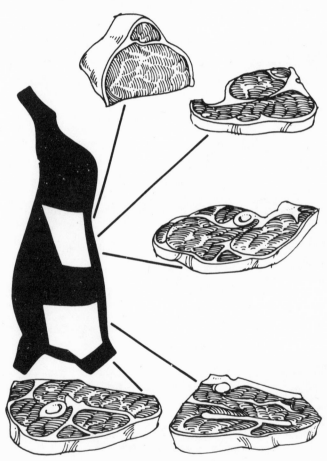

PORTERHOUSE (T-BONE) STEAK

- look for T-shaped backbone
- a tender cut—cook with dry heat
- *lean* beef

SIRLOIN STEAK

- look for cross section of pel (hip) bone
- a tender cut—cook with dry heat
- *lean* beef

BLADE POT ROAST

- look for blade (shoulder) bone parts of rib bone
- a less tender cut—cook with m heat
- *medium lean* beef

ARM POT ROAST

- look for round (arm) bone—may also contain cross section of rib bones
- a less tender cut—cook with moist heat
- *very lean* beef

Pork

PORK LOIN
and
HAM SECTIONS

CENTER HAM SLICE

- look for round (leg) bone
- a tender cut—cook with dry heat
- *lean* meat

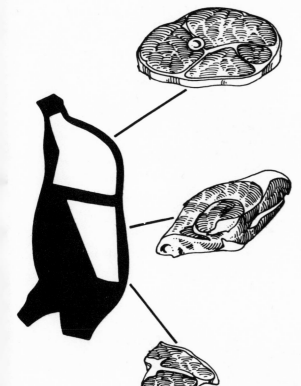

SIRLOIN ROAST

- look for T-shaped backbone and cross section of hip bone
- a tender cut—cook with dry heat
- *medium lean* meat

LOIN CHOP

- look for T-shaped backbone
- a tender cut—cook with dry heat (use moist heat for thin chops)
- *medium lean* meat

Lamb

LEG OF LAMB ROAST

- look for round (leg) bone
- a tender cut—cook with dry heat
- *very lean* meat

LAMB SHOULDER, LOIN and LEG SECTIONS

LEG CHOP (STEAK)

- look for round (leg) bone
- a tender cut—cook with dry heat
- *very lean* meat

LOIN CHOPS

- look for T-shaped backbone
- a tender cut—cook with dry heat
- *lean meat*

SIRLOIN CHOP

- look for pelvic (hip) bone
- a tender cut—cook with dry heat
- *very lean* meat

ARM CHOP

- look for round (arm) bone—may often contain cross section of rib bone
- a tender cut—cook with dry heat
- *lean* meat

Veal

**VEAL SHOULDER,
RIB, LOIN,
and
LEG SECTIONS**

VEAL CUTLET
(Round Steak)

- look for round (leg) bone
- a less tender cut—cook with moist heat
- *very lean* meat

LOIN CHOP

- look for T-shaped backbone
- a less tender cut—cook with moist heat
- *very lean* meat

RIB CHOP

- look for rib bone
- a less tender cut—cook with moist heat
- *very lean* meat

BLADE STEAK

- look for blade (shoulder) bone
- a less tender cut—cook with moist heat
- *very lean* meat

Roasting, baking, broiling, braising and sautéing are recommended cooking methods for meat, fish and poultry, because they require little additional fat and tend to remove interstitial fat (the fat contained in the meat).

ROASTING, done in an uncovered cooking utensil in the oven, is a dry-heat method of cooking. Lean meats may require basting, but this is not usually necessary with beef, pork or lamb, which are virtually self-basting, and thus lose much of their fat in a useful way during the cooking process. Always place the meat on a rack in the roasting pan to allow fat to drip away during cooking. Use low roasting temperatures (about 350°) to increase the fat drip-off. High temperatures sear the meat, sealing in the fat.

BAKING, also an oven method, differs from roasting in utilizing a covered container and a little additional cooking liquid. Ideal for less fatty meats, such as lean pork chops and fish, baking retains moisture and blends flavors.

BRAISING AND STEWING are done in closed containers either in the oven or on top of the stove. More liquid is used in stewing than in braising. These are slow cooking methods excellent for tenderizing tougher cuts of meat, but may yield unwanted fat, which stays in the cooking liquid. For this reason, it is a good idea to cook such meat dishes hours or even a day ahead of serving time, and then to refrigerate them so that hardened fat can be removed. It is less efficient to skim fat while the cooking liquid is still hot, and in many braised and stewed dishes, flavors are improved by standing.

BROILING, cooking over or under direct heat, allows meat fat to drip away either into coals or into a broiling pan if a rack is used. The same result may be achieved with pan-broiling if the pan has a ridged surface. Less tender meats may be broiled after being cubed, scored, pounded, ground or marinated. Fruit juices or wine make excellent marinades.

SAUTÉ, from the French *"sauter"* meaning "to jump" refers to a pan method using so little fat that food is constantly agitated or made to jump in the pan to prevent sticking. Chinese stir-frying has the same objective—to keep the food in motion so that it will not burn.

FRYING is usually avoided in low-fat cookery since it often involves the use of batters that can absorb the cooking fat. Instead, foods to be fried or deep-fried may be dredged in flour, or dipped in egg white and then in cracker meal. Corn oil is a good choice for deep-fat frying because its smoking point is higher than the correct cooking temperature for most foods. Fat that begins to smoke releases undesirable chemicals and will not cook correctly. When cooked until done and not overdone, food absorbs only a minimal amount of oil. It will absorb excessive amounts only if it is immersed too long, or if the oil is improperly heated. The food itself will lower the fat temperature. Use a thermometer so that you will know when the correct frying temperature has been reached and allow it to return to that correct temperature before adding each new batch of food. Timing is important. Watch carefully for the moment of doneness.

MEAT DRIPPINGS. The rich meat essence that drips into the roasting pan or broiler along with the fat from roasts, steaks or other meats, may be salvaged for future use by pouring the contents of the pan, fat and all, into a refrigerator dish and chilling it. The dark, protein-rich juice that separates out beneath the fat will add zest to meat pies, brown sauces, hashes or meat loaves, and will be a help in using left-over meats. Discard the hardened fat.

GRAVIES. It is possible to make a thickened gravy without that seemingly indispensable meat fat to blend with the thickening agent. Use a cup or so of clear defatted broth (canned, made from bouillon cubes, or, best of all, homemade). In a jar with a tight fitting lid, place 1 tablespoon of cornstarch; or 1 tablespoon of uncooked flour; or 1 to 2 tablespoons of browned flour for each ½ cup of liquid. Shake until smooth. Heat the remaining liquid in a saucepan, pour flour mixture into it and simmer, adding seasonings as desired. Flour is browned to give the sauce a mahogany color where desired. This can be done by placing flour in a shallow pan over low heat, stirring frequently, or in an oven at 300° for about 15 minutes.

BROTH. Rich, homemade broth is heartier and more flavorful than the canned variety. Make it the day before you plan to use it to allow for defatting after refrigeration. Use it to make soups or stews, defatting the finished dish whenever necessary. Canned broth as well as canned soups and stews are usually relatively free of fat, but to be sure, refrigerate the can before opening it, then remove any visible fat before using the product.

TRIM all visible fat from meats before cooking. Much fat will remain as interstitial marbling although it may not be obvious to the eye, and this will lubricate the meat sufficiently during cooking. Consult Shopping Tips section for the leanest cuts.

. . . . **Other Cooking Hints**

WINES AND SPIRITS FOR COOKING: The wines and spirits you cook with need not be very old or expensive *but* they should be good enough for you to drink and enjoy.

VINEGAR: Try a good wine or herb vinegar for salads.

WHOLE-GRAIN FLOUR should be kept in the refrigerator or better yet in the freezer to keep it from becoming rancid.

You may substitute 1 cup of whole wheat *pastry flour* for 1 cup all-purpose flour.

You may substitute 1 cup whole wheat flour for ⅞ cup all-purpose flour.

IODIZED SALT should be used to add this essential nutrient to your diet. Put a few grains of rice in the salt shaker to keep it free flowing.

The American Heart Association Cookbook

Appetizers

Beginning and end shake hands with each other.

GERMAN PROVERB

A good beginning is an appetizer that shakes hands with the dinner, neither duplicating it nor displacing it, but acting as a graceful introduction. Serve a light, delicate appetizer before a heavy meal, and a hearty appetizer before a light meal. Except where appetizers must stand alone, as at a cocktail party, with no dinner to follow, plan them to tease the appetite, not drown it.

Serve hot foods hot, and cold ones cold. Raw vegetables should be crisp from the refrigerator. Hot meat tidbits should be kept hot in a chafing dish or on a warming tray.

Most of the foods on the following pages can be made well in advance, particularly the dip sauces, which should be chilled before serving. Two surprise dips (Basic Cheese and Mock Sour Cream) lend themselves to many tasty variations that are not confined to appetite teasing and appear elsewhere in this book. Of course, you would not plan to use the same sauce twice in a single meal. A well-planned appetizer sends the guest to the dinner table with high expectations.

• • • • • • • • • • • • *Tuna–Dill Pâté*

½ CUP COLD VEGETABLE JUICE COCKTAIL
2 ENVELOPES (2 TABLESPOONS) UNFLAVORED GELATIN
1 CUP BOILING VEGETABLE JUICE COCKTAIL
2 CUPS MOCK SOUR CREAM (p. 175)
1 TABLESPOON DILL WEED
⅛ TEASPOON WORCESTERSHIRE SAUCE
1 7-OUNCE CAN TUNA (WATER PACKED), DRAINED

Place cold vegetable juice cocktail and gelatin in container of blender; cover and run at low speed until gelatin is soft.

Add boiling vegetable juice cocktail, and blend at high speed until gelatin dissolves.

Add Mock Sour Cream (p. 175), dill weed and Worcestershire sauce. Blend until smooth.

By turning blender on and off quickly, chop drained tuna into mixture. Do not overblend.

Pour into a 5-cup mold and chill until set. Unmold. Garnish with fresh dill weed and lemon wedges. Serve with crackers or tiny bread rounds.

YIELD: 4 CUPS
APPROX. CAL/SERV.: 1 CUP = 180   1 TABLESPOON = 10

Guests may hesitate to nibble from this pretty holiday creation, but it is rich in nutrients and low in calories. So enjoy without fear of spoiling your appetite or your figure.

• • • • • • • • *Christmas Tree Relish Tray*

1 STYROFOAM CONE, ABOUT 10 TO 12 INCHES HIGH
MUSTARD GREENS, CHICORY, OR CURLY ENDIVE
TOOTHPICKS
CHERRY TOMATOES
ZUCCHINI SLICES
CAULIFLOWER FLORETS
CARROT STICKS
RADISH ROSES

Begin at the base and encircle the styrofoam cone with a layer of greens, attaching them with wire staples or upholstery pins. Add a second layer overlapping the first. Working upward, continue adding layers until entire cone is covered. Decorate with vegetables speared with toothpicks.

Set "tree" on a tall compote or footed cake stand, and position extra vegetables around the base. Place a bowl of dip sauce nearby.

Raw Vegetables

Fresh raw vegetables make excellent low-calorie appetizers. These are some suggestions. Arrange vegetables in groups on a platter and serve with one of the dips on the following pages.

ASPARAGUS SPEARS

BROCCOLI FLORETS

GREEN ONIONS

CARROT STRIPS

CELERY STICKS

TURNIP WEDGES

GREEN PEPPER STRIPS

Recipe continues...

RUTABAGA WEDGES

CAULIFLOWER FLORETS

RADISH ROSES

KOHLRABI WEDGES

CUCUMBER SLICES

CHERRY TOMATOES

GREEN BEANS

ZUCCHINI

· · · · · · · · · · · · · · · · *Fruits*

Try serving a tray of fresh fruits. Cut the larger ones into wedges or bite-size pieces. Add a bowl of cheese dip or other fruit dressing. The following fruits make refreshing snacks.

PINEAPPLE—½ CUP

STRAWBERRIES—1 CUP

GRAPES—12

PRUNES—2 MEDIUM

APPLES—1 SMALL

WINTER PEARS—½ SMALL

MELON—½ SMALL CANTALOUPE

KUMQUATS—4 SMALL

APPROX. CAL/SERV.: 40

· · · · · · · · · · · · · · *Fruit Kabobs*

Combine several kinds of fresh melon balls (cantaloupe, honeydew, Persian) in a marinade of dry white wine or lemon juice for a few hours. Alternate balls on tiny skewers. Serve garnished with fresh mint.

APPROX. CAL/SERV.: 4 MELON BALLS = 20

Nibbles

5 CUPS DRY CEREAL (SUCH AS OAT CIRCLES, WHEAT SQUARES, RICE SQUARES, PUFFED CORN CEREALS)
2 CUPS PRETZEL STICKS, BROKEN IN HALF
1 CUP PEANUTS OR OTHER NUTS
⅓ CUP MARGARINE
4 TEASPOONS WORCESTERSHIRE SAUCE
1 TEASPOON CELERY SALT
1 TEASPOON ONION SALT
½ TEASPOON GARLIC POWDER
1 TEASPOON SEASONED SALT

Heat oven to 275°F.

Combine dry cereals to make 5 cups, and add broken pretzel sticks.

In a saucepan, melt margarine and combine with Worcestershire sauce and seasonings. Toss with the cereals and add peanuts.

Place in a shallow roasting pan. Bake in preheated oven for 1 hour, stirring every 10 minutes.

YIELD: ABOUT 8 CUPS
APPROX. CAL/SERV.: 1 CUP = 320   1 TABLESPOON = 20

Poor Man's Caviar

A dark mixture with flavor tones from the Middle East, this is not only a delicious snack, but a nutritious one as well.

1 LARGE EGGPLANT
2 TABLESPOONS OLIVE OIL
1 SMALL ONION, FINELY CHOPPED
1 CLOVE GARLIC, MINCED
¼ CUP RAW GREEN PEPPER, FINELY CHOPPED
1½ TABLESPOONS LEMON JUICE
½ TEASPOON SALT
COARSLEY GROUND PEPPER

Recipe continues...

Slice eggplant in half and rub with 1 tablespoon of the oil. Place halves cut side down on baking pan.

Broil on middle rack of oven for 20 to 25 minutes, or until eggplant is quite soft. Cool slightly. Scoop out pulp and mash well with fork.

Sauté onion and garlic in remaining oil until brown. Stir into eggplant pulp with remaining ingredients. Add more salt if necessary. Chill for 2 or 3 hours. Sprinkle with chopped parsley and serve with bread rounds or toast.

YIELD: ABOUT 2½ CUPS

APPROX. CAL/SERV.: ½ CUP = 75   1 TABLESPOON = 10

. . . . *Aspic Canapés*

A refreshing, piquant flavor surprise when served alone or with a canapé assortment.

1 10½-OUNCE CAN BEEF CONSOMME

1 TABLESPOON GELATIN

2 TABLESPOONS MARSALA WINE

CHOPPED PARSLEY

8 PIMIENTO STRIPS

3 HARD-COOKED EGG WHITES

Oil 24 miniature muffin tins very lightly. In each, sprinkle a few grains of coarsely ground pepper, and some chopped parsley with a few pimiento strips or chopped hard-cooked egg white.

Heat the beef consommé in a saucepan and dissolve gelatin in the hot liquid. Remove from heat; add the wine. Pour mixture into muffin tins. Chill until firm. When set, loosen around the edges with a knife and unmold onto thin bread rounds. Serve immediately.

YIELD: 24 CANAPÉS

APPROX. CAL/SERV.: 1 CANAPÉ = 20

Marinated Garbanzos (chick peas)

1 20-OUNCE CAN GARBANZOS, DRAINED
½ CUP OIL
3 TABLESPOONS VINEGAR
½ CUP FRESH CHOPPED PARSLEY
¼ CUP CHOPPED SCALLIONS
DASH GARLIC SALT
SALT AND PEPPER TO TASTE

Combine all ingredients and allow to marinate in the refrigerator for at least 2 hours. Drain. Serve with toast rounds, or as part of an antipasto tray with tuna fish, pimientos and olives. Place cocktail plates and forks for the convenience of guests.

YIELD: 2½ CUPS
APPROX. CAL/SERV.: ½ CUP = 135   1 TABLESPOON = 20

Miniature Meat Balls

These flavorful meat balls taste even better when made a day ahead and reheated before serving.

2 TABLESPOONS SOY SAUCE
¼ CUP WATER
½ CLOVE GARLIC, MINCED
½ TEASPOON GINGER
1 POUND LEAN GROUND BEEF

Preheat oven to 450°F.

In a large bowl, combine soy sauce, water, minced garlic and ginger. Add ground beef and mix lightly, but thoroughly. Form into balls about 1-inch in diameter.

Arrange on a lightly oiled baking dish. Bake, uncovered, for 15 minutes. Spear with toothpicks and serve from a hot chafing dish.

YIELD: ABOUT 32 MEATBALLS
APPROX. CAL/SERV.: 1 MEATBALL = 30

Garbanzo Dip

1 1 POUND, 4-OUNCE CAN GARBANZOS (CHICK PEAS)

2 TABLESPOONS OIL

2 TABLESPOONS OLIVE OIL

½ TEASPOON SESAME SEEDS OR 1½ TABLESPOONS TAHINI

½ TEASPOON SALT

FRESHLY GROUND PEPPER

1 LARGE CLOVE GARLIC, MINCED

2 TABLESPOONS LEMON JUICE

Drain chick peas thoroughly. Combine with other ingredients in blender jar. Blend until creamy.

Serve chilled, sprinkled with chopped parsley, as a dip for raw vegetables, or as a spread. Especially good on matzos or with pita bread.

For a more flavorful dip, increase the garlic and lemon juice.

YIELD: ABOUT 1½ CUPS

APPROX. CAL/SERV.: 1 TABLESPOON = 45

Chili Sauce Dip

1 12-OUNCE BOTTLE CHILI SAUCE

2 TABLESPOONS LEMON JUICE

3–4 DROPS TABASCO SAUCE

2 TABLESPOONS HORSERADISH

¼ CUP FINELY CHOPPED CELERY

¼ TEASPOON SALT

1 TABLESPOON MINCED PARSLEY

Combine all ingredients and chill. Serve with crisp raw vegetables.

YIELD: ABOUT 1½ CUPS

APPROX. CAL/SERV.: 1 TABLESPOON = 5

· · · · · · · · · *Cucumber and Yogurt Dip*

1 CUCUMBER
1 8-OUNCE CONTAINER PLAIN LOW-FAT YOGURT
GARLIC POWDER TO TASTE
DASH WORCESTERSHIRE SAUCE

Scrub cucumber to remove wax. Grate the unpeeled cucumber, and drain *very well* until almost dry. Combine with other ingredients. Serve with crackers.

YIELD: 1 ¾ CUPS
APPROX. CAL/SERV.: ½ CUP = 45   1 TABLESPOON = 5

· · · · · · · · · · · *Curry-Yogurt Dip*

1 CUP PLAIN LOW-FAT YOGURT
3 TABLESPOONS MAYONNAISE
2–3 TEASPOONS CURRY POWDER
SALT TO TASTE

Combine all ingredients. Use as a dip for vegetables.

YIELD: ABOUT 1 CUP
APPROX. CAL/SERV.: ½ CUP = 210   1 TABLESPOON = 25

· · · · · · · · · · · *Basic Cheese Sauce*

Use this basic recipe with variations as a dip, a spread, a salad dressing or a delicious replacement for sour cream.

2 CUPS (1 POUND) LOW-FAT COTTAGE CHEESE
2 TABLESPOONS LEMON JUICE
¼ CUP SKIM MILK
SALT TO TASTE

Place all ingredients in a blender jar. Blend until creamy, adjusting the milk measure to produce desired consistency.

YIELD: 2 CUPS
APPROX. CAL/SERV.: 1 CUP = 190   1 TABLESPOON = 10

· · · · · · · · · · · · · · *variations*

BLUE CHEESE: To 1 cup of Basic Cheese Sauce, add 1 or 2 tablespoons of crumbled blue cheese and ¼ teaspoon of Worcestershire sauce. Chill for a few hours or overnight to allow flavors to blend. Excellent as a stuffing for celery.
APPROX. CAL/SERV.: 1 TABLESPOON = 15

DILL: To 1 cup of Basic Cheese Sauce, add 1 tablespoon chopped fresh dill and 1 tablespoon minced onion. Chill.
APPROX. CAL/SERV.: 1 TABLESPOON = 10

GARLIC: To 1 cup of Basic Cheese Sauce, add 2 tablespoons mayonnaise, 1 or 2 tablespoons chopped onion, a dash of garlic powder and 2 sprigs of fresh parsley. Mix in blender at high speed until smooth. Chill.
APPROX. CAL/SERV.: 1 TABLESPOON = 20

ANCHOVIES: To 1 cup of Basic Cheese Sauce, add 4 anchovy fillets, 1 teaspoon paprika and ½ teaspoon dry mustard. Mix in a blender until smooth. Serve chilled.
APPROX. CAL/SERV.: 1 TABLESPOON = 15

ONION: To 1 cup of Basic Cheese Sauce, add 2 teaspoons dry onion soup mix and 1 teaspoon finely chopped green onion. Mix. Serve chilled.
APPROX. CAL/SERV.: 1 TABLESPOON = 10

HONEY-CHEESE: To 1 cup of Basic Cheese Sauce, add 2 to 4 tablespoons of honey, depending on the degree of sweetness desired.
APPROX. CAL/SERV.: 1 TABLESPOON = 20

· · · · · · · · · · *Creamy Cheese Spread*

½ CUP LOW-FAT COTTAGE CHEESE
2 TABLESPOONS NONFAT DRY MILK

In a blender, mix the cottage cheese and milk powder until smooth. Chill to thicken before using.

YIELD: ½ CUP
APPROX. CAL/SERV.: ½ CUP = 115   1 TABLESPOON = 15

· · · · · · · · · · · · · · *variations*

Use one recipe of Creamy Cheese Spread to make any of the following:

PINEAPPLE CHEESE SPREAD: To Creamy Cheese Spread, add 2 or 3 tablespoons of well-drained crushed pineapple.
APPROX. CAL/SERV.: 1 TABLESPOON = 15

ORANGE CHEESE SPREAD: Add 1 teaspoon of grated orange rind.
APPROX. CAL/SERV.: 1 TABLESPOON = 15

PARSLEY CHEESE SPREAD: Add 1 tablespoon of finely chopped parsley.
APPROX. CAL/SERV.: 1 TABLESPOON = 15

CHIVE CHEESE SPREAD: Add 1 teaspoon of chopped chives.
APPROX. CAL/SERV.: 1 TABLESPOON = 15

· · · · · · · · · · · *Breads and Crackers*

There is a wide selection of low-fat breads and crackers for use with spreads or dips. Here are a few:

RY-KRISP—60 CALORIES

MELBA TOAST—15 CALORIES

*MINIATURE BISCUITS—65 CALORIES

*WHOLE WHEAT PITA BREAD—⅛ LOAF = 35 CALORIES

MATZOS—6-INCH DIAMETER PIECE = 78 CALORIES

*TORTILLA CHIP—60 CALORIES

WHEAT CRACKER—9 CALORIES

FINN CRISP—20 CALORIES

WHOLE WHEAT WAFERS—7 CALORIES

* Recipes included in this book.

Make these crunchy toast bits yourself.

· · · · · · · · · · · *Garlic Rye Toasties*

½ STICK (¼ CUP) MARGARINE, SOFTENED
GARLIC POWDER; OR 1 CLOVE GARLIC, MINCED
24 SLICES PARTY RYE BREAD

If you are using raw garlic, combine it with the softened margarine and spread each slice of bread with the mixture. If you use garlic powder, first spread margarine on bread and then sprinkle with the garlic powder.

Arrange slices on a baking sheet, and bake in a hot oven (400°F.) for 10 minutes, or until crisp.

YIELD: 24 GARLIC TOASTIES
APPROX. CAL/SERV.: 35

· · · · · · · · · · · *Teriyaki Canapés*

1 POUND SIRLOIN STEAK
1 TEASPOON GROUND GINGER
1 CLOVE GARLIC, MINCED
1 SMALL ONION, MINCED
1 TABLESPOON SUGAR
¼ CUP SOY SAUCE
3 TABLESPOONS WATER
1 TABLESPOON RED WINE

Remove all fat and cut steak into ½-inch cubes.

Combine all other ingredients and pour over the meat. Let stand at least 2 hours, or preferably overnight. Drain, reserving marinade. Place meat in single layer on broiler pan.

Broil 1 inch from the flame, 5 minutes on one side. Turn and broil 3 minutes more.

Spear each cube with a toothpick and put on a heated serving dish or in a chafing dish. Heat marinade and pour over the meat. Keep hot.

YIELD: 32
APPROX. CAL/SERV.: 35

· · · · · · · · · · · · · · . *Meat Balls*

Make tiny meat balls (see recipe for Basic Meat Balls, p. 88). Serve in a chafing dish with one of the following sauces. Provide toothpicks for spearing.

SWEET AND SOUR SAUCE I: In a saucepan, combine 1 16-ounce can of tomato sauce, 1 12-ounce bottle of chili sauce and ¾ cup of grape jelly. Heat until jelly is melted. Pour over meat balls and simmer 20 minutes.
APPROX. CAL/SERV.: ½ OUNCE MEAT BALL = 50
1 OUNCE MEAT BALL = 100

SWEET AND SOUR SAUCE II: Mix the contents of 1 16-ounce can of tomato sauce with an equal amount of whole cranberry sauce. Bring to a boil, add meat balls and simmer 20 minutes.
APPROX. CAL/SERV.: ½ OUNCE MEAT BALL = 60
1 OUNCE MEAT BALL = 125

SWEET AND SOUR SAUCE III: Mix 12 ounces of chili sauce with an equal amount of beer. Bring to a boil, add meat balls and simmer 20 minutes.
APPROX. CAL/SERV.: ½ OUNCE MEAT BALL = 40
1 OUNCE MEAT BALL = 85

· · · · · · · · · · . *Meat Balls in Beer Sauce*

2 SLICES BREAD, CUBED
1 12-OUNCE CAN OR BOTTLE BEER
1 POUND LEAN GROUND BEEF
½ CUP SHREDDED MOZZARELLA CHEESE
(MADE FROM PARTIALLY SKIMMED MILK)
½ TEASPOON SALT
DASH PEPPER
3 TABLESPOONS MARGARINE
½ CUP CHOPPED ONION
2 TABLESPOONS BROWN SUGAR
2 TABLESPOONS VINEGAR
2 TABLESPOONS BEEF STOCK
1–2 TABLESPOONS FLOUR (OPTIONAL)

Recipe continues...

Preheat oven to 350°F.

Soak bread cubes in ½ cup of beer.

Combine ground beef with cheese, salt, pepper and beer-soaked bread. Mix well and form into 32 cocktail-size meat balls. Arrange in single layer on a cookie sheet and bake 15 minutes.

Meanwhile, sauté onions in margarine until tender. Stir in the sugar, vinegar, beef stock and remaining beer. Thicken with flour if desired. Simmer over low heat 10 minutes.

When meat balls are done, drain on paper towels to remove fat. Then add to sauce and simmer 20 minutes. Serve with toothpicks.

YIELD: 32 SMALL MEAT BALLS

APPROX. CAL/SERV.: 1 MEAT BALL = 60

Marinated Mushrooms

½ POUND FRESH MUSHROOMS

1 CUP OIL

¼ CUP LEMON JUICE

2 TABLESPOONS CHOPPED CHIVES

½ TEASPOON SALT

Select fresh, bite-size mushrooms. Wash thoroughly.

Combine the remaining ingredients and pour over the mushrooms. Marinate several hours at least, turning occasionally.

Drain and serve on toothpicks as an appetizer. Leftover marinade makes a delicious base for salad dressing.

YIELD: 6 SERVINGS

APPROX. CAL/SERV.: 55

Lemon Pepper Mushrooms

8 LARGE MUSHROOMS

1 TABLESPOON CHOPPED CHIVES

2 TABLESPOONS LEMON JUICE

1 TABLESPOON MAYONNAISE

1 TABLESPOON OIL

1½ TEASPOONS LEMON PEPPER

1 TEASPOON SALT

Preheat oven to 450°F.

Select large firm mushrooms, wash and wipe with a damp cloth. Remove stems, discard lower half and chop upper half of the stems very fine, and in a bowl combine with the remaining ingredients.

Stuff mushrooms with the mixture. Bake in a shallow pan 8–10 minutes. Serve immediately.

YIELD: 8 SERVINGS

APPROX. CAL/SERV.: 35

· · · · · · · · · · · **Spinach Turnovers**

A variation on the classic spinach pie of Middle-Eastern origin, these are easy to make since ready-made biscuit dough is used.

1 PACKAGE REFRIGERATED BUTTERMILK BISCUITS

½ POUND FRESH SPINACH, CLEANED AND CHOPPED

1 MEDIUM ONION, DICED

1 TEASPOON SALT

¼ TEASPOON PEPPER

1 TABLESPOON LEMON JUICE

1 TABLESPOON OLIVE OIL

¼ CUP PINE NUTS (OPTIONAL)

Preheat oven to 375°F.

Remove uncooked biscuits from container, separate, cover, and let stand on a floured bread board about 10 minutes, until warm.

Mix the chopped spinach with all other ingredients to make the filling.

Roll out individual biscuits to a ⅛-inch thickness. Put 1 tablespoon of filling mixture in the center of each.

A

B

Recipe continues...

Fold to form a triangle, and press edges together with a fork. Place on a greased cookie sheet.

Bake in the oven 20 minutes. Serve hot or at room temperature.

YIELD: 10 TURNOVERS

APPROX. CAL/SERV.: 80 (OR 100 WITH PINE NUTS)

· · · · · · · · · · · · · *Antipasto*

Antipasto,* literally meaning "before the pasta," is the Italian equivalent of the French word hors d'oeuvre, or the English word appetizer. An antipasto may be simple or elaborate. It may include any or all of the following:

PROSCIUTTO

ROASTED SWEET GREEN PEPPERS

PIMIENTO

MARINATED MUSHROOMS

MARINATED GARBANZOS

CHERRY TOMATOES OR TOMATO WEDGES

OLIVES

SARDINES

SMALL STRIPS OF MOZZARELLA (MADE FROM
PARTIALLY SKIMMED MILK)

PICKLED CAULIFLOWER

TUNA FISH

ANCHOVIES

CRISP CELERY

RADISHES

* Caloric values for antipasto have not been computed, since they will vary according to the amount of the above ingredients consumed. The vegetables will add very few calories. Other items should be eaten in moderation.

. . *Ab-duq Khiar (dip for fresh vegetables or crackers)*

3 CUPS LOW-FAT YOGURT
2 CUCUMBERS, CHOPPED
3 YOUNG GREEN ONIONS, CHOPPED
2 SPRIGS BASIL, CHOPPED
2 SPRIGS SUMMER SAVORY, CHOPPED
¼ CUP CHOPPED WALNUTS
½ CUP RAISINS
½ TEASPOON SALT

Beat yogurt until smooth.
Stir in the remaining ingredients and chill.

YIELD: 4½ CUPS
APPROX. CAL/SERV.: ½ CUP = 95

This may be served as a summer salad, as a dip with sesame crackers
or vegetables, or diluted and served as cold soup.

. . . . *Party and Knapsack Special*

2 CUPS SUNFLOWER SEEDS
½ CUP WALNUTS
1 CUP SOYNUTS
1 CUP PEANUTS
1 CUP RAISINS

Combine all ingredients. Serve for a light lunch on the trail or serve
at parties.

YIELD: 10 ½-CUP SERVINGS
APPROX. CAL/SERV.: 380

. . . . *Toasted Tortilla Triangles*

12 CORN TORTILLAS
SALT

Recipe continues...

Preheat oven to 400°F.

Cut each tortilla into 6 pie-shaped pieces.

Place ½ of the tortilla triangles on a cookie sheet, spread out, and salt lightly.

Bake them for 10 minutes. Remove from oven, turn each one over, and return them to the oven for 3 more minutes.

Place second half of tortilla triangles on cookie sheet and repeat process.

YIELD: 72 TORTILLA TRIANGLES
APPROX. CAL/SERV.: 70

· · · · · · · · · · · · · · *variations*

Sprinkle the tortillas with seasoned salt, cumin, or chili powder for different flavors.

· · · · · · · · · · · · *Cream Cheese*

1 CUP LOW-FAT COTTAGE CHEESE
4 TABLESPOONS MARGARINE
1 TABLESPOON SKIM MILK
SALT TO TASTE

Mix all ingredients in blender until smooth.

YIELD: 1 CUP
APPROX. CAL/SERV.: 1 TABLESPOON = 45

· · · · · · · · · · · · · *variations*

Chopped chives, pimiento, other vegetables, herbs or seasonings may be added.

Soups

The great china tureen that sat on Grandmother's sideboard is as much a memory of the days gone by as the stock pot that simmered on the back of the stove. Soups today are more easily and quickly made but, as in those earlier times, a soup is only as good as the broth it develops from.

Before starting a soup, look through the kitchen stores. Tops of celery, vegetables that have lost their freshness, the outer leaves of salad greens, are wisely consigned to a quick stock pot. Pour canned broth over them, add some water and a few herbs and leave them to simmer for half an hour. Then strain the broth and use it to make your own soup du jour, confident that you have increased its nutrient content through thrifty use of ingredients that might have been discarded.

Soup is an economical dish. Many a leftover meat or vegetable has been saved from oblivion by becoming an addition to the soup pot. Even repeated reheating of a soup need not end its career. The broth can always be strained from limp, overcooked meats or vegetables and reused or consumed alone for its own rich flavor.

The soup of your dreams may be the hot, thick lentil soup of childhood winters, or the chilled tart summer gazpacho. Or, it may be a soup you created yourself from a hodge-podge of mealtime leftovers. There is no limit to invention when you become your own soup chef, whether you have five minutes or five hours. So, put on the soup pot, and *bon appétit!*

Cabbage Soup

1 MEDIUM HEAD CABBAGE
1 LARGE ONION
1 LARGE POTATO, PARED
3 CUPS SKIM MILK
2 TABLESPOONS MARGARINE
SALT AND PEPPER TO TASTE

Shred the cabbage. Thinly slice the onion and potato. Place vegetables in a heavy saucepan with a small amount of water. Cover and cook slowly until tender.

Mash to a pulp (cabbage should retain some texture). Add milk, margarine, salt and pepper. Simmer 10 to 15 minutes. Serve hot.

YIELD: ABOUT 1 ½ QUARTS
APPROX. CAL/SERV.: 1 CUP = 110

Borscht (Hot)

Virtually a one-dish meal, this hearty soup needs only a salad and some crusty bread or a boiled potato.

2 POUNDS BONELESS CHUCK, CUT INTO BITE-SIZE CHUNKS
4 CUPS CANNED TOMATOES, UNDRAINED
4 CUPS CANNED BEETS, UNDRAINED
1 LARGE CABBAGE, SHREDDED
2 TABLESPOONS SALT
WATER TO COVER

Purée tomatoes and beets in a blender. Pour into a stew pot with meat, cabbage and salt. Bring to a boil. Skim surface, lower heat, cover, and simmer for 3 hours, checking to see that soup does not boil. Taste for seasoning. Serve hot in soup bowls. Boiled potato is a good accompaniment.

YIELD: ABOUT 2 ½ QUARTS
APPROX. CAL/SERV.: 1 CUP = 260

. . . . *Quick Borscht (Cold)*

2 CUPS CANNED BEETS WITH LIQUID

4 TABLESPOONS SUGAR

2 CUPS WATER

½ TEASPOON SALT

1 TEASPOON GRATED ONION OR ½ TEASPOON DRIED ONION FLAKES

2 TABLESPOONS LEMON JUICE

6 TABLESPOONS MOCK SOUR CREAM (p. 175) OR PLAIN LOW-FAT YO-GURT, PLUS EXTRA FOR GARNISH

Put all ingredients in blender until smooth and creamy. If blender will not hold entire amount at one time, add everything except 1 cup of water, pour off some of the blended mixture, add the water and blend.

Pour mixture into a large pitcher and chill thoroughly.

Serve in tall glasses with mock sour cream or yogurt.

YIELD: 1¼ QUARTS

APPROX. CAL/SERV.: 1 CUP = 80 (1 TABLESPOON MOCK SOUR CREAM)

75 (1 TABLESPOON YOGURT)

. . . . *Vegetable Soup*

3 CARROTS, FINELY CHOPPED

1 HEAD CABBAGE, SHREDDED

2 RIBS CELERY, FINELY CHOPPED

1 ONION, CHOPPED

1 28-OUNCE CAN OF TOMATOES

6 BEEF BOUILLON CUBES, DISSOLVED IN 6 CUPS BOILING WATER

SALT AND PEPPER

Place vegetables in a large pot with tomatoes and bouillon. Bring to a boil, and simmer, covered, until thick, about 45 minutes. Season to taste with salt and pepper.

YIELD: 2 QUARTS

APPROX. CAL/SERV.: 1 CUP = 45

· · · · · · · · · Beef-Barley Vegetable Soup

This is a variation of the preceding recipe, but much higher in protein and calories. A meal in itself.

3 POUNDS MEATY SHIN BONE
1½ QUARTS COLD WATER
1 TEASPOON SALT
⅛ TEASPOON PEPPER
3 TABLESPOONS BARLEY
VEGETABLES, AS FOR VEGETABLE SOUP (p. 25)

Place meat in kettle; cover with cold water, add seasoning.

Heat slowly to boiling point, cover, and let simmer 2½–3 hours, or until meat is tender. Skim off fat.

Remove meat and bone, add barley and vegetables, and continue cooking for 45 minutes.

YIELD: ABOUT 2 QUARTS
APPROX. CAL/SERV.: 1 CUP = 185

· · · · · · · · · · · Tomato Corn Soup

2 TABLESPOONS OIL
¼ CUP CHOPPED ONION
2 TABLESPOONS FLOUR
2 CUPS TOMATO JUICE
1 16-OUNCE CAN (2 CUPS) CREAM STYLE CORN
2 CUPS SKIM MILK
PEPPER AND SALT TO TASTE
PARSLEY FOR GARNISH

In a 2-quart saucepan, heat oil over moderately low heat and cook chopped onion until transparent. Stir in flour and cook stirring until slightly thickened. Pour mixture into a blender with tomato juice and corn. Blend until smooth.

Pour into a 2-quart saucepan with the milk. Place over moderately low heat and cook, stirring constantly. Do not allow to boil.

Add salt and pepper to taste.
Serve hot garnished with parsley.

YIELD: ABOUT 1 ½ QUARTS
APPROX. CAL/SERV.: 1 CUP = 155

· · · · · · · · · · · · **Tomato Bouillon**

A smooth broth whose flavor develops ahead of the cooking. An excellent first course.

4 CUPS TOMATO JUICE
½ BAY LEAF
2 WHOLE CLOVES
¼ TEASPOON DILL SEED
¼ TEASPOON BASIL
¼ TEASPOON MARJORAM
¼ TEASPOON OREGANO
½ TEASPOON SUGAR
PEPPER TO TASTE
2 TEASPOONS MARGARINE
CHOPPED PARSLEY
CURRY POWDER (OPTIONAL)

Place all herbs except parsley in the tomato juice and let stand 1 hour to allow flavors to blend. Heat tomato-herb bouillon to boiling point. Remove from heat and strain.

Pour into serving bowls. Add ½ teaspoon of margarine to each bowl. Garnish with parsley and a dash of curry powder, if desired.

YIELD: 1 QUART
APPROX. CAL/SERV.: 1 CUP = 65

Fruit Soup

1 CUP DRIED PRUNES
1 CUP SMALL DRIED APRICOT HALVES
2 QUARTS WATER
1 CUP SEEDLESS WHITE OR DARK RAISINS
1 STICK CINNAMON
2 TABLESPOONS CORNSTARCH
¼ CUP COLD WATER

Soak prunes and apricots in the water for 4 hours (or follow package instructions, which may not include soaking). Add raisins and cinnamon stick and bring to a boil. Simmer gently, covered, until fruits are tender but still whole. Remove cinnamon stick.

Dissolve cornstarch in cold water, add to fruit, and cook until thickened, stirring constantly.

Serve hot or chilled.

YIELD: ABOUT 2 QUARTS
APPROX. CAL/SERV.: 1 CUP = 150

Green Split Pea Soup

1 CUP GREEN SPLIT PEAS
3 TABLESPOONS MARGARINE
¼ CUP CHOPPED ONION
4 CUPS COLD WATER
SALT AND PEPPER
½ TEASPOON GROUND MARJORAM
2 CUPS SKIM MILK

Soak peas as directed, and drain.

Melt margarine in a large saucepan and cook onion until lightly browned. Add water, peas, and seasoning; cover and simmer 1 hour, or until peas are tender, stirring occasionally.

Press soup through a sieve or purée in an electric blender.

Return to saucepan, add milk, adjust seasoning, and heat thoroughly, stirring occasionally.

Serve immediately.

YIELD: ABOUT 1½ QUARTS
APPROX. CAL/SERV.: 1 CUP = 200

· · · · · · · · · *Bean and Vegetable Soup*

A very hearty soup, as thick as a chili, but with a milder flavor.

1½ CUPS DRIED KIDNEY BEANS
2 QUARTS WATER
1 MEATY SHIN BONE, LEAN AND WELL TRIMMED
1 TABLESPOON SALT
½ CUP TOMATO SAUCE; OR 1 CUP CHOPPED FRESH TOMATO
½ CUP CHOPPED CARROTS
1 CUP FINELY SHREDDED CABBAGE OR CHOPPED WATERCRESS
½ CUP CHOPPED ONION
1 MEDIUM POTATO, CHOPPED
2 TABLESPOONS MINCED PARSLEY

Wash kidney beans and soak overnight in water.

Add shin bone and salt. Boil until beans are tender and meat well done, adding more water if necessary. Put in vegetables and cook until done. Adjust consistency if desired by adding more water. Remove shin bone. Skim off the fat before serving.

Serve hot.

YIELD: ABOUT 2 QUARTS
APPROX. CAL/SERV.: 1 CUP = 190

Black Bean Soup

1 POUND BLACK BEANS
1 ONION, STUCK WITH 2 CLOVES
1 BAY LEAF
SPRIG PARSLEY
1 MEDIUM ONION, CHOPPED
1 GREEN PEPPER, CHOPPED
2 CLOVES GARLIC, MINCED
¼ CUP OIL
1 TEASPOON OREGANO
1 TEASPOON SUGAR
1 TEASPOON VINEGAR
1 8-OUNCE CAN TOMATO SAUCE
¼ CUP DRY SHERRY
CHOPPED ONION FOR GARNISH

Soak black beans overnight in water to cover. To same water add onion stuck with cloves, bay leaf and parsley. Bring water to a boil and cook beans until tender.

Cook onion, green pepper and garlic in oil until soft. Add to the beans with the remaining ingredients and cook until thickened.

Pour in dry sherry and serve with finely chopped raw onion sprinkled on top. (If a smooth soup is desired, purée in a blender.)

YIELD: 1½–2 QUARTS
APPROX. CAL/SERV.: 1 CUP = 285

Creamy Asparagus Soup

1 16-OUNCE CAN CUT ASPARAGUS WITH LIQUID
1 CUP COOKED RICE
¼ CUP CHOPPED ONION
¼ CUP CHOPPED CELERY
1½ CUPS SKIM MILK
½ TEASPOON SALT
⅛ TEASPOON PEPPER
DASH NUTMEG

Place canned asparagus and liquid in a blender with onion, celery and cooked rice. Blend on low speed until puréed. Pour into a saucepan. Stir in milk. Season, and heat to boiling point. Serve immediately.

YIELD: ABOUT 1¼ QUARTS
APPROX. CAL/SERV.: 1 CUP = 95

· · · · · · · · · · · · · · · *variation*

ASPARAGUS WATERCRESS SOUP: Add ½ cup of chopped watercress to the blender with other ingredients. Blend until puréed, and proceed as above.

· · · · · · · · · · · · *Cold Avocado Soup*

2 10½-OUNCE CANS CHICKEN BROTH, CHILLED
2 RIPE AVOCADOS, CHILLED
DASH LEMON JUICE
1 OUNCE SHERRY, OR TO TASTE
DILL WEED

Put chilled broth in a blender. Dice avocados and add to broth with lemon juice and sherry. Blend well.

Pour into cups and sprinkle with dill weed. Serve cold.

YIELD: 3 CUPS
APPROX. CAL/SERV.: 1 CUP = 150

Fresh Mushroom Soup

1 POUND FRESH MUSHROOMS

2 TABLESPOONS OIL

2 CUPS WATER

2 CUPS NONFAT DRY MILK

1 TEASPOON ONION FLAKES

1 TABLESPOON PARSLEY FLAKES

1 TABLESPOON FLOUR

1 TABLESPOON SHERRY

SALT AND PEPPER TO TASTE

Slice caps and stems of mushrooms in thick pieces. Heat oil in a heavy saucepan and sauté the mushrooms quickly until just crisp tender.

Combine all other ingredients in blender and mix until thick and foamy. Add mushrooms and blend again at lowest speed for 4 or 5 seconds or until mushrooms are chopped into fine pieces but not pulverized.

Pour the mixture back into the saucepan and heat slowly, stirring with a wire whisk to keep from burning. Use an asbestos pad if soup is to be left on the stove.

YIELD: ABOUT 1¼ QUARTS

APPROX. CAL/SERV.: 1 CUP = 180

variation

SPINACH SOUP: Substitute 1 10-ounce package of frozen chopped spinach for the mushrooms. Cook spinach until it is just broken up and follow recipe for mushroom soup. Serve dusted with nutmeg.

APPROX. CAL/SERV.: 1 CUP = 175

. . . . *Pumpkin Soup*

3 GREEN ONIONS, SLICED
2 TABLESPOONS MARGARINE
2 CUPS PURÉED CANNED PUMPKIN
2 TABLESPOONS FLOUR
1 TEASPOON SALT
¼ TEASPOON GROUND GINGER
⅛ TEASPOON TUMERIC
2 CUPS SKIM MILK
4 TEASPOONS INSTANT CHICKEN BOUILLON DISSOLVED IN WARM WATER
1 QUART WATER
CHOPPED CHIVES OR PARSLEY

Sauté the onion in margarine, and stir in pumpkin.

Blend flour, salt and spices with ⅓ cup of milk. Stir into the pumpkin mixture.

Add remaining milk, and cook, stirring constantly, 5 to 10 minutes until thickened. Do not allow to boil. Mix in the bouillon and heat almost to boiling. (If the soup separates from overheating, whirl in a blender to restore consistency.) Serve hot, garnished with chives or parsley.

YIELD: 2 QUARTS
APPROX. CAL/SERV.: 1 CUP = 80

. . . . *Five-Minute Soup*

A quick-cooking soup, this is best served immediately while the vegetables are fresh and colorful.

4 CUPS CHICKEN BOUILLON
HALF A RAW CUCUMBER, SCRUBBED, UNPEELED AND SLICED VERY THIN
4 RAW MUSHROOMS, SLICED
2 CUPS SHREDDED RAW GREEN LEAF VEGETABLE (SPINACH, LETTUCE OR CABBAGE)
1 TOMATO, CUBED
½ CUP LEFTOVER LEAN MEAT, SHREDDED

Recipe continues...

Heat the bouillon. Add the vegetables and meat. Bring to a boil and simmer 5 minutes. Adjust seasoning. Serve immediately.

YIELD: ABOUT 1½ QUARTS
APPROX. CAL/SERV.: 1 CUP = 45

. . . . *Oriental Chicken Soup*

Use leftover chicken in this delicate Oriental soup.

1 10½-OUNCE CAN CHICKEN BROTH
½ CUP COOKED CHICKEN BREAST, CUT IN THIN SLIVERS
CHOPPED SCALLION TOPS OR THIN SLIVERS OF GREEN PEPPER
1 CUP CHINESE NOODLES

Heat the chicken broth and add the chicken, noodles and green onion or pepper.

YIELD: 3 SERVINGS
APPROX. CAL/SERV.: 115

. . . . *Mexican Chicken Soup*

A great south-of-the-border flavor. Serve with tortillas.

1 3-POUND FRYING CHICKEN, SKINNED AND CUT INTO SERVING PIECES
1 TABLESPOON SALT
2 CUPS CANNED TOMATOES
1 CLOVE GARLIC, MINCED
½ CUP CHOPPED ONION
⅔ CUP CANNED MILDLY HOT CALIFORNIA CHILES, DICED (OR ⅓ CUP
    FOR A MILDER FLAVORED SOUP)
2 CUPS COOKED, DRAINED PINTO BEANS OR GARBANZOS

Place chicken pieces in a large saucepan. Add salt and enough water to cover. Cook until tender, about 25 minutes.

Remove chicken pieces from the broth and put in the tomatoes, garlic, onion and chiles. Slide chicken meat off the bones and return meat to the broth. Add beans and simmer about 15 minutes.

YIELD: ABOUT 2 QUARTS

APPROX. CAL/SERV.: 1 CUP = 190   1 TORTILLA = 60

. . . . New England Fish Chowder

  2 CUPS CUBED POTATOES
1½ CUPS CUBED ONIONS
1½ TEASPOONS SALT
 ⅛ TEASPOON COARSELY GROUND BLACK PEPPER
  2 CUPS BOILING WATER
  1 POUND FROZEN OR FRESH HADDOCK FILLETS, CUT IN ¾-INCH CUBES
  2 CUPS SKIM MILK MIXED WITH EITHER 1 CUP OF NONFAT DRY
    MILK OR 1 12-OUNCE CAN OF EVAPORATED SKIM MILK, UNDILUTED
  1 TABLESPOON CHOPPED FRESH PARSLEY
PAPRIKA

In the water with the seasonings added, cook the potatoes and onions until barely tender, about 10 minutes.

Add fish and cook 10 minutes more. Stir in milk. Simmer 15 minutes longer. Do not boil.

Pour into a soup tureen or bowls, garnish with chopped parsley and sprinkle with paprika.

YIELD: ABOUT 1¾ QUARTS

APPROX. CAL/SERV.: 1 CUP = 175

· · · · · · · · · · · · · *Gazpacho*

    6 CUPS FRESH RIPE TOMATOES, PEELED AND CHOPPED; OR CANNED
      PLUM TOMATOES
    1 ONION, ROUGHLY CHOPPED
    ½ CUP GREEN PEPPER CHUNKS
    ½ CUP CUCUMBER CHUNKS
    2 CUPS TOMATO JUICE
    ½ TEASPOON CUMIN (OPTIONAL)
    1 GARLIC CLOVE, MINCED
    1 TABLESPOON SALT
  FRESHLY GROUND PEPPER
    ¼ CUP OLIVE OIL
    ¼ CUP WINE VINEGAR
    ½ CUP EACH FINELY CHOPPED ONION, PEPPER AND CUCUMBER
    1 CUP FINELY CHOPPED TOMATO
  GARLIC CROUTONS

In a blender, purée tomatoes, onion, green pepper and cucumber. Add tomato juice, cumin, garlic, salt and pepper. Put in a bowl; cover and chill.

Before serving add oil and vinegar. Serve accompanied by side dishes of finely chopped tomatoes, onion, green pepper and cucumber. Garnish with croutons.

    YIELD: ABOUT 1 ¾ QUARTS
    APPROX. CAL/SERV.: 1 CUP = 155

· · · · · · · · · · · · · *Onion Soup*

    2 TABLESPOONS OIL OR MARGARINE
  1½ CUP THINLY SLICED ONIONS
    6 CUPS BEEF BROTH
  BLACK PEPPER
  PARMESAN CHEESE
    6 SLICES FRENCH BREAD, TOASTED

Sauté onions in oil until transparent and thoroughly cooked. Add broth and black pepper. Simmer 30 minutes.

Divide into 6 ovenproof casseroles or bowls. Top each with a slice of toasted French bread; sprinkle with Parmesan cheese.

Place in the oven or under the broiler until cheese is melted. Serve immediately.

YIELD: ABOUT 1 ½ QUARTS

APPROX. CAL/SERV.: 1 CUP = 165

· · · · · · · · · · · · · **Soupe Au Pistou**

Two unusually good pungent garnishes distinguish this delicious soup.

  8 CUPS WATER

1 ½ TABLESPOONS COARSE OR KOSHER SALT

1 ½ POUNDS ZUCCHINI AND/OR SUMMER SQUASH, SLICED ½ INCH THICK

  1 POUND GREEN BEANS, TRIMMED AND CUT IN 1-INCH PIECES

  1 15-OUNCE CAN FAVA OR NAVY BEANS

  1 CUP SMALL ELBOW OR SHELL MACARONI

Bring the 8 cups of water to a boil. Add all ingredients except macaroni. Simmer 10 minutes. Add macaroni, return to a boil, then simmer for another 12 minutes.

Serve hot with Summer or Winter Pistou (p. 38) and grated Parmesan cheese.

YIELD: ABOUT 2 QUARTS

APPROX. CAL/SERV.: 1 CUP = 140   1 CUP SUMMER PISTOU = 200

1 CUP WINTER PISTOU = 195

· · · · · · · · · · · · **Summer Pistou**

1 ½ TEASPOONS GARLIC, FINELY CHOPPED

  1 TEASPOON COARSE OR KOSHER SALT

  ½ CUP FRESH BASIL LEAVES, FINELY CHOPPED

  2 TABLESPOONS OIL

  4 TOMATOES, PEELED AND COARSELY CHOPPED

Recipe continues…

Crush the garlic and salt together with the flat of a knife or mortar and pestle until it combines in a thick paste. In a bowl, combine with all other ingredients and mash to a thick purée. Serve *very cold* spooned into hot soup.

APPROX. CAL/SERV.: 60

Winter Pistou

½ TEASPOON COARSE OR KOSHER SALT
½ TEASPOON FINELY CHOPPED GARLIC
½ TEASPOON DRIED SWEET BASIL LEAVES
1 16-OUNCE CAN ITALIAN PLUM TOMATOES, DRAINED THOROUGHLY
2 TABLESPOONS OIL

Crush salt, garlic and basil to a dry paste. Add the Italian plum tomatoes broken up, and the oil, and continue mixing to a paste. Serve *cold* spooned into hot soup.

APPROX. CAL/SERV.: 55

Lentil Porridge

1 CUP LENTILS
1 CARROT, GRATED
2 MEDIUM POTATOES, DICED
2 TABLESPOONS OIL
1 TABLESPOON FLOUR
4 CUPS WATER
SALT
PEPPER

Cover lentils with 4 cups of water in a large pot. Bring to a boil and cook 1 hour.

Add potatoes and carrots. Cook 20 minutes more, or until vegetables are tender.

Blend the oil and the flour over medium heat. Cook, stirring until smooth. Pour into the lentils, mix well, and bring to a boil. Season to taste.

Imitation bacon bits or cubes of lean Canadian bacon may be used for additional flavoring.

YIELD: ABOUT 1 QUART
APPROX. CAL/SERV.: 1 CUP = 300   ½ CUP = 150

. . . . **Salad Bowl Soup**

1 18-OUNCE CAN SPICY TOMATO COCKTAIL JUICE
1 CUP GARBANZO BEANS, DRAINED
¾ CUP CUBED COOKED CHICKEN OR TURKEY
1 PEELED AND MASHED AVOCADO
¼ AVOCADO SLICED IN 4 PIECES FOR GARNISH (OPTIONAL)

Heat the tomato cocktail juice with garbanzos and chicken or turkey meat.
Simmer about 5 minutes. Stir in the mashed avocado.
Serve immediately garnished with extra avocado slices, if desired.

YIELD: ABOUT 1 QUART
APPROX. CAL/SERV.: 1 CUP = 290

. . . . **Greek Egg Lemon Soup**

1 QUART WATER
4 PACKAGES INSTANT CHICKEN BROTH
¼ CUP UNCOOKED RICE
4 TABLESPOONS FRESH LEMON JUICE
   EGG SUBSTITUTE EQUIVALENT TO 3 EGGS

Bring water to a boil in a saucepan. Add chicken broth and stir until dissolved. Add rice and cook until tender. Remove from heat.
Bring egg substitute to room temperature. Beat lemon juice into egg substitute. Whisk half the broth, a little at a time, into egg substitute mixture. Pour egg substitute mixture back into remaining broth, mixing well. Return to low heat and cook, stirring constantly, just until soup is thickened.
Caution: Do not boil.

YIELD: 1 QUART
APPROX. CAL/SERV.: 60

Meats

Meat is one of the foods Americans enjoy most as the mainstay of their daily meals. Many people have come to equate the concepts of "flavorful" and "tender" with large servings of meat that have a high fat content; however, it is possible to have flavorful, tender meat without the heavy marbling. Learning to be satisfied with smaller servings of meat will be easier if you round out meals with tastily prepared vegetables, fruits, bread and beverage.

Choose lean meat cuts with more muscle than fat such as round or rump. As a rule, young animals provide the leanest cuts. Quality is important. Firm, dry, fine-textured lean meat is preferable to soft, moist, coarse-textured lean meat. Good quality lean beef is a uniform, bright, light-to-deep red. Very young veal is light pink; meat from slightly older animals is darker grayish-pink, and is just as acceptable. Very young lamb is bright pink; older lamb is dark pink to red. There is less fat in the younger animals. Take advantage of special meat prices in retail groceries, where good lean cuts are often made available at lower cost. Grass-fed beef is leanest and contains more protein and less fat than grain-fed beef. The recipes in this section adapt well to the preparation of grass-fed beef.

Pork, ham, beef and lamb are the fattiest of the meats. Plan to serve them less frequently than fish, poultry and veal.

Few meat eaters will turn down a good steak. And believe it or not, you can still have a tender steak without choosing a heavily marbled piece of beef. London broil, round and flank steaks are very good choices, but they benefit from tenderizing. You may want to use a marinade, and one of the most efficient ways to do this is in a roasting bag. Fruit juices and wines make elegant marinades. For a dark, rich flavor, refrigerate the meat in a combination of dry red wine and water. Or use lemon juice, orange juice or white wine. Add flavor to the marinade with fresh orange or lemon slices, herbs or garlic. Dry the steak before broiling it Watch carefully for that state of doneness when the meat is rare or medium rare. The result: a juicy, tender meat.

Veal is lower in fat than beef or the other meats, although it is slightly higher in cholesterol because it comes from very young animals. Like poultry and fish, veal may be served more often during the week than beef, pork or lamb. It is a favorite of many grand cuisines for its delicate flavor and versatility in combining with other ingredients.

The aroma of roasting fresh pork has a robust outdoors quality. Because pork is likely to be quite high in saturated fat, roasting and broiling are the preferred cooking methods. It is a happy fact, however, that most pork on the market today has far less fat and hence more protein per serving than in previous years. This is the result of scientific breeding and feeding practices. Sirloin roast, tenderloin and loin chops are relatively lean when closely trimmed. Pork requires long, slow cooking, but is easily overdone to dry tastelessness. Thorough cooking is necessary to kill trichinae, but contrary to the belief of many an otherwise good cook, this is accomplished when the meat registers an internal temperature of only 140°. At 170°, a mere 30° more, pork reaches its peak of flavor and tenderness. Though still slightly pink in color, it is entirely safe to eat.

Of the smoked cuts, Canadian bacon is acceptable, being medium lean. The butt end of a ham is leaner than the shank end; a good indicator of leanness is the center ham slice, because marbling and seam fat are most evident there.

Lamb is another meat that is particularly good when it has been cooked over an open fire. Its flavor has a special affinity for herbs, including dill and mint, which are seldom used with other meats. Lamb comes from young sheep, generally less than one year old. An animal between one and two years old provides yearling mutton. The leg and the loin sections of a lamb yield the leanest meat. Lamb is at its juiciest and is most flavorful when served medium rare. Leftover lamb makes good sandwiches or finds its way easily into an aromatic moussaka.

Choose very lean meats for grinding. Do not grind meats in which interstitial fat is visible. Trim all remaining fat from cooked meats.

Because meats are a major source of saturated fat, their careful selection and preparation are prime factors in lowering total saturated fat intake. Accordingly, all recommendations concerning meats assume the greatest importance in planning fat-controlled meals. It would be wise to consult Shopping Tips and Cooking Tips before preparing the following Meat recipes.

Beef Bourguignon

5	MEDIUM ONIONS, SLICED
4	TABLESPOONS OIL
2	POUNDS LEAN BEEF, CUT INTO 1-INCH CUBES
1½	TABLESPOONS FLOUR
¼	TEASPOON MARJORAM
¼	TEASPOON THYME
1½	TEASPOONS SALT
½	TEASPOON PEPPER
½	CUP BOUILLON
1	CUP DRY RED WINE
½	POUND FRESH MUSHROOMS, SLICED

In a heavy skillet, cook the onions in the oil until tender. Remove them to another dish.

In the same pan, sauté the beef cubes until browned. Sprinkle with flour and seasonings.

Add bouillon and wine. Stir well and simmer slowly for 1½ to 2 hours. Add more bouillon and wine (1 part stock to 2 parts wine) as necessary to keep beef barely covered.

Return onions to the stew, add the mushrooms and cook stirring 30 minutes longer, adding more bouillon and wine if necessary. Sauce should be thick and dark brown.

YIELD: 8 SERVINGS
APPROX. CAL/SERV.: 375

. . . . *Braised Sirloin Tips*

2 TABLESPOONS MARGARINE
2 POUNDS BEEF SIRLOIN TIP, CUT INTO 1-INCH CUBES
1 10½-OUNCE CAN BEEF CONSOMMÉ
⅓ CUP RED BURGUNDY OR CRANBERRY COCKTAIL
2 TABLESPOONS SOY SAUCE
1 CLOVE GARLIC, MINCED
¼ TEASPOON ONION SALT
2 TABLESPOONS CORNSTARCH
¼ CUP WATER
4 CUPS HOT COOKED RICE

Melt margarine in a large skillet and brown meat on all sides.

Stir in the consommé, wine (or cranberry cocktail), soy sauce, garlic and onion salt. Heat to boiling. Reduce heat, cover, and simmer 1 hour, or until meat is tender.

Blend cornstarch and water and stir gradually into the stew. Cook, stirring constantly, until gravy thickens and boils. Cook 1 minute more. Serve over rice.

YIELD: 8 SERVINGS
APPROX. CAL/SERV.: 415

. . . . Beef Kabobs

1 CUP RED WINE

½ CUP SOY SAUCE

1 CUP PINEAPPLE JUICE

1 TEASPOON THYME

1 TEASPOON ROSEMARY

¼ CUP WORCESTERSHIRE SAUCE

1 ONION, FINELY CHOPPED

½ TEASPOON PEPPER

1½ POUNDS SIRLOIN, CUT INTO CUBES

3 TOMATOES, CUT INTO EIGHTHS, IF LARGE; OR USE WHOLE CHERRY TOMATOES

3 ONIONS, CUT IN 1-INCH WEDGES, OR SMALL WHOLE BOILING ONIONS

12 WHOLE MUSHROOMS

1 SMALL EGGPLANT, PEELED AND CHOPPED IN 1-INCH PIECES

1 GREEN PEPPER, CUT IN LARGE CUBES

12 SMALL WHOLE POTATOES, COOKED FRESH, OR CANNED

Make a marinade by mixing the first 8 ingredients together. Pour over the meat. Let stand 2 hours at room temperature, or overnight in the refrigerator.

Alternate the beef on skewers with the vegetables. Broil 3 inches from the heat for about 15 minutes, or grill over charcoal turning frequently and basting with the marinade.

YIELD: 8 SERVINGS

APPROX. CAL/SERV.: 320

. . . . *Marinated Steak*

1 THICK FLANK STEAK OR LONDON BROIL (ABOUT 1½ POUNDS)
⅔ CUP DRY RED WINE
1 TABLESPOON SOY SAUCE
⅛ TEASPOON OREGANO, CRUMBLED
⅛ TEASPOON MARJORAM, CRUMBLED
⅛ TEASPOON PEPPER

Mix together the wine, soy sauce and seasonings. Place the steak in a long glass baking dish and pour the marinade over the meat. Cover and chill at least 12 to 18 hours, turning meat once or twice.

Preheat the broiler. Remove the steak from the marinade. Pat dry and broil 4 inches from the heat for about 5 minutes on each side.

To serve, cut thin slices diagonally across the grain.
Serve with rice.

YIELD: 6 SERVINGS
APPROX. CAL/SERV.: 270

. . . . *Chinese Beef Skillet*

1 7-OUNCE PACKAGE FROZEN CHINESE PEA PODS
3 TABLESPOONS OIL
1 POUND BEEF TENDERLOIN TIPS, SLICED PAPER-THIN (ACROSS THE GRAIN)
¼ CUP CHOPPED ONION
1 SMALL CLOVE GARLIC, MINCED
4 CUPS THINLY SLICED RAW CAULIFLOWER FLORETS (1 MEDIUM HEAD)
1 CUP CONDENSED BEEF BROTH
2 TABLESPOONS CORNSTARCH
¼ CUP SOY SAUCE
½ CUP COLD WATER

Recipe continues...

Pour boiling water over frozen pea pods and carefully separate them with a fork. Drain immediately.

Preheat electric skillet to about 400°F. Heat 2 tablespoons of the oil; add half the beef. Cook briskly, turning meat constantly for 1 or 2 minutes, or until just browned. Remove meat at once. Let skillet heat about 1 minute and repeat with remaining beef. Remove beef. Cook onion and garlic a few seconds in remaining oil. Add cauliflower and broth. Cook, stirring gently, about 3 minutes until cauliflower is tender-crisp.

Mix cornstarch, soy sauce and water. Stir into the broth in the skillet. Add beef and pea pods. Cook, stirring constantly, until the sauce thickens. Serve with rice.

YIELD: 6 SERVINGS, ABOUT 1½ QUARTS
APPROX. CAL/SERV.: 285

· · · · · · · · · *Good and Easy Sauerbraten*

You can make this tangy sauerbraten in less than three hours.

3 POUNDS LEAN BONELESS SHOULDER ROAST
1 CUP WATER
1 CUP WINE VINEGAR
SALT AND PEPPER TO TASTE
1 MEDIUM ONION, SLICED
2 BAY LEAVES
16 GINGERSNAPS, CRUSHED TO FINE CRUMBS

Preheat oven to 475°F.

Season the roast with salt and pepper, place in a Dutch oven and roast, uncovered, in preheated oven until both sides are browned, turning once—about 4 or 5 minutes on each side.

Remove from the oven, pour vinegar and water over the roast. Arrange onion slices on top, add bay leaves to the pot liquid. Cover and return to the oven.

Reduce heat to 350°F. and cook 1½ hours, or until tender. Add gingersnaps, replace cover, and cook ½ hour longer. Additional water may be added to thin the gravy.

Remove meat from gravy and slice as thin as possible. Serve with sour red cabbage and applesauce.

YIELD: 8 SERVINGS

APPROX. CAL/SERV.: 275

· · · · · · · · · · · *Lazy Beef Casserole*

A delicious gravy forms during the cooking of this very easy and tender beef dish.

1 POUND LEAN BEEF CHUCK, CUT INTO 1½-INCH CUBES

½ CUP RED WINE

1 10½-OUNCE CAN CONSOMMÉ, UNDILUTED

¾ TEASPOON SALT

⅛ TEASPOON PEPPER

1 MEDIUM ONION, CHOPPED

¼ CUP FINE DRY BREAD CRUMBS

¼ CUP ALL-PURPOSE FLOUR

Preheat the oven to 300°F. Put meat in a casserole with the wine, consommé, seasonings and onion. Mix flour and bread crumbs and stir into the liquid.

Cover and bake about 3 hours. (Or, a lower temperature and longer cooking time may be used if it is more convenient.)

Serve with rice or noodles.

YIELD: 4 SERVINGS

APPROX. CAL/SERV.: 350 (OR 450 WITH ½ CUP RICE OR PASTA)

. . . . *Nigerian Beef-Spinach Stew*

If you were a member of the Yoruba tribe in Nigeria, you would make this dish with melon seed and call it *Efo Egusi*, "Efo" for "spinach," "Egusi" for "melon seed." In other parts of West Africa, it is known as "Palaver Sauce." Whatever its name, this classic African dish is usually a mixture of meat and fish. Here it has a modern addition to the sauce in the form of ginger ale.

¼ CUP OIL
2 POUNDS LEAN STEWING BEEF, CUT INTO CUBES
1 12-OUNCE BOTTLE GINGER ALE
½ TEASPOON CRUSHED RED PEPPER
¼ TEASPOON BLACK PEPPER
1 TEASPOON SALT
1 MEDIUM TOMATO, CHOPPED
1 10-OUNCE PACKAGE FRESH SPINACH
4 MEDIUM ONIONS
2 MEDIUM WHOLE TOMATOES
2 TEASPOONS CORNSTARCH

Heat 2 tablespoons of the oil in a heavy saucepan and brown the beef cubes on all sides, adding more oil as it is needed and removing cubes to add others. Return all meat to the pan and add ginger ale, red pepper, black pepper, salt and the chopped tomato. Cover and simmer 1½ hours or until meat is tender.

Meanwhile, wash the spinach, and remove tough stems. Tear leaves into small pieces. Slice the onions thinly and separate the slices into rings. Slice the whole tomatoes.

Mix the cornstarch with 1 tablespoon of cold water. Stir into the stew and cook 1 minute until slightly thickened.

Add onion rings, tomato slices and spinach. Return to simmer. Cover and simmer until the vegetables are just tender—about 5 minutes.

Serve with rice.

YIELD: 8 SERVINGS
APPROX. CAL/SERV.: 370 (OR 470 WITH ½ CUP RICE)

. . . . *Beef Stroganoff*

1 POUND BEEF TENDERLOIN, LEAN BEEF ROUND OR SIRLOIN
SALT AND PEPPER
½ POUND MUSHROOMS, SLICED
1 ONION, SLICED
3 TABLESPOONS OIL
3 TABLESPOONS FLOUR
2 CUPS BEEF BOUILLON
2 TABLESPOONS TOMATO PASTE
1 TEASPOON DRY MUSTARD
PINCH OF OREGANO AND DILLWEED
2 TABLESPOONS SHERRY
⅓ CUP LOW-FAT YOGURT

Remove all visible fat from the meat and cut into thin strips, about 2 inches long. Sprinkle with salt and pepper and let stand in a cool place for 2 hours.

In a heavy skillet, sauté mushrooms in oil until tender. Remove from skillet, and sauté onions in the same oil until brown. Remove from skillet.

Brown meat quickly on all sides until rare. Remove and set aside.

Blend the flour into the oil in the skillet and gradually add the bouillon, stirring constantly until smooth and slightly thick. Add the tomato paste, dry mustard, oregano, dill weed and sherry. Blend well. Combine the sauce with the meat, mushrooms and onions in the top of a double boiler. Cook for 20 minutes. Blend in the yogurt 5 minutes before serving.

YIELD: 6 SERVINGS
APPROX. CAL/SERV.: 275 (OR 375 WITH ½ CUP RICE OR PASTA)

. . . . *Sukiyaki*

2 POUNDS TENDERLOIN OR SIRLOIN STEAK

3 TABLESPOONS OIL

½ CUP SOY SAUCE

½ CUP BEEF STOCK, OR CANNED CONDENSED BEEF BROTH

1 TABLESPOON HONEY

1 CUP GREEN ONION CUT DIAGONALLY INTO ½-INCH LENGTHS

1 CUP CELERY CUT DIAGONALLY INTO 1-INCH LENGTHS

1 CUP THINLY SLICED MUSHROOMS

4 CUPS FRESH SPINACH LEAVES, WASHED AND WELL-DRAINED; OR SHREDDED CHINESE CABBAGE

1 5-OUNCE CAN WATER CHESTNUTS, DRAINED AND THINLY SLICED

1 5-OUNCE CAN BAMBOO SHOOTS, DRAINED AND SLIVERED

1 16-OUNCE CAN BEAN SPROUTS, DRAINED AND RINSED IN COLD WATER; OR 1 POUND FRESH BEAN SPROUTS

For best results, partially freeze the steak before slicing. Remove excess fat. Lay the steak flat on a board. Using a sharp knife, thinly slice the meat across the grain, diagonally from top to bottom.

Just before cooking, arrange the sliced steak and vegetables neatly on a large platter or tray for easy handling. Preheat a large (12-inch) electric fry pan to 400°F. Heat the oil in the pan and quickly sauté the steak strips a few at a time until browned on both sides (about 2 minutes).

Combine the beef stock, soy sauce and honey and pour over the cooked steak strips. Push the meat to one side of the pan, allow the sauce to begin bubbling and, keeping each vegetable grouping separate, add the onions, celery and mushrooms. Cook, tossing over high heat about 2 minutes. Push each aside as it is cooked.

Again keeping in separate groups, add the spinach or Chinese cabbage, separately, then the sliced water chestnuts, bamboo shoots and drained bean sprouts, keeping each group apart from the others. Cook and toss stirring each food until just heated through. Season with pepper.

Serve immediately with rice, accompanied by soy sauce. If more gravy is desired, add an additional ½ cup of broth to the pan before serving.

YIELD: 10 SERVINGS

APPROX. CAL/SERV.: 280 (OR 380 WITH ½ CUP RICE)

Stuffed Beef Roll-Ups

¼ CUP MARGARINE

1 CUP BOILING BEEF BROTH (CANNED OR MADE FROM A BOUILLON CUBE)

2 CUPS PACKAGED HERB STUFFING MIX

¼ CUP MINCED ONION

2 POUNDS LEAN ROUND STEAK, CUT ¼ INCH THICK

1 TEASPOON SALT

¼ TEASPOON PEPPER

2 TABLESPOONS FLOUR

2 TABLESPOONS MARGARINE OR OIL

1 CAN ONION SOUP, UNDILUTED

Melt the ¼ cup of margarine in the broth. Mix lightly with the stuffing mix and onion.

Cut the steak into 8 portions. Season with salt and pepper. Place a spoonful of stuffing on each steak piece; roll and secure with a string or a toothpick.

Coat each roll in flour and brown in the remaining margarine in a heavy skillet.

Pour the soup over all. Cover and simmer about 1½ hours or until tender.

YIELD: 8 SERVINGS

APPROX. CAL/SERV.: 430

B

A

C

. . . . *Sweet-and-Sour Tongue*

4 POUNDS COOKED SMOKED BEEF TONGUE
1 16-OUNCE CAN CRANBERRY JELLY
½ CUP CHILI SAUCE
½ CUP HOT WATER
½ CUP WHITE RAISINS

Peel and slice the smoked tongue and arrange in a baking dish.

Combine the jelly, chili sauce, water and raisins. Cook until jelly melts.

Pour over the slices and allow to stand overnight to marinate.

Before serving, heat in oven at 350°F. for 30 minutes.

YIELD: 16 SERVINGS
APPROX. CAL/SERV.: 345

. . . . *Barbecued Beef Ribs*

2 POUNDS LEAN BEEF RIBS
¼ CUP PEACH PRESERVES
½ CUP WATER
JUICE OF 1 LEMON
1½ TABLESPOONS BROWN SUGAR
1 TABLESPOON MARGARINE
1 TABLESPOON OIL
1 TABLESPOON VINEGAR
½ TEASPOON PAPRIKA
1½ TEASPOONS SALT
½ TEASPOON PEPPER
2 TABLESPOONS WORCESTERSHIRE SAUCE

Preheat the oven to 450°F.

Place the ribs on a rack in shallow baking pan and roast for 30 minutes.

In a small saucepan, combine all other ingredients and cook over medium heat until thickened, stirring constantly. Set sauce aside.

Remove the ribs and rack from pan and pour off the fat. Reduce oven heat to 350°F. Return ribs to the pan, and pour the sauce over them. Bake uncovered, basting occasionally, until ribs are tender, about 1 hour.

YIELD: 4 SERVINGS

APPROX. CAL/SERV.: 385

Chinese Flank Steak

 1 POUND LEAN FLANK STEAK
¼ CUP SOY SAUCE
¼ CUP COOKING SHERRY
 1 TEASPOON SUGAR
 1 TABLESPOON CORNSTARCH
¼ CUP OIL
 1 6-OUNCE PACKAGE OF FROZEN PEA PODS OR FROZEN ITALIAN GREEN BEANS, THAWED AND DRAINED
¼ TO ½ POUND FRESH MUSHROOMS, SLICED
¼ CUP CHOPPED GREEN ONIONS
 8 WATER CHESTNUTS, THINLY SLICED

Slice flank steak across the grain into thin strips, 2 to 3 inches long, ½ to 1 inch wide, and ½ to 1 inch thick.

Mix soy sauce, sherry, sugar and cornstarch, add meat and marinate the mixture for at least 30 minutes at room temperature or 2 hours in the refrigerator.

When ready to cook, heat skillet with about 1½ tablespoons oil until very hot. Add pea pods or green beans and stir rapidly until lightly brown and crisp tender. Remove from skillet.

Add another tablespoon oil and brown mushrooms (more oil may be needed). Remove from skillet.

Add remaining 1½ tablespoons oil, heat, and add green onions, meat, and all of the marinade. Stir rapidly until all of the meat is browned on all sides.

Add all other ingredients, including water chestnuts, and stir until heated through.

YIELD: 4 SERVINGS

APPROX. CAL/SERV.: 365

Veal

. . . . *Veal with Artichokes*

2 CLOVES GARLIC
2 TABLESPOONS OIL
2 POUNDS VEAL ROUND, CUT INTO BITE-SIZE PIECES (HAVE BUTCHER
  FLATTEN PIECES TO ¼ INCH THICK)
1 1-POUND CAN SOLID-PACK TOMATOES
½ CUP SHERRY OR SAUTERNE
¼ TEASPOON OREGANO
2 10-OUNCE PACKAGES FROZEN ARTICHOKE HEARTS

In a heavy skillet, sauté the garlic in oil. Remove the garlic.
Season the veal with salt and pepper. Brown in the oil.
Add the tomatoes, wine and oregano, mixing well, and the artichoke
hearts.
Cover and simmer 45 to 60 minutes, or until the meat is tender.

YIELD: 8 SERVINGS
APPROX. CAL/SERV.: 310

· · · · · · · · · · *Paupiettes de Veau*

2 POUNDS VEAL ROUND, SLICED ¼ INCH THICK AND CUT INTO SIX
  3 × 4-INCH RECTANGLES
1 6-OUNCE CAN MUSHROOMS
1 TABLESPOON CHOPPED ONION
¼ CUP PLUS 2 TABLESPOONS OIL
  3 SLICES BREAD, BROKEN INTO SMALL PIECES
½ TEASPOON DRIED PARSLEY
¼ TEASPOON THYME
¼ TEASPOON SALT
⅛ TEASPOON PEPPER

Preheat the oven to 350°F.

Brown the mushrooms and onion in the 2 tablespoons of oil.

Combine the bread, parsley, thyme, salt and pepper in a bowl. Mix in the browned mushrooms and onions. Divide this mixture into 6 portions and place each portion on a piece of meat, wrap the meat around the filling to form a cylinder. Overlap the ends and secure with a toothpick.

Brown the paupiettes on all sides in the ¼ cup of oil.

While meat is browning, make the sauce.

· · · · · · · · · · · · · · · *sauce*

2 TABLESPOONS FLOUR
¼ TEASPOON SALT
PEPPER TO TASTE
1 TABLESPOON OIL
½ CUP BROTH
½ CUP DRY WHITE WINE

In a saucepan, combine the flour and seasoning with the oil. Blend until smooth. Gradually stir in the broth and wine.

Place the browned paupiettes in a casserole dish and pour the sauce over all. Cover and bake 1½ hours. About 15 minutes before end of bak-

Recipe continues...

ing time, remove cover, spoon some of the sauce over the paupiettes, and continue cooking, uncovered, to glaze the meat.

YIELD: 8 SERVINGS

APPROX. CAL/SERV.: 390

Veal Columbo

1 ½ POUNDS VEAL CUTLET, CUT IN SERVING PIECES
⅓ CUP WHEAT GERM
2 TABLESPOONS FLOUR
½ TEASPOON SALT
½ TEASPOON CRUSHED OREGANO
⅛ TEASPOON GARLIC POWDER
⅛ TEASPOON ONION POWDER
⅛ TEASPOON PEPPER
3 TABLESPOONS MARGARINE
1 3-OUNCE CAN MUSHROOMS WITH LIQUID
3 TABLESPOONS TOMATO PASTE
¼ CUP MARSALA WINE, SHERRY OR WATER
2 TABLESPOONS CHOPPED PARSLEY

Coat the veal pieces with 3 tablespoons of the wheat germ and pound it into the meat with a mallet or knife.

Stir together the remaining wheat germ, flour, salt and spices and spread mixture over a sheet of wax paper. Dip the pieces of veal into the mixture, coating each piece well. Sauté the veal in margarine until golden on both sides. Remove from skillet.

Drain the mushrooms, measure the liquid and add water to make ⅓ cup. Pour into the skillet.

Add the mushrooms, tomato paste and the water or wine. Mix well. Return the veal to the skillet and simmer 10 minutes.

Arrange the veal on a heated platter. Cover with the sauce and serve garnished with parsley.

YIELD: 6 SERVINGS

APPROX. CAL/SERV.: 330

Cutlet of Veal with Zucchini

- 6 VEAL CUTLETS
- 2 EGG WHITES, SLIGHTLY BEATEN
- ⅔ CUP FINE BREAD CRUMBS
- 2 TABLESPOONS OIL
- 2 CUPS CANNED TOMATOES
- 1½ TEASPOONS SALT
- ¼ TEASPOON OREGANO
- 3 MEDIUM ZUCCHINI, SLICED ½ INCH THICK

Dip the cutlets in egg white, then in crumbs. Brown them in oil.

Pour off excess oil. Add the tomatoes, salt and oregano. Cover tightly and simmer for 30 minutes.

Add the zucchini, cover and continue cooking 20 minutes.

YIELD: 6 SERVINGS
APPROX. CAL/SERV.: 355

Veal Stew with Fennel

- 1½ POUNDS LEAN VEAL STEW MEAT, CUT IN 1-INCH CUBES
- 3 TABLESPOONS OIL
- SALT AND PEPPER
- 1 LARGE ONION, CHOPPED
- ¼ CUP WATER
- ½ TEASPOON CRUSHED FENNEL SEED
- 3 SMALL GREEN ONIONS, CHOPPED
- 2 PACKAGES FROZEN SPINACH LEAVES

Brown the meat in the oil in a Dutch oven or heavy kettle. Season meat with salt and pepper, stir in the onion and sauté until limp, but not brown.

Add water and fennel seed to the pot, cover and simmer the stew over low heat for about 1 hour, or until the meat is tender. Add more water if necessary during cooking.

Recipe continues…

Put in the onions and spinach. Cover and simmer until the spinach is tender, about 5 to 10 minutes. Season to taste.

Arrange the meat on a heated serving platter, surround with a border of spinach and garnish with lemon wedges.

YIELD: 6 SERVINGS

APPROX. CAL/SERV.: 320

. . . . *Veal Scallopini*

4 VEAL CUTLETS

1 SMALL CLOVE GARLIC, QUARTERED

2 TABLESPOONS OIL

1 TABLESPOON FLOUR

1/2 TEASPOON SALT

FEW GRAINS PEPPER

FEW GRAINS NUTMEG

1 SMALL ONION, THINLY SLICED

1/2 CUP MARSALA WINE

1 4-OUNCE CAN SLICED MUSHROOMS, DRAINED; OR 1/2 POUND FRESH MUSHROOMS

1/2 TEASPOON PAPRIKA

2 TABLESPOONS COARSELY CHOPPED PARSLEY

Sauté garlic in oil over low flame for 5 minutes. Discard garlic. Brown cutlets in the oil.

Mix flour, salt, pepper and nutmeg. Sprinkle over the browned meat. Add onion and wine. Cover skillet and simmer about 20 minutes, turning the meat several times. Add more liquid (wine or tomato juice) if necessary.

Add mushrooms, cover and cook 8 to 10 minutes longer.

Serve on a warm platter with the sauce, garnished with the paprika and parsley.

YIELD: 4 SERVINGS

APPROX. CAL/SERV.: 360

. . . . *Veal Paprika*

 1 TEASPOON SALT
¼ TEASPOON PEPPER
¼ CUP PLUS 1 TABLESPOON FLOUR
1½ POUNDS VEAL CUBES
 3 TABLESPOONS OIL
 1 TEASPOON PAPRIKA
¾ CUP WATER
 1 TABLESPOON VINEGAR
 1 CUP SKIM MILK

Mix ¼ cup of flour with the pepper and ½ teaspoon of the salt. Coat the veal cubes with the mixture.

Brown meat in hot oil.

Combine the paprika, the remaining ½ teaspoon of salt and water. Pour over the browned veal. Cover and simmer about 1 hour, or until meat is tender. Remove to a hot platter.

Add the tablespoon of flour to the drippings in the skillet. Combine the vinegar and skim milk, and add slowly to the drippings. Do not boil. Heat sauce thoroughly, and pour over veal. Serve at once.

YIELD: 6 SERVINGS
APPROX. CAL/SERV.: 335

. . . . *Stuffed Veal Breast*

 4 OR 5 POUND VEAL BREAST
1½ TEASPOONS SALT
 1 CUP RAW BROWN RICE
 1 MEDIUM ONION, FINELY CHOPPED
 2 TABLESPOONS OIL
½ TEASPOON POULTRY SEASONING
 2 TABLESPOONS MINCED PARSLEY
 1 TEASPOON GRATED ORANGE RIND
⅓ CUP SEEDLESS RAISINS

Recipe continues…

Have the butcher cut a large pocket in the side of the veal breast. Wipe the veal with moist paper towels. Sprinkle salt over the surface of the meat and inside the pocket. Set aside.

Preheat the oven to 300°F.

Rinse the brown rice. In a 2-quart saucepan, bring 3 cups of water to a boil, add 1 teaspoon of salt and brown rice. Cover saucepan and simmer over medium heat for 25–30 minutes, or until the rice is almost tender. Remove from heat, drain and allow to cool. Meanwhile, sauté the chopped onion in the oil until tender but not brown (about 5 minutes). Remove from heat.

In a mixing bowl, combine the cooked rice, sautéed onion, remaining ½ teaspoon of salt, poultry seasoning, minced parsley, orange rind and raisins. Mix thoroughly. Correct seasoning.

Fill the pocket in the veal breast with the stuffing and close the pocket with a skewer or heavy, round toothpicks. Place breast rib side down in a shallow roasting pan. Brush with oil. Place in preheated oven and bake for 2½ to 3 hours, or until tender, basting occasionally with accumulated liquid. Do not cover—veal should brown nicely during baking.

YIELD: 10 SERVINGS
APPROX. CAL/SERV.: 340

. . . . *Veal Stufino*

1½ POUNDS SHOULDER OF VEAL, CUT IN CHUNKS
  3 TABLESPOONS OIL
  1 CARROT, FINELY CHOPPED
  2 STALKS CELERY, FINELY CHOPPED
  1 ONION, FINELY CHOPPED
  1 CLOVE GARLIC, MINCED
 ½ CUP DRY WHITE WINE
  2 CUPS SKINNED, CHOPPED TOMATOES
SALT AND PEPPER TO TASTE

Brown the veal in the oil. Add the carrot, celery, onion and garlic. Pour in the wine, scraping the pan and stirring. Cook for 3 minutes.

Add the tomatoes, salt and pepper. Cook over medium-high heat for a few minutes to reduce the sauce. Then cover and simmer over low heat, or bake in a 300°F. oven for 1½ hours. Serve garnished with parsley.

YIELD: 6 SERVINGS

APPROX. CAL/SERV.: 340

. . . . *Scaloppine Al Limone*

1½ POUNDS VEAL SCALLOPS, CUT ⅜ INCH THICK AND POUNDED UNTIL ¼ INCH THICK*

SALT

FRESHLY GROUND PEPPER

  2 TABLESPOONS FLOUR

  2 TABLESPOONS MARGARINE

  2 TABLESPOONS OLIVE OIL

  ¾ CUP BEEF STOCK, FRESH OR CANNED

  6 PAPER-THIN LEMON SLICES

  1 TABLESPOON LEMON JUICE

Season the veal scallops with salt and pepper, then dip them in flour and shake off the excess. In a heavy 10- to 12-inch skillet, melt 2 tablespoons of margarine with the 2 tablespoons of olive oil over moderate heat. When the foam subsides, add the veal, 4 or 5 scallops at a time, and sauté them for about 2 minutes on each side, or until they are golden brown.

With tongs, transfer the veal scallops to a plate. Now pour off almost all of the fat from the skillet, leaving a thin film on the bottom. Add ½ cup of beef stock and boil it briskly for 1 or 2 minutes, stirring constantly and scraping in any browned bits clinging to the bottom and sides of the pan.

Return the veal to the skillet and arrange the lemon slices on top. Cover the skillet and simmer over low heat for 10 to 15 minutes, or until the veal is tender when pierced with the tip of a sharp knife.

To serve, transfer the scallops to a heated platter and surround with

* Veal cubes (stewing meat) may be substituted. Pound as flat as possible. Follow directions above, but cooking time will be increased to 45 minutes to an hour over low heat, or until tender.

Recipe continues...

the lemon slices. Add the ¼ cup of remaining beef stock to the juices in the skillet and boil briskly until the stock is reduced to a syrupy glaze. Add the lemon juice and cook, stirring, for 1 minute. Remove the pan from the heat, and pour the sauce over the scallops.

YIELD: 6 SERVINGS

APPROX. CAL/SERV.: 325

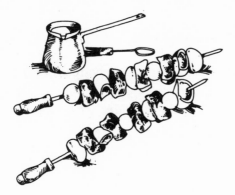

Lamb

Lamb Kabobs

1 ½ TO 2 POUNDS LEAN LAMB, CUT IN CUBES
SELECT VEGETABLES FROM THE FOLLOWING:
  FIRM FRESH TOMATO WEDGES OR CHERRY TOMATOES
  FRESH MUSHROOM CAPS
  EGGPLANT CUBES
  SMALL CANNED WHOLE POTATOES
  SMALL CANNED ONIONS, OR FRESH ONIONS CUT IN 1-INCH WEDGES,
    OR RAW PEARL ONIONS
  GREEN PEPPER, CUT IN SQUARES

Place meat in a shallow glass dish, pour the desired marinade over meat. Let stand 2 hours at room temperature, turning occasionally, or let stand overnight in the refrigerator.

Drain meat, reserving the marinade. Thread meat and vegetables onto skewers.

Broil 4 inches from a preheated broiler, about 15 minutes, turning once; or grill over hot coals. Baste with the marinade.

LAMB MARINADE I: Mix together 4 tablespoons of oil, 1 tablespoon of soy

Recipe continues...

sauce, ¼ teaspoon of pepper, 2 onions (chopped fine) and 3 table-spoons of lemon juice.

LAMB MARINADE II: Prepare 1 envelope of dry garlic salad dressing mix as directed.

YIELD: 8 SERVINGS
APPROX. CAL/SERV.: 330

· · · · · · · · · · · **Lamb Chop Casserole**

6 LEAN SHOULDER LAMB CHOPS
1½ CUPS WATER
1 8-OUNCE CAN TOMATO SAUCE
¼ CUP CATSUP
1 TABLESPOON WORCESTERSHIRE SAUCE
½ TEASPOON OREGANO
1 CLOVE GARLIC, CRUSHED
1 TEASPOON SALT
½ TEASPOON PEPPER

Preheat oven to 350°F.

In a large heavy skillet, brown the chops well on both sides.

Place chops in a shallow baking pan. Pour the water into skillet in which chops were browned; stir to loosen particles in the bottom of the pan.

Mix together the remaining ingredients and pour over the chops. Cover and bake for 1 hour.

YIELD: 6 SERVINGS
APPROX. CAL/SERV.: 265

· · · · · · · · · · **Julep Lamb Chops, Flambé**

4 LEAN LOIN LAMB CHOPS
2 TEASPOONS DRIED MINT
2 TABLESPOONS BOURBON, WARMED
2 TEASPOONS OIL
4 SLICES CANNED PINEAPPLE
SALT AND BLACK PEPPER TO TASTE

Cut all excess fat from the lamb chops. Press the dried mint into the surface of the chops.

Broil about 4 inches from the heat in a broiler or over charcoal for 12 to 16 minutes, depending on the thickness of the chops.

Meanwhile, heat the oil in a skillet and brown the pineapple slices slightly on each side.

When the chops are done, season with salt and pepper. Arrange in a serving dish on top of the pineapple slices.

Sprinkle the bourbon over the chops, ignite and take to the table aflame.

YIELD: 4 SERVINGS

APPROX. CAL/SERV.: 325

Easy Lamb Curry

1 TABLESPOON OIL

3 TABLESPOONS CHOPPED ONION

1 CUP DICED CELERY

1 TABLESPOON FLOUR

1 TEASPOON CURRY POWDER

2 CUPS BOILING WATER

2 BOUILLON CUBES

¼ CUP CATSUP

½ TEASPOON SALT

2 CUPS DICED COOKED LAMB

½ CUP CHOPPED APPLE (UNPEELED IF COLOR IS GOOD AND SKIN IS CRISP)

In a skillet, sauté the onions and celery lightly in the oil.

Stir in flour mixed with curry powder. Blend until smooth. Add bouillon cubes dissolved in water and catsup and salt. Simmer about 1 hour, stirring occasionally.

Add the cooked lamb and the chopped apple. Simmer another 20 minutes.

Serve over rice.

YIELD: 4 SERVINGS

APPROX. CAL/SERV.: 325 (OR 425 WITH ½ CUP RICE)

· · · · · · · · · · *Armenian Lamb Casserole*

1   POUND LEAN LAMB, CUT IN 1-INCH CUBES
2   TABLESPOONS OIL
1   ONION, SLICED
1   CLOVE GARLIC, MINCED
1   CUP CANNED TOMATOES
1   GREEN PEPPER, QUARTERED
2   CARROTS, SLICED
3   SLICES LEMON
1   MEDIUM EGGPLANT, CUT IN 2-INCH CUBES
2   ZUCCHINI, CUT IN 1-INCH CUBES
$\frac{1}{2}$ TEASPOON PAPRIKA
$\frac{1}{8}$ TEASPOON CUMIN
$1\frac{1}{2}$ TEASPOONS SALT
$\frac{1}{2}$ TEASPOON PEPPER
$\frac{1}{2}$ CUP OKRA, SLICED (OPTIONAL)

Heat the oil in a skillet. Brown the lamb cubes, then add onions and garlic and brown slightly. Add the tomatoes, and cook over low heat for 1 hour, adding a small amount of water, if necessary.

Preheat the oven to 350°F.

Transfer the meat mixture to a large porcelain-coated or glass casserole. (Plain cast iron will discolor the vegetables.) Add all remaining ingredients, bring to a boil on top of the stove. Cover tightly, place in oven and bake 1 hour, or until vegetables are tender.

YIELD: 4 SERVINGS
APPROX. CAL/SERV.: 390

Baked Lamb Shanks

4 LAMB SHANKS, WITH EXCESS FAT REMOVED
SALT AND FRESHLY GROUND BLACK PEPPER
2 CLOVES GARLIC, MINCED
2 SMALL CARROTS, CUT IN THIN STRIPS
1 LARGE ONION, THINLY SLICED
2 RIBS CELERY, THINLY SLICED LENGTHWISE
2 BAY LEAVES, BROKEN
1 TEASPOON OREGANO
½ TEASPOON THYME
1 CUP TOMATO SAUCE, FRESH OR CANNED
1 CUP WATER
2 TABLESPOONS OLIVE OIL
8 OR MORE NEW POTATOES, PEELED

Preheat oven to 375°F. Season the lamb shanks with the salt and pepper to taste and the garlic.

In the bottom of a roasting pan place the carrots, onion, celery and bay leaves. Place the lamb shanks on the bed of vegetables and sprinkle with oregano and thyme. Add tomato sauce diluted with the water and the oil. Cover tightly and bake 1½ to 2½ hours, depending on the size of the shanks.

During the last 30 minutes of cooking, raise the temperature of the oven to 400°F. and uncover the roasting pan. Add the potatoes and continue cooking, uncovered, basting with the pan drippings.

When the potatoes are done, pour off the sauce and strain it. Skim the fat. Serve the shanks surrounded by the potatoes. Serve the sauce separately.

YIELD: 4 SERVINGS
APPROX. CAL/SERV.: 375

Lamb-Stuffed Cabbage

½ POUND COOKED LAMB, GROUND
1 CUP COOKED RICE (WHITE OR BROWN)
1 EGG
1 SMALL CLOVE GARLIC, CRUSHED
½ TEASPOON SALT
⅛ TEASPOON THYME, CRUMBLED
⅛ TEASPOON ROSEMARY, CRUMBLED
⅛ TEASPOON PEPPER
1 15-OUNCE CAN TOMATO SAUCE
1 HEAD CABBAGE (ABOUT 2 POUNDS)
2 TABLESPOONS MARGARINE
1 CUP CHOPPED ONION
2 TABLESPOONS SUGAR
½ TEASPOON SALT
½ CUP WATER

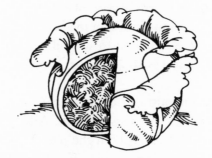

Combine the first 8 ingredients in a large bowl.

Add ⅓ of the tomato sauce and mix well with a fork.

Trim the outside leaves from the cabbage. Cut a small slice, about 3 inches in diameter, from the top end; set aside. Hollow out the cabbage leaving a shell about ½ inch thick. Make sure the core end is even, so the cabbage will sit level.

Spoon lamb mixture into the cabbage shell, pressing it down firmly. Fit top back into place. Tie with a string.

Sauté onion in margarine until soft.

Add remaining tomato sauce, sugar, salt and water. Bring to a boil, stirring constantly. Remove from heat.

Place cabbage, core end down, in a deep casserole or Dutch oven. Preheat oven to 350°F.

Pour sauce over cabbage. Cover and bake 1½ hours, basting with the sauce 2 or 3 times.

Place the cabbage on a heated serving platter, remove the string and spoon the sauce over. Cut into wedges to serve.

YIELD: 4 SERVINGS

APPROX. CAL/SERV.: 325

Lamb Chops Oriental

4 LEAN LAMB SHOULDER CHOPS, 1 INCH THICK

1 13-OUNCE CAN PINEAPPLE CHUNKS, DRAINED (RESERVE JUICE)

¼ CUP SOY SAUCE

¼ CUP VINEGAR

½ TEASPOON DRY MUSTARD

1 TABLESPOON OIL

¼ CUP BROWN SUGAR

1 TEASPOON CORNSTARCH

Place the chops in a shallow glass dish. Drain the pineapple and combine the syrup with the soy sauce, vinegar and mustard. Pour over the chops. Cover and refrigerate at least 4 hours, turning the chops occasionally.

Drain the chops, reserving the marinade. Heat the oil in a large skillet and brown the chops over medium heat. Add ¼ cup of the reserved marinade to the chops in the skillet. Cover tightly and cook over low heat 30 to 45 minutes, or until tender.

Mix the sugar and cornstarch in a small saucepan, stir in the remaining marinade. Heat to boiling, stirring constantly. Reduce heat, simmer 5 minutes. Add pineapple chunks and heat through. Serve the sauce over the chops.

YIELD: 4 SERVINGS

APPROX. CAL/SERV.: 335

Lamb Stew with Caraway

1 TABLESPOON OIL

1½ POUNDS BONELESS LAMB, CUT IN 1-INCH CUBES

2 TABLESPOONS FLOUR

SALT AND PEPPER TO TASTE

1 CLOVE GARLIC, MINCED

¼ CUP DRY WHITE WINE

WATER TO COVER

1 TEASPOON CARAWAY SEEDS

4 MEDIUM POTATOES, PEELED AND CUT IN LARGE CUBES

8 SMALL WHOLE ONIONS, PEELED

4 TO 6 CARROTS, CUT IN THICK SLICES

CHOPPED PARSLEY

Heat oil in a skillet. Brown lamb cubes well on all sides. Sprinkle with flour, salt, pepper and garlic, stirring well to coat lamb. Add wine and water to cover meats. Sprinkle with caraway seeds. Cover and simmer 1 hour, adding more water if necessary.

Add potatoes, onions and carrots, cover tightly and cook slowly until lamb is tender, about 30 minutes. Sprinkle with chopped parsley.

YIELD: 6 SERVINGS

APPROX. CAL/SERV.: 385

Pork

Canadian Bacon in Wine Sauce

1 POUND SLICED CANADIAN BACON
1½ TABLESPOONS OIL
1½ TABLESPOONS FLOUR
1 10½-OUNCE CAN CONSOMMÉ
PINCH OF THYME
PINCH OF DRIED SWEET BASIL
2 TABLESPOONS SHERRY

Cook the Canadian bacon in a skillet for 5 minutes, turning often. Remove to a heated serving platter. Discard the drippings.

Heat the oil in a sauce pan, blend in the flour and brown it slowly. Add the consommé, stirring to keep the sauce smooth. Add the thyme and sweet basil, simmer for 15 minutes over a low flame. Strain the sauce, add the sherry, heat through and pour over the bacon slices.

YIELD: 4 SERVINGS
APPROX. CAL/SERV.: 330

. . . . *Apricot Ham Steak*

1 1½-POUND HAM SLICE CUT 2 INCHES THICK
WHOLE CLOVES
¼ CUP FIRMLY PACKED BROWN SUGAR
1 16-OUNCE CAN PEELED WHOLE APRICOTS

Preheat oven to 325°F.

Remove any fat around the slice of ham. Place in a shallow baking pan. Sprinkle with sugar and stud the sides with cloves.

Drain the apricot juice. Pour ⅓ cup of the juice over the ham.

Bake 1 hour, basting often with the juice in the pan. Arrange the drained apricots on top of the ham and bake 15 minutes longer, or until richly glazed.

YIELD: 6 SERVINGS
APPROX. CAL/SERV.: 270

. . . . *Baked Ham Slice Sauterne*

1 2-POUND HAM SLICE, CUT 1½ INCHES THICK
½ CUP FIRMLY PACKED BROWN SUGAR
3 TABLESPOONS CORNSTARCH
1½ CUPS WATER
1 TABLESPOON MARGARINE
½ CUP RAISINS
½ CUP SAUTERNE, OR OTHER WHITE DINNER WINE

Preheat the oven to 350°F.

Place the ham in a shallow baking pan.

Mix the sugar and cornstarch in a saucepan. Stir in water and margarine. Cook, stirring constantly, 5 minutes.

Remove from the heat and stir in the raisins and wine. Pour over the ham. Bake uncovered for 45 minutes or until tender.

YIELD: 8 SERVINGS
APPROX. CAL/SERV.: 365

. . . . *Hawaiian Ham*

Perk up leftover ham in this sweet-and-sour dish.

3 CUPS LEAN COOKED HAM, DICED
1 MEDIUM ONION, SLICED
1 SMALL GREEN PEPPER, SLICED IN RINGS
1 CUP CANNED PINEAPPLE CUBES WITH JUICE
½ CUP SEEDLESS RAISINS
2 TEASPOONS DRY MUSTARD
¼ CUP BROWN SUGAR
1 TABLESPOON CORNSTARCH
¼ TEASPOON SALT
⅓ CUP VINEGAR
1 TEASPOON WORCESTERSHIRE SAUCE
1 TABLESPOON SOY SAUCE (OPTIONAL)

Preheat oven to 350°F.

Put the cubed ham in a 2½-quart casserole. Arrange the onion and green pepper rings on top. Drain the pineapple cubes. Reserve the juice and add water to make 1 cup. Place the fruit over the vegetables. Sprinkle with the raisins. Blend the mustard, sugar, cornstarch and salt in a small saucepan. Stir in the pineapple juice and vinegar and cook while stirring until the mixture boils and is clear. Blend in the Worcestershire and soy sauces. Pour over the ham and vegetables in the casserole.

Bake uncovered 45 to 60 minutes. Serve over boiled rice.

YIELD: 8 SERVINGS, ABOUT 1½ QUARTS
APPROX. CAL/SERV.: 270 (OR 370 WITH ½ CUP RICE)

. . . . *Ham Roll-Up*

8 THIN SLICES BAKED HAM
8 SLICES LOW-FAT CHEESE (MOZZARELLA, OR LOW-FAT CHEDDAR)
16 ASPARAGUS SPEARS (CANNED OR FROZEN), IF FROZEN, COOK FIRST

Recipe continues...

Roll each slice of ham around 2 asparagus spears and pin with tooth-picks.

Place 1 slice of cheese on top of each roll, and run under the broiler until the cheese melts. Serve immediately.

YIELD: 8 SERVINGS

APPROX. CAL/SERV.: 1 ROLL = 200

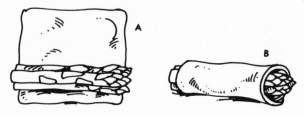

Bayou Red Beans and Rice

1 POUND DRIED RED KIDNEY BEANS (2½ CUPS)

4 CUPS WATER

1 HAM BONE WITH 1 CUP CHOPPED HAM

1 LARGE ONION, CHOPPED

2 STALKS CELERY WITH LEAVES, CHOPPED

1 TEASPOON SALT

2 TEASPOONS TABASCO SAUCE

Soak beans overnight in water.

Pour into a large heavy pan or Dutch Oven.

Add remaining ingredients.

Simmer 3 hours or until beans are tender.

Remove ham bone, cut off meat and add to beans.

Add water when necessary during cooking. Water should barely cover beans at end of cooking time.

Remove 1 cup of beans at end of cooking time and mash to a paste (a blender may be used for this procedure).

Add to remaining beans and stir until liquid is thickened.

Serve hot over white rice.

YIELD: 8 1-CUP SERVINGS

APPROX. CAL/SERV.: 225

Sweet-and-Sour Pork

1 ½ POUNDS LEAN PORK LOIN
2 TABLESPOONS OIL
1 20-OUNCE CAN PINEAPPLE CHUNKS WITH JUICE
½ CUP WATER
⅓ CUP VINEGAR
¼ CUP BROWN SUGAR
2 TABLESPOONS CORNSTARCH
1 TABLESPOON SOY SAUCE
¾ CUP THINLY SLICED GREEN PEPPER
½ CUP THINLY SLICED ONION

Trim all visible fat from the pork loin and cut meat into thin strips. Heat the oil in a skillet and brown the meat strips. Remove the meat and set aside.

Drain the pineapple and combine the pineapple juice with the water, vinegar, brown sugar, cornstarch and soy sauce. Shake in a glass jar until well mixed.

Cook sweet-and-sour sauce in the skillet until clear and slightly thickened. Add the meat and cook over low heat for about 1 hour.

About 5 minutes before serving, add the green pepper and onion slices and the pineapple chunks. Serve over steamed rice.

YIELD: 6 SERVINGS
APPROX. CAL/SERV.: 395 (OR 495 WITH ½ CUP RICE)

. . . . *Pork with Steamed Spiced Sauerkraut*

2 POUNDS SAUERKRAUT, DRAINED, WASHED AND SQUEEZED DRY
½ CUP CHOPPED ONIONS
1 TABLESPOON MARGARINE
1 TABLESPOON SUGAR
2 CUPS COLD WATER
1 LARGE RAW POTATO, GRATED
GARNI (IN CHEESECLOTH BAG)
     5 WHOLE JUNIPER BERRIES
     6 PEPPERCORNS
     2 BAY LEAVES
     ¼ TEASPOON OF CARAWAY SEEDS
     1 WHOLE ALLSPICE
6 PIECES PORK LOIN (18 OUNCES)

Preheat oven to 325°F.

Brown onions lightly in margarine, add sugar, water and sauerkraut. Toss with a fork until well separated.

Add grated potato.

Put sauerkraut mixture in 2-quart casserole; burrow hole in sauerkraut and bury garni bag.

Brown the meat and place it on top of the sauerkraut.

Cover and bake for 1½–2 hours.

Cover may be removed if meat needs browning.

YIELD: 6 SERVINGS
APPROX. CAL/SERV.: 250

· · · · · · · · *Costolette Di Maiale Pizzaiola*
(Braised Pork Chops with Tomato and Garlic Sauce)

2   TABLESPOONS OLIVE OIL

2   TABLESPOONS OIL

6   CENTERCUT LOIN PORK CHOPS, VERY LEAN, 1 TO 1½ INCHES THICK

1   TEASPOON FINELY CHOPPED GARLIC

½   TEASPOON DRIED OREGANO, CRUMBLED

¼   TEASPOON DRIED THYME, CRUMBLED

½   BAY LEAF

½   TEASPOON SALT

½   CUP DRY RED WINE

1   CUP DRAINED CANNED TOMATOES, PURÉED THROUGH A SIEVE OR FOOD MILL

1   TABLESPOON TOMATO PASTE

½   POUND GREEN PEPPERS, SEEDED AND CUT IN 2-BY-¼ INCH STRIPS (ABOUT 1½ CUPS)

½   POUND FRESH MUSHROOMS, WHOLE IF SMALL, QUARTERED OR SLICED IF LARGE

Trim all fat from pork chops.

In a heavy 10- to 12-inch skillet, heat 2 tablespoons of olive oil until a light haze forms over it. Brown the chops in this oil for 2 or 3 minutes on each side, then transfer them to a plate.

Pour off almost all of the fat. In what remains, cook the garlic, oregano, thyme, bay leaf and salt for 30 seconds, stirring constantly. Add the wine and boil briskly to reduce it to about ¼ cup, scraping in any bits of meat or herbs in the pan.

Stir in the tomatoes and tomato paste and return the chops to the skillet. Baste with the sauce, cover, and simmer over low heat, basting once or twice, for 40 minutes.

Meanwhile, heat the unused oil in another large skillet. Fry the green peppers in the oil for about 5 minutes, stirring frequently. Add the mushrooms and toss them with the peppers for a minute or two, then transfer both to the pan with the pork chops. Cover and simmer for 5 minutes. Simmer uncovered, stirring occasionally, for 10 minutes longer,

Recipe continues…

until the pork and vegetables are tender and the sauce is thick enough to coat a spoon heavily. (If the sauce is too thin, remove the chops and vegetables and boil the sauce down over high heat, stirring constantly.) To serve, arrange the chops on a heated platter and spoon the vegetables and sauce over them.

YIELD: 6 SERVINGS

APPROX. CAL/SERV.: 315

Costolette Di Maiale Alla Modenese (Pork Chops Braised in White Wine)

1 TEASPOON DRIED SAGE LEAVES, CRUMBLED

1 TEASPOON DRIED ROSEMARY LEAVES, CRUMBLED

1 TEASPOON FINELY CHOPPED GARLIC

1 TEASPOON SALT

FRESHLY GROUND BLACK PEPPER

4 CENTER-CUT LOIN PORK CHOPS, VERY LEAN, ABOUT 1 INCH THICK (12 OUNCES)

2 . TABLESPOONS MARGARINE

1 TABLESPOON OLIVE OIL

¾ CUP DRY WHITE WINE

1 TABLESPOON FINELY CHOPPED FRESH PARSLEY

Trim all fat from pork chops. Combine the sage, rosemary, garlic, salt and a few grindings of pepper. Press a little of this mixture firmly into both sides of each pork chop.

In a heavy 10- to 12-inch skillet, melt the margarine with the olive oil over moderate heat. When the foam subsides, place the chops in the hot fat and brown them for 2 or 3 minutes on each side, turning them carefully with tongs. When the chops are golden brown, remove them from the pan to a platter.

Pour off all but a thin film of fat from the pan, add ½ cup of the wine and bring it to a boil. Return the chops to the pan, cover and reduce the heat to the barest simmer. Basting with the pan juices occasionally, cook the chops for 25 to 30 minutes, or until they are tender when pierced with the tip of a sharp knife.

Transfer the chops to a heated serving platter and pour into the skillet the remaining ¼ cup of wine. Boil it briskly over high heat, stirring and scraping in any browned bits that cling to the bottom and sides of the pan, until it has reduced to a few tablespoons of syrupy glaze. Remove the skillet from the heat. Taste for seasoning and stir in the parsley.

Pour the sauce over the pork chops and serve.

YIELD: 4 SERVINGS

APPROX. CAL/SERV.: 300

. . . . ***Baked Stuffed Eggplant***

1	LARGE EGGPLANT
1	CUP CHOPPED ONIONS
1	CUP CHOPPED MUSHROOMS
1½	TEASPOONS BASIL
½	TEASPOON CHERVIL
¼	TEASPOON PEPPER
1	TEASPOON SALT
2	TABLESPOONS MARGARINE
1	POUND LEAN GROUND BEEF
¼	CUP TOMATO PASTE
¼	CUP WHEAT GERM
2	TABLESPOONS FRESH CHOPPED PARSLEY

Preheat oven to 350°F.

Wash eggplant, and cut in half lengthwise. Carefully remove the pulp leaving ½ inch of the outer shell. Dice the pulp.

Sauté the onions, mushrooms, seasonings and meat in the margarine. Stir in the tomato paste, wheat germ and eggplant pulp. Cook until meat is slightly done.

Spoon meat mixture into the eggplant shell and place in an oiled ovenproof dish and bake 20 to 30 minutes. Garnish with parsley.

YIELD: 6 SERVINGS

APPROX. CAL/SERV.: 270

· · · · · · · · · · · · *Basic Meat Loaf*

2 POUNDS LEAN GROUND BEEF

1 TEASPOON SALT

½ TEASPOON SEASONED SALT

½ TEASPOON FRESHLY GROUND BLACK PEPPER

3 SLICES BREAD, SOAKED IN ½ CUP SKIM MILK

1 LARGE ONION, GRATED

1 CLOVE GARLIC, MINCED

2 TABLESPOONS WORCESTERSHIRE SAUCE

3 TABLESPOONS CHILI SAUCE

1 TEASPOON DRY MUSTARD

Preheat oven to 375°F.

Combine all ingredients and mix well. Pat the meat mixture into a loaf shape, and place on an oiled, flat baking dish. Bake 50 to 60 minutes.

YIELD: 8 SERVINGS

APPROX. CAL/SERV.: 285

. . . . *Meat Loaf*

1 POUND LEAN GROUND BEEF
3 MEDIUM CARROTS, SHREDDED
1 CUP LOW-FAT COTTAGE CHEESE
1 SMALL ONION, CHOPPED
1 TEASPOON SALT
¼ TEASPOON PEPPER
½ TEASPOON BASIL
1 EGG WHITE

Preheat oven to 350°F.

Mix all ingredients. Shape into a loaf and place on an ungreased shallow baking pan.

Bake for 50 minutes or until brown.

YIELD: 6 SERVINGS
APPROX. CAL/SERV.: 210

. . . . *Southern Meat Loaf*

1½ POUNDS LEAN GROUND BEEF
1 MEDIUM ONION, DICED
5 SLICES BREAD
1 TEASPOON BASIL
1 TABLESPOON PARSLEY
2 TABLESPOONS GRATED PARMESAN CHEESE
½ TEASPOON GARLIC SALT
1 TEASPOON SALT
½ TEASPOON BLACK PEPPER
2 EGG WHITES (SLIGHTLY BEATEN)
1 1-POUND CAN TOMATO SAUCE
1 TABLESPOON PREPARED MUSTARD

Preheat oven to 350°F.

Combine the first 10 ingredients and ¼ cup of the tomato sauce and gently mold into a loaf.

Pour the tomato sauce from the can into a bowl and, using the can as a measure, add the same amount of water. Mix in the prepared mustard. Pour sauce over loaf and bake 1 hour.

YIELD: 6 SERVINGS
APPROX. CAL/SERV.: 350

. . . . *Greek Meat Loaf*

1¼ POUNDS LEAN GROUND ROUND
1 8-OUNCE CAN TOMATO SAUCE
½ CUP CHOPPED ONION
2 TABLESPOONS CHOPPED GREEN PEPPER
1½ TEASPOONS SALT
1 BAY LEAF, CRUSHED
½ TEASPOON THYME
½ TEASPOON MARJORAM
¾ CUP COARSELY CRUSHED SALTINES
2 PIECES BREAD (SOAKED IN WATER A FEW MINUTES, THEN SQUEEZED
  SLIGHTLY AND LEFT FAIRLY MOIST)
1 TEASPOON OREGANO
½ TEASPOON GARLIC POWDER

Recipe continues...

Preheat oven to 350°F.

Mix all ingredients gently and pack lightly into a loaf pan. Bake about 1 hour. Pour off accumulated drippings before serving.

YIELD: 6 SERVINGS

APPROX. CAL/SERV.: 310

· · · · · · · · · · · · · *variation*

Substitute 2 tablespoons mint leaves for bay leaf, thyme and marjoram in the above recipe.

· · · · · · · · · · · · · *Basic Meat Balls*

1 POUND LEAN GROUND ROUND
¼ TEASPOON GARLIC SALT
1 MEDIUM ONION, FINELY CHOPPED
¼ CUP SKIM MILK
½ TEASPOON SALT
¼ TEASPOON PEPPER
¼ CUP WHEAT GERM
1 TEASPOON DRY MUSTARD
1 TABLESPOON OIL
1 10½-OUNCE CAN BEEF CONSOMMÉ
1 TEASPOON PARSLEY FLAKES, DRIED OR FRESH
1 TABLESPOON CORNSTARCH

Mix all ingredients, except the consommé. Form into 12 medium-size meat balls. Heat the oil in a skillet and brown meat balls on all sides. Pour off any fat remaining in skillet, and add the consommé. Sprinkle in the parsley flakes. Cover and cook gently for 20 minutes. Thicken the gravy with cornstarch.

YIELD: 6 SERVINGS
APPROX. CAL/SERV.: 230

Chili Meat Balls

1 POUND LEAN GROUND ROUND
2 ONIONS, MINCED
1½ TEASPOONS SALT
⅛ TEASPOON GARLIC POWDER (OPTIONAL)
2 TEASPOONS CHILI POWDER
¼ CUP WHEAT GERM
1 CUP TOMATO JUICE

Preheat oven to 350°F.

Combine the first 6 ingredients with ¼ cup of the tomato juice. Shape into 18 balls. Arrange in a 1½-quart casserole, and pour over the remaining ¾ cup of tomato juice. Cover and bake 1 hour, adding more tomato juice if necessary.

YIELD: 6 SERVINGS
APPROX. CAL/SERV.: 205

Sauerbraten Meat Balls

1 POUND LEAN GROUND ROUND
¾ CUP SOFT COARSE BREAD CRUMBS
¼ CUP MINCED ONION
2 TEASPOONS SALT
¼ TEASPOON BLACK PEPPER
7 TABLESPOONS LEMON JUICE
2 TABLESPOONS WATER
2 TABLESPOONS MARGARINE
3 BEEF BOUILLON CUBES
2½ CUPS WATER
¼ CUP BROWN SUGAR
¾ CUP GINGERSNAP CRUMBS

Recipe continues...

Combine meat, bread crumbs, onion, salt, pepper, the 2 tablespoons of water and 3 tablespoons of the lemon juice. Mix well and form into 1-inch balls.

Heat margarine in a skillet and brown meat balls. Remove from pan. To the drippings in the pan, add 2½ cups of water and the rest of the lemon juice. Bring to a boil and stir in the beef bouillon cubes, sugar and gingersnap crumbs. Add the meat balls to the sauce and simmer covered for 10 minutes.

Stir and cook uncovered 5 minutes longer. Serve over noodles and sprinkle with poppy seeds.

YIELD: 6 SERVINGS
APPROX. CAL/SERV.: 325 (OR 425 WITH ½ CUP NOODLES)

· · · · · · · · **Beef-and-Stuffing Patties**

Hamburger "cups" that hold herbed stuffing are cooked in a chili-flavored sauce.

  1 10½-OUNCE CAN TOMATO SOUP
1½ POUNDS LEAN GROUND ROUND
  1 TEASPOON SALT
1½ TEASPOONS CHILI POWDER
  1 CUP PACKAGED HERB STUFFING MIX
  2 TABLESPOONS CHOPPED SWEET PICKLE
  2 TABLESPOONS CHOPPED CELERY
  ¼ CUP WATER
  ½ TEASPOON PREPARED MUSTARD

Preheat oven to 450°F.

Combine ¼ cup of the soup, with the beef, salt and 1 teaspoon of the chili powder. Mix well. Shape into 6 patties with 1-inch standing rims. Place in shallow ovenproof dish; bake 15 minutes. Pour off the fat.

Combine the stuffing, prepared according to package directions, with the pickle and celery. Place ⅓ cup of the mixture in the center of each patty.

Blend the remaining soup with the remaining ½ teaspoon of chili powder, the water and mustard. Pour over and around the patties.

Return to the oven and bake 10 more minutes.

YIELD: 6 SERVINGS
APPROX. CAL/SERV.: 345

. . . . **Annette's Dutch Cabbage Rolls**

use variation

1 LARGE HEAD CABBAGE
2 CUPS WATER
1 POUND LEAN GROUND CHUCK
1 CUP QUICK-COOKING RICE, RAW
1 EGG (OPTIONAL)
2 TABLESPOONS CHOPPED ONION
½ TEASPOON SALT
1 16-OUNCE CAN SAUERKRAUT, DRAINED *subst cabbage, chopped*
1 8-OUNCE CAN TOMATO SAUCE (OPTIONAL) *unsalted*

Remove the core from the cabbage head and pull off about a dozen of the large outer leaves for stuffing. Rinse in cold water.

Recipe continues...

Cut the heavy stem from the base of each cabbage leaf and place leaves in 2 cups of boiling water to soften. Cover pan and turn off heat to let leaves steam while preparing the stuffing.

Meanwhile, prepare the stuffing: Mix ground beef, rice, egg (optional), chopped onion and salt in mixing bowl.

Carefully remove cabbage leaves from the pot and put sauerkraut into the same water for a few minutes while stuffing the cabbage leaves.

Place a heaping tablespoon of beef mixture in the center of each cabbage leaf. Fold over half of leaf, tuck in both ends and roll up, enclosing the mixture. Secure rolled leaf with toothpicks.

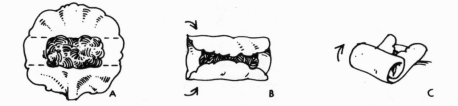

Remove sauerkraut from the hot water and place in a single layer in the bottom of a 2-quart casserole. Place each roll, folded side down, on the bed of sauerkraut. Pour in tomato sauce if desired. Cover with a tight-fitting lid and cook over low heat for 1 hour, or until cabbage rolls are firm.

YIELD: 8 SERVINGS
APPROX. CAL/SERV.: 190

· · · · · · · · · · · · · · · *variation*

Omit the sauerkraut. Make cabbage rolls as directed above and place in a casserole. Pour over them a sauce made of 1 diced onion, 2 tablespoons of lemon juice, 2 tablespoons of brown sugar, 1 10-ounce can tomato purée and 1 cup of water. Cover and simmer 1½ hours, basting occasionally and adding water if necessary.

APPROX. CAL/SERV.: 215

. . . . *Spanish Rice*

Is leftover rice taking up refrigerator space? Try this colorful dish.

1 TABLESPOON OIL
1 SMALL ONION, CHOPPED
½ GREEN PEPPER, CHOPPED
1 POUND LEAN GROUND BEEF
1 TEASPOON SALT
¼ TEASPOON BLACK PEPPER
1 TABLESPOON PREPARED MUSTARD *dry*
2 TABLESPOONS CATSUP
1 TABLESPOON WORCESTERSHIRE SAUCE
3 CUPS COOKED RICE
1 28-OUNCE CAN TOMATOES *unsalted*

Sauté onion and green pepper in the oil until soft.

Add ground beef and seasonings, stirring until meat loses its pink color. Stir in the cooked rice, the tomatoes, and the catsup and Worcestershire sauce. Mix thoroughly.

Reduce heat and simmer, covered, for 15 minutes.

YIELD: 8 SERVINGS
APPROX. CAL/SERV.: 255

. . . . *variation*

Stuffed Pepper España. Remove tops and seeds from 4 medium green peppers. Parboil peppers in 1 quart of water for 5 minutes. (Reserve the water.) Fill peppers with Spanish Rice, top with ¼ cup of bread crumbs and dot with margarine. Stand peppers in a baking dish in the reserved water in which they were parboiled. Bake 30 minutes at 350°F.

APPROX. CAL/SERV.: ½ STUFFED PEPPER = 290

· · · · · · · · · *Hamburger Corn-Pone Pie*

    1 POUND LEAN GROUND BEEF
    ⅓ CUP CHOPPED ONION
    1 TABLESPOON OIL
    2 TEASPOONS CHILI POWDER
    ¾ TEASPOON SALT
    1 TEASPOON WORCESTERSHIRE SAUCE
    1 CUP CANNED TOMATOES
    1 CUP DRAINED KIDNEY BEANS, CANNED
    1 CUP CORN BATTER BREAD (½ STANDARD CORN BREAD RECIPE)
        see p. 300.

Preheat oven to 425°F.

Brown meat and chopped onion in melted oil, then drain off the fat. Add the seasonings and tomatoes, cover, and simmer over low heat for 15 minutes.

Add the kidney beans, adjust seasoning to taste.

Pour the meat mixture into a lightly oiled 1½-quart casserole, and top with the corn bread batter.

Bake for 20 minutes.

YIELD: 6 SERVINGS
APPROX. CAL/SERV.: 365

. . . . *Chili Con Carne*

 2 TABLESPOONS OIL
½ CUP CHOPPED GREEN PEPPER
½ CUP CHOPPED ONION
 1 POUND LEAN GROUND BEEF
 2 CUPS CANNED TOMATOES *unsalted*
 1 10½-OUNCE CAN TOMATO SOUP ✗
½ TEASPOON PAPRIKA
⅛ TEASPOON CAYENNE PEPPER
 1 BAY LEAF
 1 TABLESPOON CHILI POWDER
 1 CLOVE GARLIC, MASHED
 1 TEASPOON SALT ✗
 1 16-OUNCE CAN RED KIDNEY BEANS WITH LIQUID *washed*

Heat oil in a 10-inch skillet, then brown the green pepper, onion and ground beef in the oil, stirring occasionally. Add the tomatoes, tomato soup, paprika, cayenne pepper, bay leaf and chili powder. Cover, simmer over low heat for about 1 hour, stirring occasionally. (Add more water if the mixture becomes too thick.) Then add the garlic, salt and kidney beans with liquid and heat thoroughly.

YIELD: 6 SERVINGS
APPROX. CAL/SERV.: 345

. . . . *Barbecued Hamburger*

Easy to make and serve in quantity, this barbecued burger mix is great for outdoor eating.

 1 POUND LEAN GROUND BEEF
 1 ONION, DICED
½ CUP CATSUP
 2 TABLESPOONS CHILI SAUCE
 1 TEASPOON PREPARED MUSTARD
 1 TEASPOON VINEGAR
 1 TEASPOON SUGAR
½ TEASPOON SALT

Recipe continues...

Brown meat and onions in a large skillet. Pour off the fat that accumulates.

Add all other ingredients, mixing well, and simmer 20 to 30 minutes, uncovered.

Spoon into hamburger buns.

YIELD: 6 ½-CUP SERVINGS

APPROX. CAL/SERV.: 200 (OR 320 WITH BUN)

· · · · · · · · *Goulash*
Macaroni-Beef Skillet Supper

1 CUP ELBOW MACARONI
1 POUND LEAN GROUND BEEF
1 CUP DICED ONIONS
1 CLOVE GARLIC, MASHED
2 TABLESPOONS OIL
1 8-OUNCE CAN TOMATO SAUCE *unsalted*
1 TEASPOON SALT
¼ TEASPOON BLACK PEPPER
1 CUP CATSUP
1 8-OUNCE CAN MUSHROOM STEMS AND PIECES, DRAINED
2 TABLESPOONS WORCESTERSHIRE SAUCE
½ TEASPOON ITALIAN SEASONING

Cook the macaroni in boiling salted water according to package directions. Drain and set aside.

Sauté the meat, onion, and garlic in oil until the meat loses its pink color and the onions are tender. Add salt and pepper, tomato sauce, catsup, mushrooms, Worcestershire sauce and Italian seasoning.

Bring mixture to a boil, and then simmer gently for about 5 minutes. Mix in the cooked macaroni and simmer for 5 more minutes.

YIELD: 8 SERVINGS

APPROX. CAL/SERV.: 270

· · · · · · · · · · · · · · ## *Kibbee*

A ground-meat dish from the Middle East, this is traditionally made with lamb.

1 POUND LEAN GROUND BEEF OR LAMB
1 CUP FINELY CRUSHED BULGUR WHEAT*
¼ CUP CHOPPED WALNUTS OR PINE NUTS
1 SMALL ONION, MINCED OR GRATED
1½ TEASPOONS SALT
¼ TEASPOON BLACK PEPPER
1 TEASPOON CINNAMON
½ CUP WATER
1 TABLESPOON MARGARINE
1½ CUPS PLAIN LOW-FAT YOGURT

Preheat oven to 350°F.

Rinse the crushed wheat, drain and let stand for 10 minutes. Meanwhile, brown the nuts in a skillet with a small amount of oil or margarine. Mix the wheat with the ground meat, onion, salt, pepper and cinnamon. Mix well, adding ½ cup of water as you mix.

Pat half the meat mixture in a flat layer in the bottom of an oiled cake pan (8 × 8 inch or 8 × 10 inch). Sprinkle the toasted nuts over the meat layer and pat out the remaining meat mixture over the nuts.

Leave in the pan, but cut into squares or diamond-shaped pieces. Dot with margarine and bake for about 30 minutes. Serve warm, with a side dish of plain yogurt.

YIELD: 6 SERVINGS

APPROX. CAL/SERV.: 330

* *Bulgur wheat may be found in health food stores.*

Picadillo

1½ POUNDS LEAN GROUND BEEF
2 TABLESPOONS MARGARINE
1 CLOVE GARLIC, CHOPPED
1 LARGE ONION, CHOPPED
1 GREEN PEPPER, CHOPPED
4 SPRIGS PARSLEY, CHOPPED
¼ CUP SEEDLESS RAISINS
¼ CUP SLICED BLANCHED ALMONDS
2 TABLESPOONS SLICED PIMIENTO
12 STUFFED OLIVES, SLICED
1 TABLESPOON CAPERS
1 BAY LEAF
1 TEASPOON SALT
¼ TEASPOON PEPPER
½ CUP TOMATO PASTE
¼ CUP DRY RED WINE

In a large skillet, melt the margarine and saute the garlic until brown. Discard the garlic.

Sauté the onion, green pepper and parsley until the vegetables are soft. Add the ground beef; brown, stirring with a fork to prevent lumps. Mix in the remaining ingredients.

Simmer, covered, stirring occasionally, for about 15 minutes. Serve over white rice.

YIELD: 6 SERVINGS
APPROX. CAL/SERV.: 380 (OR 480 WITH ½ CUP RICE)

Beef Tostadas

Beef Mixture

1 ONION, CHOPPED
1 TABLESPOON OIL
1 POUND LEAN GROUND BEEF
2 WHOLE CANNED TOMATOES, DRAINED
OREGANO, CHILI POWDER AND GARLIC, TO TASTE

Ingredients

TORTILLAS FRIED CRISP (8)

BEEF MIXTURE

MOZZARELLA CHEESE (MADE FROM PARTIALLY SKIMMED MILK)

SALSA CRUDA

SHREDDED LETTUCE, RED CABBAGE OR OTHER GREENS

Sauté onion in 1 tablespoon of oil. Add ground beef and cook until meat loses its red color. Drain off the fat that accumulates. Add tomatoes and seasoning, and cook for a minute or two.

Cover tortillas with ground beef mixture, top with grated mozzarella and grill under broiler.

Serve with shredded lettuce or red cabbage and salsa cruda.

YIELD: 4 SERVINGS

APPROX. CAL/SERV.: 225

· · · · · · · · · · · · **Salsa Cruda**

2 LARGE RIPE TOMATOES, PEELED

2 CANNED SERRANO OR JALAPEÑO CHILIES

1 SMALL ONION

1 TABLESPOON CILANTRO (FRESH CORIANDER), OR A FEW CORIANDER SEEDS

PINCH OF SUGAR

SALT AND PEPPER

Mix all ingredients together in a blender. Serve cold.

Pickled Watermelon Rind

3 POUNDS WHITE PART OF THE WATERMELON RIND, CUBED
3 CUPS SUGAR
2 CUPS CIDER VINEGAR
1 CUP COLD WATER
1 TABLESPOON WHOLE CLOVES
1 TABLESPOON WHOLE ALLSPICE
1 TABLESPOON CINNAMON STICK PIECES
1 SLICED LEMON
SALT

Make a brine of 2 tablespoons salt to 1 quart of water. Cover rind with brine and let stand overnight. Drain. Cover with fresh water and cook about 10 minutes, until tender, then drain.

In a large pot, combine sugar, vinegar, and 1 cup of cold water. Heat until sugar dissolves. Enclose allspice, cloves, cinnamon and lemon in a cheesecloth bag, and add to the vinegar mixture.

Put in the watermelon rind and cook until transparent, about 45 minutes. Pour into sterilized jars and seal.

YIELD: 3 PINTS
APPROX. CAL/SERV.: 1 CUP = 845   1 TABLESPOON = 50

. . . . *Spiced Peaches*

Use this method of pickling with pears or peaches. Serve with baked ham or as part of a fruit salad.

$\frac{1}{2}$ CUP VINEGAR
8 CANNED PEACH HALVES
1 CUP JUICE FROM THE PEACHES
$\frac{1}{4}$ CUP SUGAR
1 STICK CINNAMON
1 TEASPOON WHOLE CLOVES

Combine the vinegar, the juice from the peaches, the sugar, cinnamon and cloves. Boil until reduced by about half. Remove the spices. Stick the cloves into the peach halves and pour the syrup over peaches; let stand overnight in the refrigerator.

YIELD: 8 SERVINGS
APPROX. CAL/SERV.: 80

. . . . *Cranberry Chutney*

1 CUP LIGHT SEEDLESS RAISINS
1 8-OUNCE PACKAGE PITTED DATES, CHOPPED
2 16-OUNCE CANS WHOLE CRANBERRY SAUCE
$\frac{3}{4}$ CUP SUGAR
$\frac{1}{8}$ TEASPOON SALT
$\frac{1}{4}$ TEASPOON EACH GROUND GINGER, CINNAMON AND ALLSPICE
$\frac{1}{8}$ TEASPOON GROUND CLOVES
$\frac{3}{4}$ CUP CIDER VINEGAR

Combine all ingredients and cook, stirring occasionally, for 30 minutes. Spoon into hot sterilized jars; seal. Excellent with turkey or chicken.

YIELD: 6 HALF PINTS
APPROX. CAL/SERV.: 1 CUP = 570   1 TABLESPOON = 35

. . . . *Baked Curried Fruit*

1 20-OUNCE CAN PEACHES

1 20-OUNCE CAN BING CHERRIES

1 20-OUNCE CAN PINEAPPLE CHUNKS

2 11-OUNCE CANS MANDARIN ORANGES

⅔ CUPS LIGHT BROWN SUGAR

2 TEASPOONS CURRY POWDER

JUICE OF 1 LEMON

¼ CUP MARGARINE

Drain fruits well in a colander until all juice has run off, 1 to 2 hours.
Prepare a shallow casserole (8 × 12 inches or similar size) by
greasing it with margarine. Add fruit, cover with a mixture of brown
sugar and curry powder, sprinkle with the lemon juice and dot with
margarine.

Cover and bake 1 hour in oven at 300°F.

YIELD: 12 SERVINGS, ABOUT 2 QUARTS

APPROX. CAL/SERV.: ½ CUP = 115

Fish

$\mathcal{T}$he most wonderful fish of all is the one you catch yourself. But after the tackle has been stowed away and the catch delivered to the kitchen, the most wonderful fish is the one that has been properly prepared, its flavor lightly enhanced with herbs, garlic or lemon, its flesh moist and tender.

"Show me a fish-hater," someone once said, "and I'll show you a person who has never tasted properly cooked fish." At any rate, it is scarcely possible for one to dislike all fish. From the spring-fresh taste of trout and the chickenlike texture of the blowfish, to the dark, beefy richness of red salmon, there are countless flavor variations to be sampled out of the salt and freshwater seas.

Fish has fewer calories than meat. All fish is low in fat and extremely nutritious. An average serving supplies one-third to one-half of the daily protein requirements, as well as B vitamins, thiamin, riboflavin and niacin. Most fish also provide iodine, copper and iron and, if cooked with the bones, calcium and phosphorus.

Fish requires more attention from the cook than meat, whether it is cooked whole, filleted or cut into steaks. Leaving fish whole with head and tail intact prevents loss of natural juices, particularly when broiling is the cooking method. The skin of broiled fish is deliciously crisp.

A quick and easy method of cooking fillets or steaks is to dip them in flour or cracker meal and sauté them in oil, turning once and basting after turning. When the fish is done, remove to a heated platter, squeeze raw garlic through a press into the cooking oil, add lemon juice and pour over the fish.

Fish is also excellent baked, steamed, poached or in stews. When poaching or stewing, do not allow the cooking liquid to boil, only to shimmer a little on the surface.

Fish may be served several times a week.

If you usually catch your fish in the market, look for firm flesh, shiny scales and bright, protruding eyes. Use within two days of purchase.

Thaw frozen fish in the refrigerator. Do not refreeze fish.

Despite its many excellent qualities, fish is not served as often as it might be. Certain rules attend its preparation: It must not be overcooked, and when done, it will not wait on the diner. Perhaps these requirements frighten away too many cooks.

Low in calories and higher in polyunsaturated fat, fish has a place on the breakfast table, goes well in salads, makes tempting appetizers, delicious dinners or light lunches. It is time this versatile food was rediscovered.

· · · · · · · · · · . *Crispy Baked Fillets*

This method produces a crisp coating; looks almost like deep-fried fish.

1 POUND FISH FILLETS
¼ TEASPOON SALT
DASH FRESHLY GROUND PEPPER
2 TABLESPOONS OIL
⅓ CUP CORNFLAKE CRUMBS

Preheat oven to 500°F.

Wash and dry fillets and cut into serving pieces. Season, dip in oil, and coat with cornflake crumbs. Arrange in a single layer in a lightly oiled shallow baking dish. Bake 10 minutes without turning or basting.

YIELD: 4 SERVINGS
APPROX. CAL/SERV.: 260

· · · · · · · · · · · *Ginger Broiled Fish*

2 POUNDS FRESH OR FROZEN FISH PIECES OR STEAKS, ABOUT ¾ OF
AN INCH THICK
¾ CUP DRY WHITE WINE
3 TABLESPOONS OIL
3 TABLESPOONS SOY SAUCE
1½ TEASPOONS INSTANT MINCED ONION
1½ TEASPOONS SEASONED SALT
¾ TEASPOON GINGER
½ TEASPOON HORSERADISH

Preheat broiler.

Cut fish into 6 serving portions; arrange in a single layer in a well-oiled, preheated pan.

Combine all ingredients except fish. Pour sauce over fish and broil 10 to 12 minutes about 2 inches from the heat, turning once and basting several times. Fish is done when it flakes easily with a fork.

YIELD: 8 SERVINGS
APPROX. CAL/SERV.: 235

· · · · · · · · · · · *Puffy Broiled Fillets*

1 POUND FISH FILLETS, WITH SKINS
SALT AND PEPPER TO TASTE
2 TABLESPOONS MELTED MARGARINE
¼ CUP TARTAR SAUCE
1 EGG WHITE, BEATEN UNTIL STIFF

Preheat broiler.

Place fillets skin side down in a well-oiled, shallow baking pan. Season with salt and pepper and brush with melted margarine.

Broil about 10 minutes, 3 to 4 inches from the heat.

Meanwhile, gently fold tartar sauce into stiffly beaten egg white. When fish flakes easily, spread mixture over the fillets and broil 2 minutes more or until topping is golden brown.

YIELD: 4 SERVINGS
APPROX. CAL/SERV.: 300

• • • • • • • • *Broiled Marinated Fish Steaks*

1 ½ POUNDS FISH STEAKS, CUT 1 INCH THICK

• • • • • • • • *marinade for fish steaks*

2 TABLESPOONS OIL

⅓ CUP TARRAGON VINEGAR

1 TEASPOON SALT

1 TEASPOON WORCESTERSHIRE SAUCE

¼ TEASPOON PEPPER

1 BAY LEAF

2 TABLESPOONS CHOPPED PARSLEY

In a shallow pan, combine oil, vinegar, salt, Worcestershire sauce, pepper, bay leaf and parsley. Add fish steaks; cover and refrigerate for at least 3 hours, turning occasionally so that steaks are well coated. Remove from marinade. Place in a hot broiler pan 3 inches from the heat. Broil 15 to 20 minutes, turning once and basting with the sauce until fish is done.

YIELD: 6 SERVINGS

APPROX. CAL/SERV.: 210

• • • • • • • • *Stuffed Fish Beachcomber*

1 WHOLE FISH (ABOUT 2½–3 POUNDS)

2 TABLESPOONS MARGARINE

6 TABLESPOONS DICED ONIONS

¾ CUP SLICED MUSHROOMS

3 TABLESPOONS VINEGAR

1½ CUPS DAY-OLD BREAD CRUMBS

½ CUP SKIM MILK

1 EGG WHITE, SLIGHTLY BEATEN

SALT AND PEPPER TO TASTE

½ TEASPOON CURRY POWDER

2 TABLESPOONS CHOPPED PICKLES OR RELISH

Preheat oven to 375°F.

Sauté onions and mushrooms in margarine 10 minutes. Add vinegar and simmer 10 minutes. Remove from heat and cool 10 minutes.

Soak bread crumbs in skim milk, then squeeze out excess milk and add crumbs to onion mixture. Add beaten egg white, salt and pepper and pickles or relish mixed with curry powder.

Sprinkle fish on all sides with salt and pepper. Stuff with bread mixture; close opening with skewers or picks.

Grease a baking dish or line it with unglazed parchment paper; place fish in it. Brush with oil and bake 45 minutes, or until fish flakes easily when tested with a fork.

YIELD: 6 SERVINGS

APPROX. CAL/SERV.: 320

· · · · · · · · · · · · · · · *variation*

Use 1½-pound fillets or steaks in place of whole fish. Place 3 or 4 tablespoons stuffing between 2 fillets or steaks, and place on a greased baking dish. Bake 25 to 30 minutes at 350°F.

· · · · · · · · · · · **Broiled Fish Roll-Ups**

2 TABLESPOONS CHOPPED ONION

½ CUP CHOPPED CELERY

3 TABLESPOONS WATER

2 CUPS COARSE BREAD CRUMBS

½ TEASPOON SALT

PEPPER

¼ CUP COOKED, CHOPPED SPINACH

½ TEASPOON THYME

1½ POUNDS FISH FILLETS

1 EGG WHITE, SLIGHTLY BEATEN

¼ CUP SKIM MILK

2 TABLESPOONS FLOUR

½ CUP FINE CRACKER CRUMBS

Recipe continues...

Preheat broiler.

Combine onion, celery and water in a saucepan. Bring to a boil; cover and simmer until vegetables are tender. Add bread crumbs, salt, pepper, spinach and thyme. Mix well, adding liquid to moisten if necessary. Place some of the mixture on each fillet. Sprinkle with salt, roll up and fasten with toothpicks. Roll the stuffed fillets in a mixture of egg white and skim milk, then in a mixture of flour and cracker crumbs.

Place fish rolls on a lightly oiled broiler rack and place in the broiler. When almost done on one side, turn carefully and cook until tender (about 10 minutes).

Remove toothpicks, garnish with parsley and serve immediately.

YIELD: 6 SERVINGS

APPROX. CAL/SERV.: 350

Foil Fish Bake

4 FRESH LAKE TROUT, MACKEREL OR OTHER WHOLE WHITE FISH (2 POUNDS IN ALL)

2 TABLESPOONS MARGARINE

½ CUP CHOPPED PARSLEY

½ CUP CHOPPED DILL SPRIGS

¼ CUP CHOPPED CHIVES

¼ CUP CHOPPED ONION

2 TABLESPOONS LEMON JUICE

Preheat oven to 400°F.

Clean and rinse fish; allow to drain. Sprinkle lightly with salt.

Make stuffing: Mix together margarine, parsley, dill sprigs, chives, onion and lemon juice. Stuff and wrap each fish separately in aluminum foil, sealing the edges carefully. Bake 20 minutes. Unwrap, remove to a hot platter, garnish with parsley and lemon slices.

YIELD: 4 SERVINGS

APPROX. CAL/SERV.: 220

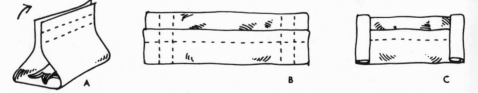

A   B   C

. . . . *Plaki Greek Fish with Vegetables*

3 POUNDS WHOLE FISH
¼ CUP OIL
1½ CUPS CHOPPED ONION
2 CLOVES GARLIC, MINCED
1½ CUPS CANNED TOMATOES
½ CUP SNIPPED FRESH PARSLEY
¼ CUP SNIPPED FRESH DILL, OR 1 TABLESPOON OF DRIED
½ TEASPOON SALT
¼ TEASPOON PEPPER
2 TABLESPOONS LEMON JUICE
1 POUND FRESH SPINACH
½ CUP DRY WHITE WINE

About 1 hour before serving, heat oven to 350°F.

In a large skillet, sauté onions in oil until soft. Add garlic, tomatoes, parsley, dill, ½ teaspoon salt and the pepper. Cook 10 minutes.

Sprinkle fish lightly with salt and lemon juice. Arrange tomato mixture in 9 × 13 × 2-inch baking dish. Lay the fish on top and arrange the spinach around it. Pour wine over all; cover with foil and bake 30 minutes. Then uncover and continue baking 15 minutes longer.

YIELD: 6 SERVINGS
APPROX. CAL/SERV.: 315

. . . . *Curried Fillets Amandine*

1 POUND FRESH OR FROZEN FILLETS (HADDOCK, PERCH, FLOUNDER, COD OR SOLE)
¼ CUP FLOUR
2 TEASPOONS CURRY POWDER
¼ TEASPOON SALT
¼ CUP MARGARINE
⅓ CUP CHOPPED BLANCHED ALMONDS
CHUTNEY

Combine flour, curry powder and salt and thoroughly coat fillets with the mixture.

Recipe continues...

Heat margarine in a large skillet, sauté the fillets in the margarine over moderate heat until browned (about 4 minutes). Turn and brown on the other side, cooking until fish flakes easily with a fork. Remove to a heated platter.

Add almonds to the margarine remaining in the pan and cook, stirring until browned. Pour over fish, serve with chutney.

YIELD: 4 SERVINGS
APPROX. CAL/SERV.: 360

Fillets in Lemon Dressing

4 FILLETS OF FIRM-TEXTURED WHITE FISH
2 TABLESPOONS GRATED ONION
1 TABLESPOON FINELY CHOPPED CELERY
4 TABLESPOONS OIL
4 SLICES TOAST, CUBED
1 TABLESPOON CHOPPED PARSLEY
JUICE OF 1 LEMON
GRATED RIND OF ½ LEMON
1 TEASPOON SALT
PEPPER
DASH NUTMEG

Preheat oven to 375°F.
Sauté onion and celery in oil. Mix in remaining ingredients.
Place 2 fillets on the bottom of an oiled baking dish. Spread dressing over fish, and top with remaining 2 fillets. Dust with paprika, dot with margarine, and bake 40 minutes.

YIELD: 4 SERVINGS
APPROX. CAL/SERV.: 365

. . . . *Braised Fish*

A beautiful dish with its own delectable sauce. Pour the sauce over rice or soak it up with crusty French bread.

¼ CUP OIL

1½ POUNDS PAN-DRESSED FISH; OR 1 POUND OF FIRM-TEXTURED FISH FILLETS, SUCH AS HADDOCK

2 TABLESPOONS FLOUR

½ TEASPOON SUGAR

½ TEASPOON GINGER

¼ TEASPOON GARLIC POWDER OR 1 CLOVE GARLIC, MINCED

1 TABLESPOON SOY SAUCE

1 TABLESPOON SHERRY

WATER

½ TEASPOON FRESHLY MILLED BLACK PEPPER

CHIVES OR GREEN ENDS OF SPRING ONIONS

2 MEDIUM-SIZE RIPE TOMATOES, CHOPPED

1 TABLESPOON CHOPPED PARSLEY

1 TEASPOON CORNSTARCH

½ CUP WATER

SALT TO TASTE

Dust fillets lightly with flour.

In a heavy skillet, heat oil and brown fish on both sides.

Combine sugar, ginger and garlic with soy sauce, sherry and enough water to make 1 cup. Pour over fish, cover and braise 10 minutes. Uncover, add black pepper, chives, parsley and chopped tomatoes. Cook uncovered another 5 minutes. Mix together the cornstarch, salt and water; blend well. Simmer 5 minutes more.

YIELD: 4 SERVINGS

APPROX. CAL/SERV.: 335

Baked Cod

1 POUND COD FILLET, CUT IN 2-SQUARE-INCH PIECES
4 MEDIUM POTATOES, PEELED AND QUARTERED
4 MEDIUM CARROTS, SCRAPED AND CUT INTO 2-INCH PIECES
1 TABLESPOON LEMON JUICE
1 TABLESPOON MARGARINE
1½ TEASPOONS SALT
¼ TEASPOON PEPPER
½ CUP SHREDDED MOZZARELLA CHEESE (MADE FROM PARTIALLY SKIMMED MILK)
1 TO 2 TABLESPOONS CHOPPED PARSLEY

Preheat oven to 375°F.

Slightly grease a 13 × 9-inch baking dish. Put fish pieces into the dish and sprinkle with lemon juice. Place carrots and potatoes between pieces, and place dabs of margarine and pieces of potato over fish. Season with salt and pepper.

Sprinkle cheese over all; cover and bake 1 hour.

Serve garnished with chopped parsley.

YIELD: 4 SERVINGS
APPROX. CAL/SERV.: 330

Flounder Fillets in Foil

4 FLOUNDER FILLETS
MARGARINE OR OIL
SALT AND PEPPER
1 TABLESPOON SHALLOTS OR GREEN ONIONS
½ POUND CHOPPED MUSHROOMS
3 TABLESPOONS DRY WHITE WINE
1 TABLESPOON LEMON JUICE
1 TABLESPOON CHOPPED PARSLEY

Preheat oven to 400°F.

Sauté shallots or green onions in margarine till soft; add mushrooms and cook 5 minutes. Stir in wine, lemon juice and parsley, and cook until most of the liquid evaporates.

Lightly grease 4 pieces of heavy duty foil with margarine or oil. Place a fillet on each piece; season with salt and pepper. Spoon some mushroom sauce over each fillet. Draw edges of, foil together and seal. Bake 20 minutes, or until fish flakes. Serve in the foil.

YIELD: 4 SERVINGS
APPROX. CAL/SERV.: 225

Tomato Crown Fish

1½ POUNDS FISH FILLETS
1½ CUPS WATER
  2 TABLESPOONS LEMON JUICE
  2 LARGE FRESH TOMATOES, OR CANNED ONES, SLICED
½ GREEN PEPPER, MINCED
  2 TABLESPOONS ONION, MINCED
½ CUP BREAD CRUMBS
  1 TABLESPOON OIL
½ TEASPOON BASIL

Preheat oven to 350°F.

Freshen fish several minutes in mixture of water and lemon juice. Place in a greased baking dish, season lightly, and spread tomato slices over fillets.

Sprinkle with green pepper and onion. Mix bread crumbs, oil and basil; sprinkle evenly over the vegetables. Bake 10 to 15 minutes.

YIELD: 6 SERVINGS
APPROX. CAL/SERV.: 240

Teriyaki Halibut

  2 POUNDS HALIBUT FILLETS
  6 SLICES CANNED PINEAPPLE
¼ CUP SOY SAUCE
  1 TABLESPOON BROWN SUGAR
  2 TABLESPOONS OIL
  1 TEASPOON FLOUR
½ CUP DRY WHITE WINE
½ TEASPOON DRY MUSTARD

Recipe continues...

In a small saucepan, combine soy sauce, brown sugar, oil, flour, wine and mustard. Bring to a boil, reduce heat, and simmer for 3 minutes. Allow to cool. Marinate fillets for 15 minutes in this liquid. Brush pineapple with the marinade and place with the fish in an oiled broiling pan. Broil 5 to 6 inches from the heat for about 5 minutes on each side, or until fish is done.

Remove to a warm platter, and spoon sauce over the fish and fruit.

YIELD: 8 SERVINGS
APPROX. CAL/SERV.: 255

Hearty Halibut

    2 POUNDS HALIBUT OR OTHER FISH STEAKS
   ⅔ CUP THINLY SLICED ONION
 1½ CUPS SLICED FRESH MUSHROOMS
   ⅓ CUP CHOPPED TOMATO
   ¼ CUP CHOPPED GREEN PEPPER
   ¼ CUP CHOPPED PARSLEY
    3 TABLESPOONS CHOPPED PIMIENTO
   ½ CUP DRY WHITE WINE
    2 TABLESPOONS LEMON JUICE
    1 TEASPOON SALT
   ¼ TEASPOON DILL WEED
   ⅛ TEASPOON PEPPER
LEMON WEDGES

Preheat oven to 350°F.

Arrange onion slices in the bottom of a greased baking dish and place fish on top. Combine remaining vegetables and spread over fish.

Combine wine, lemon juice and seasonings and pour over all. Cover and bake 25 to 30 minutes, or until fish flakes easily when tested with a fork. Serve with lemon wedges.

YIELD: 8 SERVINGS
APPROX. CAL/SERV.: 200

. . . . *Halibut Steaks Brazilian*

Coffee adds a new taste to broiled halibut steaks.

2 POUNDS HALIBUT OR OTHER FISH STEAKS
2 TABLESPOONS LEMON JUICE
1 TABLESPOON INSTANT COFFEE
¼ CUP MELTED MARGARINE OR OIL
1 TEASPOON SALT
1 TEASPOON ONION SALT
CHOPPED PARSLEY

Place fish steaks in shallow baking dish. Dissolve coffee in lemon juice, add remaining ingredients, except parsley, and mix thoroughly.
Pour over fish and let stand 30 minutes, turning once.
Remove fish, reserving the sauce, and broil 4 or 5 minutes about 3 inches from the heat. Turn carefully and brush with remaining sauce. Broil 4 or 5 minutes longer, or until fish is done. Garnish with chopped parsley.

YIELD: 8 SERVINGS
APPROX. CAL/SERV.: 220

. . . . *Tuna Chop Suey*

2 TABLESPOONS OIL
1 LARGE CLOVE GARLIC, MINCED
1½ CUPS CELERY STRIPS
1 LARGE ONION, CUT IN 8 WEDGES
1 MEDIUM GREEN PEPPER, CUT IN STRIPS
2 TABLESPOONS CORNSTARCH
1 CUP WATER
1 TABLESPOON SOY SAUCE
1 TEASPOON SALT
1 9-OUNCE CAN TUNA, DRAINED AND FLAKED
2 CUPS COOKED RICE
⅓ CUP SAUTÉED ALMONDS (OPTIONAL)

Recipe continues...

In a skillet, sauté garlic, celery, onion and green pepper in oil until tender but still crisp.

Blend cornstarch with 2 tablespoons water. Add remaining water and soy sauce to vegetables in skillet; gradually stir in cornstarch mixture. Add salt and tuna. Cook and stir until liquid thickens and vegetables are glazed.

Serve over rice, garnished with sautéed almonds, if desired.

YIELD: 4 SERVINGS

APPROX. CAL/SERV.: 385 (OR 425 WITH ALMONDS)

. . . . *Halibut Ragout*

A quick and nutritious stew. Serve with your favorite bread.

2 POUNDS HALIBUT, FRESH OR FROZEN

2 TABLESPOONS OIL

½ CUP CHOPPED ONION

1 CLOVE GARLIC, MINCED

¼ CUP CHOPPED GREEN PEPPER

3 STALKS CELERY, SLICED DIAGONALLY

3 CARROTS, CUT JULIENNE

1 28-OUNCE CAN TOMATOES

1 CUP WATER

2 CHICKEN BOUILLON CUBES

1 TEASPOON SALT

⅛ TEASPOON PEPPER

¼ TEASPOON THYME

¼ TEASPOON BASIL

3 TABLESPOONS MINCED PARSLEY

Thaw the halibut if it is frozen. Cut into 1-inch pieces. Sauté onion, garlic, green pepper, celery and carrots in oil.

Add tomatoes, water, bouillon cubes and all seasonings, except 2 tablespoons parsley. Cover and simmer 20 minutes.

Add the halibut. Cover and simmer 5 to 10 minutes more, or until done. Sprinkle with the remaining parsley.

YIELD: 8 SERVINGS, MEASURES ABOUT 2 QUARTS

APPROX. CAL/SERV.: 235

Tuna Ring

2 7-OUNCE CANS TUNA, DRAINED
1 CUP WATER
¾ CUP DRY BREAD CRUMBS
½ CUP COOKED GREEN PEAS
⅓ CUP NONFAT DRY MILK
¼ CUP SLIVERED ALMONDS
1 EGG
2 TABLESPOONS FINELY CHOPPED ONION
2 TABLESPOONS FINELY CHOPPED GREEN PEPPER
2 TABLESPOONS FINELY CHOPPED PIMIENTO
2 TEASPOONS WORCESTERSHIRE SAUCE
1 TEASPOON SALT
⅛ TEASPOON PEPPER

Preheat oven to 350°F.

Combine tuna with all other ingredients; spoon into a well-oiled 8-inch ring mold. Bake in preheated oven for 45 minutes. Unmold at once. Serve garnished with more pimiento and fresh parsley.

YIELD: 6 SERVINGS
APPROX. CAL/SERV.: 300

Red Snapper À L' Orange

1½ POUNDS RED SNAPPER FILLETS, CUT INTO 6 SERVING PIECES
1 TEASPOON SALT
DASH PEPPER
2 TABLESPOONS ORANGE JUICE
1 TEASPOON GRATED ORANGE RIND
3 TABLESPOONS OIL
NUTMEG

Preheat oven to 350°F.

Combine salt, pepper, orange juice, rind and oil. Place fish pieces

Recipe continues...

in a single layer in an oiled pan, and pour sauce on top of fish. Sprinkle with nutmeg, and bake 20 to 30 minutes.

YIELD: 6 SERVINGS
APPROX. CAL/SERV.: 230

. . . . *California Cioppino*

For this fish stew use a firm-textured fish, such as rock, cod or red snapper. Serve steaming hot with garlic bread and a green salad.

1 MEDIUM ONION, CHOPPED
2 CLOVES GARLIC, CHOPPED
2 TABLESPOONS CHOPPED PARSLEY
¼ CUP TOMATO JUICE
4 MEDIUM TOMATOES, CHOPPED
2 POUNDS FISH, CUT IN BITE-SIZE PIECES
SALT AND PEPPER TO TASTE

Sauté onion, garlic and parsley about 5 minutes in just enough oil to brown lightly. Add tomatoes and juice. Simmer about 15 minutes.

Add fish and cook gently 20 to 30 minutes. Season with salt and pepper. Serve at once in soup plates.

YIELD: 8 SERVINGS
APPROX. CAL/SERV.: 185

. . . . *Mushroom Baked Sole*

1 MEDIUM ONION, FINELY CHOPPED
¼ CUP CHOPPED PARSLEY
1 CUP SLICED MUSHROOMS
¼ CUP MARGARINE
1½ POUNDS SOLE FILLETS
SALT AND PEPPER
¼ CUP DRY WHITE WINE
½ CUP SKIM MILK
1 TABLESPOON FLOUR
PAPRIKA

Preheat oven to 350°F.

Sauté onion, parsley and mushrooms in 3 tablespoons of the margarine, stirring constantly until onions are soft.

Place half the fillets in a greased baking dish. Sprinkle lightly with salt and pepper and spread sautéed mixture evenly over fish. Top with remaining fillets, season with salt and pepper, pour wine over all, and dot with remaining margarine. Bake uncovered for 15 minutes. Remove from oven and drain, reserving the pan liquid. In a small saucepan, combine flour and milk. Add the reserved pan liquid, and cook, stirring constantly, until thickened.

Pour over the fish and bake 5 minutes longer. Sprinkle with paprika and parsley.

YIELD: 6 SERVINGS
APPROX. CAL/SERV.: 265

Fillet of Sole with Walnuts and White Wine

1 POUND FILLET OF SOLE
½ CUP DRY WHITE WINE
½ CUP LIGHT STOCK (FISH OR CHICKEN) OR CANNED CLAM JUICE
CAYENNE PEPPER
SALT

sauce

2 TABLESPOONS OIL
2 TABLESPOONS FLOUR
¼ CUP SKIM MILK
¼ CUP LIGHT STOCK
½ CUP WHITE WINE
½ TEASPOON SALT
½ CUP CHOPPED WALNUTS
DASH WHITE PEPPER

Preheat oven to 325°F.

To cook the fish, place skinned fillets in a shallow oiled baking pan.

Recipe continues...

Add salt, a dash of cayenne pepper, the ½ cup of wine and ½ cup stock. Cover with foil and bake 20 minutes, or until tender.

Meanwhile, make the sauce: Heat oil in a small saucepan over a low flame. Blend in the flour and cook but do not brown. Add seasonings and, over medium heat, pour in milk, stock and wine, and stir constantly until mixture thickens. Reduce heat, add walnuts and simmer 1 minute.

When fillets are done, remove them to a serving platter, pour sauce over them and garnish with fresh parsley.

YIELD: 4 SERVINGS
APPROX. CAL/SERV.: 400

· · · · · · · · · · · · · **Sole Venetian**

1 POUND FILLET OF SOLE
2 TABLESPOONS OIL
1 TABLESPOON FRESH MINT, CHOPPED
1 GARLIC CLOVE, CHOPPED
2 TABLESPOONS MINCED PARSLEY
1 GREEN ONION, CHOPPED
½ CUP DRY WHITE WINE
¼ TEASPOON WHITE PEPPER
½ TEASPOON SALT
¼ CUP WATER

Wash and dry the sole. Rub with a paste made of mint, garlic, parsley and 1 tablespoon of oil.

Sauté green onion in the remaining tablespoon of oil, add wine, water and seasonings.

Meanwhile, broil the fillets until just done and remove to a warm platter. Pour the pan juice into the wine sauce. Heat sauce and pour over sole. Serve at once.

YIELD: 4 SERVINGS
APPROX. CAL/SERV.: 255

Poached Fish ✓

2 POUNDS FISH FILLETS, SKINNED
2 TABLESPOONS OIL
1 SMALL ONION, CHOPPED
¼ CUP CHOPPED CELERY
2 TABLESPOONS LEMON JUICE
1 TEASPOON SALT
3 OR 4 PEPPERCORNS
1 BAY LEAF
1 CUP HOT WATER
2 SPRIGS PARSLEY

In a large shallow pan, sauté the onion and celery in oil until tender. Place skinned fillets on top of vegetables, or roll each fillet, secure with a toothpick, and place on vegetables. Add water and seasonings. Cover and simmer about 8 minutes, or until fish flakes when tested with a fork.

Carefully transfer fillets to a heated platter. Serve with Lemon Parsley Sauce or Horseradish Sauce (p. 124).

YIELD: 8 SERVINGS
APPROX. CAL/SERV.: 200

Lemon Parsley Sauce

½ CUP MARGARINE
JUICE OF 1 LARGE LEMON (ABOUT 3 TABLESPOONS)
1 TEASPOON GRATED LEMON RIND
1 TABLESPOON CHOPPED PARSLEY

Heat margarine and lemon juice in a saucepan. Add grated lemon rind. Pour over fish.

YIELD: ¾ CUP
APPROX. CAL/SERV.: 1 TABLESPOON = 70

· · · · · · · · · · · **Horseradish Sauce**

1 TABLESPOON MARGARINE
4 TEASPOONS FLOUR
2 TABLESPOONS HORSERADISH, DRAINED
1 CUP FISH STOCK OR CANNED CLAM JUICE

Melt the margarine, blend in the flour and cook briefly. Add horse-radish and fish stock. Cook, stirring, until thick.
Serve over poached fish.

YIELD: 1¼ CUPS
APPROX. CAL/SERV.: 1 TABLESPOON = 10

· · · · · · · · · · · **Crab Meat Maryland**

3 CUPS FLAKED CRAB MEAT, FRESH, FROZEN OR CANNED
3 TABLESPOONS OIL
2 TABLESPOONS MINCED ONIONS
3 TABLESPOONS FLOUR
2 CUPS SKIM MILK
½ TEASPOON CELERY SALT
⅛ TEASPOON GRATED ORANGE PEEL
1 TABLESPOON SNIPPED PARSLEY
1 TABLESPOON MINCED GREEN PEPPER
1 PIMIENTO, MINCED
DASH TABASCO SAUCE
2 TABLESPOONS DRY SHERRY
1 EGG, BEATEN
DASH PEPPER
DASH SALT
2 SLICES BREAD, TOASTED LIGHTLY AND REDUCED TO CRUMBS
1 TABLESPOON OIL

Preheat oven to 350°F.
Thaw or drain crab meat if it is canned or frozen.
Sauté onion in oil until transparent. Add the flour, and cook, stirring,

1 minute. Pour in milk and cook over low flame until sauce is thickened. Put in the celery salt, orange peel, parsley, pepper, pimiento and Tabasco sauce. Remove from heat and add the sherry.

Stir some of the sauce into the beaten egg; then pour the egg mixture slowly into the sauce, stirring constantly. Add pepper and crab meat. Turn into 8 greased individual casseroles or shells. Mix oil with toasted bread crumbs and salt.

Bake, uncovered, 15 to 20 minutes or until lightly browned.

YIELD: ABOUT 8 SERVINGS
APPROX. CAL/SERV.: 1 CUP = 190

. . . . *Shrimp Gumbo*

⅓ CUP OIL
2 CUPS SLICED FRESH OKRA OR 1 10-OUNCE PACKAGE FROZEN OKRA, SLICED
1 POUND FRESH OR FROZEN SHRIMP, PEELED AND DEVEINED
⅔ CUP CHOPPED GREEN ONIONS AND TOPS
3 CLOVES GARLIC, FINELY CHOPPED
1½ TEASPOONS SALT
½ TEASPOON PEPPER
2 CUPS WATER
1 CUP CANNED TOMATOES
2 WHOLE BAY LEAVES
6 DROPS TABASCO SAUCE
1½ CUPS COOKED RICE

Sauté okra in oil 10 minutes. Add shrimp, onions, garlic, salt and pepper. Cook about 5 minutes. Add water, tomatoes and bay leaves. Cover and simmer 20 minutes. Remove the bay leaves and sprinkle in the Tabasco.

Place ¼ cup of cooked rice in each of 6 soup bowls. Fill with gumbo and serve.

YIELD: 6 SERVINGS
APPROX. CAL/SERV.: 260

· · · · · · · · · · · *Cold Salmon Mousse*

Serve this elegant mousse with a sauce and a green salad. Attractive and light—a good summer meal.

    2 CUPS CANNED SALMON
    1 ENVELOPE GELATIN
    ¼ CUP COLD WATER
    ½ CUP BOILING WATER
    ½ CUP MAYONNAISE
    1 TABLESPOON LEMON JUICE
    1 TEASPOON GRATED ONION
    ½ TEASPOON TABASCO SAUCE
    ¼ TEASPOON PAPRIKA
    1 TEASPOON SALT
    1 TABLESPOON CHOPPED CAPERS
 1 ½ CUPS COTTAGE CHEESE

Remove skin and bones from salmon. Drain and flake. Soften gelatin in cold water, add boiling water and stir until dissolved. Cool, and mix well with the mayonnaise, lemon juice, onion, Tabasco, paprika, salt and capers. Chill to the consistency of beaten egg white, and mix in the salmon.

Whip cottage cheese in a blender until smooth and creamy, fold into an oiled 1½-quart mold. (Use a fish mold if possible.) Chill until set.

Serve with 5 tablespoons Cucumber and Yogurt Dip Sauce or 10 tablespoons Basic Cheese Sauce with Dill (see Appetizers).

YIELD: 8 SERVINGS, ABOUT 4½ CUPS
APPROX. CAL/SERV.: 215

. . . . *Scallops Oriental*

2 POUNDS FRESH OR FROZEN SCALLOPS
¼ CUP HONEY
¼ CUP PREPARED MUSTARD
1 TEASPOON CURRY POWDER
1 TEASPOON LEMON JUICE
LEMON WEDGES

Preheat broiler.

Rinse fresh scallops well in cold water, or thaw frozen scallops. Place in a baking pan.

In a saucepan, combine honey, mustard, curry powder and lemon juice.

Brush scallops with the sauce. Broil 4 inches from the flame for 10 minutes, or until browned. Turn scallops, brush with remaining sauce and broil 10 minutes longer.

Garnish with lemon wedges.

YIELD: 8 SERVINGS
APPROX. CAL/SERV.: 155

. . . . *Salad Nicoise*

Dressing

4 TEASPOONS DIJON MUSTARD
¼ CUP WINE VINEGAR
1 TABLESPOON SALT
3 CLOVES GARLIC, MINCED
¾ CUP OIL
FRESHLY GROUND PEPPER
2 TEASPOONS CHOPPED FRESH THYME OR 1 TEASPOON DRIED THYME

Recipe continues...

Salad

2 POUNDS FRESH GREEN BEANS CUT 1½ INCHES LONG
4 RIBS CELERY, CUT IN ONE-INCH PIECES
2 GREEN PEPPERS, CUT IN RINGS
1 PINT CHERRY TOMATOES
5 RED-SKINNED POTATOES, FLAKED
3 7-OUNCE CANS TUNA FISH, FLAKED
10 RIPE OLIVES, SLICED
10 STUFFED GREEN OLIVES, SLICED
1 LARGE RED ONION
⅓ CUP CHOPPED PARSLEY
2 TABLESPOONS CHOPPED FRESH BASIL OR 1 TEASPOON DRIED BASIL
¼ CUP FINELY CHOPPED GREEN ONION

Make dressing combining listed ingredients and chill while preparing salad ingredients.

Steam green beans until tender-crisp.

Drain and set aside. Blanch celery by putting it in boiling water for 15 seconds.

Arrange into a *large* salad bowl with all remaining ingredients. Add dressing.

YIELD: 12 SERVINGS
APPROX. CAL/SERV.: 300

· · · · · · · · **Bean Sprout Tuna Chow Mein**

1 CHICKEN BOUILLON CUBE

1 CUP WATER

1 TABLESPOON SOY SAUCE

SALT AND PEPPER TO TASTE

2 TABLESPOONS CORNSTARCH

6 STALKS CELERY, CUT DIAGONALLY

2 MEDIUM ONIONS, SLIVERED

1 SIX-OUNCE CAN BAMBOO SHOOTS, DRAINED

1 FOUR-OUNCE CAN MUSHROOMS, DRAINED, OR 4 OUNCES SLICED FRESH
  MUSHROOMS

2 CUPS FRESHLY GROWN BEAN SPROUTS OR 1 CAN BEAN SPROUTS,
  DRAINED

2 TABLESPOONS OIL

1 7-OUNCE CAN WATER-PACKED TUNA, DRAINED

Dissolve bouillon in water, add soy sauce, salt and pepper. Stir in cornstarch until dissolved.

Slice celery diagonally ⅛ inch thick. Slice onions in very thin slices or slivers. Cut mushrooms in slices.

Heat oil in frying pan or wok over highest heat. When hot, toss in celery and onion; stir-fry one minute. Add bamboo shoots, mushrooms and bean sprouts.

Stir broth mixture and add to vegetables. Stir and cook just until sauce is thickened. Add tuna and stir until hot and sauce is clear.

Serve immediately over fluffy rice.

YIELD: 4 SERVINGS

APPROX. CAL/SERV.: 218

Wild game has little fat, life in the wild being what it is, strenuous with little opportunity for overeating. Domesticated game, on the other hand, has a softer life and the leisure time to accumulate fat in quantities that can make it unacceptable to a fat-controlled eating plan. Domesticated duck and goose are in this category.

Wild duck and pheasant are acceptably lean, as are partridge, quail and other small birds. Venison is very lean, and rabbit, with a flavor somewhat like chicken, has only a fraction of a chicken's fat.

Recipes for preparing lean game usually call for the addition of cooking fat, and basting is a must if the meat is to be roasted. But braising and fricaseeing are also excellent means of cooking game, do not require additional cooking fat and produce tender results.

· · *Herbed Rabbit in Wine Sauce (European Method)*

1 3-POUND RABBIT, CUT UP

1 TEASPOON LEMON JUICE

½ CUP DRY WHITE WINE

2 TABLESPOONS SUGAR

1 TEASPOON PEPPER

¼ TEASPOON MARJORAM

1 SMALL BAY LEAF

3 WHOLE CLOVES

3 TABLESPOONS FLOUR

2 TABLESPOONS OIL

½ CUP CHOPPED ONION

¼ CUP CHOPPED GREEN PEPPER

To make marinade mix lemon juice, wine, sugar, pepper, marjoram, bay leaf and cloves; let rabbit pieces rest in mixture for at least 12 hours in the refrigerator.

Remove pieces from marinade and dry them well. Strain marinade and set aside. Roll rabbit pieces lightly in flour, and brown in oil. Place rabbit and marinade in a heavy stew pot and let simmer until tender (1½–2 hours). Add onions and green peppers during last 15 minutes of cooking.

Remove rabbit to a serving platter. Strain sauce again and heat, but do not allow to boil. Pour over rabbit, and serve with brown rice.

YIELD: 6 SERVINGS

APPROX. CAL/SERV.: 240 (OR 340 WITH ½ CUP RICE)

Venison Stew

2 POUNDS BREAST OR SHOULDER VENISON
2 TABLESPOONS OIL
6 CUPS BOILING WATER
2 TEASPOONS SALT
¼ TEASPOON PEPPER
2 TABLESPOONS FLOUR
4 MEDIUM POTATOES, DICED
4 CARROTS, DICED
2 TURNIPS, DICED
4 ONIONS, DICED
SEASONED FLOUR

Cut the venison into 1-inch cubes. Roll in seasoned flour and brown in a small amount of oil in a heavy skillet. Add the boiling water, salt and pepper to the browned meat; cover and simmer for 2 to 3 hours.

Add the diced vegetables and cook until tender. Using 2 tablespoons of flour moistened with water, thicken the remaining liquid.

YIELD: 8 SERVINGS
APPROX. CAL/SERV.: 250

Roast Pheasant in Red Wine

1 LARGE PHEASANT
2 CUPS RED WINE
SALT
PEPPER

Preheat oven to 350°F.

Place the pheasant in roasting pan; roast uncovered until almost tender. When nearly done, season with salt and pepper, add the wine, and continue roasting for 10 minutes until the meat is tender.

YIELD: 4 SERVINGS
APPROX. CAL/SERV.: 325

Hasenpfeffer

½ CUP VINEGAR
2 CUPS WATER
2 TEASPOONS SALT
¼ TEASPOON PEPPER
½ TEASPOON WHOLE CLOVES
2 TEASPOONS SUGAR
4 BAY LEAVES
1 MEDIUM ONION, SLICED
1 2½-TO-3-POUND RABBIT, CUT UP
FLOUR
3 TABLESPOONS OIL
2 TEASPOONS WORCESTERSHIRE SAUCE
3 TABLESPOONS FLOUR

To make the pickling mixture, combine the vinegar, water, salt, pepper, cloves, sugar, bay leaves and sliced onion in a bowl. Add the rabbit pieces and refrigerate for 8 to 12 hours; turn the pieces occasionally so they will absorb the flavor evenly.

Remove the rabbit pieces from the pickling mixture and drain on absorbent paper. Save the liquid and onions but discard bay leaves and cloves. Dredge the rabbit pieces in flour and brown in oil. Pour liquid and onions over the rabbit and add Worcestershire sauce. Thicken the liquid with a mixture of 3 tablespoons flour and cold water.

YIELD: 4 SERVINGS
APPROX. CAL/SERV.: 370

Brunswick Stew

1 SQUIRREL, CUT UP
1 TEASPOON SALT
½ TEASPOON PEPPER
2 CUPS WATER
1 SMALL ONION, CHOPPED
1 CUP CORN
1 CUP LIMA BEANS
2 POTATOES, DICED
2 CUPS TOMATOES
1 TEASPOON SUGAR

Season squirrel with salt and pepper; simmer in water with onion for 2 hours. Add corn, lima beans, potatoes, tomatoes and sugar to the squirrel and simmer for 30 minutes or until vegetables are tender.

YIELD: 4 SERVINGS

APPROX. CAL/SERV.: 270

· · · · · · · · *Grouse, Pheasant or Partridge in Wine*

1 GROUSE, PHEASANT OR PARTRIDGE, CUT UP

2 CUPS PORT OR SHERRY

6 WHOLE CLOVES

1 MEDIUM ONION, SLICED

1 BAY LEAF

1 TEASPOON SAGE

SEASONED FLOUR

2 TABLESPOONS OIL

2 TABLESPOONS FLOUR

2 TABLESPOONS COLD WATER

To make marinade, mix port or sherry, cloves, onion, bay leaf and sage; let pieces rest in mixture for 2 days in the refrigerator in a covered container.

Remove the bird from marinade and dry pieces well. Strain the marinade and set aside. Dip pieces in seasoned flour and brown in oil. Place the browned bird and liquid in a casserole. Cover and bake in slow oven (300°) for 1 to 1½ hours or until tender.

Strain the liquid from the bird; bring to rapid boil for 15 minutes or until reduced in quantity by one half. Thicken the liquid with flour and cold-water mixture. Serve over the bird.

YIELD: 4 SERVINGS

APPROX. CAL/SERV.: 425

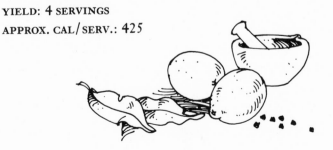

· · · · · · Marinade for Venison, Elk or Antelope

1 CUP BEEF BROTH

1 TEASPOON SALT

1 TABLESPOON PICKLING SPICE

½ TEASPOON CELERY SEEDS

½ TEASPOON BASIL

½ TEASPOON MARJORAM

½ TEASPOON THYME

½ TEASPOON SAGE

1 BAY LEAF

3 PEPPERCORNS, CRUSHED

3 WHOLE ALLSPICE, CRUSHED

2 TABLESPOONS LEMON JUICE

¼ CUP VINEGAR

Combine all of the ingredients. Cover venison, elk or antelope with the marinade. Marinate in the refrigerator for 10 to 12 hours.

Remove the meat from the marinade and drain well. Cook as desired.

YIELD: 1¼ CUPS

APPROX. CAL/SERV.: 1¼ CUPS = 25

Poultry

*P*oultry is universally loved and as widely available. At its flavorful best when freshly killed, it does not require lengthy preparation, and may appear as easily in a peasant dish redolent of garlic as in an elegantly sauced creation suited to champagne tastes.

Because its delicate flesh is easily digested, chicken is one of the first meats eaten in life and one of the last. Turkey is the favorite holiday bird of many poultry lovers, and the tiny Cornish hens are as delightful a novelty to the formal diner as they are to the picnicker.

Poultry carries a layer of fat under the skin and several large fat deposits near the tail. The latter are easily removed. A whole chicken destined for the roasting oven, needs its skin as a protective layer to prevent the meat from drying out during cooking, but the skin is easily removed once the chicken is cooked. Individual pieces of chicken may be skinned before or after cooking. Whether broiled, fried, roasted or simmered in a pot, the chicken and its relatives deserve the high position they hold in world cookery.

·   ·   ·   ·   ·   ·   ·   ·   ·   · *Crispy Baked Chicken*

Cornflake crumbs give this skinless chicken a crisp new coating. A favorite finger food for children and for taking on picnics.

1 FRYING CHICKEN (2½ TO 3 POUNDS), CUT INTO SERVING PIECES
1 CUP CORNFLAKE CRUMBS
1 CUP SKIM MILK
SEASONING, IF DESIRED

Preheat oven to 400°F.

Remove all skin from the chicken; rinse and dry the pieces thoroughly. Season. Coat each piece with oil or dip in milk, shake to remove excess, and roll in the crumbs. Let stand briefly so coating will adhere.

Place chicken in an oiled baking pan. (Line pan with foil for easy clean-up.) Do not crowd; pieces should not touch. Bake 45 minutes or more. Crumbs will form a crisp "skin."

YIELD: 4 SERVINGS
APPROX. CAL/SERV.: 270

·   ·   ·   ·   ·   ·   ·   ·   ·   ·   · *Sesame Chicken*

2 TABLESPOONS MARGARINE
2 TABLESPOONS OIL
1 FRYING CHICKEN (2½ TO 3 POUNDS), CUT INTO SERVING PIECES
⅓ CUP FLOUR SEASONED WITH SALT AND PEPPER
¼ CUP SESAME SEEDS
3 TABLESPOONS MINCED GREEN ONION
½ CUP DRY WHITE WINE
JUICE OF ½ LEMON

Preheat oven to 375°F.

Melt margarine with oil in baking pan. Allow to cool slightly but not harden. In a paper bag, shake chicken in seasoned flour until coated.

Then roll pieces in oil in baking pan, and arrange so that pieces do not touch. Sprinkle with lemon juice and sesame seeds. Bake 30 minutes, or until lightly browned. Turn chicken; sprinkle with sesame seeds and minced onion. Pour wine into bottom of pan and cook for 30–45 minutes, basting occasionally, until done.

YIELD: 4 SERVINGS
APPROX. CAL/SERV.: 400

Lemon-Baked Chicken

A touch of lemon gives this golden baked chicken a delicate flavor.

1 FRYING CHICKEN (2½–3 POUNDS), CUT INTO SERVING PIECES
2 TABLESPOONS OIL OR MELTED MARGARINE
3 TABLESPOONS FRESH LEMON JUICE
1 CLOVE GARLIC, CRUSHED
½ TEASPOON SALT
DASH PEPPER

Preheat oven to 350°F.

In a bowl, combine lemon juice, oil, garlic, salt and pepper. Arrange chicken in a shallow casserole or baking pan, and pour over it the lemon and oil mixture. Cover and bake until tender, about 40 minutes, basting occasionally. Uncover casserole and bake 10 minutes longer to allow chicken to brown. To serve, sprinkle with chopped parsley.

YIELD: 4 SERVINGS
APPROX. CAL/SERV.: 215

. . . . *Chicken Mandarin*

1 FRYING CHICKEN (2½ TO 3 POUNDS), CUT INTO SERVING PIECES
¼ CUP SEASONED FLOUR
2 TABLESPOONS MARGARINE
2 TABLESPOONS OIL
4 TABLESPOONS LEMON JUICE
½ CUP ORANGE JUICE
2 TABLESPOONS HONEY
½ TABLESPOON SOY SAUCE
½ TEASPOON POWDERED GINGER
1 11-OUNCE CAN MANDARIN ORANGES, WITH JUICE

Wash and dry chicken pieces. Shake in a paper bag with seasoned flour to coat. In a skillet, heat oil and margarine; add chicken and brown each piece. Drain mandarin oranges and set aside. Mix juice from the can with the lemon juice, orange juice, honey, soy sauce, and ginger. Pour sauce over the chicken in skillet. Cover and simmer for 30 minutes, or until tender. Add mandarin orange sections 5 or 10 minutes before chicken is done.

Serve with rice.

YIELD: 4 SERVINGS
APPROX. CAL/SERV.: 360 (OR 460 WITH ½ CUP RICE)

. . . . *Chicken with Apricot Glaze*

1 FRYING CHICKEN (2½–3 POUNDS) CUT INTO SERVING PIECES
¼ CUP SEASONED FLOUR
2 TABLESPOONS MARGARINE
2 TABLESPOONS OIL
½ CUP APRICOT JAM
1 TEASPOON MARJORAM
1 TEASPOON GRATED LEMON RIND
1 TABLESPOON SOY SAUCE
1 16-OUNCE CAN WHOLE PEELED APRICOTS, WITH JUICE (THERE SHOULD BE ABOUT 1½ CUPS OF JUICE)
1 LARGE GREEN PEPPER, CUT INTO ½ INCH SQUARES

Wash and dry chicken, coat with flour. In a large skillet, brown each piece in heated margarine and oil. After browning, coat chicken pieces with apricot jam. Combine marjoram, lemon rind, soy sauce and apricot juice. Pour over chicken.

Cover pan and simmer until tender, about 40 minutes, basting occasionally. Add green pepper and cook 5 minutes more. Meanwhile, pit the apricots. Add them to pan just before serving and heat through.

Serve with rice.

YIELD: 4 SERVINGS

APPROX. CAL/SERV.: 445 (OR 545 WITH ½ CUP RICE)

· · · · · · · · · ***Oven Barbecued Chicken***

 1 2½ TO 3 POUND FRYING CHICKEN, CUT INTO SERVING PIECES
 ¼ CUP WATER
 ¼ CUP VINEGAR
 3 TABLESPOONS OIL
 ½ CUP CHILI SAUCE OR CATSUP
 3 TABLESPOONS WORCESTERSHIRE SAUCE
 1 TABLESPOON DRY MUSTARD
1½ TEASPOONS SALT
 ½ TEASPOON PEPPER
 2 TABLESPOONS CHOPPED ONION (OPTIONAL)

Preheat oven to 350°F.

Combine all ingredients except chicken in a saucepan; simmer 10 minutes. Wash and dry chicken and place in a large baking pan. Pour half of the barbecue sauce over chicken and bake, uncovered, for 50–60 minutes; basting with remaining sauce every 15 minutes.

Or, chicken may be immersed in sauce, then removed and cooked over charcoal, basting frequently.

YIELD: 4 SERVINGS

APPROX. CAL/SERV.: 260

. . . . . *Chicken in White Wine and Yogurt Sauce*

4 CHICKEN BREASTS, SPLIT AND SKINNED
4 TABLESPOONS MARGARINE
3 TABLESPOONS FLOUR
½ CUP CHICKEN BOUILLON
¾ CUP LOW-FAT YOGURT
¼ CUP WHITE WINE
2 TEASPOONS GRATED LEMON RIND
1 TEASPOON SALT
½ TEASPOON PEPPER
½ CUP SLICED MUSHROOMS

Preheat oven to 350°F.

Melt 2 tablespoons margarine in a shallow baking pan; place chicken breasts in the pan. Bake, uncovered, about 30 minutes. Meanwhile, melt remaining margarine in a saucepan, add flour and cook briefly, stirring. Add bouillon, stirring constantly until mixture is thick and smooth. Add yogurt, wine, lemon rind, salt and pepper, stirring until blended.

Remove pan from oven. Turn each chicken breast. Cover each with sliced mushrooms, and pour sauce over all. Bake, uncovered, for 30 minutes, or until tender.

Serve garnished with a lemon twist or sprig of parsley.

YIELD: 8 SERVINGS
APPROX. CAL/SERV.: 230

. . . . *Chicken in Tomato-Wine Sauce*

1 DICED ONION
1 CLOVE GARLIC, CRUSHED
1 2½–3-POUND CHICKEN, CUT INTO SERVING PIECES
1 8-OUNCE CAN TOMATO SAUCE
1 CUP HOT WATER
SALT AND PEPPER
1 4-OUNCE CAN MUSHROOM STEMS AND PIECES, DRAINED
½ CUP WHITE WINE

Place all ingredients, except mushrooms and wine, in a large pot. Cover and simmer 45 minutes over a flame so low that liquid barely quivers on top. Add mushrooms and wine and cook 5 minutes more.

Serve garnished with parsley.

YIELD: 4 SERVINGS

APPROX. CAL/SERV.: 210

Chicken in Rosé Sauce

4 CHICKEN BREASTS, SPLIT AND SKINNED
4 TABLESPOONS MARGARINE
2 TABLESPOONS FLOUR
¾ CUP CHICKEN BROTH
½ CUP ROSÉ WINE
¼ CUP THINLY SLICED GREEN ONION
½ CUP SLICED MUSHROOMS
1 10-OUNCE PACKAGE FROZEN ARTICHOKE HEARTS, COOKED ACCORDING TO PACKAGE DIRECTIONS; OR 1 14-OUNCE CAN ARTICHOKE HEARTS PACKED IN WATER

Preheat oven to 350°F.

Melt 2 tablespoons margarine in baking pan, add chicken breasts and bake for 30 minutes.

Melt remaining margarine in a saucepan, add flour and cook briefly, stirring. Add chicken broth and wine, stirring constantly until sauce is thick and smooth.

Remove chicken breasts from oven, turn, and cover each with sliced mushrooms, green onion and artichokes. Pour sauce over all and bake for 30 minutes, or until tender.

YIELD: 8 SERVINGS

APPROX. CAL/SERV.: 230

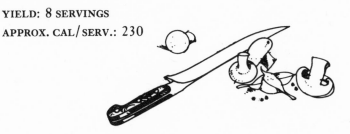

· · · · · · · · **Chicken with Spanish Sauce**

1 2½–3-POUND FRYER, CUT INTO SERVING PIECES
2 TABLESPOONS OIL
½ CUP MINCED ONION
½ CUP CHOPPED GREEN PEPPER
1 MINCED CLOVE GARLIC
1 28-OUNCE CAN TOMATOES
½ CUP WHITE WINE
½ TEASPOON THYME
2 BAY LEAVES

Preheat oven to 350°F.

Heat oil in heavy skillet and quickly brown chicken pieces. Remove to a casserole; add salt and pepper to taste.

In same skillet, lightly brown onions, green pepper and garlic. Add to casserole along with tomatoes, wine and herbs. Cover and bake until chicken is tender, about 1 hour.

YIELD: 4 SERVINGS
APPROX. CAL/SERV.: 290

· · · · · · · · · · · **Chicken Jerusalem**

2 TABLESPOONS OIL
1 2½–3 POUND FRYER, CUT INTO SERVING PIECES
SEASONED FLOUR
½ POUND FRESH MUSHROOMS, CUT IN PIECES
1 6-OUNCE JAR MARINATED ARTICHOKE HEARTS, DRAINED
2 CLOVES GARLIC, MINCED
1¼ TEASPOONS SALT
½ TEASPOON OREGANO
½ TEASPOON PEPPER
2 CUPS CANNED OR FRESH TOMATOES
½ CUP SHERRY

Preheat oven to 350°F.

Heat oil in frying pan. Dredge chicken pieces in seasoned flour and brown in oil. Place in casserole with mushrooms and artichoke hearts. Stir garlic and spices with tomatoes; pour over chicken.

Bake 1–1½ hours, or until tender, adding sherry during last few minutes of cooking time.

YIELD: 4 SERVINGS
APPROX. CAL/SERV.: 320

Baked Chicken Parmesan

1 2½–3-POUND FRYER, CUT INTO SERVING PIECES
1 TEASPOON SALT
¼ TEASPOON PEPPER
¼ TEASPOON GARLIC SALT
¼ TEASPOON PAPRIKA
⅛ TEASPOON THYME
¼ CUP PARMESAN CHEESE
1 TABLESPOON MINCED PARSLEY
⅓ CUP FINE BREAD CRUMBS
⅓ CUP WATER
1 TABLESPOON OIL
¼ CUP MARGARINE (MELTED)
⅓ CUP MARSALA WINE

Preheat oven to 350°F.

In a paper bag, place seasonings, cheese, parsley and crumbs; coat chicken by shaking a few pieces at a time in the bag.

Oil a shallow roasting pan, pour in the water and arrange chicken pieces. Sprinkle chicken with oil and melted margarine and bake, uncovered, in the oven for 45 minutes.

Pour wine over chicken. Lower oven heat to 325°F.; cover pan with foil, and bake 15 minutes longer. Remove foil; raise oven heat to 350°F., and bake 10 minutes longer.

YIELD: 4 SERVINGS
APPROX. CAL/SERV.: 365

. . . . *Chicken Jambalaya*

3 CHICKEN BREASTS, SPLIT AND SKINNED
½ CUP CHOPPED ONION
¼ CUP CHOPPED GREEN PEPPER
1 CUP BOUILLON
1 CUP WHITE WINE
¼ CUP CHOPPED PARSLEY
½ TEASPOON BASIL
1 SMALL BAY LEAF
½ TEASPOON THYME
1 CUP RAW RICE
½ CUP LEAN HAM, CUBED
1 CUP CANNED TOMATOES, DRAINED

Preheat oven to 350°F.

In a saucepan, bring to a boil the bouillon, wine, herbs, onion and green pepper. Place rice, ham, tomatoes and chicken in a large casserole; pour herb sauce over all. Cover tightly and bake for 25 or 30 minutes. Add seasoning. Turn heat off; allow casserole to remain in the oven for 10–15 minutes.

YIELD: 6 SERVINGS
APPROX. CAL/SERV.: 350

. . . . *Chicken Salad Casserole*

A hot dish with the character of a salad, this is a good luncheon offering, summer or winter.

2 CUPS CUBED, COOKED CHICKEN
1 SMALL GREEN PEPPER, SLICED
1 4-OUNCE CAN MUSHROOMS, DRAINED
½ CUP SLIVERED WATER CHESTNUTS
¼ CUP MAYONNAISE
¼ CUP SKIM MILK
1 2-OUNCE JAR SLICED PIMIENTO, DRAINED
½ TEASPOON SALT

Preheat oven to 350°F.

Simmer green pepper slices in water until nearly tender. Drain.

Combine milk with mayonnaise; add pimiento, green pepper, mushrooms, water chestnuts, chicken and salt. Place in a 1-quart casserole. Cover and bake 20 minutes.

YIELD: 4 SERVINGS (ABOUT 3 CUPS)
APPROX. CAL/SERV.: 260

· · · · *Chicken and Broccoli with Mushroom Sauce*

1 10-OUNCE PACKAGE FROZEN BROCCOLI
3 TABLESPOONS MARGARINE
3 TABLESPOONS FLOUR
1 CUP CHICKEN BROTH
1 4-OUNCE CAN MUSHROOM SLICES, WITH LIQUID
1 POUND COOKED CHICKEN, SLICED (OR 2 CUPS COOKED CHICKEN OR
   TURKEY)
2 TABLESPOONS CHOPPED PARSLEY
2 TABLESPOONS BREAD CRUMBS

Preheat oven to 375°F.

Cook broccoli according to package directions.

Mix margarine and flour together in saucepan. Cook briefly over medium heat. Blend in chicken broth, stirring constantly until thickened and smooth. Stir in mushrooms and their liquid. Season to taste.

Place broccoli pieces in a shallow baking pan. Cover with sliced chicken and pour mushroom sauce over all. Top with parsley and bread crumbs. Bake, uncovered, 15–25 minutes, or until bubbly and brown on top.

YIELD: 4 SERVINGS
APPROX. CAL/SERV.: 330

· · · · · · · · · · · · *variation*

This recipe may be made with asparagus.

· · · · · · · · **Chicken Curry—in a hurry**

Leftover roast or boiled chicken can come to no better end than in this zesty dish of Eastern origin.

2 CUPS COOKED DICED CHICKEN OR TURKEY
½ POUND THINLY SLICED FRESH MUSHROOMS
1 TABLESPOON OIL OR MARGARINE
⅓ CUP CHOPPED ONION
3 TABLESPOONS FLOUR
1 CHICKEN BOUILLON CUBE
½ TEASPOON SALT
1½ TEASPOONS CURRY POWDER
1 CUP FINELY CHOPPED APPLE
¼ CUP CHOPPED PARSLEY
¾ CUP SKIM MILK
1 CUP WATER

In a large skillet, sauté chicken, mushrooms and onions in oil until chicken is lightly browned on all sides.

Stir in flour, bouillon cube, salt and curry powder. Add apple and parsley; then pour in milk and water. Simmer, stirring constantly, for 3 minutes or until apple pieces are tender-crisp.

Serve over rice.

YIELD: 4–6 SERVINGS
APPROX. CAL/SERV.: 235 (OR 335 WITH ½ CUP RICE)

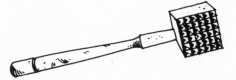

Chicken À La King

3 TABLESPOONS OIL
4 TABLESPOONS FLOUR
1 TEASPOON SALT
PEPPER TO TASTE
3 CUPS CHICKEN STOCK
⅓ CUP NONFAT DRY MILK
½ POUND SLICED MUSHROOMS
¼ CUP DICED GREEN PEPPER
¼ CUP CHOPPED PIMIENTO
2 CUPS COOKED CHICKEN
4 TABLESPOONS SHERRY
1 TABLESPOON CHOPPED PARSLEY

Heat oil in a saucepan, add flour, and cook briefly, stirring. Pour in chicken stock, stirring constantly until thick and smooth. Season and stir in nonfat dry milk. Cook 1 minute.

Sauté sliced mushrooms and add to sauce, along with chicken, green pepper and pimiento. Heat through, then add sherry. Adjust seasoning, and garnish with parsley. Serve with rice.

YIELD: 6 SERVINGS (ABOUT 1 QUART)
APPROX. CAL/SERV.: 1 CUP = 205 (OR 305 WITH ½ CUP RICE)

. . . . *Chicken Pot Pie*

The vegetables in this pot pie may be any you happen to have on hand. The dish may also be made with other meats, such as beef or pork.

2 CUPS COOKED CHICKEN
1½ CUPS WATER
½ CUP NONFAT DRY MILK
3 TABLESPOONS FLOUR
1 TEASPOON SALT
¼ TEASPOON TARRAGON
¼ TEASPOON PARSLEY
⅛ TEASPOON PEPPER
¾ CUP SMALL WHITE ONIONS, COOKED
COOKED CARROT SLICES, LIMA BEANS AND GREEN PEAS TO TOTAL 1½
  CUPS (A PACKAGE OF MIXED FROZEN VEGETABLES MAY BE USED)
ONE RECIPE FOR PASTRY CRUST OR MASHED POTATO TOPPING

Preheat oven to 400°F.
Beat nonfat dry milk and flour with water until smooth. Add salt, tarragon, parsley and pepper. Cook over medium heat, stirring constantly, until mixture thickens.
Mix in chicken and vegetables. Pour into 1½-quart casserole. Cover with Pastry Crust or Mashed Potato Topping. Bake 20 minutes, or until lightly browned.

YIELD: 4 SERVINGS
APPROX. CAL/SERV.: 225 (OR 340 WITH TOPPING)

. . . . *pastry crust*

½ CUP FLOUR
⅛ TEASPOON SALT
2 TABLESPOONS OIL

Stir salt and oil into flour. Form into a ball, flatten slightly and place on a sheet of wax paper. Place another sheet on top of dough and roll out quickly. Peel off top layer of paper, invert dough over filling and seal pie by pressing dough firmly to edge of casserole. Cut steam holes and bake pie at 400°F. for about 20 minutes.

YIELD: 4 SERVINGS
APPROX. CAL/SERV.: 110

mashed potato topping

2 CUPS MASHED POTATOES
½ CUP HOT SKIM MILK
¼ TEASPOON PEPPER
2 TABLESPOONS MARGARINE (MELTED)
1 TEASPOON SALT
⅛ TEASPOON NUTMEG
PAPRIKA

Beat together mashed potatoes, margarine, milk, salt, pepper and nutmeg until light and fluffy.

Spread over top of chicken mixture and sprinkle lightly with paprika. Bake at 400°F. for about 20 minutes.

YIELD: 4 SERVINGS
APPROX. CAL/SERV.: 110

Chicken Dinner in the Pot

A very good one-pot dinner. Children like it, too.

2 CHICKEN BREASTS, SPLIT AND SKINNED
4 MEDIUM-SIZE POTATOES
2 LARGE CARROTS
½ POUND FRESH GREEN BEANS, OR 1 10-OUNCE PACKAGE FROZEN
1 LARGE ONION
1 TABLESPOON DRIED PARSLEY FLAKES
SALT AND PEPPER
½ CUP DRY SHERRY

Recipe continues…

Preheat oven to 300°F.

Place chicken breasts in a large, heavy ovenware pot. (An enamel-coated cast-iron pot is best.) Peel potatoes, slice ½ inch thick and place on top of chicken.

Peel and quarter the onion. Peel carrots, quarter lengthwise, and cut into 2 inch lengths. Cut ends off the green beans, or separate frozen beans, and place in the pot with onions and carrots. Sprinkle contents of pot with parsley flakes. Season lightly with salt and pepper. Pour sherry over all and cover tightly. Bake 2 hours, or until vegetables are tender.

YIELD: 4 SERVINGS

APPROX. CAL/SERV.: 310

. . . . . . *Curried Turkey with Water Chestnuts*

After the holidays, use left-over turkey in this deliciously different mild curry. Grand for entertaining.

¼ CUP OIL

1 BUNCH GREEN ONIONS

1 SMALL STALK CELERY

1 GREEN PEPPER, SLICED

2 TABLESPOONS SLIVERED SALTED ALMONDS

2 CUPS WATER CHESTNUTS, THINLY SLICED

2 CUPS DICED COOKED TURKEY OR CHICKEN

3 TABLESPOONS FLOUR

1 TEASPOON CURRY POWDER

1 TEASPOON PAPRIKA

½ TEASPOON SWEET BASIL

1½ CUPS CHICKEN BROTH OR BOUILLON

¼ CUP CHOPPED PIMIENTO

1 CUP DRAINED PINEAPPLE TIDBITS

Slice green onions and celery diagonally, about ½ inch thick. Heat oil in a skillet and sauté onions, celery and peppers until slightly browned. Add almonds, water chestnuts and cooked turkey. Mix well with flour, paprika, curry powder and basil. Sauté lightly, stirring constantly, until well blended.

Mix in broth, pimiento and pineapple. Cover and let steam briefly. Season with salt and pepper.

Serve on rice. A good accompaniment is Cranberry Chutney, page 101.

YIELD: 6 SERVINGS

APPROX. CAL/SERV.: 280 (OR 380 WITH ½ CUP RICE)

. . . . *Almond Chicken*

A quick and satisfying oriental dish. Cook vegetables only until crisp.

2 WHOLE RAW CHICKEN BREASTS, SKINNED AND THINLY SLICED (SEMI-THAWED CHICKEN IS BETTER FOR SLICING HERE)

2 TABLESPOONS OIL

1 SMALL ONION, THINLY SLICED

1 CUP CELERY, THINLY SLICED

1 CUP SLICED WATER CHESTNUTS

1 5-OUNCE CAN BAMBOO SHOOTS

2 CUPS CHICKEN BROTH OR BOUILLON

2 TABLESPOONS SOY SAUCE

1 TEASPOON SUGAR

2 TABLESPOONS CORNSTARCH

¼ CUP COLD WATER

SALT

¼ CUP TOASTED ALMOND SLIVERS

Preheat oil in heavy frying pan, and sauté chicken for 2–3 minutes. Add onion and celery. Cook 5 minutes. Then add water chestnuts, bamboo shoots, chicken broth and soy sauce. Cover and cook 5 minutes more.

Blend sugar, cornstarch and cold water. Pour over chicken and cook until thick, stirring constantly. Add salt to taste. Garnish with toasted almonds. Serve over rice.

YIELD: 4 SERVINGS

APPROX. CAL/SERV.: 340 (OR 440 WITH ½ CUP RICE)

. . . . *variation*

WITH SNOW PEAS: Omit almonds and add 1 10-ounce package of frozen snow pea pods with the water chestnuts and bamboo shoots.

APPROX. CAL/SERV.: 290 (OR 390 WITH ½ CUP RICE)

· · *Shredded Chicken with Green Pepper and Carrots*

Color and texture make this a beautiful dish. Quick to cook, and delicious.

3 CHICKEN BREASTS, BONED, SPLIT AND SKINNED
4 TEASPOONS CORNSTARCH
4 TEASPOONS SOY SAUCE
1 TABLESPOON DRY SHERRY
1 EGG WHITE, SLIGHTLY BEATEN
5 TABLESPOONS OIL
1 WHOLE CARROT, THINLY SHREDDED
1 GREEN PEPPER, THINLY SLICED
1 TEASPOON FRESH GINGER, THINLY SHREDDED; OR 1 STALK SCALLION SLICED INTO ½-INCH LENGTHS
1 TEASPOON SUGAR
2 TABLESPOONS COLD WATER

Use a very sharp knife to slice chicken breasts horizontally, paper thin. This is easier if breasts are slightly frozen. Cut the slices into strips about ⅛ inch wide and 1½–2 inches long. Place in bowl.

Combine half of the cornstarch and half of the soy sauce with the sherry and egg white. Pour over chicken slivers and let stand 30 minutes.

Heat 1 tablespoon oil in a skillet. Sauté carrot slivers 1 minute. Add green pepper and sauté for 1 minute. Remove vegetable mixture from pan and set to one side.

In the same pan, heat the remaining 4 tablespoons of oil and sauté ginger or scallion for 30 seconds. With a slotted spoon, remove chicken from the soy sauce, and add to pan, cooking and stirring until it shreds and turns white. Add reserved vegetable mixture, sugar and remaining soy sauce. Cook until heated through, then stir in remaining 2 teaspoons of cornstarch dissolved in 2 teaspoons of cold water. Cook briefly until all ingredients are coated with a clear glaze.

Serve at once.

YIELD: 6 SERVINGS
APPROX. CAL/SERV.: 275

· · · · · · · · · Chicken Philippine Style

A sour tang relates this interesting dish with the Philippine *adobo*.

1 2½- TO 3-POUND BROILER CHICKEN, CUT INTO PIECES
½ CUP VINEGAR
½ CUP SOY SAUCE
1 CLOVE GARLIC, MINCED
⅛ TEASPOON GROUND BLACK PEPPER

Marinate chicken in mixture of other ingredients for about 30 minutes. This can be done in skillet to be used for cooking. Heat on top of stove until it comes to a boil, cover and simmer about 40 minutes, or until almost all liquid has evaporated.

Serve hot or cold.

YIELD: 4 SERVINGS
APPROX. CAL/SERV.: 170

· · · · · · · · · · · Sesame-Soy Chicken

Charcoal-broiled chicken with a difference, this finger food makes good outdoor eating.

Recipe continues...

1 2½–3-POUND FRYER, CUT INTO SERVING PIECES
½ CUP SOY SAUCE
2 TABLESPOONS SUGAR
1 TEASPOON SALT
1 2-INCH PIECE FRESH GINGER, FINELY CHOPPED; OR 1 TEASPOON
   GROUND GINGER
2 TABLESPOONS SESAME SEEDS, TOASTED
2 TABLESPOONS OIL

Marinate chicken for 1–2 hours in soy sauce, sugar, salt and ginger. Remove from marinade and broil over charcoal or in the oven, basting with marinade and oil.

When chicken is done and nicely browned on both sides, in about 30 minutes, sprinkle with toasted sesame seeds, and arrange on a platter. Serve with rice and a salad.

YIELD: 4 SERVINGS
APPROX. CAL/SERV.: 285

. . . . *Turkey Mousse*

2 CUPS DICED TURKEY, COOKED
1 ENVELOPE GELATIN
¼ CUP COLD WATER
1 BOUILLON CUBE
½ CUP BOILING WATER
½ CUP MAYONNAISE
1 TABLESPOON LEMON JUICE
1 TEASPOON GRATED ONION
1 TEASPOON SALT
½ TEASPOON TABASCO SAUCE
¼ TEASPOON PAPRIKA
1½ CUPS LOW-FAT COTTAGE CHEESE
¼ CUP CHOPPED GREEN PEPPER
¼ CUP DICED CELERY
¼ CUP CHOPPED PIMIENTO

Soften gelatin in cold water. Dissolve bouillon cube in boiling water and add to softened gelatin, stirring until dissolved. Cool. Add mayonnaise, lemon juice, onion, salt, Tabasco and paprika.

Whip the cottage cheese in blender until smooth and creamy. Add to gelatin mixture. Then fold in turkey, green pepper, celery and pimiento. Pour into a 1½-quart mold. Chill until firm.

YIELD: 10 SERVINGS
APPROX. CAL/SERV.: 160

· · · · · · · · · · · *Roast Chicken*

Choose a plump chicken, about 4 pounds. Wash and dry it well. Rub inside and out with salt, pepper and a little basil or tarragon. Grease the skin with 1 teaspoon oil. Truss the chicken. Place on a rack in a roasting pan and roast about 1 hour at 400°F., basting frequently with a mixture of white wine and defatted chicken broth or bouillon. Serve with chicken gravy, if desired.

YIELD: 6 SERVINGS
APPROX. CAL/SERV.: 165

· · · · · · · · · · · *Chicken Gravy*

1 CUP CLEAR CHICKEN BROTH OR DEFATTED CHICKEN ESSENCE FROM
   THE ROASTING PAN
¼ CUP SKIM MILK
2 TABLESPOONS FLOUR
SALT AND PEPPER TO TASTE

Combine flour and skim milk, beating until smooth, or shake the mixture in a tightly capped jar. Gradually add to the chicken broth or essence in a saucepan.

Cook over medium heat, stirring constantly until thick. Add seasoning; reduce heat and continue to cook, stirring, 5 minutes longer.

YIELD: 1 CUP
APPROX. CAL/SERV.: 1 CUP = 80   1 TABLESPOON = 5

· · · · · · · · · *Roast Stuffed Cornish Hen*

6 CORNISH HENS (ABOUT 14 OUNCES EACH)
1 PACKAGE WILD RICE MIX OR LONG GRAIN AND WILD RICE COMBINA-
   TION
1 MEDIUM ONION, CHOPPED
2 TABLESPOONS MARGARINE
½ TEASPOON SAGE
¼ CUP BRANDY
1 CUP ORANGE SECTIONS

To make the stuffing, cook rice until it is still slightly firm. Drain. In a skillet, melt margarine and cook chopped onion until browned. Add rice and sage; toss gently.

Preheat oven to 350°F.

Clean, wash and dry hens. Stuff lightly and skewer or sew the vents closed.

Brush hens with ½ cup melted margarine and place breasts side up on a rack in a shallow pan. Roast uncovered about 1 hour, basting occasionally with the melted margarine.

Make a sauce by adding ½ cup water to the drippings in the roasting pan, stirring to dislodge browned particles from the pan. Add ¼ cup brandy and 1 cup orange sections. Cook 2 minutes. Serve with hens.

YIELD: 12 SERVINGS
APPROX. CAL/SERV.: 250

· · · · · · · · · · · *Rice Dressing*

6 CUPS CHICKEN BOUILLON
2 CUPS UNCOOKED RICE
2 TEASPOONS SALT
PEPPER TO TASTE
3 ONIONS, CHOPPED
4 STALKS CELERY, CHOPPED
1 GREEN PEPPER, CHOPPED
½ POUND CHOPPED MUSHROOMS
1 TABLESPOON CHOPPED PARSLEY
3 EGG WHITES

Cook rice in chicken bouillon. Simmer onions, celery and green pepper in water until tender.

Fold in the egg whites and mushrooms. Pack loosely into cavity of a turkey or bake in a casserole.

YIELD: STUFFING FOR A 12- TO 15-POUND TURKEY
APPROX. CAL/SERV.: 12-POUND TURKEY = 135
15-POUND TURKEY = 110

· · · · · · · · · · · · *Celery Stuffing*

  1 CHICKEN BOUILLON CUBE
  1 CUP WATER
  ½ CUP CHOPPED ONION
1 ½ CUPS DICED CELERY, INCLUDING LEAVES
  3 CUPS SKIM MILK
  2 8-OUNCE PACKAGES POULTRY STUFFING MIX

Dissolve bouillon cube in water. Add onion and celery; cook about 10 minutes, or until tender.

Add skim milk and bring almost to a boil.

Stir liquid into stuffing mix until well moistened. If too dry, add a little boiling water.

Use as stuffing for roasting turkey.

Put extra stuffing in a covered pan and bake at 350°F. for 20 minutes.

YIELD: STUFFING FOR A 10- TO 12-POUND TURKEY OR 12 SERVINGS
APPROX. CAL/SERV.: 80

· · · · · · · · · · · · ·   *Apple Stuffing*

¼ CUP CHOPPED ONIONS

¼ CUP CHOPPED CELERY

2 TABLESPOONS MARGARINE

4 CUPS DRY BREAD CUBES

1 CUP DICED UNPEELED APPLES

½ TEASPOON POULTRY SEASONING

½ TEASPOON DRIED SAGE

¼ TEASPOON SALT

⅛ TEASPOON GROUND BLACK PEPPER

1 CHICKEN BOUILLON CUBE

½ CUP HOT WATER

Cook onions and celery in margarine for 5 minutes, or until tender. Dissolve bouillon cube in hot water.

Combine onions and celery with all other dry ingredients. Add bouillon and toss lightly.

Use to stuff a turkey.

YIELD: STUFFING FOR A 10- TO 12-POUND TURKEY OR 12 SERVINGS
APPROX. CAL/SERV.: 130

· · · · · · · · · · · · ·   *variation*

WITH MIXED DRIED FRUITS: Combine 1 cup of dried chopped fruits, (apricots, prunes or peaches) with ½ cup of raisins. Simmer in water in a covered saucepan for 20 minutes. Cool slightly and combine with all other ingredients in Apple Stuffing.

APPROX. CAL/SERV.: 190

· · · · · · · · · · **Corn Bread Dressing**

3 CUPS CRUMBLED CORN BREAD

1 CUP BREAD CRUMBS

2 CUPS CHICKEN BOUILLON

3 STALKS CELERY, FINELY CHOPPED

1 LARGE ONION, FINELY CHOPPED

2 EGG WHITES

½ TEASPOON SALT

½ TEASPOON PEPPER

½ TEASPOON SAGE OR POULTRY SEASONING

Combine all ingredients in a mixing bowl. Mix well.

Turn into an oiled baking dish and bake at 350°F. for 45 minutes. Or use as stuffing in a turkey.

YIELD: STUFFING FOR A 10- TO 12-POUND TURKEY

APPROX. CAL/SERV.: 115

· · · · · · · · · · · **Chicken with Orange**

1 2½–3-POUND FRYER, CUT INTO SERVING PIECES

½ TEASPOON PAPRIKA

1 MEDIUM ONION, SLICED

½ CUP FROZEN ORANGE JUICE CONCENTRATE

2 TABLESPOONS BROWN SUGAR

2 TABLESPOONS CHOPPED PARSLEY

2 TEASPOONS SOY SAUCE

½ TEASPOON GROUND GINGER

⅓ CUP WATER

Brown chicken pieces under the broiler.

Place in casserole; add salt and paprika.

Arrange onion slices over chicken.

Combine juice concentrate, brown sugar, parsley, soy sauce, ginger and water. Pour over chicken and onions.

Cover and simmer until chicken is tender, about 35–40 minutes.

YIELD: 4 SERVINGS

APPROX. CAL/SERV.: 195

Molly's Chicken Casserole

3 CHICKEN BREASTS SPLIT AND SKINNED

sauce

1 CUP SPAGHETTI SAUCE (YOUR OWN OR YOUR FAVORITE BRAND)
1 TEASPOON WORCESTERSHIRE SAUCE
DASH TABASCO
DASH DRY MUSTARD
¼ CUP VINEGAR

Preheat oven to 350°F.

Place chicken breasts in a 2-quart casserole dish with a little water. Bake, uncovered, for one hour.

Meanwhile, combine sauce ingredients and simmer for 30 minutes.

Pour the sauce over the chicken; broil in oven, basting several times but turning only once for about 20 minutes.

Watch carefully so that the chicken does not burn.

YIELD: 6 SERVINGS
APPROX. CAL/SERV.: 130

Sauces

. . . . *Barbecue Sauce*

¼ CUP WATER
¼ CUP VINEGAR
 3 TABLESPOONS OIL
½ CUP CHILI SAUCE OR CATSUP
 3 TABLESPOONS WORCESTERSHIRE SAUCE
 1 TABLESPOON DRY MUSTARD
1½ TEASPOONS SALT
½ TEASPOON PEPPER
 2 TABLESPOONS CHOPPED ONION

Combine all ingredients and simmer for 15 to 20 minutes. Good with beef, pork or chicken.

YIELD: ABOUT 1½ CUPS
APPROX. CAL/SERV.: ¼ CUP = 95   1 TABLESPOON = 25

· · · · · · · · · · · · · *Tomato Sauce*

1 CUP DICED ONION
2 CLOVES GARLIC, MINCED
1 28-OUNCE CAN ITALIAN PLUM TOMATOES
3 TABLESPOONS TOMATO SAUCE
1 TEASPOON SEASONED SALT
⅛ TEASPOON BLACK PEPPER
½ TEASPOON OREGANO
½ TEASPOON BASIL

Combine all ingredients in a heavy saucepan. Bring to a boil, reduce heat and simmer about 20 minutes.

Use over stuffed green peppers, meat loaf or stuffed cabbage.

YIELD: ABOUT 1 QUART
APPROX. CAL/SERV.: 1 CUP = 70   1 TABLESPOON = 5

· · · · · · · · · · · · · · *variation*

WITH GREEN PEPPERS: Add 1 green pepper, diced, and ½ cup of sliced mushrooms to the other ingredients. Cook as directed.

APPROX. CAL/SERV.: 1 CUP = 80   1 TABLESPOON = 5

· · · · · · · · · · · *Lemon-Chablis Sauce*

1 LEMON
1 TABLESPOON CORNSTARCH
1 CUP CHABLIS OR OTHER DRY WHITE WINE
¼ TEASPOON SALT
1½ TABLESPOONS MARGARINE

Thinly slice half of the lemon. Squeeze the juice from the other half and grate the rind.

Make a smooth paste of the cornstarch, wine and salt.

Melt the margarine in a small saucepan. Add the wine paste and cook, stirring constantly, until the sauce is clear and slightly thickened.

Add the grated lemon rind, juice and slices. Heat a few minutes longer, and pour over baked, broiled or poached fish.

YIELD: 1 ¼ CUPS

APPROX. CAL/SERV.: 1 TABLESPOON = 20

· · · · · · · · · · · · · **Fish Sauce**

1 CUP MAYONNAISE
1 CUP CHILI SAUCE
3 TO 4 TABLESPOONS DRAINED HORSERADISH
DASH HOT PEPPER SAUCE

Mix the mayonnaise and chili sauce together. Stir in the remaining ingredients and chill. Serve with fish. (May also be used as an appetizer dip sauce.)

YIELD: 2 ¼ CUPS

APPROX. CAL/SERV.: 1 CUP = 740   1 TABLESPOON = 45

· · · · · · · · · · · · · **Tartar Sauce**

1 CUP MAYONNAISE
1 TABLESPOON MINCED PICKLE
1 TABLESPOON MINCED PARSLEY
1 TABLESPOON MINCED CAPERS
1 TABLESPOON MINCED ONION

Combine all ingredients. Mix well and refrigerate. Serve with fish.

YIELD: 1 ¼ CUP

APPROX. CAL/SERV.: 1 TABLESPOON = 80

· · · · · · · · · · · **Mock Béarnaise Sauce**

1 TABLESPOON OIL
1 TABLESPOON CORNSTARCH
¾ CUP CHICKEN BROTH
1 EGG YOLK, LIGHTLY BEATEN
1–2 TABLESPOONS VINEGAR ESSENCE (p. 172), ACCORDING TO TASTE

Recipe continues…

Combine the cornstarch and oil in a small saucepan. Add the broth, and cook over medium heat, stirring constantly until the mixture thickens.

Remove from the heat, add a small amount of the sauce to the beaten egg yolk, and pour egg mixture slowly into the sauce.

Cook over low heat, stirring constantly, for 1 minute. Remove from heat and add the Vinegar Essence. Serve over steamed fish or vegetables.

YIELD: 1 CUP

APPROX. CAL/SERV.: 1 TABLESPOON = 15

· · · · · · · · · · · · · · *variation*

MOCK HOLLANDAISE. Substitute 1 to 2 tablespoons of fresh lemon juice for the Vinegar Essence.

· · · · · · *Vinegar Essence for Béarnaise Sauce*

¼ CUP WINE VINEGAR

¼ CUP DRY WHITE WINE OR DRY VERMOUTH

1 TABLESPOON MINCED SHALLOTS OR GREEN ONIONS

1 TABLESPOON MINCED FRESH TARRAGON OR ½ TABLESPOON OF DRY TARRAGON

⅛ TEASPOON WHITE PEPPER

PINCH SALT

Combine vinegar, vermouth, onions, tarragon, salt and pepper. Bring to a boil and over medium heat reduce to about 2 tablespoons. Set aside.

APPROX. CAL/SERV.: 1 TABLESPOON = 25

· · · *Quick-and-Easy Mock Hollandaise Sauce*

½ CUP MAYONNAISE

2 TABLESPOONS HOT WATER

1 TABLESPOON LEMON JUICE

In the top of a double boiler blend hot water with mayonnaise, stirring until heated through. Add the lemon juice.

Pour over broccoli, asparagus or other vegetables.

YIELD: ABOUT ½ CUP
APPROX. CAL/SERV.: 800   1 TABLESPOON = 90

Basic White Sauce I

1 TABLESPOON MARGARINE
1 TABLESPOON FLOUR
¼ TEASPOON SALT
⅛ TEASPOON PEPPER
1 CUP SKIM MILK

Melt margarine in a saucepan over low heat. Blend in the flour, salt and pepper to make a roux. Cook over low heat, stirring until the mixture is smooth and bubbly.

Stir in the milk. Heat to boiling and cook 1 minute, stirring constantly.

NOTE: for a medium-thick white sauce, increase margarine and flour to 2 tablespoons each; for a thick sauce, increase each to 4 tablespoons.

YIELD: 1 CUP
APPROX. CAL/SERV.: 215   1 TABLESPOON = 15
    MEDIUM THICK: 1 CUP = 340   1 TABLESPOON = 20
    THICK: 1 CUP = 590   1 TABLESPOON = 35

Basic White Sauce II

2 TABLESPOONS MARGARINE
2 TABLESPOONS FLOUR
4 TABLESPOONS NONFAT DRY MILK
½ TEASPOON SALT
PEPPER TO TASTE
1 CUP WATER

Melt margarine, stir in the flour and make a roux. Add the nonfat dry milk and water.

Recipe continues...

Place over a low heat and cook, stirring constantly, until sauce is thick and smooth. Season to taste.

NOTE: this recipe may also be made with skim milk or evaporated skim milk.

YIELD: 1 CUP
APPROX. CAL/SERV.: 310   1 TABLESPOON = 20

· · · · · · · · · · **Quick Madeira Sauce**

1 10-OUNCE CAN BOUILLON
⅓ CUP PLUS 1 TABLESPOON MADEIRA OR PORT WINE
2 TEASPOONS CORNSTARCH

Combine the bouillon and ⅓ cup of the wine in a saucepan. Bring to a boil and reduce rapidly to 1 cup.

Mix the remaining tablespoon of wine with the cornstarch and stir into the sauce. Cook over medium heat until thickened.

Serve with pheasant or other game.

YIELD: ABOUT 1 CUP
APPROX. CAL/SERV.: 164   1 TABLESPOON = 10

· · · · · · · · · · · **Basic Gravy**

2 TABLESPOONS BROWNED FLOUR*
1 CUP LIQUID (MEAT DRIPPINGS OR BOUILLON OR BOTH)

Use 2 tablespoons of flour for each cup of liquid. Put half of the liquid in a jar and add the flour. Cover tightly and shake until mixture is smooth.

Pour into a pan, add the remaining liquid. Bring to a simmer and cook for a few minutes, stirring constantly. Season to taste.

Add gravy coloring, if desired.

---

* Browned flour adds color and flavor to the gravy. To brown, spread flour in a shallow pan and cook over very low heat, stirring occasionally, until lightly colored.

NOTE: for a thick gravy, increase flour to 4 tablespoons for each cup of liquid.

YIELD: 1 CUP

APPROX. CAL/SERV.: 1 TABLESPOON = 5   1 TABLESPOON (THICK) = 10

· · · · · · · · · · · · · *variation*

MUSHROOM GRAVY: Add ¼ cup of sliced mushrooms for each cup of gravy.

· · · · · · · · · · *Mock Sour Cream* ✓

2 TABLESPOONS SKIM MILK
1 TABLESPOON LEMON JUICE
1 CUP LOW-FAT COTTAGE CHEESE
¼ TEASPOON SALT

Place all ingredients in a blender and mix on medium-high speed until smooth and creamy.

Use as a sour cream substitute.

This sauce may be added to hot dishes at the last moment. Or serve it cold, with the addition of flavoring or herbs, as a dressing for salad or a sauce for a mousse.

YIELD: ABOUT 1¼ CUPS

APPROX. CAL/SERV.: 1 CUP = 160   1 TABLESPOON = 10

Vegetarian

More planning is required to get adequate nutrition from a vegetarian diet than from a diet that includes meat. The difficulty is in getting enough of the right kind of protein.

Protein is made up of twenty-two amino acids, eight of which must be acquired from food; our bodies cannot make them. If one of the eight is missing in the correct quantity from the food we eat, then all of the others are useless. Without the missing link, they are powerless to build a single protein molecule, a situation that can lead to a deficiency in this vital body-building element. Some vegetable sources, such as beans, seeds and grains, contain high quality protein, but are better eaten in combination rather than alone because they can supplement one another to make far more of it available for body use. The key word here is "available."

Vegetable protein does not contain fat, and is less costly than animal protein; but to get sufficient amounts of it, one must consume vegetables in greater bulk than is necessary with animal products. Eggs and low-fat dairy products have all the necessary amino acids, making them high-quality sources, and therefore excellent dietary supplements. Unfortunately, the high cholesterol content of the egg yolk makes it unacceptable for regular daily consumption, but no such limitation applies to the egg white—and the protein is in the egg white.

The vegetarian (vegan) who does not eat animal products must combine plant products very carefully to obtain enough usable protein, matching vegetables that lack certain amino acids with others that supply them. For example, wheat and beans supplement each other if eaten together, as do peanuts and sunflower seeds, and rice and beans.

The chart on the following page will serve as a useful guide in meal planning to obtain quality protein nutrition from vegetable sources.

FOR QUALITY PROTEIN* FROM VEGETABLE SOURCES, USE ANY FOOD FROM COLUMN I IN COMBINATION WITH A FOOD FROM COLUMN II

	COLUMN I	COLUMN II
Legumes	Beans: Aduki, Black, Cranberry, Fava, Kidney, Limas, Pinto, Marrow, Mung, Navy, Pea, Soy (Tofu) (Sprouts)	Low-fat dairy products
	Peas: Black-eyed, Chick, Cow, Field, Split	Grains
	Lentils	Nuts & seeds
Grains	Whole Grains: Barley; Corn (Cornbread) (Grits) Oats; Rice; Rye; Wheat (Bulgur, Wheat Germ) Sprouts	Low-fat dairy products Legumes
Nuts & seeds	Nuts: Almonds, Beechnuts, Brazil nuts. Cashews, Filberts, Pecans, Pine nuts (Pignolia), Walnuts	Low-fat dairy products Legumes
	Seeds: Pumpkin, Sunflower	

* Low-fat dairy products (milk, yogurt, cheese, eggs, cottage cheese), in addition to being used as a supplement to the above, may be used alone as quality protein.

Before cooking, most legumes should be soaked overnight. The soaking mixture should be refrigerated to avoid fermentation. Black-eyed peas, lentils, pinto beans and split peas, however, require no soaking before cooking. Legumes should be simmered for approximately 2½ hours in the same water in which they are soaked to allow for greater retention of nutrients. To further improve flavor, salt, herbs and onions can be added to the simmering mixture. Avoid overstirring the legumes as they cook, since it can lead to mushiness. To reduce the soaking time, dried beans may be cooked in boiling water for 2 minutes and then soaked for 1 hour. Then they may be simmered for the normal period of time.

Drain beans when they are still hot to prepare bean pulp or puree. Any leftover bean stock can be used for soups or stews.

There is a great variety of legumes from which to choose in making meatless meals. Remember, it is a good idea to cook, then freeze, a large enough quantity of dried legumes so that you may use them in various recipes.

The recipes in this section contain skim milk, eggs and cheese in small amounts. They are balanced to give you the right combination of amino acids. So relax and enjoy eating lower on the food chain.

· · · · · · · · · · *Fluffy Fondue Casserole*

This delicate dish puffs up like a soufflé.

4 SLICES BREAD, TOASTED
2 TABLESPOONS MARGARINE
1½ CUPS LOW-FAT COTTAGE CHEESE
4 LARGE EGG WHITES
1¼ CUPS SKIM MILK FORTIFIED WITH ¼ CUP NONFAT DRY MILK
¼ TEASPOON DRY MUSTARD
¼ TEASPOON PAPRIKA
¼ TEASPOON WORCESTERSHIRE SAUCE
½ TEASPOON SALT
¼ TEASPOON BLACK PEPPER
1 HEAPING TABLESPOON CHOPPED CHIVES
1 TABLESPOON SHERRY

Preheat oven to 350°F.

Grease an oblong baking dish (about 8 × 13 inches). Spread the toast with margarine and cut into cubes. Place evenly over bottom of the baking dish.

Beat egg whites in a large bowl until stiff.

In a blender, beat cottage cheese until creamy. Add the milk and all other ingredients. Blend thoroughly.

Carefully fold this mixture into the stiffly beaten egg whites, and pour into the baking dish. Bake 45 minutes to an hour or until a knife inserted in the center comes out clean.

YIELD: 6 SERVINGS
APPROX. CAL/SERV.: 160

. . . . *Baked Soybeans*

1½ CUPS DRY SOYBEANS

½ TEASPOON PEPPER

1 TEASPOON SALT

2 ONIONS, CHOPPED

2 TABLESPOONS MARGARINE

¼ CUP CATSUP

¼ CUP MOLASSES

1 TABLESPOON DRY MUSTARD

Soak soybeans overnight.

Bring to a boil, cover, and simmer until nearly tender (about 3 hours).

Meanwhile, sauté the onions in the margarine until soft. Season with salt and pepper. Add to the beans with the catsup, molasses and mustard.

Cover and bake in a 300°F. oven for 1 hour, or until the beans are tender, uncovering now and then to allow excess liquid to evaporate.

YIELD: 2 QUARTS

APPROX. CAL/SERV.: ½ CUP = 115

. . . . *Soybean Chili*

1 CUP SOYBEANS

1 CUP WHOLE WHEAT BERRIES*

6 CUPS WATER

2 TABLESPOONS OIL

2 TEASPOONS CHILI POWDER

⅛ TEASPOON HOT RED PEPPER

1 TEASPOON OREGANO

1 CLOVE GARLIC, FINELY CHOPPED

2 ONIONS, CHOPPED

1 CANNED JALAPEÑO HOT PEPPER, CHOPPED

4 TOMATOES, CHOPPED

SOY SAUCE

COOKED BROWN RICE

CHOPPED SCALLIONS

* *Whole wheat berries are the kernels of whole wheat before grinding and may be found in health food stores.*

Soak soybeans and wheat berries overnight in enough water to cover them.

Transfer to a heavy saucepan, bring to a boil, cover, and simmer 3 to 4 hours, or until beans are nearly tender.

Heat oil in a skillet. Add the chili powder, red pepper and oregano, and cook, stirring, 2 minutes. Add garlic and onion and cook 5 minutes more. Add chili peppers and chopped tomato. Bring to a boil. Pour into the soybean mixture and continue cooking until beans and wheat are tender. Season with soy sauce to taste.

Garnish with scallions and serve with brown rice.

YIELD: 12 SERVINGS

APPROX. CAL/SERV.: ½ CUP = 170 (OR 285 WITH ½ CUP BROWN RICE, ONIONS AND SOY SAUCE)

. . . . *Old-Fashioned Baked Beans*

  1 POUND NAVY BEANS
  3 TABLESPOONS BROWN SUGAR
1½ TEASPOONS SALT
  1 TEASPOON DRY MUSTARD
 ⅓ CUP DARK MOLASSES
  2 ONIONS, CUT IN QUARTERS

Wash the beans and soak overnight in enough water to cover them. Drain. Place in a saucepan, cover with water and simmer 1 to 2 hours, until tender. Mix in the brown sugar, salt, mustard and molasses.

Place onion quarters in the bottom of a 2-quart casserole. Pour in the beans. If necessary, add enough boiling water to cover them.

Cover casserole, place in oven and bake at 325°F. for 5 to 6 hours, adding more water if needed.

Remove the casserole lid for the last 30 to 40 minutes of cooking.

YIELD: 12 SERVINGS

APPROX. CAL/SERV.: ½ CUP = 170

. . . . **Cottage Cheese-Nut Croquettes**

2 CUPS LOW-FAT COTTAGE CHEESE
2 CUPS BREAD CRUMBS
½ CUP COARSELY CHOPPED PECANS
¼ TEASPOON PAPRIKA
SKIM MILK TO MOISTEN, IF NEEDED
¼ CUP CHOPPED GREEN PEPPER
1 ½ TABLESPOONS CHOPPED ONIONS
½ TEASPOON SALT
1 EGG
¼ CUP SKIM MILK
1 CUP CORN FLAKE CRUMBS

Preheat oven to 325°F.

Combine first 8 ingredients and mix well. Divide into 10 equal portions and shape into croquettes.

Lightly beat together the egg and milk. Dip each croquette into the mixture, then roll in corn flake crumbs.

Place croquettes on a greased cookie sheet and bake 25 minutes.

Serve with basic Tomato Sauce (p. 170) or Créole Sauce (p. 244).

YIELD: 20 CROQUETTES
APPROX. CAL/SERV.: 1 CROQUETTE = 100 (OR 110 WITH 2 TABLESPOONS SAUCE)

· · · · · · · · · · · · · *Enchilada Bake*

½ CUP DRY BEANS, COOKED
1 ONION, CHOPPED
1 CLOVE GARLIC, MINCED
5 OR 6 MUSHROOMS, SLICED
1 GREEN PEPPER, CHOPPED
1½ CUPS STEWED TOMATOES
1 TABLESPOON CHILI POWDER
1 TEASPOON CUMIN SEED, GROUND
SALT TO TASTE
½ CUP DRY RED WINE
8 CORN TORTILLAS
¼ CUP GRATED MOZZARELLA CHEESE (MADE FROM PARTIALLY
  SKIMMED MILK)
½ CUP RICOTTA CHEESE (MADE FROM PARTIALLY SKIMMED MILK)
¼ CUP LOW-FAT YOGURT
6 BLACK OLIVES, SLICED

Preheat the oven to 350°F.

Sauté onion, garlic, mushrooms and pepper.

Add the beans, tomatoes, spices, salt and wine. Simmer gently for about 30 minutes.

Mix ricotta cheese and yogurt.

In an oiled 1½-quart casserole, put a layer of tortillas, a layer of sauce, 1½ tablespoons of grated cheese and 4 tablespoons of cheese-yogurt mixture. Repeat until all ingredients are used, ending with a layer of sauce. Top with cheese-yogurt mixture and black olives.

Bake for 15 to 20 minutes.

YIELD: 6 SERVINGS
APPROX. CAL/SERV.: 195

· · · · · · · · · *Ricotta Lasagna Swirls*

8 LASAGNA NOODLES, COOKED

· · · · · · · · · · · · · · *filling*

1 PACKAGE FRESH SPINACH
2 TABLESPOONS PARMESAN CHEESE
1 CUP RICOTTA CHEESE (MADE FROM PARTIALLY SKIMMED MILK)
¼ TEASPOON NUTMEG
SALT AND PEPPER

· · · · · · · · · · · · · · *sauce*

2 CUPS TOMATO SAUCE
2 CLOVES GARLIC, MINCED
½ CUP ONIONS, CHOPPED
1 TABLESPOON OIL
½ TEASPOON BASIL
SALT AND PEPPER TO TASTE

Wash spinach thoroughly, chop finely and put in a pan with a tight fitting lid. Cook over low heat for 7 minutes. Drain and squeeze out excess juice. Mix spinach with cheeses, nutmeg, salt and pepper.

Spread mixture evenly along entire length of each noodle, roll each one and place on its side, not touching, in an oiled 8 × 8-inch shallow baking dish.

To make sauce, sauté garlic and onions in oil, add tomato sauce, basil and seasonings. Simmer 15 to 20 minutes.

Cover lasagna swirls with the sauce—bake in oven at 350°F. for 20 minutes.

YIELD: 4 SERVINGS
APPROX. CAL/SERV.: 380

Stuffed Cabbage Leaves

1¼ CUPS RAW BROWN RICE
⅛ CUP OF SOY GRITS
1 ONION, CHOPPED
½ CUP PINE NUTS (OR TOASTED SUNFLOWER SEEDS)
1 SCANT TABLESPOON CARAWAY SEEDS
¼ CUP RAISINS
½ TEASPOON SALT
1 15-OUNCE CAN TOMATO SAUCE
12 WHOLE CABBAGE LEAVES, STEAMED BRIEFLY
1 CUP LOW-FAT YOGURT

Cook the rice and soy grits together until done. Sauté onion. Mix the rice and soy grits with onion, nuts, caraway seed, raisins and salt. Add enough tomato sauce to moisten mixture.

Steam cabbage for a few minutes only, until leaves can be separated. Place about 3 tablespoons of the rice mixture on each leaf. Roll up and secure with a toothpick, if necessary. Place the rolled leaves in a covered skillet and pour the remaining tomato sauce over all. Cook about 15 minutes, or until cabbage is tender. This is especially good topped with yogurt.

YIELD: 6 SERVINGS
APPROX. CAL/SERV.: 230

variation

Instead of stuffing and rolling the leaves, cut out the center of the cabbage. Boil cabbage 10 minutes, and fill cavity with stuffing.

Tostadas

This is a meal that has nearly everything in taste and nutrition. The tostado is not as complicated as it seems. The beans and sauce are easily prepared ahead of time.

Recipe continues...

· · · · · · · · · · · · · *sauce*

6 MEDIUM TOMATOES, SEEDED AND CHOPPED
1 CUP FINELY CHOPPED ONIONS
1 TEASPOON OREGANO, DRIED
½ TEASPOON MINCED GARLIC
1 TEASPOON HONEY
1 TEASPOON SALT
½ CUP RED WINE VINEGAR

Combine these ingredients in a small bowl. Mix thoroughly and set aside.

· · · · · · · · · · · · *frijoles refritos*

1½ CUPS DRY KIDNEY BEANS
5 CUPS WATER OR STOCK
1 CUP ONIONS, CHOPPED
2 MEDIUM TOMATOES, CHOPPED; OR ⅔ CUP CANNED
½ TEASPOON GARLIC, MINCED
1 TEASPOON CHILI POWDER
PINCH CAYENNE
1 TEASPOON SALT

Soak the beans overnight.

Cook beans with ½ cup of onions, ¼ cup of tomatoes, ¼ teaspoon of garlic, the chili, cayenne and 5 cups of water. When beans are tender, add 1 teaspoon of salt.

In a large frying pan, heat 2 tablespoons of oil; sauté the remaining onions and garlic until the onions are transparent. Add remaining tomatoes and cook 3 minutes. With a fork, mash ¼ cup of beans into the mixture. Continue mashing and adding the beans by quarter cups. Cook about 10 minutes more, then turn off the heat and cover the pan to keep the frijoles warm.

· · · · · · · · · · · · · · *dressing*

2 TABLESPOONS OIL
2 TABLESPOONS OLIVE OIL
2 TABLESPOONS RED WINE VINEGAR
¼ TEASPOON SALT
3 CUPS SHREDDED ICEBERG LETTUCE

Combine the dressing ingredients and mix thoroughly. Drop the lettuce into the mixture and toss to coat well.

· · · · · · · · · · · · · · *tostadas*

12 CORN TORTILLAS
OIL FOR FRYING

Fry each tortilla in oil; drain on paper towels. (Fry about ½ minute per side.)

· · · · · · · · · · · *to assemble the tostadas*

1 CUP CHOPPED ONIONS
¼ CUP GRATED PARMESAN CHEESE

For each serving, place 1 or 2 tostadas on a plate, and spread each one with about ⅓ cup of frijoles refritos. Top with ¼ cup of lettuce, some chopped onions, tomato sauce, and 1 tablespoon of grated cheese.

YIELD: 12 TOSTADAS
APPROX. CAL/SERV.: 1 TOSTADA = 325

. . . . ***Green Pepper Tostadas***

    1 TABLESPOON OIL
    2 SWEET GREEN PEPPERS, DICED
    3 WHOLE CANNED TOMATOES, DICED
    1 MEDIUM ONION, DICED
    ¼ CUP "WHIPPED" LOW-FAT COTTAGE CHEESE
    4 TORTILLAS
    ½ CUP GRATED MOZZARELLA CHEESE (MADE FROM PARTIALLY
        SKIMMED MILK)
    ½ CUP SHREDDED LETTUCE

Sauté green peppers, onion, and tomatoes in the oil; add the whipped cheese and cook for 5 minutes.

Broil tortillas until slightly crisp. (Tortillas will curl up and form a pocket.)

Place 3 tablespoons of pepper-tomato mixture in the center of each tortilla. Sprinkle with the grated Mozzarella cheese, and broil until the cheese is melted.

Serve topped with shredded lettuce.

YIELD: 4 TOSTADAS
APPROX. CAL/SERV.: 1 TOSTADA = 190

. . . . ***Complementary Pizza***

Sauce
    3 TABLESPOONS OLIVE OIL
    1 CUP ONIONS, FINELY CHOPPED
    1 TABLESPOON MINCED GARLIC
    4 CUPS CANNED TOMATOES, CHOPPED
    1 SMALL CAN TOMATO PASTE
    1 TABLESPOON DRIED OREGANO
    1 TABLESPOON FRESH BASIL; OR 1 TEASPOON OF DRIED BASIL
    1 BAY LEAF
    2 TEASPOONS HONEY
    1 TABLESPOON SALT
PEPPER TO TASTE

Dough

 2 TABLESPOONS DRY YEAST
 1¼ CUPS WARM WATER
 1 TEASPOON HONEY
 ¼ CUP OLIVE OIL
 1 TEASPOON SALT
 2½ CUPS WHOLE WHEAT FLOUR
 1 CUP SOY FLOUR

Topping

 1 CUP MOZZARELLA CHEESE (MADE FROM PARTIALLY SKIMMED
 MILK), GRATED AND COMBINED WITH 1 CUP GRATED PARMESAN
 CHEESE, SLICED ONIONS, MUSHROOMS, OR GREEN PEPPER FOR GAR-
 NISH.

To make the sauce, heat the oil and sauté the onions until soft but not brown. Add garlic and cook 2 minutes more.

Add the remaining ingredients and bring the sauce to a boil; then lower the heat and simmer, uncovered, for about 1 hour, stirring occasionally. Remove bay leaf. If a smoother sauce is desired, purée or sieve it.

To make the dough, dissolve the yeast in a mixture of water and honey. Blend with the oil, salt, whole wheat and soy flour in a large bowl.

Knead until smooth and elastic on a floured board. Place in the bowl and let rise in a warm place until doubled in volume (about 1½ hours).

Punch down and knead again for a few minutes to make the dough easy to handle.

Preheat oven to 500°F.

To make 4 10-inch pizzas, divide the dough into quarters, stretch each quarter to a 5-inch circle while you hold it in your hands, then roll it out to 10 inches, about ⅛ inch thick.

Dust a large cookie sheet or pizza pan with cornmeal. Place the dough circles in the pan and pinch a small rim around the edge. Spread ½ cup of tomato sauce on each pizza and sprinkle on ½ cup of the cheese. If desired, add the sliced mushrooms, onions or other garnishes.

Bake 10 to 15 minutes in the hot oven.

 YIELD: 4 10-INCH PIZZAS
 APPROX. CAL/SERV.: 1 CHEESE PIZZA = 885   ¼ PIZZA = 220
 1 VEGETABLE PIZZA = 800

· · · · · · · · · · *Nutty Noodle Casserole*

12 OUNCES NOODLES (WHOLE WHEAT OR SOY) COOKED AND DRAINED
½ CUP MARGARINE
2 MEDIUM ONIONS, CHOPPED
⅔ CUP DRY SOYBEANS, COOKED
1½ CUPS PEANUTS
1 CUP CASHEWS
4 CUPS LOW-FAT YOGURT
⅔ CUP RAW SESAME BUTTER
SALT AND PEPPER TO TASTE
1 TEASPOON NUTMEG
½ CUP SESAME MEAL, TOASTED

Sauté onions in margarine until transparant. Stir in peanuts and cashews. Cook until lightly browned. Combine with noodles and soybeans. Place in an oven at 350°F. until thoroughly heated. Remove to a serving dish or casserole and stir in the yogurt, sesame butter and nutmeg, which have been thoroughly blended. Season with salt and pepper, and sprinkle sesame seed meal over the top.

YIELD: 15 SERVINGS (¾ CUP)
APPROX. CAL/SERV.: 460

· · · · · · · · · · *Macaroni Salad Ricotta*

¼ POUND WHOLE WHEAT MACARONI, COOKED UNTIL TENDER, DRAINED
  AND CHILLED
1 CUP RICOTTA CHEESE (MADE FROM PARTIALLY SKIMMED MILK)
2 TEASPOONS MUSTARD
1 TABLESPOON OR MORE LOW-FAT YOGURT
¼ CUP SLICED OR CHOPPED RIPE OLIVES
1 GREEN PEPPER, CHOPPED COARSELY
2 SCALLIONS WITH TOPS, CHOPPED
1 TABLESPOON CHOPPED PARSLEY
RED PIMIENTO TO TASTE
½ TEASPOON EACH DILL AND BASIL
SALT AND PEPPER TO TASTE

Make a dressing of the consistency of mayonnaise by thinning the mustard with a tablespoon or more of yogurt and mixing with the Ricotta. Stir in all other ingredients.

Serve on a bed of salad greens.

YIELD: 4 SERVINGS
APPROX. CAL/SERV.: 170

. . . . *Melenzana Alla Griglia (Broiled Eggplant)*

1 LARGE EGGPLANT
½ CUP ITALIAN SALAD DRESSING
1 TEASPOON ROSEMARY
¼ TEASPOON OREGANO
1 CUP TOMATO SAUCE
SALT AND PEPPER
2 OUNCES GRATED PARMESAN CHEESE

Peel eggplant and cut crosswise in ¾-inch slices. Place in a bowl with salad dressing, rosemary and oregano, being certain dressing and herbs are spread over each eggplant slice. Let stand 1 hour. Drain.

Arrange eggplant slices on a baking sheet. Broil 3 inches from a medium-low flame about 5 minutes on each side until the slices are tender and lightly browned.

Arrange the eggplant and tomato sauce in alternate layers in an 8-inch-square baking dish, seasoning each layer lightly with salt and pepper. Top with grated cheese.

Place under broiler again for about 2 minutes or until cheese is brown. Serve immediately.

YIELD: 6 SERVINGS
APPROX. CAL/SERV.: 135

Growing your own sprouts can be an adventure. You can grow sprouts from a wide variety of seeds and grains. The growing process requires very little space, and you end up with a delicious and nutritious product. Research shows that the nutritional value of seeds greatly increases during the first few days of sprouting. You can sprout alfalfa seeds, mung beans, soybeans, wheat or lentils with no special equipment. And your yield is fantastic—2 tablespoons of seeds produce 1 cup of sprouts. You can use sprouts as an ingredient in salads, sauté them as a vegetable, add them to soups or stews, or bake your own sprouted wheat or rye bread.

· · · · · · · · · · · · · ·   *Sprouts*

2 TABLESPOONS ALFALFA SEEDS

Buy seeds that are specifically intended for sprouting—not for planting. Put seeds in a jar, rinse with cold water, then cover with fresh cold water.

Soak overnight in a dark place, pour off liquid and rinse, leaving seeds slightly moist. Rinse two times a day for 3–5 days. A pint jar with a screen lid makes rinsing easy. Store seeds in the refrigerator. Sprouts are ready to use when they are 1–1½ inches long.

YIELD: 1 CUP
APPROX. CAL/SERV.: 25

· · · · · · · · · · · · ·   *variation*

Mung beans, soybeans, lentils or wheat berries may be substituted for alfalfa seeds to obtain sprouts.

. . . . *Pizza Sandwiches*

Sauce

2 TABLESPOONS OIL

½ CUP CHOPPED ONION

2½ TABLESPOONS CHOPPED CELERY

2½ TABLESPOONS CHOPPED GREEN PEPPER

1 CUP CANNED TOMATOES

6 TABLESPOONS TOMATO PASTE

1 TEASPOON OREGANO

⅛ TEASPOON SWEET BASIL

¾ TEASPOON SALT

⅛ TEASPOON PEPPER

¼ TEASPOON ROSEMARY (OPTIONAL)

Sauté onion, celery and pepper in vegetable oil until tender and translucent.

Add tomatoes, tomato paste and seasonings.

Cook over low heat on stove top for approximately 30 minutes, stirring occasionally.

YIELD: APPROX. 1½ CUPS SAUCE

Sandwich

1½ CUPS PIZZA SAUCE

1½ CUPS LOW-FAT COTTAGE CHEESE

6 ENGLISH MUFFINS, TOASTED

4 TABLESPOONS PARMESAN CHEESE, GRATED

Mix 2 tablespoons cottage cheese with 2 tablespoons sauce.

Spread mixture on ½ toasted English muffin.

Sprinkle 1 teaspoon Parmesan cheese over top.

Broil in oven for approximately 5 minutes or until Parmesan cheese just starts to turn golden.

YIELD: 12 PIZZA SANDWICHES

APPROX. CAL/SERV.: 136

. . . . . . *Vegetable Cottage Cheese Sandwich*

1½ CUPS RINSED LOW-FAT COTTAGE CHEESE
1½ TABLESPOONS DRY SKIM MILK POWDER
 2 TABLESPOONS WATER
 ¼ TEASPOON SALT
 ½ TEASPOON SUGAR
 1 TEASPOON LEMON JUICE
 1 TABLESPOON CHOPPED ONION
 ⅓ CUP CHOPPED CARROT
 ¼ CUP CHOPPED CELERY
DASH OF GARLIC SALT AND WORCESTERSHIRE SAUCE

Place the cottage cheese, skim milk powder, water, salt, sugar and lemon juice in a blender and blend until smooth.

Scrape mixture out of the blender and into bowl.

Stir in vegetables, garlic and Worcestershire sauce.

Spread ½ cup of mixture on two slices of bread to make a sandwich.

YIELD: 5 HALF-CUP SERVINGS OF SPREAD
APPROX. CAL/SERV.: 90   SANDWICH: 225

SERVING IDEAS: Serve on whole wheat, pumpernickel, Vienna, rye, or French bread. For a sack lunch, make a poor-boy sandwich of the vegetable spread, lettuce, and tomato slices.

. . . . *Hominy Grits Casserole*

 ¾ CUP HOMINY
1½ TEASPOONS SALT
1½ CUPS BOILING WATER
 1 CUP SKIM MILK
 6 TABLESPOONS MARGARINE
1½ TABLESPOONS SUGAR
EGG SUBSTITUTE EQUIVALENT TO 2 EGGS
 2 CUPS SKIM MILK

Preheat oven to 300°F.

Combine hominy, salt, and water. Stir, then add 1 cup of skim milk.

Place in an oiled 1 ½ quart casserole.
Add margarine, sugar, eggs, and skim milk.
Bake 1 hour.

YIELD: 6 SERVINGS
APPROX. CAL/SERV.: 290

. . . . *Meatless Moussaka*

2 LARGE EGGPLANTS, SLICED ½ -INCH THICK AND PEELED
2 TEASPOONS SALT

. . . . *Tomato Sauce*

3 MEDIUM-SIZE ONIONS, PEELED AND CHOPPED
1 CLOVE GARLIC, PEELED AND CRUSHED
4 MEDIUM-SIZE TOMATOES, PEELED, CORED AND COARSELY CHOPPED
   (RESERVE JUICE)
¼ TEASPOON LEAF ROSEMARY, CRUMBLED
2 TABLESPOONS MINCED FRESH MINT OR 1 TABLESPOON MINT FLAKES
   (OPTIONAL)
2 TABLESPOONS MINCED PARSLEY
2 TEASPOONS SUGAR
1 TEASPOON SALT
¼ TEASPOON PEPPER
1 8-OUNCE CAN TOMATO SAUCE

. . . . *Cheese Filling*

1 POUND LOW-FAT COTTAGE CHEESE, RINSED
2 EGG WHITES
⅛ TEASPOON LEAF ROSEMARY, CRUMBLED
⅛ TEASPOON MACE
¼ TEASPOON SALT
⅛ TEASPOON PEPPER
¼ CUP OLIVE OR VEGETABLE OIL
½ CUP GRATED PARMESAN CHEESE

Recipe continues...

Sprinkle both sides of each eggplant slice with salt; place between several thicknesses of paper toweling; weight down and let stand 1 hour.

Meanwhile, make tomato sauce. Mix all ingredients except tomato sauce in heavy saucepan and heat, uncovered, stirring occasionally, until tomatoes begin to release their juices. Cover, lower heat and simmer 1 hour, stirring occasionally. Stir in tomato sauce and simmer uncovered, 15 minutes longer.

Prepare cheese filling while tomato sauce simmers. Mix together all remaining ingredients except the ½ cup Parmesan cheese and ¼ cup oil; refrigerate until needed.

Brush both sides of each eggplant slice lightly with olive or vegetable oil, then broil quickly on each side to brown. To assemble moussaka, spoon half the tomato sauce over the bottom of a 13 × 9 × 2-inch baking pan. Sprinkle with grated Parmesan, then arrange half the browned eggplant slices on top. Spread with cheese filling. Arrange remaining eggplant slices on top. Finally, cover with remaining tomato sauce and one last sprinkling of Parmesan.

Note: Dish can be prepared up to this point several hours ahead of time and refrigerated until about an hour before serving. In fact, it will be better if it is, because the flavors get together better.

Bake, uncovered, 45 to 50 minutes in moderate oven (375°F.), until bubbling and browned. Remove from oven and let stand 15 minutes before cutting into serving-size squares.

YIELD: 8 SERVINGS
APPROX. CAL/SERV.: 240

Vegetable Sukiyaki

6 OUNCES BEAN CURD

1 BEEF BOUILLON CUBE (DISSOLVED IN 1 CUP WATER)

¼ CUP SOY SAUCE

1 TABLESPOON OIL

1 GREEN PEPPER, SLICED

2 CARROTS, SLICED

1 MEDIUM ONION, SLICED

12 GREEN ONIONS, CUT INTO 2-INCH PIECES

½ POUND FRESH MUSHROOMS, SLICED

1 HEAD CHINESE CABBAGE CHOPPED CROSSWISE INTO 1-INCH PIECES

1 CUP BEAN STARCH NOODLES

3 TABLESPOONS SUGAR

Clean and slice carrots, green pepper, onions, and mushrooms. Cut bean curd into bite-sized pieces. Cook noodles in boiling, unsalted water until tender.

Pour beef bouillon mixture and oil into a large frying pan and heat. Add vegetables and bean curd one at a time, keeping each food in a separate section. Cook 3 minutes. Add noodles, soy sauce and sugar. Cook for 2 more minutes; vegetables should be crisp. Serve in saucepan with rice as side dish.

YIELD: 6 SERVINGS

APPROX. CAL/SERV.: 150

Eggplant Parmesan

1 WHOLE EGGPLANT

½ POUND SLICED MOZZARELLA CHEESE (MADE FROM PARTIALLY SKIMMED MILK)

2 WHOLE TOMATOES, SLICED VERY THIN

½ POUND FRESH MUSHROOMS, SLICED

¼ CUP OIL

½ CUP BREAD CRUMBS

EGG SUBSTITUTE EQUIVALENT TO 1 EGG

1 CUP TOMATO SAUCE

Recipe continues…

Peel eggplant and slice in ½-inch rounds. Sprinkle with salt and allow to stand for 1–2 hours. Rinse with cold water.

Using mallet, pound eggplant slices to ¼-inch thickness.

Dip eggplant slices in egg substitute, then in bread crumbs.

Sauté breaded eggplant in oil. Drain on absorbent paper.

Place eggplant in bottom of 10 × 10-inch oven baking dish.

Arrange tomato slices on eggplant; then sliced mushrooms.

Top with tomato sauce.

Arrange mozzarella cheese over top.

Bake at 450°F. for 15–20 minutes.

Finish browning cheese under broiler, if necessary.

YIELD: 6 SERVINGS

APPROX. CAL/SERV.: 250

· · · · · · · · · · · *Quick and Easy Yogurt*

½ TEASPOON UNFLAVORED GELATIN

1 TABLESPOON SUGAR (OPTIONAL)

3 CUPS INSTANT NONFAT DRY MILK GRANULES

6 CUPS WATER

1 13-OUNCE CAN EVAPORATED SKIM MILK

3 TABLESPOONS PLAIN LOW-FAT YOGURT

Soften the unflavored gelatin by placing 1 tablespoon water in measuring cup and sprinkling gelatin over the water and allowing it to soak for 3 minutes, or until it has absorbed the moisture and is translucent. Use only the amount of gelatin specified, because too much results in a rubbery and unpleasant product.

Next add enough boiling water to the gelatin mixture to measure 1 cup.

At this point, sugar may be added to take the edge off the sharp taste.

Stir, then allow the mixture to cool.

Preheat oven to 275°F.

Measure remaining ingredients.

Mix nonfat dry milk with 3 cups water in large mixing bowl.

Add 2 cups tepid water, evaporated milk, and the gelatin mixture.

Next add the yogurt. (You must buy yogurt as a starter for this first batch; always save 3 tablespoons from each batch you make to be used as a starter the next time around.)

After adding yogurt, stir mixture thoroughly and pour into clean jars and loosely cover, put it in the oven, and *turn the oven off.*

Leave mixture overnight, or about 8 to 10 hours. Refrigerate.

From here on, you're on your own. Yogurt is remarkably versatile. Salad dressings, milk shakes, and desserts are just a few of the delights you can create. A variety of flavors to suit every taste can be made. Try adding fresh or canned fruit, molasses, spices or honey. You have 2 quarts to experiment with, and possibilities are endless. Just remember to save those few tablespoons to form the starter for your next batch.

YIELD: 8 CUPS
APPROX. CAL/SERV.: 140

· · · · · · · · · · · *Chef's Spinach Salad*

 1 POUND RAW SPINACH
⅔ CUP COOKED CHICK PEAS
½ CUP SLICED MUSHROOMS
½ CUP SLICED BEETS
 8 OUNCES FARMER OR RICOTTA CHEESE (MADE FROM PARTIALLY
   SKIMMED MILK)
⅓ CUP PUMPKIN OR SUNFLOWER SEEDS
JUICE OF 1 LEMON
 2 TABLESPOONS OIL

Wash spinach and break into bite-sized pieces.

Toss chick peas, mushrooms, beets, and crumbled farmer cheese with spinach.

Just before serving, sprinkle in seeds and add the lemon juice and oil as dressing.

YIELD: 10 SERVINGS
APPROX. CAL/SERV.: 100

. . . . *Spaghetti Cheese Amandine*

    8 OUNCES SPAGHETTI, BROKEN IN 1-INCH PIECES
    ⅓ CUP MARGARINE
    1 CUP LOW-FAT COTTAGE CHEESE
    ½ CUP SLIVERED BLANCHED ALMONDS
    ½ TEASPOON SALT

Cook spaghetti according to package directions, then drain.
Melt the margarine in a large skillet.
Sauté the almonds in the melted margarine.
Add the spaghetti, cottage cheese and salt and toss constantly until heated.
Serve hot.

YIELD: 6 SERVINGS
APPROX. CAL/SERV.: 260

. . . . *Cottage Cheese–Nut Loaf*

    ¼ CUP SOFT MARGARINE
    1 MEDIUM ONION, CHOPPED
    1 PACKAGE LIGHT BROTH
    2 EGGS, WELL BEATEN
    2 CUPS LOW-FAT COTTAGE CHEESE
    ½ CUP CHOPPED WALNUTS
    2 CUPS FORTIFIED FLAKE-TYPE CEREAL

Preheat oven to 350°F.
Sauté onions in margarine.
Add the broth powder, eggs, and remaining ingredients and mix well.
Bake for 1 hour in an oiled 9 × 5 × 3-inch loaf pan.

YIELD: 6 SERVINGS
APPROX. CAL/SERV.: 300

· · · · · · · · **Quick and Easy Baked Beans**

2 16-OUNCE CANS VEGETARIAN BAKED BEANS IN TOMATO SAUCE
½ CUP CHOPPED ONION
2 TABLESPOONS MOLASSES OR BROWN SUGAR
2 TEASPOONS DRY MUSTARD
2 TABLESPOONS MARGARINE
1 CUP TOMATO SAUCE
2 16-OUNCE CANS BARBECUE BEANS

Preheat oven to 350°F.
Combine all ingredients and place in a 3-quart casserole dish.
Bake uncovered for 45 to 60 minutes.

YIELD: 24 SERVINGS
APPROX. CAL/SERV.: 100

· · · · · · · · · · · · · · **Lentil Loaf**

1 CUP COOKED LENTILS OR BEANS
½ CUP CHOPPED WALNUTS
1 EGG
1 13-OUNCE CAN EVAPORATED SKIM MILK
1½ CUPS CORNFLAKES OR BREAD CRUMBS
1 SMALL ONION, CHOPPED
¼ TEASPOON SAGE
½ TEASPOON SALT
¼ CUP OIL

Preheat oven 350° F.
Mix all ingredients together thoroughly.
Place in an oiled 9 × 5 × 3-inch loaf pan and bake for 45 minutes.
Serve with plain brown gravy or cranberry sauce.

YIELD: 6 SERVINGS
APPROX. CAL/SERV.: 300

. . . . *Soybean Bake*

$\frac{1}{2}$ CUP DRIED SOYBEANS

WATER TO COVER BEANS

1 CUP BULGUR

2 TABLESPOONS OIL

1 ONION, FINELY CHOPPED

1 GREEN PEPPER, FINELY CHOPPED

SALT, PEPPER, AND TABASCO SAUCE TO TASTE

2 TABLESPOONS CHOPPED PARSLEY

1 POUND FETA CHEESE, CRUMBLED

1 1-POUND 14-OUNCE CAN ITALIAN PLUM TOMATOES, CHOPPED

1 TEASPOON GROUND CUMIN

1 TABLESPOON BEEF FLAVORING OR BOUILLON (OPTIONAL)

Soak the soybeans overnight in water to cover. The next day, drain the beans and place them in an electric blender. Add 1 cup water and blend until smooth.

Preheat the oven to 375°F.

Pour 1 cup boiling water over the bulgur and set aside.

Heat the oil in a skillet and sauté the onion and green pepper until tender. Add the soybeans, then the bulgur after it has absorbed all of the water, salt, pepper, tabasco, and parsley.

Spread half of the mixture in the bottom of an oiled 3-quart casserole and sprinkle with half the cheese.

Combine the tomatoes, cumin and beef flavoring, if used, and spoon half the mixture over the cheese. Repeat the layers.

Cover and bake 1 hour, removing the cover for the last 15 minutes of cooking.

YIELD: 8 SERVINGS

APPROX. CAL/SERV.: 330

Zucchini Cheese Casserole

3 MEDIUM ZUCCHINI SQUASH
¼ CUP CHOPPED ONION
2 TABLESPOONS OIL
1 POUND LOW-FAT COTTAGE CHEESE
1 TEASPOON BASIL
⅓ CUP PARMESAN CHEESE

Preheat oven to 350°F.
Sauté zucchini and chopped onion in oil.
Whip cottage cheese with basil in blender.
Place alternating layers of zucchini and cottage cheese in a 1½-quart casserole dish. Top with Parmesan cheese.
Bake uncovered for 25 to 30 minutes.

YIELD: 6 SERVINGS
APPROX. CAL/SERV.: 130

Sunflower Spaghetti Sauce

2½ CUPS TOMATO SAUCE
1 6-OUNCE CAN TOMATO PASTE
1 TEASPOON OREGANO
1 CLOVE GARLIC, MINCED
½ TEASPOON CUMIN
1 OR 2 BAY LEAVES
½ CUP SUNFLOWER SEED MEAL
½ CUP SUNFLOWER SEEDS

Mix ingredients together in heavy 2-quart saucepan.
Simmer for 20 minutes.

YIELD: 6 SERVINGS
APPROX. CAL/SERV.: 195 (OR 295 WITH ½ CUP PASTA)

. . . . **Scalloped Eggplant Italian**

1 LARGE EGGPLANT, PARED AND SLICED THIN

1 EGG PLUS 1 EGG WHITE, BEATEN WELL

1 ½ CUPS FINE BREAD CRUMBS

1 8-OUNCE PACKAGE SLICED MOZZARELLA CHEESE (MADE FROM PARTIALLY SKIMMED MILK)

2 8-OUNCE CANS (2 CUPS) SEASONED TOMATO SAUCE

1 TEASPOON OREGANO

½ TEASPOON SALT

½ TEASPOON GARLIC POWDER

DASH OF TABASCO

PEPPER TO TASTE

Preheat oven to 350°F.

Dip eggplant into beaten egg, then into crumbs. Brown in hot oil.

Place ¼ of the eggplant slices in the bottom of a 2-quart casserole and top with ¼ of the cheese slices.

Combine the tomato sauce with the remaining ingredients and spoon ¼ of the sauce over the eggplant and cheese.

Repeat layers until all of the ingredients are used, ending with the sauce.

Cover and bake for about 1 hour.

YIELD: 8 SERVINGS

APPROX. CAL/SERV.: 190

. . . . **Spinach Soufflé**

2 TABLESPOONS MARGARINE

2 TABLESPOONS FLOUR

½ TEASPOON SALT

½ CUP SKIM MILK

½ PACKAGE (⅔ CUP) FROZEN CHOPPED SPINACH, COOKED AND DRAINED

1 TABLESPOON FINELY CHOPPED ONION

6 EGG WHITES

In a small, heavy saucepan, melt margarine. Blend in flour and salt.
Cook over low heat, stirring, until mixture is smooth and bubbly.
Remove from heat and gradually stir in milk.
Return to heat and bring mixture to a boil, stirring constantly.
Cook 1 minute longer.
Remove from heat.
Stir in spinach and onion.
Beat egg whites at high speed for 5 minutes. Fold in spinach mixture.
Grease bottom of 2-cup casserole; pour in spinach mixture.
Bake at 325°F. for 50 minutes. Serve immediately.

YIELD: 4 SERVINGS
APPROX. CAL/SERV.: 100

· · · · · · · · · · *Lentil Spaghetti Sauce*

1 MEDIUM ONION, CHOPPED
1 CLOVE GARLIC, MINCED
½ CUP OIL
1½ CUP DRIED LENTILS, WASHED
1 DRIED HOT RED PEPPER, CRUMBLED
2½ TEASPOONS SALT
½ TEASPOON PEPPER
4 CUPS WATER
2 BEEF BOUILLON CUBES
¼ TEASPOON DRIED BASIL, CRUMBLED
¼ TEASPOON DRIED OREGANO, CRUMBLED
1 16-OUNCE CAN TOMATOES
1 6-OUNCE CAN TOMATO PASTE
1 TABLESPOON VINEGAR

Sauté onion and garlic in oil for 5 minutes.
Add lentils, red pepper, salt, pepper, and water.
Cover and simmer for 30 minutes.

Recipe continues...

Add remaining ingredients and simmer uncovered about 1 hour, stirring occasionally.

YIELD: 12 SERVINGS

APPROX. CAL/SERV.: 150 (OR 250 WITH ½ CUP PASTA)

· · · · · · · · · · *Stuffed Acorn Squash I*

1½ CUPS COOKED RICE

½ CUP CHOPPED WALNUTS

¾ CUP CRACKER CRUMBS

1 MEDIUM ONION, CHOPPED FINE

2 EGG WHITES, SLIGHTLY BEATEN

½ TEASPOON SAGE

2 TEASPOONS CHOPPED PARSLEY

1 TEASPOON SALT

GENEROUS AMOUNT OF PEPPER

3 ACORN SQUASH, CUT IN HALF AND CLEANED

Combine all ingredients except squash. Place mixture loosely in squash halves. Bake stuffed squash in pan covered with foil. Bake for 1 hour at 350°F. or until squash is tender.

YIELD: 6 SERVINGS

APPROX. CAL/SERV.: 320

Salads and Salad Dressing

There is a salad for everyone. It is difficult to think of a munchable food that would not fit into a salad. There are meat salads, rice salads, wheat salads, vegetable and fruit salads, fish salads, hot, cold, wet and dry salads. Even the ordinary green salad can be astonishing and extraordinary in its variety, for there are dozens of kinds of greenery that may be used alone or in combination.

Most salads have in common a low-fat content and high nutritional value. A salad-lover's dream (although perhaps a gourmet's nightmare) might be a salad that answered a full day's nutritionl needs—a succulent mountainous heap on the order of a giant antipasto with crisp greens, slender strips of meat, cooked or raw vegetables, green onions, olives, anchovies, herbs and any other ingredient that suits one's fancy. Whether a salad has its origins in the vegetable garden or in the cans on the larder shelf, it can provide an excellent means for getting a day's vitamins, minerals, and protein and for fitting that extra portion of polyunsaturated oil into the meal plan.

There are few rules in salad making. However, it is important to have greens dry and crisp and to mix them with the dressing just before serving. Let your own imagination be your guide. As a main dish or a side dish, a good salad is a jewel in the crown of the successful cook.

. . . . *Perfection Salad*

2 TABLESPOONS UNFLAVORED GELATIN
½ CUP COLD WATER
2 CUPS BOILING WATER
½ CUP SUGAR
½ CUP VINEGAR
¼ CUP LEMON JUICE
2 TEASPOONS SALT
3 TABLESPOONS CHOPPED ONIONS
1 CUP SHREDDED CABBAGE
1 CUP DICED CELERY
3 TABLESPOONS CHOPPED PIMIENTO
3 TABLESPOONS GREEN PEPPER

Soak unflavored gelatin in cold water. Mix in the boiling water, sugar, vinegar, lemon juice and salt.

Cool until mixture starts to thicken. Fold in onions, cabbage, celery, pimiento and green pepper.

Pour into a 1-quart mold and chill.

YIELD: 8 SERVINGS
APPROX. CAL/SERV.: 60

. . . . *Vegetable Salad Mold*

1 ENVELOPE UNFLAVORED GELATIN
1¾ CUPS CHICKEN BROTH OR BOUILLON
2 TABLESPOONS LEMON JUICE
¼ TEASPOON SALT
½ CUP CHOPPED FRESH SPINACH
6 THIN SLICES CUCUMBER, HALVED
½ CUP SLICED CELERY
¼ CUP THINLY SLICED RADISHES

Sprinkle gelatin over ¾ cup of chicken broth in a small saucepan. Heat slowly until gelatin is dissolved, stirring constantly. Remove from heat and add remaining 1 cup of chicken broth, lemon juice and salt. Chill until slightly thickened. Stir in remaining ingredients. Pour into individual ½-cup molds and chill until set.

YIELD: 4 SERVINGS

APPROX. CAL/SERV.: 15

· · · · · · · · · · ·   *Tart Asparagus Salad*

2 ENVELOPES UNFLAVORED GELATIN

½ CUP COLD WATER

½ CUP SUGAR

½ CUP VINEGAR

1 CUP WATER

1 TABLESPOON MINCED ONION

2 TABLESPOONS LEMON JUICE

1 10-OUNCE CAN CUT GREEN ASPARAGUS

1 CUP PIMIENTO, CUT INTO STRIPS

1 TEASPOON SALT

1 5-OUNCE CAN WATER CHESTNUTS, SLICED

1 CUP CHOPPED CELERY

Dissolve gelatin in cold water. Combine sugar, vinegar and 1 cup water. Bring to a boil. Remove from heat, and add gelatin, onion and lemon juice.

Allow to cool, then add asparagus, pimiento, salt, water chestnuts and celery.

Pour into a 1½-quart mold and chill until set.

YIELD: 10 SERVINGS

APPROX. CAL/SERV.: 76

· · · · · · · · · · · *Tomato Aspic Salad*

1 ¾ CUPS TOMATO JUICE
 ½ TEASPOON SALT
 ⅛ TEASPOON PEPPER
 1 BAY LEAF
 ½ TEASPOON PAPRIKA
 1 TEASPOON LEMON JUICE
 1 TABLESPOON GRATED ONION
 1 TABLESPOON UNFLAVORED GELATIN (1 ENVELOPE)
 ¼ CUP COLD WATER
 ½ CUP CHOPPED CELERY
 2 TABLESPOONS CHOPPED GREEN ONION
 2 TABLESPOONS FINELY CHOPPED PARSLEY

Heat together tomato juice, salt, pepper and bay leaf. Remove from heat, take out bay leaf and add paprika, lemon juice and onion.

Soften gelatin in the cold water and combine with the hot tomato juice. Stir until dissolved. Cool.

Add chopped vegetables. Pour into 6 individual molds and refrigerate until set.

YIELD: 6 SERVINGS
APPROX. CAL/SERV.: 20

· · · · · · · · · · *Carrot and Pineapple Mold*

 1 3-OUNCE PACKAGE ORANGE OR LEMON GELATIN
 1 CUP BOILING WATER
 ½ CUP MIXED ORANGE AND PINEAPPLE JUICE
 1 CUP DRAINED CRUSHED PINEAPPLE
 1 CUP RAW GRATED CARROTS
 ¼ CUP CHOPPED ALMONDS
 1 TABLESPOON MINCED GREEN PEPPER

Dissolve the gelatin in boiling water. Add fruit juice, and chill until slightly thickened. Fold in remaining ingredients, and pour into individual molds, or 1-quart mold.

YIELD: 6 SERVINGS
APPROX. CAL/SERV.: 135

· · · · · · · *Jellied Strawberry Apple Salad*

1 3-OUNCE PACKAGE STRAWBERRY GELATIN
1 CUP BOILING WATER
1 CUP ORANGE JUICE
1 CUP SHREDDED, PARED APPLE (PREPARED JUST BEFORE ADDING)

Dissolve gelatin in boiling water. Add orange juice. Chill until mixture is the consistency of slightly beaten egg white.

Fold in apple, and pour into a 3½-cup mold. Chill until firm.

Serve with a dressing made by stirring 1 teaspoon of cinnamon and 2 tablespoons of sugar into 1 cup of Basic Cheese Sauce (p. 11).

YIELD: 6 SERVINGS
APPROX. CAL/SERV.: 135

· · · · · · · *Festive Cherry Salad Ring*

2 CUPS CANNED DARK SWEET CHERRIES, PITTED
1 CUP CHERRY SYRUP AND WATER
1 3-OUNCE PACKAGE CHERRY FLAVORED GELATIN
¾ CUP SHERRY OR CHIANTI WINE
40 TINY MARSHMALLOWS; OR 10 LARGE MARSHMALLOWS, CUT IN QUARTERS

Drain syrup from cherries into a measure and add water to make one cup. In a saucepan, bring syrup almost to boiling and add to cherry flavored gelatin, stirring until dissolved. Add sherry or Chianti.

Pour into an 8-inch ring mold and chill till mixture begins to set. Add pitted cherries and marshmallows. Chill until firm.

Recipe continues...

Unmold on salad greens. Center of ring may be filled with Waldorf Salad (p. 228) if desired.

YIELD: 8 SERVINGS
APPROX. CAL/SERV.: 145

· · · · · · · · · · · *Peach-Ginger Ale Mold*

1   16-OUNCE CAN CLING PEACH SLICES
2   3-OUNCE PACKAGES ORANGE OR LEMON GELATIN
1½ CUPS BOILING WATER
12 OUNCES GINGER ALE
½   CUP CHOPPED WALNUTS

Drain the peaches. Overlap slices in the bottom of a 1½-quart mold. Reserve some peach slices.

Dissolve gelatin in boiling water. Add ginger ale. Chill until slightly thickened, then beat until fluffy.

Chop the reserved peach slices and fold into the gelatin with the walnuts. Spoon over the peaches in the mold. Refrigerate.

YIELD: 8 SERVINGS
APPROX. CAL/SERV.: 195

· · · · · · · · · *Cranberry-Orange Salad*

1   3-OUNCE PACKAGE LEMON GELATIN
1   CUP BOILING WATER
1   CUP ORANGE JUICE
1   16-OUNCE JAR CRANBERRY-ORANGE RELISH
1   UNPEELED APPLE, CHOPPED
½   CUP CHOPPED PECANS

Dissolve gelatin in boiling water. Add orange juice and let stand until almost jelled.

Combine cranberry-orange relish, chopped apple and pecans; fold into the almost-jelled mixture. Pour into a 1-quart mold. Chill until firm.

YIELD: 10 SMALL SERVINGS
APPROX. CAL/SERV.: 180

· · · · · · · · · · *Yogurt-Gelatin Delight*

1 3-OUNCE PACKAGE FRUIT-FLAVORED GELATIN
8 OUNCES LOW-FAT YOGURT OF THE SAME FLAVOR

Prepare the gelatin according to package directions. Chill until it just begins to set.

Add the yogurt, stirring to combine thoroughly with the gelatin. Pour into molds. Chill until set.

YIELD: 6 SERVINGS
APPROX. CAL/SERV.: 95

· · · · · · · · · · · · *variation*

FLUFFY WHIP: When gelatin has started to set, whip it with an electric mixer until it is light and fluffy. Then fold in yogurt.

· · · · · · · · · · *Molded Waldorf Salad*

1 3-OUNCE PACKAGE LEMON GELATIN
1 CUP BOILING WATER
¾ CUP APPLE JUICE
1 LARGE UNPEELED APPLE, FINELY CHOPPED
½ CUP FINELY DICED CELERY
½ CUP RAISINS
¼ CUP BASIC CHEESE SAUCE (p. 11)
¼ CUP CHOPPED PECANS (OPTIONAL)

Dissolve gelatin in water. Add apple juice and chill until syrupy. Fold in remaining ingredients and pour into a 1-quart mold. Chill until set.

YIELD: 6 SERVINGS
APPROX. CAL/SERV.: 160

· · · · · · · · · · **Parsley Potato Salad**

2 CUPS DICED COOKED POTATOES
½ TABLESPOON CHOPPED PIMIENTO
½ CUP DICED CELERY
1 TABLESPOON CHOPPED ONION
2 TABLESPOONS CHOPPED PARSLEY
½ TABLESPOON CIDER VINEGAR
1 TEASPOON DRY MUSTARD
½ TEASPOON CELERY SEED
⅛ TEASPOON PEPPER
½ TEASPOON SALT
¼ CUP MAYONNAISE

Combine all ingredients except mayonnaise. Toss lightly and chill.

A few hours before serving time, add mayonnaise and return salad to the refrigerator. Serve in lettuce cups, garnished with small strips of pimiento.

YIELD: 4 SERVINGS
APPROX. CAL/SERV.: 145

· · · · · · · · · · · **Cauliflower Salad**

1 CUP SHREDDED CARROTS
1 CUP SLICED CAULIFLOWER
½ CUP CHOPPED PECANS
1 CUP SPINACH OR OTHER DARK GREENS
SALT

Slice the cauliflower in about ¼-inch to ½-inch cuts. Slice the part near the stalk very thin.

Tear the greens into small pieces. Toss all ingredients together lightly; add salt to taste. Chill and serve with your choice of dressing.

YIELD: 4 SERVINGS
APPROX. CAL/SERV.: 125

· · · · · · · · · · · · *Chef's Salad*

This is a one-dish meal, a main course that needs only a crusty loaf of bread to make it complete.

2 CUPS CLEANED, CRISPED SALAD GREENS
1 CUCUMBER, CUBED
3 CARROTS, SCRAPED AND SLICED
1 3½-OUNCE CAN ARTICHOKE HEARTS, DRAINED AND QUARTERED
4 SLICES TOMATO
4 SCALLIONS, CHOPPED
3 OUNCES LOW-FAT CHEESE, CUT IN THIN STRIPS
2 CUPS COLD LEAN MEAT (ROAST BEEF, HAM OR PORK) CUT IN THIN STRIPS, OR SHRIMP OR TUNA FISH

Group the vegetables and meat on top of the salad greens. Serve with your favorite salad dressing.

YIELD: 4 SERVINGS
APPROX. CAL/SERV.: MEAT OR TUNA TOPPING = 380
SHRIMP TOPPING = 235

· · · · · · · · · *Fresh Vegetable Salad Bowl*

1 HEAD ROMAINE LETTUCE
½ POUND FRESH BUTTON MUSHROOMS
1 POUND CHERRY TOMATOES
1 SMALL HEAD CAULIFLOWER
1 POUND VERY YOUNG RAW ASPARAGUS SPEARS

Remove outer leaves of romaine, separate stems from mushrooms, and snap off stem ends of tomatoes. Break cauliflower into florets, and trim stalk end from asparagus.

Wash all vegetables under cold running water. Drain well.

Place inner leaves of romaine upright, around the sides of a deep round salad bowl. Arrange remaining ingredients neatly in the center. Chill until serving time. Serve with your favorite dressing.

YIELD: 8 SERVINGS
APPROX. CAL/SERV.: 50

Sukiyaki Salad

½ CUP RAW SPINACH LEAVES, COARSELY BROKEN UP
½ CUP OTHER SALAD GREENS BROKEN INTO SMALL PIECES
½ CUP BEAN SPROUTS, DRAINED
½ CUP CELERY, THINLY SLICED, DIAGONALLY
¼ CUP WATER CHESTNUTS, THINLY SLICED
½ CUP RAW MUSHROOMS, THINLY SLICED, LENGTHWISE
½ CUP GREEN PEPPER, THINLY SLICED, LENGTHWISE
½ CUP CABBAGE, THINLY SLICED
½ CUP WATERCRESS

In a large bowl, combine ingredients.

Blend 2 tablespoons of soy sauce and garlic to taste with ½ cup of your favorite French dressing. Toss with the salad.

YIELD: 4 SERVINGS
APPROX. CAL/SERV.: 130

Grapefruit and Orange Salad

1 HEAD CHICORY
1 GRAPEFRUIT
1 ORANGE
1 SMALL GREEN ONION, THINLY SLICED

Wash the chicory, drain well and pat dry. Break or cut up into serving pieces.

Peel the grapefruit and orange, taking care to remove all the white membrane. Separate each fruit into sections.

Combine the chickory with the grapefruit and orange sections and the green onion. Toss well with oil and vinegar dressing just before serving.

YIELD: 4 SERVINGS
APPROX. CAL/SERV.: 50 (OR 125 WITH 1 TABLESPOON DRESSING)

Spinach-Avocado-Orange Toss

½ TEASPOON GRATED ORANGE PEEL
¼ CUP ORANGE JUICE
½ CUP OIL
2 TABLESPOONS SUGAR
2 TABLESPOONS WINE VINEGAR
1 TABLESPOON LEMON JUICE
¼ TEASPOON SALT
6 CUPS SPINACH OR OTHER GREENS, TORN INTO BITE-SIZE PIECES
1 SMALL CUCUMBER, THINLY SLICED
1 AVOCADO, PEELED AND SLICED
1 11-OUNCE CAN MANDARIN ORANGES, DRAINED
2 TABLESPOONS SLICED GREEN ONIONS

Combine first 7 ingredients in a jar. Cover tightly and shake until thoroughly blended.

Mix remaining ingredients in a bowl and pour the dressing over all. Toss lightly.

YIELD: 10 SERVINGS
APPROX. CAL/SERV.: 170

Cucumbers in Sour Cream

3 MEDIUM CUCUMBERS, PEELED AND SLICED
1 SMALL ONION, CHOPPED FINE
1 TEASPOON SALT
1 TEASPOON SUGAR
1 CUP MOCK SOUR CREAM (p. 175)
2 TABLESPOONS CHOPPED PARSLEY
FRESHLY GROUND BLACK PEPPER TO TASTE

Sprinkle cucumbers and onion with salt and sugar. Mix well. Chill in the refrigerator several hours. Drain off water that accumulates.

Mix in Mock Sour Cream, parsley, and black pepper. Correct seasonings, if necessary. Chill until serving time.

YIELD: 6 SERVINGS
APPROX. CAL/SERV.: 50

Recipe continues...

. . . . *variation*

WITH YOGURT DRESSING: Mix ½ cup plain low-fat yogurt with 1 teaspoon lemon juice; add salt, pepper and dill to taste. Pour over cucumbers.

WITH LEMON-HERB DRESSING: Marinate drained cucumber slices in ¼ cup fresh lemon juice combined with 1 tablespoon sugar and ⅛ teaspoon marjoram or thyme.

APPROX. CAL/SERV.: YOGURT DRESSING = 30

LEMON-HERB DRESSING = 25

. . . . *Carrot-Raisin Salad*

2 CUPS SHREDDED RAW CARROTS
½ CUP SEEDLESS RAISINS
¼ CUP MAYONNAISE
¼ CUP LOW-FAT YOGURT
2 TABLESPOONS FRESH LEMON JUICE
⅛ TEASPOON SALT

Scrub the carrots, scrape them and shred to make 2 cups. Combine with raisins.

Mix together mayonnaise, yogurt, lemon juice, and salt.

Pour over salad and mix thoroughly.

YIELD: 6 SERVINGS
APPROX. CAL/SERV.: 130

. . . . *Any Bean Salad*

1 16-OUNCE CAN BEANS (GREEN, RED OR WHITE KIDNEY BEANS OR A
   COMBINATION)
1 TABLESPOON CHOPPED GREEN PEPPERS
1 TABLESPOON CHOPPED PIMIENTO
1 TABLESPOON CHOPPED GREEN ONION
½ CUP OIL
¼ CUP VINEGAR
1 TABLESPOON SUGAR
1 TEASPOON SALT
¼ TEASPOON PEPPER
2 RADISHES, SLICED

Drain the beans; reserve the liquid and add water to it if necessary to make ⅓ cup.

Combine the beans, green peppers, pimiento and onion in a bowl.

Mix together oil, vinegar, sugar, salt, pepper and the reserved bean liquid. Pour over the vegetables; marinate in the refrigerator at least 3 hours.

Add radishes just before serving.

With a slotted spoon, lift the beans onto a bed of salad greens.

YIELD: 6 SERVINGS
APPROX. CAL/SERV.: 135

. . . . *Bean Sprout Salad*

2 CUPS CANNED BEAN SPROUTS
2 CUPS CANNED SLICED GREEN BEANS
½ BUNCH PARSLEY
½ TEASPOON DILL SEED

Drain bean sprouts and green beans thoroughly.

Chop the parsley.

Toss together all 3 items, sprinkle with dill seed and serve with lemon wedges.

Recipe continues...

· · · · · · · · · · · · · · *dressing*

  1 TABLESPOON OIL
  2 TABLESPOONS LOW-FAT YOGURT
  1 TABLESPOON CATSUP
  ½ TEASPOON WORCESTERSHIRE SAUCE

Mix all dressing ingredients together. Serve with Bean Sprout Salad.

YIELD: 6 SERVINGS
APPROX. CAL/SERV.: 50

· · · · · · · *Bean Sprout-Bean Curd Salad*

  3 CUPS MUNG BEAN OR SOYBEAN SPROUTS
  4 RIBS CELERY, FINELY CHOPPED
  ½ CUP CHOPPED WALNUTS
  1 TEASPOON CARAWAY SEEDS
  ½ CUP CUBED BEAN CURD

Combine all ingredients. Toss lightly with Vinaigrette Sauce, and serve on salad greens.

YIELD: 6 SERVINGS
APPROX. CAL/SERV.: 225

· · · · · · · · · · · *vinaigrette sauce*

  ⅔ CUP OIL
  ⅓ CUP WINE VINEGAR
  2 TEASPOONS OREGANO
  1 TEASPOON SALT
  ½ TEASPOON PEPPER
  ½ TEASPOON DRY MUSTARD
  2 CLOVES GARLIC, CRUSHED

Combine all ingredients in a jar, cover tightly and shake to blend.

. . . . **Sauerkraut Salad**

1 28-OUNCE CAN SAUERKRAUT
½ CUP SUGAR
1 CUP DICED CELERY
1 CUP DICED GREEN PEPPER
¼ CUP DICED ONION
¼ TEASPOON SALT
⅛ TEASPOON PEPPER
1 TEASPOON CELERY SEED
3 TABLESPOONS DICED PIMIENTO
3 TABLESPOONS VINEGAR

Drain the sauerkraut 15 minutes in a colander.
Cut with scissors into 1-inch pieces.
Mix all ingredients together in a large bowl; cover and store in the refrigerator for 24 hours. (This salad will store indefinitely.)

YIELD: 10 SERVINGS
APPROX. CAL/SERV.: 60

. . . . **Celery Seed Cole Slaw**

3 CUPS FINELY SHREDDED CABBAGE
3 TABLESPOONS OIL
⅓ CUP VINEGAR, WARMED
1 TABLESPOON FINELY CHOPPED ONION
1 TABLESPOON CHOPPED PIMIENTO
2 TABLESPOONS SUGAR
½ TEASPOON DRY MUSTARD
1 TEASPOON SALT
½ TEASPOON CELERY SEEDS

In a large bowl, toss the shredded cabbage, oil and warm vinegar. Add the remaining ingredients and toss again. Cover and refrigerate until serving time.

YIELD: 6 SERVINGS
APPROX. CAL/SERV.: 90

· · · · · · · **Cole Slaw with Green Peppers**

½ CUP SUGAR
⅔ CUP VINEGAR
½ CUP OIL
1 TEASPOON SALT
¼ TEASPOON PEPPER
2 POUNDS CABBAGE, SHREDDED
1 MEDIUM ONION, CHOPPED
1 GREEN PEPPER, SLICED

Combine the sugar, vinegar, oil and seasonings and pour over the cabbage, onion and pepper in a bowl. Toss to mix.

Cover and let stand several hours before serving. (Salad can be stored in the refrigerator for several days.)

Drain before serving.

YIELD: 10 SERVINGS
APPROX. CAL/SERV.: 155

· · · · · · · · · · · · **Vegetable Salad**

1 MEDIUM HEAD CABBAGE, THINLY SLICED
3 TABLESPOONS COARSE OR KOSHER SALT
½ POUND CARROTS, SLICED ACROSS TO FORM THIN CIRCLES
2 GREEN PEPPERS, DICED IN ¼-INCH CUBES
2 CUCUMBERS, THINLY SLICED
1 BUNCH RADISHES, THINLY SLICED
½ CUP OIL
½ CUP VINEGAR
¼ CUP SUGAR
1 TEASPOON PEPPER
1 TEASPOON GARLIC POWDER
1 TEASPOON PAPRIKA

Slice cabbage, put into a large bowl, and sprinkle with coarse salt. Add other ingredients and stir. Let stand about 15 minutes.

Add oil, vinegar, sugar, pepper, garlic powder and paprika. Cover and refrigerate. This will keep for several weeks in the refrigerator.

YIELD: 15 SERVINGS
APPROX. CAL/SERV.: 95

Parsley Salad

2 BUNCHES PARSLEY, WASHED AND CRISPED
½ CUP FINELY CRUSHED BULGUR WHEAT
1 CUCUMBER, DICED
2 MEDIUM TOMATOES, CUT IN LARGE PIECES
4 GREEN ONIONS, FINELY CHOPPED
¼ CUP CHOPPED FRESH GREEN MINT, OR 1 TABLESPOON DRIED MINT
1 TEASPOON SALT
PEPPER TO TASTE

Wash and drain the crushed wheat and let stand while preparing the vegetables.

Chop parsley and combine with chopped cucumber, tomatoes, onions and mint. Mix in the crushed wheat.

dressing

JUICE OF 1½ LEMONS
1 CLOVE GARLIC, CRUSHED
1 TABLESPOON OLIVE OIL

Mix all dressing ingredients together and let stand for several hours. Remove garlic from dressing. Toss together with the Parsley Salad. Let stand for several hours before using.
Serve on salad greens.

YIELD: 6 SERVINGS
APPROX. CAL/SERV.: 105

· · · · · · · · · · · · · *Waldorf Salad*

2 CUPS DICED UNPEELED APPLES
1 CUP DICED CELERY
¼ CUP COARSELY CHOPPED WALNUTS
½ CUP RAISINS, OR SEEDLESS GRAPES, HALVED
1 TEASPOON LEMON JUICE
DASH SALT
½ CUP CREAMY CHEESE SPREAD (p. 12)

Mix all ingredients together.
Chill. Serve on salad greens.

YIELD: 6 SERVINGS
APPROX. CAL/SERV.: 135

· · · · · · · · · · *Avocado-Pineapple Salad*

2 AVOCADOS
4 CANNED PINEAPPLE SLICES
SALAD GREENS
1 PINT LOW-FAT COTTAGE CHEESE
¼ CUP SYRUP FROM THE CANNED PINEAPPLE
¼ CUP HONEY
¼ CUP LEMON JUICE
CHOPPED MINT (OPTIONAL)

Cut avocados lengthwise into halves; remove peel and seeds. Cut each half into 8 pieces crosswise; sprinkle with a little lemon juice or canned pineapple syrup to prevent discoloration.

Cut the pineapple slices into halves.

Line 4 salad plates with greens. Spoon cottage cheese over the greens to make a base for the pineapple and avocado slices.

Reassemble one avocado half over each serving of cottage cheese, alternating avocado pieces with pineapple halves.

Combine the pineapple syrup, honey, lemon juice and mint. Pour over pineapple and avocado slices.

YIELD: 8 SERVINGS
APPROX. CAL/SERV.: 190

. . . . **Dilled Shrimp Salad**

3 POUNDS CLEANED AND DEVEINED SHRIMP
1 TABLESPOON SHRIMP SPICE
½ ONION, PEELED AND SLICED
1 5-OUNCE CAN WATER CHESTNUTS, SLICED
4 TABLESPOONS ITALIAN SALAD DRESSING
2 TABLESPOONS CHOPPED FRESH DILL; OR 1 TEASPOON POWDERED DILL
3 RIPE TOMATOES
6 FRESH MUSHROOMS, SLICED
PARSLEY
1 SMALL HEAD ROMAINE

Cook shrimp in water with the shrimp spice. Drain and chill.
Toss with the onion, water chestnuts and dressing. Sprinkle with dill.
Serve on romaine lettuce and surround with sliced tomatoes and mushrooms.

YIELD: 16 SERVINGS
APPROX. CAL/SERV.: 110

. . . . **Chicken-Vegetable Salad**

2 CUPS CHUNKED WHITE MEAT OF CHICKEN OR TURKEY
½ CUCUMBER, PEELED AND DICED
½ CUP DICED CELERY
½ CUP WATER CHESTNUTS, DRAINED AND SLICED
¼ CUP DICED GREEN PEPPER
¼ CUP CHOPPED PIMIENTO
¼ CUP SLICED SCALLIONS
¼ CUP MAYONNAISE
6 LETTUCE CUPS
2 TABLESPOONS CAPERS
PAPRIKA

Toss the first 7 ingredients with mayonnaise. Serve in lettuce cups, garnished with capers and paprika.

YIELD: 6 SERVINGS
APPROX. CAL/SERV.: 170

Chicken-Fruit Salad

Delicate flavor, a pretty yellow color and crunchy texture make this a delightful salad combination.

2 CUPS DICED WHITE MEAT OF CHICKEN
2 APPLES, DICED
1 CUP PINEAPPLE CHUNKS, DRAINED
3 TABLESPOONS MAYONNAISE
¾ TEASPOON CURRY POWDER
¼ CUP CHOPPED ALMONDS

Toss all ingredients together. Spoon individual portions into lettuce cups.

YIELD: 6 SERVINGS
APPROX. CAL/SERV.: 220

Chinese Chicken Salad

4 CUPS COOKED CHICKEN, CUT IN BITE-SIZE PIECES

sauce A

4 TABLESPOONS SOY SAUCE
2 TABLESPOONS HONEY
1 CLOVE GARLIC, CRUSHED

sauce B

3 TABLESPOONS OIL
2 SCALLIONS, CHOPPED
4 SLICES PEELED FRESH GINGER ROOT*
1½ TEASPOONS BLACK PEPPER OR SZECHWAN PEPPER (OBTAINABLE AT CHINESE FOOD STORES)
¼ TABLESPOON CRUSHED RED PEPPER

* Ginger roots should be peeled, covered with sherry and refrigerated before use.

Arrange chicken pieces on a platter of Boston or Bibb lettuce. Combine all ingredients for Sauce A, and set aside for 5 minutes. Combine all ingredients for Sauce B in a saucepan and heat for 3 minutes. Mix Sauce B into Sauce A. Pour over the chicken.

YIELD: 10 SERVINGS
APPROX. CAL/SERV.: 155

· · · · · · · · · *Cooked Salad Dressing*

2 TABLESPOONS CORNSTARCH
2 TABLESPOONS SUGAR
1 TEASPOON DRY MUSTARD
½ TEASPOON SALT
⅛ TEASPOON PAPRIKA
½ CUP WATER
1 TABLESPOON VINEGAR
¼ CUP MARGARINE
⅔ CUP SKIM MILK OR BUTTERMILK

Mix together cornstarch, sugar, mustard, salt and paprika.
Add water and cook over low heat, stirring until thickened.
Stir in vinegar. Blend in margarine and gradually add milk. Stir until creamy.
Store and use as needed. Vary the flavor by adding poppy or caraway seeds or honey.

YIELD: 1½ CUPS
APPROX. CAL/SERV.: 1 TABLESPOON = 25

. . . . **Special Green Goddess Dressing**

1 EGG
1 TABLESPOON CHOPPED PARSLEY
3 CANNED ANCHOVY FILLETS, DRAINED
4 GREEN ONIONS WITH TOPS
2 TABLESPOONS TARRAGON VINEGAR
¼ CUP OIL

Place all ingredients, except oil, in a blender. Whip to a liquid consistency.

Gradually add the oil, increasing the flow as the mixture thickens. Continue to blend for a few seconds after all the oil has been added. Store in a closed container in the refrigerator until needed.

YIELD: ¾–1 CUP
APPROX. CAL/SERV.: 1 TABLESPOON = 45

. . . . **Tomato Dressing**

1 CUP TOMATO JUICE
¼ CUP LEMON JUICE OR VINEGAR
2 TABLESPOONS ONION, FINELY CHOPPED
⅛ TEASPOON PEPPER
¼ TEASPOON SALT
1 TEASPOON CHOPPED PARSLEY (OPTIONAL)

Combine all ingredients in a blender and mix thoroughly, or shake vigorously in a tightly covered jar. Store in the refrigerator.

YIELD: 1¼ CUPS
APPROX. CAL/SERV.: 1 TABLESPOON = 5

Chef's Dressing I

⅓ CUP TOMATO JUICE
⅓ CUP OIL
¼ CUP VINEGAR
¼ TEASPOON PEPPER
½ TEASPOON OREGANO
½ TEASPOON MUSTARD
¼ TEASPOON SOY SAUCE

Combine all ingredients and shake well.

YIELD: 1 CUP
APPROX. CAL/SERV.: 1 TABLESPOON = 40

variation

ONION OR CHIVE DRESSING: Add 2 tablespoons of finely chopped chives or scallions.

Chef's Dressing II

¾ CUP BUTTERMILK
3 ROUND TABLESPOONS LOW-FAT COTTAGE CHEESE
¼ TEASPOON SALT
¼ TEASPOON PREPARED MUSTARD
A DROP OF TABASCO SAUCE
½ SMALL WHITE ONION, MINCED
1 TABLESPOON PARSLEY
½ TABLESPOON MINCED CHIVES

Mix all ingredients together in a blender until smooth.
Serve over tossed greens.

YIELD: 1 CUP
APPROX. CAL/SERV.: 1 TABLESPOON = 10

· · · · · · · · · · *Tomato Soup Dressing*

1 CAN TOMATO SOUP
½ CUP VINEGAR
½ CUP OIL
½ CUP SUGAR
1 TEASPOON SALT
1 SMALL ONION, FINELY CHOPPED

Shake all ingredients together in a jar to combine well. Refrigerate and use as needed.

YIELD: 2½ CUPS
APPROX. CAL/SERV.: 1 TABLESPOON = 40

· · · · · · · · · · · · · *variations*

To this basic dressing add any of the following, to taste:

DRY MUSTARD
GARLIC POWDER
WORCESTERSHIRE SAUCE
OREGANO
CURRY POWDER

· · · · · · · · · *Oil and Vinegar Dressing*

¾ CUP OIL
¼ CUP VINEGAR
1 TEASPOON SALT
⅛ TEASPOON FRESHLY GROUND BLACK PEPPER

Place in a tightly closed jar and shake to blend. Use as is or with the addition of any of the following:

⅛ TEASPOON PAPRIKA OR DRY MUSTARD
¼ TEASPOON BASIL, TARRAGON OR OTHER SALAD HERBS
¼ TEASPOON OREGANO AND ¼ TEASPOON GARLIC POWDER
PINCH CURRY POWDER
FEW GRAINS RED PEPPER OR CAYENNE OR A DASH OF TABASCO SAUCE
YIELD: 1 CUP
APPROX. CAL/SERV.: 1 TABLESPOON = 90

· · · · · · Honey-Poppy Seed Salad Dressing

1 CUP HONEY
1 TEASPOON DRY MUSTARD
1 TEASPOON PAPRIKA
¼ TEASPOON SALT
2 TEASPOONS POPPY SEED
5 TEASPOONS VINEGAR
1 TEASPOON LEMON JUICE
1 TEASPOON GRATED ONION, IF DESIRED
1 CUP OIL

In a blender or with an electric mixer, blend together all ingredients except the oil.

Gradually add the oil, beating constantly until mixture thickens.

Store in a covered jar in the refrigerator.

YIELD: 2 CUPS
APPROX. CAL/SERV.: 1 TABLESPOON = 95

· · · · · · · · · Celery Seed Dressing

⅓ CUP UNDILUTED FROZEN LEMONADE CONCENTRATE
2 TABLESPOONS HONEY
⅓ CUP OIL
½ TEASPOON CELERY SEEDS

Combine all ingredients and blend thoroughly until smooth.
Serve on fruit salad.

YIELD: ABOUT 1 CUP
APPROX. CAL/SERV.: 1 TABLESPOON = 60

· · · · · · *Creamy Cottage Cheese Dressing*

1 CUP LOW-FAT COTTAGE CHEESE
⅓ CUP BUTTERMILK

Mix in a blender on medium speed until smooth and creamy. More buttermilk may be added for a thinner dressing.

YIELD: 1⅓ CUPS
APPROX. CAL/SERV.: 1 TABLESPOON = 10

· · · · · · · · · · · · · · *variations**

BLUE CHEESE: Add 1 tablespoon blue cheese, and salt and pepper to taste.

CREAMY FRENCH: Add 1 teaspoon paprika with dry mustard, Worcestershire sauce, onion and garlic salt to taste. Thin with tomato juice to the desired consistency.

GREEN GODDESS: Add 3 anchovies, 1 teaspoon chopped green onion, 1 tablespoon chopped green parsley, and tarragon to taste.

ITALIAN: Add oregano, garlic powder, and onion salt to taste.

HORSERADISH: Add 1 to 2 tablespoons of grated horseradish. (Excellent with cold roast beef.)

THOUSAND ISLAND: Add 2 tablespoons pickle relish or chili sauce, and dry mustard to taste.

DILLWEED: Add ½ to 1 teaspoon of dried dillweed, or 1 tablespoon of chopped fresh dillweed.

* Variations may add up to 5 additional calories per tablespoon.

. , ... **Buttermilk-Herb Dressing**

1 CUP BUTTERMILK
1 TABLESPOON PREPARED MUSTARD
1 TEASPOON MINCED ONION
⅛ TEASPOON DRIED DILL WEED
2 TEASPOONS FINELY CHOPPED PARSLEY; OR 1 TEASPOON DRIED
   PARSLEY FLAKES
⅛ TEASPOON SALT
BLACK PEPPER

Combine all ingredients in a jar, cover tightly and shake to blend.
Chill overnight or for several hours. Shake well before serving. Can
be stored in the refrigerator tightly covered, about one week.

YIELD: 1 CUP
APPROX. CAL/SERV.: 1 TABLESPOON = 5

. . . . **Yogurt Dressing**

2 TEASPOONS LEMON JUICE
1 TABLESPOON OIL
½ CUP PLAIN LOW-FAT YOGURT
½ TEASPOON PAPRIKA
DASH TABASCO
½ TEASPOON SALT
⅛ TEASPOON GARLIC POWDER (OPTIONAL)

Mix all ingredients together in a blender on medium speed for 5
seconds.

YIELD: ⅔ CUP
APPROX. CAL/SERV.: 1 TABLESPOON = 20

Salad Dressing

2 TABLESPOONS DIJON MUSTARD
2 TABLESPOONS RED WINE VINEGAR
6 TABLESPOONS OIL

Blend mustard and vinegar.
Add oil one tablespoon at a time.

YIELD: ½ CUP
APPROX. CAL/SERV.: 1 TABLESPOON = 95

Vegetables

$\mathscr{A}$ vegetable can be many things: a flower (broccoli), a berry (tomato), a root, bulb or tuber (potatoes, carrots, radishes), stems or shoots (celery, rhubarb), or leaves (spinach, cabbage, romaine). The vegetable is defined as any kitchen garden plant used for food, whereas a fruit, strictly speaking, is the ovary of a plant. Whatever you call them, plant products are practically fat free and generally high in minerals and vitamins. Broccoli, tomatoes, sweet potatoes and many other dark green and bright yellow vegetables are good sources of vitamins A and C. They also contain iron and other minerals. Vegetables should be eaten freely because of their high nutrient, low calorie content.

Because vegetables combine well with each other and with other foods, they are great in soups or salads, as appetizers or snacks or with meat or fish. Fresh vegetables keep their color and texture best when they are cooked until barely tender. Steaming is an ideal method for cooking vegetables and retaining nutrients and flavor. When overcooked or held for a period in a warming oven, vegetables suffer loss of color, texture and nutrients. Frozen vegetables are partially cooked, so they require careful attention to prevent mushiness. Canned vegetables need only reheating.

Vegetables can be made even more tempting by adding garlic, onion, lemon juice, herbs or spices. The calorie-conscious will soon learn that margarine and oil are not the only vegetable flavor enhancers. For example, these combinations can result in new, subtle flavors: basil with asparagus, green beans, squash or tomatoes; oregano with zucchini, broccoli, cabbage, mushrooms, tomatoes or onions; dill with green beans, carrots, peas or potatoes; cinnamon with spinach, squash or sweet potatoes; marjoram with celery, eggplant or greens or with the trio of brussels sprouts, carrots and spinach; nutmeg with corn, cauliflower or beans; thyme with artichokes, mushrooms, peas or carrots; and rosemary with the combination of peas, cauliflower and spinach. Chopped parsley and chives, sprinkled on just before serving, can also enhance the flavor of many vegetables.

The important thing to remember is that it is easier to ruin a good vegetable in the cooking than it is to ruin a good steak, and a single perfectly prepared dish has been known to convert a vegetable-hater to a vegetable-lover for life.

• • • • • • • • • • • • • • • • *Colache*

2 TABLESPOONS OIL
1 POUND UNPEELED ZUCCHINI, SLICED
1 SMALL ONION, SLICED
½ CUP DICED GREEN PEPPER
¼ CUP WATER
⅔ CUP DICED FRESH TOMATO
1½ CUPS FROZEN WHOLE KERNEL CORN

Heat oil in a heavy skillet. Sauté zucchini, onion and pepper until limp. Add water, tomato and corn. Cover and cook 5 minutes or until squash is tender, adding more water if necessary. Season with salt and pepper.

YIELD: 8 SERVINGS
APPROX. CAL/SERV.: ½ CUP = 85

. . . . **Ratatouille**

¼ CUP OIL
2 CLOVES GARLIC, CHOPPED
4 ONIONS, THINLY SLICED
3 GREEN PEPPERS, CUT IN STRIPS
1 EGGPLANT, DICED
4 ZUCCHINI SQUASH, CUBED
4 OR 5 FRESH TOMATOES, PEELED; OR 1 LARGE CAN, DRAINED
2 TEASPOONS SALT
½ TEASPOON PEPPER
½ TEASPOON OREGANO
½ TEASPOON DILL
¼ CUP LEMON JUICE

Heat oil until a haze forms. Sauté onions and garlic until golden brown, then add green pepper strips, eggplant and squash; continue cooking for about 5 minutes, stirring occasionally.

Put in the tomatoes, salt, pepper, oregano and dill. Cover and cook over a low flame for about 45 minutes, stirring occasionally. Uncover and continue cooking for 15 to 20 minutes to allow excess liquid to evaporate. Sprinkle on lemon juice.

Serve hot or cold.

YIELD: 2 QUARTS
APPROX. CAL/SERV.: ½ CUP = 150

. . . . **Créole Eggplant**

1 MEDIUM EGGPLANT, SLICED OR CUBED
½ CUP SEASONED BREAD CRUMBS
1 TABLESPOON MARGARINE
CRÉOLE SAUCE

Preheat oven to 350°F.
Parboil eggplant about 10 minutes.
Put a layer of eggplant in the bottom of a casserole, then a layer of

Recipe continues...

sauce, another layer of eggplant and a layer of sauce. Continue until all the eggplant is used, finishing with a layer of sauce. Sprinkle seasoned bread crumbs over the top, dot with margarine and bake for 30 minutes, or until bubbling.

· · · · · · · · · · · · · · *Créole sauce*

    3 TABLESPOONS OIL
    2 TABLESPOONS CHOPPED ONION
    2 TABLESPOONS CHOPPED GREEN PEPPER
    ¼ CUP SLICED MUSHROOMS
    2 CUPS STEWED OR FRESH TOMATOES
    1 CUP WATER
    ½ TEASPOON SALT
    DASH PEPPER
    FEW DROPS TABASCO SAUCE (OPTIONAL)
    ½ TEASPOON BASIL (OPTIONAL)

Cook onion, green pepper and mushrooms in the oil over low heat for about 5 minutes. Add tomatoes, water and seasonings, and simmer until sauce is thick, about 30 minutes.

    YIELD: 10 ½-CUP SERVINGS
    APPROX. CAL/SERV.: 90

· · · · · · · · · · · · · · *variations*

CRÉOLE SQUASH: Substitute squash for the eggplant and proceed as above.
CRÉOLE CELERY: Boil 1 cup of diced celery in ½ cup water for about 10
    minutes, or until barely tender. Mix with Créole sauce and heat
    through.

· · · · · · · · · · · · · · *Caponata*

A delicious vegetable combination that is especially good served with sliced meats for a buffet. Also makes an excellent appetizer.

1 MEDIUM EGGPLANT
6 TABLESPOONS OIL
1 CLOVE GARLIC, MINCED
1 ONION, COARSELY CHOPPED
4 TABLESPOONS TOMATO SAUCE
½ CUP CELERY, CHOPPED
½ GREEN PEPPER, DICED
2 TABLESPOONS CAPERS
12 LARGE STUFFED GREEN OLIVES, SLICED
2 TABLESPOONS WINE VINEGAR
1 TABLESPOON SUGAR
SALT AND FRESHLY GROUND BLACK PEPPER TO TASTE

Peel eggplant and cut into slices ½ inch thick. Cut slices into cubes measuring ½ inch.

In a large heavy skillet, heat 5 tablespoons of the oil and sauté eggplant until brown. Remove eggplant and set aside.

Add the remaining tablespoon of oil to the pan and sauté the garlic and onion. Then add tomato sauce, celery and green pepper. Simmer, covered, for 15 to 20 minutes, adding water if needed. Return eggplant to skillet with capers and olives.

Heat vinegar and sugar together and pour over vegetables. Season, and simmer 15 minutes longer, stirring occasionally to prevent sticking.

Chill and serve on lettuce leaves or with slices of Italian bread.

YIELD: 8 ½-CUP SERVINGS
APPROX. CAL/SERV.: 135

• • • • • • • • • *Asparagus par Excellence*

¼ CUP ONION, DICED
1 GREEN PEPPER, CHOPPED
1 TEASPOON SALT
¼ TEASPOON PEPPER
½ CUP WATER
2 10-OUNCE PACKAGES FROZEN ASPARAGUS SPEARS
2 TEASPOONS PIMIENTO, DICED
½ TEASPOON CRUMBLED TARRAGON
2 TEASPOONS FINELY CHOPPED PARSLEY

Recipe continues...

Place onion, green pepper, salt, pepper and water in skillet. Bring to a boil. Cover and simmer 5 minutes. Add asparagus and steam for 12 to 15 more minutes. Garnish with remaining ingredients.

YIELD: 6 SERVINGS

APPROX. CAL/SERV.: 30

· · · · · · · · · · *Bean Sprouts Piquant*

1 TABLESPOON MARGARINE

½ POUND FRESH MUSHROOMS; OR USE CANNED, DRAINED MUSHROOMS

1 20-OUNCE CAN BEAN SPROUTS

½ TEASPOON SALT

¼ TEASPOON MARJORAM

¼ TEASPOON BASIL

1 TEASPOON LEMON JUICE

Melt margarine in a large saucepan and cook mushrooms until golden. Stir in drained bean sprouts, salt, herbs and lemon juice. Cover and let steam 1 minute.

YIELD: 6 SERVINGS

APPROX. CAL/SERV.: 40

· · · · · · · · · · · *Dilled Green Beans*

Very simple, very quick and very good!

2 BEEF BOUILLON CUBES

1 CUP WATER

2 TABLESPOONS CHOPPED ONION

¼ CUP CHOPPED GREEN PEPPER

½ TEASPOON DILL SEED

2 9-OUNCE PACKAGES FROZEN CUT GREEN BEANS

In a saucepan, dissolve bouillon cubes in water over medium heat. Add onion, pepper and dill seed to bouillon and cook several minutes. Add beans. Cook, covered, 8 to 10 minutes, or until beans are just tender.

YIELD: 0 SERVINGS

APPROX. CAL/SERV.: 25

. . . . *French Green Beans with Water Chestnuts*

2 9-OUNCE PACKAGES FROZEN GREEN BEANS, FRENCH STYLE
1 5-OUNCE CAN WATER CHESTNUTS, DRAINED AND SLICED

Cook beans according to directions on package. Add drained water chestnuts and heat thoroughly. Season to taste with salt and pepper.

YIELD: 6 SERVINGS
APPROX. CAL/SERV.: 40

. . . . *variation*

Top beans with sautéed or canned mushroom caps or slices, or with ½ cup of toasted, slivered almonds.

APPROX. CAL/SERV.: 90

. . . . *Spicy Green Beans*

Crisp celery and onion bits impart color and fresh texture to this pretty bean dish which is spiced with vinegar and dill.

1 9-OUNCE PACKAGE FROZEN FRENCH-STYLE GREEN BEANS
1 TABLESPOON MARGARINE
1 TABLESPOON WATER
½ CUP FINELY CHOPPED CELERY
¼ CUP FINELY CHOPPED ONION
2 TABLESPOONS CHOPPED PIMIENTO
1 TABLESPOON VINEGAR
SALT
¼ TEASPOON DILL SEED
⅛ TEASPOON PEPPER

Place margarine, water and salt in a saucepan. Add frozen beans and heat slowly, using a fork to separate. Cover and cook until beans are tender. Add remaining ingredients, toss lightly and heat through. (Celery and onion should remain crisp.)

YIELD: 4 SERVINGS
APPROX. CAL/SERV.: 50

. . . . *Green Beans Risi*

1 16-OUNCE CAN FRENCH-STYLE GREEN BEANS; OR 1 9-OUNCE PACKAGE
FROZEN GREEN BEANS, COOKED AS DIRECTED
⅓ CUP MARGARINE
2 CUPS COOKED RICE
SALT AND PEPPER
¼ CUP TOASTED FILBERTS, SLICED
¼ CUP PIMIENTO, CHOPPED

Drain green beans. Heat margarine and add beans; stir in rice, salt
and pepper. When heated through, turn into a serving dish and sprinkle
with filberts and pimiento.

YIELD: 8 SERVINGS
APPROX. CAL/SERV.: 145

✓. . . . . *Green Beans Oregano*

1 9-OUNCE PACKAGE FROZEN ITALIAN GREEN BEANS
1 CUP DICED TOMATO (ABOUT 1 MEDIUM TOMATO)
½ CUP DICED CELERY
¼ CUP DICED GREEN PEPPER
2 TABLESPOONS CHOPPED ONION
½ TEASPOON SALT
¼ TEASPOON DRIED OREGANO LEAVES
⅓ CUP WATER

Combine all ingredients in a saucepan and bring to a boil. Separate
beans with a fork.

Reduce heat, cover, and simmer 6 to 8 minutes or until beans are
tender-crisp.

YIELD: 4 SERVINGS
APPROX. CAL/SERV.: 30

. . . . *Green Beans with Mushrooms*

1 9-OUNCE PACKAGE FROZEN CUT GREEN BEANS
1 TABLESPOON OIL
1 GREEN ONION, FINELY CHOPPED; OR 1 TABLESPOON SHALLOTS,
  FINELY CHOPPED
¼ POUND MUSHROOMS, CLEANED AND SLICED
1 TEASPOON LEMON JUICE
1 TEASPOON PAPRIKA
1 TEASPOON FLOUR

Cook green beans according to directions on package; drain and
place in a serving dish. Keep hot. Meanwhile, sauté shallots or green onions
in oil over medium heat until tender. Add sliced mushrooms and lemon
juice. Cook, stirring constantly, until mushrooms are tender.

Combine paprika and flour. Sprinkle over mushrooms and cook,
stirring, 1 minute. Add mushrooms to green beans in serving dish and toss
lightly to mix.

Serve at once.

YIELD: 4 SERVINGS
APPROX. CAL/SERV.: 60

. . . . *Panned Broccoli* ✓

1 POUND FRESH BROCCOLI
2 TABLESPOONS OIL
1 TABLESPOON MINCED ONION
1 CLOVE GARLIC, MINCED
⅛ TEASPOON FRESHLY GROUND PEPPER
¼ TEASPOON SALT
1 TABLESPOON LEMON JUICE

Wash broccoli and trim. Peel stems and cut into 2-inch lengths.
Separate florets by cutting into halves or quarters so they are of uniform
size. Blanch (parboil about 10 minutes for stems, less for florets). Plunge

Recipe continues...

into cold water for about 3 minutes to set the color and texture. Sauté onion and garlic in oil. Add drained broccoli, and cook gently until it is tender-crisp. This will take only a few minutes. Season with salt, pepper and lemon juice. Serve at once.

YIELD: 4 SERVINGS

APPROX. CAL/SERV.: 95

· · · · · · · · · · · · · · · *variation*

Omit lemon juice and salt. Increase the oil. Add 2 or 3 anchovies to sautéed onion and garlic. When broccoli is done, pour entire mixture, including oil, over cooked pasta. Serve sprinkled with Parmesan cheese.

APPROX. CAL/SERV.: ½ CUP = 220

✓ · · · · · · · *Broccoli with Mustard Dill Sauce*

1 10-OUNCE PACKAGE OF FROZEN BROCCOLI; OR 1 POUND OF BROCCOLI, WASHED, TRIMMED AND CUT UP

Cook broccoli according to package instructions if frozen, or in rapidly boiling water if fresh. Do not overcook. It should be just tender-crisp.

Pour Mustard Dill Sauce over broccoli. Serve immediately.

· · · · · · · · · · · *mustard dill sauce*

1 CUP WATER

⅓ CUP NONFAT DRY MILK

3 TABLESPOONS FLOUR

3 TEASPOONS PREPARED MUSTARD × dry

1 TEASPOON SALT +

¼ TEASPOON DILL SEED

In a saucepan, combine water, nonfat dry milk, flour, prepared mustard, salt and dill seed. Beat with a rotary beater until well blended. Cook over medium heat, stirring constantly, until it thickens.

This sauce is good served on many kinds of vegetables.

YIELD: 4 SERVINGS

APPROX. CAL/SERV.: 65

. . . . *Party Walnut Broccoli*

A winner for the party buffet. Make enough for "seconds" all around.

3 10-OUNCE PACKAGES FROZEN CHOPPED BROCCOLI

6 TABLESPOONS MARGARINE

4 TABLESPOONS FLOUR

2 CHICKEN BOUILLON CUBES, DISSOLVED IN 1 CUP HOT WATER

2 CUPS SKIM MILK

⅔ CUP WATER

2 CUPS HERBED POULTRY STUFFING (CRUMBLY TYPE)

⅔ CUP CHOPPED WALNUTS

Preheat oven to 400°F.

Cook broccoli according to package directions until just barely tender. Drain well and place in an oiled 2-quart casserole.

Melt 2 tablespoons of the margarine in a saucepan. Stir in the flour; cook briefly, and then add the milk. Add the bouillon and cook, stirring constantly, until thickened. Set aside.

Melt the remaining 4 tablespoons of margarine in the ⅔ cup of water. Mix with the herb dressing and walnuts. Pour the bouillon sauce over the broccoli; sprinkle evenly with walnut mixture and bake 20 minutes, or until crusty on top.

YIELD: 6 SERVINGS

APPROX. CAL/SERV.: 205

. . . . **Spiced Red Cabbage**

4 CUPS SHREDDED RED CABBAGE
¼ CUP CIDER VINEGAR
½ CUP WATER
¼ TEASPOON GROUND ALLSPICE
¼ TEASPOON GROUND CINNAMON
⅛ TEASPOON GROUND NUTMEG
1 TEASPOON SALT
2 TART APPLES, PEELED, CORED AND DICED
1 TABLESPOON SUGAR

In a saucepan, combine shredded cabbage with all other ingredients, except apples. Cover and cook over moderate heat for 15 minutes, tossing several times so the cabbage will cook evenly.

Add apples, and toss again. Cover, and cook 5 minutes longer. Add **sugar**.

If more water is needed during cooking, add 2 or 3 tablespoons, but when the dish is done, all moisture should have cooked away.

YIELD: 6 SERVINGS
APPROX. CAL/SERV.: 45

. . . . **Honey Carrots**

10–12 SMALL YOUNG CARROTS
2 TABLESPOONS MARGARINE
1 TABLESPOON BROWN SUGAR
1 TABLESPOON HONEY
2 TABLESPOONS FINELY CHOPPED PARSLEY OR FRESH MINT

Wash and trim carrots. Cook in a small amount of boiling salted water for 15 minutes, or until tender. Drain.

Melt margarine in a skillet or saucepan. Add sugar, honey and carrots. Cook over low heat, turning carrots frequently until well glazed. Sprinkle with chopped parsley or mint, and serve immediately.

YIELD: 4 SERVINGS
APPROX. CAL/SERV.: 100

. . . . **Baked Grated Carrots**

A colorful combination of bright orange and green, this dish has a fresh texture and flavor. It will be liked by people who prefer raw carrots to cooked ones, since the vegetable retains a garden fresh crispness.

3 CUPS GRATED CARROTS
2 TABLESPOONS MARGARINE
1 TABLESPOON LEMON JUICE
½ TEASPOON SALT
1 TABLESPOON CHOPPED CHIVES
2 TABLESPOONS DRY SHERRY

Preheat oven to 350°F.
Place grated carrots in a casserole. Pour over them the melted margarine, lemon juice, salt and sherry. Sprinkle with chives. Bake for 30 minutes.

YIELD: 6 SERVINGS
APPROX. CAL/SERV.: 65

. . . . **Cauliflower with Cheese**

1 SMALL CAULIFLOWER
1 ENVELOPE INSTANT CHICKEN BROTH
MINCED FRESH PARSLEY
4 1-OUNCE SLICES MOZZARELLA CHEESE (MADE FROM PARTIALLY
   SKIMMED MILK)
PAPRIKA

Preheat oven to 400°F.
Remove leaves and stalks from the cauliflower. Cut off stem so that cauliflower will stand securely. Place the vegetable on a rack in a steamer over 1 inch of water. Cover tightly. When water comes to a boil, quickly remove cover and sprinkle the chicken broth powder over the cauliflower. Cover again, and finish steaming (about 10 minutes), until vegetable is barely tender. Then lift it carefully from the steamer

Recipe continues...

to a pie plate. Sprinkle with parsley. While still hot, place cheese slices on top, pressing them down and around the cauliflower. The heat will make them easy to mold.

Place the cauliflower in the oven and bake until cheese is bubbly and brown. Sprinkle with paprika and serve immediately. (Do not delay or mozzarella will harden.)

YIELD: 6 SERVINGS
APPROX. CAL/SERV.: 70

· · · · · · · · · *Creamy Corn Casserole*

2 TABLESPOONS MELTED MARGARINE
1 TEASPOON FLOUR
1 TEASPOON POWDERED CHICKEN BOUILLON
1 TEASPOON SEASONED SALT
¼ TEASPOON DRY MUSTARD
2 TEASPOONS DRIED CHOPPED CHIVES
1 TEASPOON PARSLEY FLAKES
2 CUPS WHOLE KERNEL CORN, DRAINED
1 CUP WHIPPED LOW-FAT COTTAGE CHEESE

Preheat oven to 325°F.

Whip cottage cheese in blender for 2 minutes.

Blend the margarine with the flour until smooth. Add seasonings, drained canned or cooked frozen corn, and cottage cheese. Mix well and pour into a 1½-quart casserole. Bake 25 to 30 minutes or until heated through. Garnish with green pepper rings and pimiento curls if desired.

YIELD: 6 SERVINGS
APPROX. CAL/SERV.: 120

· · · · · · · · · ***Fresh Greens, Southern Style***

2 POUNDS FRESH GREENS (COLLARD, MUSTARD, KALE, SWISS CHARD, TURNIP OR BEET)
1 BEEF BOUILLON CUBE
2 TABLESPOONS OIL
¼ TEASPOON DRIED HOT RED PEPPER BITS
SALT

Rinse fresh greens thoroughly in several changes of cold water to remove all sand and grit. Drain in a colander.

Remove tough stems and tear large leaves into pieces. Place greens in a large cooking pan and add bouillon cube, oil and red pepper. Cover and bring to a boil. (There is no need to add water; greens will cook in the moisture clinging to the leaves.) Uncover briefly and toss greens with a fork to dissolve bouillon cube. Cover again and simmer gently for 5 to 8 minutes for young tender greens, 15 to 20 minutes for older greens. Salt to taste.

Frozen greens may be used. Follow cooking directions on package; add other ingredients.

YIELD: 6 SERVINGS
APPROX. CAL/SERV.: 75

Stuffed Mushrooms

1 POUND MUSHROOMS
2 TABLESPOONS OIL
1 10-OUNCE PACKAGE FROZEN CHOPPED SPINACH
2 CLOVES GARLIC, MINCED
2 EGG WHITES, SLIGHTLY BEATEN
½ TEASPOON SALT
¼ TEASPOON PEPPER
½ CUP ITALIAN SEASONED BREAD CRUMBS

Preheat oven to 350°F.

Wash mushrooms and remove caps. Sauté whole caps quickly in oil.

Chop mushroom stems. Cook spinach according to package directions along with chopped mushrooms. Drain and squeeze to eliminate excess water; combine with egg whites and bread crumbs. Fill mushroom caps with the spinach mixture. Place caps in an oiled ovenproof dish and bake 10 to 15 minutes.

Use as garnish around roast meat or chicken. Also may be served as an appetizer.

YIELD: 6 SERVINGS
APPROX. CAL/SERV.: 110

Creamed Onions

2 CUPS RAW OR CANNED PEARL ONIONS
¾ CUP SKIM MILK
1½ TABLESPOONS MARGARINE
1½ TABLESPOONS FLOUR
SALT TO TASTE
DASH PEPPER
DASH NUTMEG (OPTIONAL)

If raw onions are used, parboil them until tender.

Meanwhile, make a white sauce: melt margarine in a saucepan, blend in flour and add milk gradually. Cook over low heat, stirring constantly, until mixture has thickened.

Drain onions and add to cream sauce. Season to taste.

YIELD: 4 SERVINGS
APPROX. CAL/SERV.: 95

· · · · · · · · · · · · · *Minted Peas*

A great idea! No one will guess the surprise ingredient. Very easy, very elegant!

1   10-OUNCE PACKAGE FROZEN PEAS
2   TABLESPOONS WATER
½   TEASPOON SALT
1   TABLESPOON GREEN CRÈME DE MENTHE
1   TABLESPOON MARGARINE

Place peas, water and salt in a saucepan. Bring to a boil, reduce heat, and cook, covered, 3 to 5 minutes. Remove cover, dot with margarine and pour in crème de menthe.

YIELD: 4 SERVINGS
APPROX. CAL/SERV.: 90

· · · · · · · · · · · · · · *Pea Pods*

1   POUND CHINESE PEA PODS, OR 1 10-OUNCE PACKAGE FROZEN PEA PODS
3   TABLESPOONS CHOPPED GREEN ONION
1   TABLESPOON SOY SAUCE
2   TABLESPOONS OIL

Use Chinese peas, sometimes called snow peas or sugar peas. To prepare, wash pods, break off ends and remove string that runs along the spine. Cut pods in half if they are very large.

Sprinkle with soy sauce and sauté quickly with a few chopped green onions in margarine or oil.

YIELD: 4 SERVINGS
APPROX. CAL/SERV.: 120

Recipe continues...

· · · · · · · · · · · · · · · *variation*

Pea pods may be combined with meat or vegetable dishes, in stews or in soups, if added at the last.

· · · · · · · · · · · · · **French Peas**

1 TABLESPOON OIL
2 GREEN ONIONS, DICED
1 CUP FINELY SHREDDED LETTUCE
1 TEASPOON FLOUR
3 TABLESPOONS WATER OR CHICKEN BROTH
1 10-OUNCE PACKAGE FROZEN PEAS, COOKED
1 5-OUNCE CAN WATER CHESTNUTS, DRAINED
¾ TEASPOON SEASONED SALT

In a saucepan, cook green onions and lettuce in oil over low heat for 5 minutes.

Combine flour with water or broth. Add to lettuce mixture and stir until thickened. Put in the cooked peas, sliced water chestnuts and seasoning. Heat through and serve.

YIELD: 6 SERVINGS
APPROX. CAL/SERV.: 80

· · · · · · · · **Seasoned Black-Eyed Peas**

1 POUND DRIED BLACK-EYED PEAS
¼ POUND CRISP FRIED CANADIAN BACON, CHOPPED
2 MEDIUM ONIONS, CHOPPED
2 STALKS CELERY, CHOPPED
1 SMALL BAY LEAF
1 CLOVE GARLIC, CHOPPED
1 RED PEPPER POD
1 6-OUNCE CAN TOMATO PASTE
WATER
2 TEASPOONS SALT
¼ TEASPOON PEPPER

Wash the peas and let soak for 45 minutes. Drain. Pour in just enough fresh water to cover the peas; add the remaining ingredients. Bring to a boil. Reduce heat. Cover and simmer until tender, about 3 hours. Season to taste.

YIELD: 16 ½-CUP SERVINGS
APPROX. CAL/SERV.: 130

· · · · · · · · · · · *Oven French Fries*

French fries without frying—a surprise for those who thought this crispy treat was a forbidden food.

4 MEDIUM POTATOES (IRISH POTATOES ARE GOOD)
1 TABLESPOON OIL

Preheat oven to 475°F.

Peel potatoes and cut into long strips about ½ inch wide. Dry strips thoroughly on paper towels. Toss in a bowl with oil as if making a salad.

When strips are thoroughly coated with the oil, spread them in a single layer on a cookie sheet and place in preheated oven for 35 minutes. Turn strips periodically to brown on all sides. If a crispier, browner potato is desired, run under broiler for a minute or two. Sprinkle with salt before serving.

YIELD: 6 SERVINGS
APPROX. CAL/SERV.: 80

· · · · · · · · · · · *Scalloped Potatoes*

4 CUPS THINLY SLICED, PEELED RAW POTATOES
1 ONION, PEELED AND SLICED THINLY
1 TABLESPOON CHOPPED PARSLEY, IF DESIRED
3 TABLESPOONS FLOUR
⅛ TEASPOON PEPPER
1½ TEASPOONS SALT
3 TABLESPOONS MARGARINE
1½ CUPS SKIM MILK

Recipe continues...

Preheat oven to 350°F.

In a lightly oiled casserole, place a layer of potatoes. Sprinkle with flour, then place a layer of onions. Sprinkling each layer with flour, alternate potatoes and onions until all are used. Season with salt and pepper.

Heat the milk and margarine together and pour over the potatoes. Cover casserole and bake for 1 hour, then remove cover and bake another ½ hour to brown.

YIELD: 6 SERVINGS

APPROX. CAL/SERV.: 150

Basque Potatoes

1 MEDIUM ONION, CHOPPED (½ CUP)

1 SMALL GARLIC CLOVE, CRUSHED

2 TABLESPOONS OLIVE OIL

¾ CUP CHOPPED PARSLEY

¼ CUP CHOPPED PIMIENTO

1 TEASPOON SALT

⅛ TEASPOON PEPPER

1 ENVELOPE CHICKEN BOUILLON POWDER

1 CUP WATER

6 MEDIUM POTATOES

Sauté onion and garlic in olive oil until soft. Stir in parsley, pimiento, salt, pepper, chicken bouillon and water. Remove from heat.

Pare and thinly slice the potatoes. Layer the slices in broth in the skillet. Bring to a boil. Reduce heat, cover and simmer until potatoes are tender, about 20 minutes. With a slotted spoon, lift potatoes into a heated serving dish and pour cooking liquid over them.

YIELD: 8 SERVINGS

APPROX. CAL/SERV.: 105

. . . . **Pineapple Sweet Potatoes**

4 MEDIUM SWEET POTATOES, UNPEELED (ABOUT 1 POUND)
¼ CUP PINEAPPLE JUICE
2 TABLESPOONS OIL
½ TEASPOON SALT
1 TABLESPOON CHOPPED PINEAPPLE
PINCH EACH CINNAMON, NUTMEG AND ALLSPICE
1 TABLESPOON MOLASSES
1 TEASPOON MARGARINE

Preheat oven to 425°F.

Boil potatoes until tender (about 30 minutes), and remove skins. Mash pulp. Add the fruit juice, oil and salt and whip until fluffy. Add chopped pineapple and spices.

Turn into an oiled 1-quart baking dish. Spread molasses over the top, dot with the margarine, and bake uncovered until lightly browned.

YIELD: 6 SERVINGS
APPROX. CAL/SERV.: 135

. . . . **Orange Sweet Potatoes**

4 MEDIUM SWEET POTATOES (ABOUT 1 POUND)
¼–½ TEASPOON GRATED ORANGE RIND
½ CUP ORANGE JUICE
2 TABLESPOONS BROWN SUGAR
¼ TEASPOON CINNAMON
DASH SALT
2 DASHES ANGOSTURA BITTERS (OPTIONAL)

Preheat oven to 350°F.

Boil potatoes until tender. Remove skins. Mash pulp, add remaining ingredients and whip until fluffy. Place in a 1-quart ungreased casserole. Cover and bake for about 25 minutes, or until heated through.

YIELD: 6 SERVINGS
APPROX. CAL/SERV.: 95

· · · · · · · · · *Yellow Squash-Rice Pilau*

Actually a vegetable and rice salad, this makes an excellent summer dish.

3 MEDIUM YELLOW CROOKNECK SQUASH, SLICED THIN
3 CUPS COOKED, COOLED LONG GRAIN WHITE RICE
3 GREEN ONIONS, THINLY SLICED
½ CUP TOASTED SUNFLOWER SEEDS
½ CUP WINE VINEGAR WITH GARLIC
2 TEASPOONS DILLWEED
½ TEASPOON PEPPER
½ TEASPOON SALT
1 TABLESPOON OLIVE OIL
2 TABLESPOONS OIL

Toast sunflower seeds in a low oven (about 250°F.) for 15 minutes, stirring occasionally, until lightly browned. Cover squash slices with boiling water. Cook 2 minutes. Drain well, cool, and stir together with the rice, green onions, and sunflower seeds, being careful not to break up the squash.

Combine the vinegar, dillweed, salt, pepper and oils. Pour over rice mixture and toss gently until well blended. Chill.

YIELD: 10 SERVINGS
APPROX. CAL/SERV.: 165

· · · · · · · · · · *Stuffed Zucchini*

4 MEDIUM ZUCCHINI
½ CUP CHOPPED MUSHROOMS
2 TABLESPOONS OIL
1 ONION, DICED
1 CLOVE GARLIC, CRUSHED
1 SLIGHTLY BEATEN EGG
¼ TEASPOON MARJORAM
1 TEASPOON MINCED PARSLEY
GROUND PEPPER
SALT TO TASTE

Preheat oven to 350°F.

Wash zucchini and scrub lightly to remove any grit or wax. Parboil for 10 minutes. Drain, cool and split lengthwise. Remove pulp and chop it finely.

Sauté garlic in oil until golden brown. Discard garlic and sauté mushrooms in the oil with the onions. Add herbs, salt, pepper and zucchini pulp. Cool. Mix in the slightly beaten egg, and fill the cavity of each zucchini half with the mixture. Place stuffed zucchini in an oiled shallow baking pan. Bake for 30 minutes.

YIELD: 4 SERVINGS

APPROX. CAL/SERV.: 115

· · · · · · · · · · · · *variation*

Substitute 4 ounces of ground veal or beef for the mushrooms.

APPROX. CAL/SERV.: 170

· · · · · · · · · **Stuffed Acorn Squash II**

2 ACORN SQUASH

1 CUP APPLESAUCE

2 TEASPOONS BROWN SUGAR

4 TEASPOONS MARGARINE

CINNAMON

4 TEASPOONS DRY SHERRY, IF DESIRED

Preheat oven to 400°F.

Cut each squash in half lengthwise. Place halves, cut side down, in a shallow baking pan. Cover bottom of pan with water. Bake squash for 50 to 60 minutes, or until tender. Turn squash over. Fill each cavity with applesauce and brown sugar, dot with margarine, and sprinkle with cinnamon and sherry, 1 teaspoon to each cavity. Continue baking for 15 to 20 minutes.

YIELD: 4 SERVINGS

APPROX. CAL/SERV.: 160

Stir-Fry Spinach

1 POUND LOOSE FRESH SPINACH OR OTHER LEAFY GREEN VEGETABLE
2 TABLESPOONS OIL
½ TEASPOON SALT
¼ TEASPOON SUGAR

Wash spinach thoroughly and drain well.

Heat oil in skillet over medium high heat, and add spinach, turning leaves over several times until they are well coated. Cover and cook 1 minute. Uncover, sprinkle with salt and sugar and cook, stirring, for another 30 seconds until spinach is wilted. Do not overcook. Serve at once.

YIELD: 4 SERVINGS
APPROX. CAL/SERV.: 90

Tomatoes Rockefeller

3 LARGE RIPE TOMATOES, CUT IN HALF
2 TABLESPOONS FINELY CHOPPED ONION
2 TABLESPOONS FINELY CHOPPED PARSLEY
1 TABLESPOON MARGARINE
¾ CUP CHOPPED COOKED SPINACH (DRAINED)
SALT
PEPPER
PAPRIKA
2 TABLESPOONS ITALIAN SEASONED BREAD CRUMBS

Preheat oven to 375°F.

Place tomatoes cut side up in an oiled baking dish. Combine onion, parsley, margarine, spinach, salt, pepper and paprika, and spread evenly over tomatoes. Top with crumbs and bake for 15 minutes.

YIELD: 6 SERVINGS
APPROX. CAL/SERV.: 55

· · · · · · · · · *Herbed Baked Tomatoes*

4 MEDIUM TOMATOES
¼ TEASPOON SALT
½ TEASPOON SUGAR
¼ TEASPOON ONION POWDER
⅛ TEASPOON BASIL
⅛ TEASPOON OREGANO
DASH PEPPER
½ CUP CRACKER CRUMBS
1 TABLESPOON MARGARINE
CHOPPED PARSLEY

Preheat oven to 350°F.

Cut top off the tomato, and scoop out a small portion of the pulp. Mix together with salt, sugar, onion powder, basil, oregano and pepper. Stuff tomatoes with this mixture. Top with cracker crumbs, dot with margarine and sprinkle with chopped parsley. Bake for 20 or 30 minutes, until the tomatoes are tender.

YIELD: 4 SERVINGS
APPROX. CAL/SERV.: 115

· · · · · · · · · · · · · · *variation*

TOMATOES PROVENÇALE: Mix tomato pulp with ¼ cup melted margarine; ¼ cup fine bread crumbs; 2 cloves garlic, minced; 1 teaspoon chopped parsley; ⅛ teaspoon pepper. Stuff tomatoes and bake for 30 minutes.

APPROX. CAL/SERV.: 165

. . . . *Harvard Beets*

1½ TEASPOONS CORNSTARCH
¼ CUP SUGAR
DASH PEPPER
⅛ TEASPOON GROUND CLOVES
½ TEASPOON GRATED ORANGE RIND
6 TABLESPOONS VINEGAR
¼ CUP BEET JUICE
2 CUPS DICED COOKED BEETS
1 TABLESPOON MARGARINE

Combine cornstarch, sugar, pepper, cloves and orange rind in a 1-quart saucepan. Stir in vinegar and beet juice. Cook over low heat, stirring constantly, until sauce thickens.

Add beets and simmer until they are heated through.

Just before serving, stir in the margarine.

YIELD: 4 SERVINGS
APPROX. CAL/SERV.: 115

. . . . *Deviled Beets*

1 TABLESPOON MARGARINE
¼ TEASPOON DRY MUSTARD
¼ TEASPOON GROUND CLOVES
2 TABLESPOONS VINEGAR
1 TABLESPOON BROWN SUGAR
½ TEASPOON SALT
½ TEASPOON PAPRIKA
1 TEASPOON WORCESTERSHIRE SAUCE
3 CUPS DICED COOKED BEETS, DRAINED, OR SMALL WHOLE BEETS, DRAINED

In a saucepan, melt margarine and mix well with all ingredients, except beets. Toss beets lightly in mixture to coat evenly. Cover and warm over low heat.

YIELD: 6 SERVINGS
APPROX. CAL/SERV.: 50

· · · · · · · · · · *Cold Curried Succotash*

2 CUPS CANNED WHOLE KERNEL CORN
1 12-OUNCE PACKAGE FROZEN BABY LIMA BEANS
½ CUP RAW CHOPPED ONION
½ CUP RAW CHOPPED CELERY
¼ CUP RAW CHOPPED GREEN PEPPER
¼ CUP DICED PIMIENTO
½ CUP BROWN SUGAR
1 TABLESPOON CURRY POWDER
2 3-INCH PIECES STICK CINNAMON, BROKEN UP
1 TEASPOON WHOLE CLOVES
1 TEASPOON CELERY SEED
1 TEASPOON SALT
1 CUP CIDER VINEGAR

Cook the lima beans according to package directions. Drain, reserving ½ cup of cooking liquid. In a saucepan, combine the liquid with the brown sugar, curry powder, spices, salt and vinegar. Bring to a boil, stirring constantly, reduce heat and simmer 10 minutes.

Combine the corn and limas with the raw vegetables and pimiento.

Strain the curry mixture over the vegetables. Cool. Chill overnight to blend seasonings. Serve cold as a vegetable side dish or as a relish.

YIELD: 10 SERVINGS
APPROX. CAL/SERV.: 110

· · · · · · · *Vegetables with Lemon Sauce*

1 POUND BROCCOLI (FLORETS ONLY)
1 SMALL HEAD CAULIFLOWER (FLORETS ONLY)
1 9-OUNCE PACKAGE FROZEN ARTICHOKE HEARTS
2 TABLESPOONS FINELY CHOPPED ONION
½ CUP MARGARINE
¼ TEASPOON PAPRIKA
¼ TEASPOON SALT
3 TABLESPOONS LEMON JUICE
1 PIMIENTO, DICED

Recipe continues...

Cook broccoli florets, cauliflower florets, and artichoke hearts separately in rapidly boiling water. Drain.

Sauté the onion in margarine for 2 minutes. Remove from the heat and stir in paprika, salt and lemon juice.

Arrange the vegetables in groups on a hot serving platter. Drizzle lemon sauce over all. Sprinkle the artichoke hearts with pimiento.

YIELD: 8 SERVINGS
APPROX. CAL/SERV.: 80

· · · · · · · · · · · *Curried Celery*

Vegetable course or chutney? It depends on how you serve it. Excellent with chicken, veal, pork, ham and shrimp, and just as good the following day with cold sliced meat.

2 CUPS SLICED CELERY
½ TEASPOON SALT
BOILING WATER
1 TART APPLE, PARED, CORED AND CHOPPED
½ CUP CHOPPED ONION
1 TEASPOON MARGARINE
1 TEASPOON CORNSTARCH
1 ROUNDED TEASPOON CURRY POWDER
SALT AND PEPPER TO TASTE

Put celery and salt in a saucepan over heat and pour in boiling water to ½ inch depth. Cover. Boil 5 minutes; the celery should still be crisp. Drain, reserving the cooking water, and set celery aside.

Using the same pan, sauté the chopped apple and onion in margarine over moderate heat, stirring frequently until the onion is transparent. Blend in cornstarch and curry powder. Cook 2 minutes. Add ½ cup of the reserved cooking water and cook 5 more minutes over low heat. Add the celery, salt and pepper.

YIELD: 4 SERVINGS
APPROX. CAL/SERV.: 45

. . . . **Vegetables A La Grecque**

Choose 4 cups of assorted raw fresh vegetables, prepared for cooking, (asparagus, artichoke hearts, brussel sprouts, cauliflower, broccoli, green beans, carrots, mushrooms, zucchini, eggplant). Or use frozen ones.

½ CUP OLIVE OIL
½ CUP WINE VINEGAR; OR 2 TABLESPOONS LEMON JUICE AND 1 OR 2
   SLICES LEMON
1 TEASPOON SALT
1 TEASPOON CRUSHED CORIANDER SEED
1 TEASPOON THYME
1 BAY LEAF
1 CLOVE GARLIC, CRUSHED
½ TEASPOON FRESHLY GROUND BLACK PEPPER
2 CUPS WATER

Combine oil, vinegar or lemon juice and slices, seasonings and water. Bring to a boil and put in the vegetables. Reduce heat and simmer uncovered until tender-crisp. *Do not overcook* (frozen vegetables require a shorter cooking time). Let vegetables cool in the sauce.

Vegetables à la Grecque are served cold or at room temperature.

YIELD: 8 SERVINGS
APPROX. CAL/SERV.: 140

. . . . **German-Style Wax Beans**

4 THIN SLICES CANADIAN BACON
1 TABLESPOON OIL
½ CUP SLICED GREEN ONIONS
1 16-OUNCE CAN SLICED WAX BEANS
¼ CUP WHITE WINE VINEGAR
2 TABLESPOONS SUGAR
2 TABLESPOONS DICED PIMIENTO

Fry bacon until done and dice it. Wipe pan with paper towel, pour in oil and sauté onion until limp.

Recipe continues...

Stir in the remaining ingredients. Heat through. Sprinkle in the bacon, and toss lightly.

YIELD: 4 SERVINGS
APPROX. CAL/SERV.: 150

. . . . **Glazed Onions**

20 SMALL FRESH WHITE ONIONS; OR 1 16-OUNCE CAN ONIONS
2 TABLESPOONS MARGARINE
1 TEASPOON SUGAR
¼ TEASPOON SALT

If canned onions are used, drain them. If raw, place unskinned onions in a saucepan, add 1 inch of boiling water, cover and cook until tender, about 20 minutes. Drain and cool.

Heat margarine in skillet. Add onions, sprinkle with sugar and salt, and cook slowly, shaking the pan or turning the onions until they are a light golden brown.

YIELD: 4 SERVINGS
APPROX. CAL/SERV.: 90

. . . . **Stuffed Baked Potatoes**

6 LARGE BAKING POTATOES
½ CUP OR MORE LOW-FAT COTTAGE CHEESE
GARLIC AND SALT TO TASTE
4 GREEN ONIONS, MINCED
PAPRIKA
2 TABLESPOONS PARMESAN CHEESE

Preheat oven to 425°F.

Wash and dry the potatoes. Prick the skins. Bake 60 minutes, or until done.

Cut a slice from the top of each potato and scoop out the pulp. In a blender, whip the cottage cheese until creamy. Mash the potato pulp and blend enough of the whipped cottage cheese to make a light, fluffy mixture. Stir in green onions. Spoon the mixture back into the shells, mounding it slightly.

Place the stuffed potatoes on a baking sheet, dust the tops with Parmesan cheese and paprika and return to the oven until lightly browned.

YIELD: 6 SERVINGS
APPROX. CAL/SERV.: 115

Avery Island Celery

¼ CUP MARGARINE
1 MEDIUM ONION, CHOPPED
1 16-OUNCE CAN TOMATOES
½ TEASPOON HOT PEPPER SAUCE
1 TEASPOON SALT
¼ TEASPOON SUGAR
¼ TEASPOON THYME
4 CUPS DIAGONALLY CUT CELERY
1 10-OUNCE PACKAGE FROZEN PEAS, THAWED

Melt margarine in a large skillet and cook the onion until just tender but not brown.

Drain the tomatoes reserving the liquid; combine liquid in a skillet with the hot pepper sauce, salt, sugar and thyme. Bring to a boil, and stir in the celery and peas. Cover and cook 10 minutes, or until barely tender.

Add the tomatoes, heat through and place in a serving dish.

YIELD: 10 SERVINGS
APPROX. CAL/SERV.: 85

Savory Spinach

1 10-OUNCE PACKAGE FROZEN LEAF SPINACH, THAWED
1 TEASPOON SALT
2 TABLESPOONS HORSERADISH
2 TABLESPOONS CHOPPED CANADIAN BACON (COOKED)

Recipe continues...

Cook the spinach in ¼ cup of salted water until tender, about 4 or 5 minutes.

Drain and mix in the horseradish and bacon.

YIELD: 4 SERVINGS
APPROX. CAL/SERV.: 50

· · · · · · · · · · · *Hobo Vegetables*

Having a backyard cook-out? Consider this easy way of adding vegetables to the meal.

4 CARROTS, SCRAPED
4 ONIONS, PEELED
4 POTATOES, SCRUBBED
4 TABLESPOONS MARGARINE
SALT AND PEPPER
HEAVY DUTY ALUMINUM FOIL

For each person place a carrot, a potato, and an onion on a square of foil. Add 1 tablespoon of margarine, and the salt and pepper.

Wrap snugly and seal. Place over hot coals for 45 to 60 minutes, turning occasionally, until vegetables are done.

YIELD: 4 SERVINGS
APPROX. CAL/SERV.: 250

· · · · · · · · · *Artichoke Hearts Riviera*

2 10-OUNCE PACKAGES FROZEN ARTICHOKE HEARTS
½ CUP DRY VERMOUTH
1 TABLESPOON LEMON JUICE
1 CLOVE GARLIC, CRUSHED
½ TEASPOON DRY MUSTARD
¼ TEASPOON FRESHLY GROUND BLACK PEPPER
½ TEASPOON DRIED TARRAGON
1 TABLESPOON CHOPPED PARSLEY
¼ CUP MARGARINE

Cook artichoke hearts as directed on package. Drain.

Combine vermouth, lemon juice, garlic, seasonings and margarine in a saucepan. Cover and simmer 5 minutes. Pour over cooked artichoke hearts. Garnish with chopped parsley.

YIELD: 6 SERVINGS

APPROX. CAL/SERV.: 110

· · · · · · · · · · · *Cabbage with Caraway*

1 HEAD CABBAGE (ABOUT 1½ POUNDS)

1 TEASPOON MARGARINE

1 TABLESPOON MINCED FRESH PARSLEY

1 TEASPOON SUGAR

½ TEASPOON FRESHLY GROUND BLACK PEPPER

½ CUP CHICKEN CONSOMMÉ (OR 1 CHICKEN BOUILLON CUBE)

SALT TO TASTE

CARAWAY SEEDS

Remove major section of core from the cabbage. Leave just enough to hold the head together. Slice the head into wedges about 1½ inches thick.

Melt the margarine in a large skillet. Put in the cabbage, parsley, sugar, black pepper and consommé. Cover and cook over moderate heat about 12 minutes, basting with the pan juices several times.

About 1 minute before the cabbage is done, sprinkle with caraway seeds. Remove cabbage to a serving dish. Pour the pan liquid over the cabbage.

YIELD: 6 SERVINGS

APPROX. CAL/SERV.: 30

. . . . *Brussels Sprouts and Pecans*

2 10-OUNCE PACKAGES FROZEN BRUSSELS SPROUTS, THAWED
3 TABLESPOONS MARGARINE
4 TABLESPOONS FLOUR
¾ CUP NONFAT DRY MILK
1¾ CUPS BOILING CHICKEN BROTH
¼ TEASPOON NUTMEG
¼ CUP CHOPPED PECANS
1 CUP PACKAGED STUFFING MIX

Preheat oven to 400°F.

Cook the Brussels sprouts, uncovered to preserve the color, in a small amount of boiling salt water until tender.

Prepare the sauce: Melt 3 tablespoons of margarine over low heat and blend in the flour. Cook 1 minute, stirring. Add dry milk, then boiling chicken broth all at once, beating with a wire whisk to blend. Cook and stir until sauce comes to a boil and thickens. Remove from heat and stir in nutmeg and pecans.

Place cooked sprouts in an oiled 1½-quart casserole. Pour in the cream sauce, and top with the stuffing mix.

Bake in oven till topping is lightly browned, about 10 minutes.

YIELD: 8 SERVINGS
APPROX. CAL/SERV.: 160

. . . . *Mediterranean Beans*

1 10-OUNCE PACKAGE FROZEN LIMA BEANS
¼ CUP CHOPPED ONION
1 CLOVE GARLIC, CRUSHED
1 TABLESPOON MARGARINE
1 CUP CANNED TOMATO CHUNKS (INCLUDING JUICE)
½ TEASPOON DRIED MINT LEAVES, CRUSHED

Cook lima beans according to package directions.
Sauté onion and garlic in margarine until tender.

Stir in the lima beans, tomatoes and mint leaves. Heat through and serve.

YIELD: 4 SERVINGS
APPROX. CAL/SERV.: 120

. . . . *Triple Vegetable Bake*

3 LARGE WHITE POTATOES, PARED AND CUT INTO ¾-INCH CUBES
1 POUND SMALL WHITE ONIONS, PEELED
¼ CUP MARGARINE
¼ CUP FLOUR
1 ENVELOPE INSTANT CHICKEN BROTH
2 CUPS EVAPORATED SKIM MILK
1 6-OUNCE CAN BUTTON MUSHROOMS
1 SLICE OF BREAD, CRUMBLED
1 POUND FRESH BROCCOLI, FLORETS ONLY

Preheat the oven to 375°F.

Cook potatoes and onions, covered, in boiling salted water for about 15 minutes, or until tender. Drain and return to pan.

Melt margarine in saucepan; stir in flour and chicken broth. Cook, stirring constantly, just until bubbly. Stir in the milk, and continue cooking and stirring until the sauce thickens.

Drain the canned mushrooms and stir the liquid into the sauce. Combine the mushrooms with the potatoes and onions. Fold in the sauce and place in a 1½-quart casserole. Sprinkle bread crumbs in the center. Bake for 30 minutes or until casserole is bubbly and crumbs are toasted.

While casserole bakes, cook the broccoli florets in boiling salted water for 8 minutes, or just until crisply tender. Drain, and arrange in a ring around the top of the casserole. Serve hot.

YIELD: 10 SERVINGS
APPROX. CAL/SERV.: 150

· · · · · · · · · · · · · *Vegetable Creole*

3 CUPS BOILED RICE
½ CUP DICED CELERY
⅓ CUP SLICED ONIONS
1 TABLESPOON OIL
2½ CUPS CANNED TOMATOES
1 TEASPOON CHOPPED SWEET BASIL
½ TEASPOON ROSEMARY
1 TEASPOON CELERY SALT
SALT AND PEPPER TO TASTE
2 CUPS CANNED COOKED PEAS
½ CUP CANNED KIDNEY BEANS

Simmer celery and onions in small amount of water until tender.
Drain water and add oil.
Return to low heat and sauté for 1 minute
Add tomatoes, basil, rosemary, celery salt, salt and pepper.
Cook slowly 20 minutes, stirring occasionally.
Add peas and kidney beans.
Cover; cook 5 minutes longer until thoroughly heated.
Serve over rice.

YIELD: 6 SERVINGS
APPROX. CAL/SERV.: 186

· · · · · · · · · · *Cantonese Vegetables*

1 CUP DRY PINTO BEANS

3 MEDIUM TOMATOES, CUT IN SMALL WEDGES

1 9-OUNCE PACKAGE FROZEN FRENCH-CUT GREEN BEANS

2 MEDIUM ONIONS, SLICED

1 GREEN PEPPER, CUT IN THIN STRIPS

4 STALKS OF CELERY, THIN BIAS CUT

1 TABLESPOON CORNSTARCH

2 TABLESPOONS SOY SAUCE

2 TABLESPOONS OIL

1 BEEF BOUILLON CUBE

½ CUP WATER

1 SLICE FRESH GINGER ROOT OR ½ TEASPOON GINGER

½ TEASPOON CURRY POWDER

⅛ TEASPOON PEPPER

¼ CUP PARSLEY, CHOPPED

Soak pinto beans overnight. Cook in 3 cups water until tender. Drain pinto beans and set aside.

Combine cornstarch, soy sauce, and water. Set aside.

Heat oil in heavy pan or wok; add slice of ginger, pepper, and curry powder to the oil.

Stir-fry the celery and onion until tender crisp.

Add cornstarch mixture; stir until clear.

Add cooked pinto beans, green pepper, French-cut green beans, parsley, and tomatoes.

Cook until all of the vegetables are heated through.

Serve over rice.

YIELD: 6 SERVINGS

APPROX. CAL/SERV.: 200

· · · · · · · · · · · **Dilled Green Beans**

2 BEEF BOUILLON CUBES
1 CUP WATER
2 TABLESPOONS CHOPPED ONION
½ CUP CHOPPED GREEN PEPPER
½ TEASPOON DILL SEED
2 9-OUNCE PACKAGES FROZEN CUT GREEN BEANS

Dissolve bouillon cubes in water in saucepan.
Add onion, pepper and dill seed.
Cook several minutes.
Add beans and cook, covered, for 8 to 10 minutes until the beans are tender.

YIELD: 6 SERVINGS
APPROX. CAL/SERV.: 30

· · · · · · · · · · · **Louisiana Green Beans**

1 POUND FRESH GREEN BEANS, OR 2 9-OUNCE PACKAGES FROZEN GREEN BEANS, COOKED
2 CUPS (1-POUND CAN) TOMATOES
½ CUP CHOPPED CELERY
¼ CUP CHOPPED GREEN PEPPER
½ TEASPOON ONION SALT

Cook green beans until tender.
Combine green beans, tomatoes, celery, green pepper, onion salt, and cook over medium heat about 15 minutes or until heated through.

YIELD: 8 SERVINGS
APPROX. CAL/SERV.: 20

· · · · · · · · · · · · **Carrots Deluxe**

6 MEDIUM CARROTS, PARED IN THIN STRIPS
½ TEASPOON SALT
1 TABLESPOON MARGARINE
1 TABLESPOON CHOPPED CHIVES
1 TABLESPOON CHOPPED PARSLEY
1 TABLESPOON LEMON JUICE
2 TABLESPOONS WATER

Preheat oven to 350°F.

Melt margarine in a saucepan; add lemon juice.

Arrange carrots in layers in a baking dish.

Between each layer pour in the lemon juice and margarine mixture and sprinkle with chives and parsley. Add the water.

Cover and bake until the carrots are tender, about 50 minutes.

YIELD: 4 SERVINGS
APPROX. CAL/SERV.: 60

· · · · · · · · · · · · · **Herbed Kale**

2 POUNDS FRESH KALE; OR 2 10-OUNCE PACKAGES FROZEN LEAF KALE
2 TABLESPOONS CHOPPED ONION
¾ TEASPOON SALT
½ TEASPOON SUGAR
½ CUP WATER
½ TEASPOON GROUND MARJORAM
⅛ TEASPOON GROUND BLACK PEPPER
2 TABLESPOONS POLYUNSATURATED OIL

Recipe continues...

Wash kale and cut off all tough stems.

Place in a saucepan with water, onions, salt, marjoram, sugar, and black pepper.

Cover and cook for 10 minutes or until tender.

Add oil, mix well and serve. *(+ a little vinegar)*

YIELD: 6 SERVINGS

APPROX. CAL/SERV.: 75

· · · · · · · · · · *Cabbage and Sprouts*

    2 CUPS COARSELY SHREDDED RED CABBAGE

    2 CUPS MUNG BEAN SPROUTS

2–3 TABLESPOONS OIL

    1 TEASPOON ROSEMARY

Sauté the cabbage and sprouts in the oil until tender-crisp.
Sprinkle with rosemary and serve.

YIELD: 4 SERVINGS

APPROX. CAL/SERV.: 90

· · · · · · · · · · *Sweet 'n' Sour Beans*

    1 16-OUNCE CAN PINTO BEANS, DRAINED

    1 1-POUND 4½-OUNCE CAN UNSWEETENED PINEAPPLE CHUNKS

  ¼ CUP BROWN SUGAR

    2 TABLESPOONS CORNSTARCH

  ¼ CUP VINEGAR

    1 TABLESPOON SOY SAUCE

    1 CHICKEN BOUILLON CUBE

  ½ TEASPOON SALT

    1 MEDIUM GREEN PEPPER CUT INTO STRIPS

  ½ SMALL ONION THINLY SLICED INTO RINGS

Drain pineapple, reserving juice.

Combine brown sugar and cornstarch; add reserved pineapple juice, vinegar, soy sauce, salt and bouillon cube.

Cook and stir over medium heat till thick and bubbly.

Remove from heat.

Add drained beans, pineapple, green pepper, and onion.

Cook over low heat 2 to 3 minutes or till vegetables are tender-crisp.

Serve over cooked rice.

YIELD: 6 SERVINGS

APPROX. CAL/SERV.: 150 (250 WITH ½ CUP RICE)

Rice and Pasta

As basic as bread to the diet of man are two other foods originating in the grains and grasses of the field: pasta, in its infinite variety, and rice, a staple food of more than half the peoples of the world.

Two kinds of rice are generally used in cooking—the long grain and the oval short grain. Each cooks differently, the former having a dry fluffy consistency, the latter a wetter heavier quality more suitable to dishes such as Italian Osso Bucco.

Through polishing, a process that gives rice a longer storage life (just as wheat stores longer following removal of the germ), the bran, an important source of protein, vitamins and minerals, is removed. It is fortunate that these nutrients are preserved in precooked or converted rice. Only Vitamin B is replaced in rice that has been polished. Brown, or undermilled, rice is still the best bargain in flavor and nutrients.

Rice can take on the national character of any country with the addition of herbs and spices. It is delicious hot and often very good cold, marries beautifully with all meats and fish, beans, vegetables and even fruit. With the addition of sugar, nutmeg and raisins, it becomes a dessert.

Pasta is no less versatile, and comes in hundreds of delightful shapes. It is available very thin or very thick, short or long, tubular or solid.

Good quality pasta is made from semolina flour milled from durum wheat, a type of wheat that is low in starch. Egg noodles have egg yolks added and are not recommended for use as often as other pasta.

Pasta can be a meat meal, a vegetable meal, or a fish meal, depending on the sauce served with it. Tossed with oil and a low-fat cheese, it remains uniquely a pasta meal. Possibly no one has yet been able to count the recorded recipes for sauce combinations. They must number in thousands.

Like rice, pasta suggests many interesting ways of using leftovers and both make excellent additions to soups or salads. Bland but delicious appetite appeasers, they are difficult to resist, and have lured many a weakened will power to overindulgence at the table.

· · · · · · · · · · · · · Rice Mexicali

¼ CUP OIL
1 4-OUNCE CAN MUSHROOMS
½ CUP CHOPPED ONIONS
¼ CUP CHOPPED GREEN PEPPER
1 16-OUNCE CAN TOMATOES
½ CUP WATER
1 CUP UNCOOKED RICE
2 TABLESPOONS CHOPPED PARSLEY
1½ TEASPOONS SALT
PEPPER
¼ TEASPOON SWEET BASIL
¼ TEASPOON OREGANO

Heat oil in a large, deep skillet. Add mushrooms, onions and green pepper. Cook slowly until tender and lightly browned.

Add tomatoes and water. Bring to a boil and add rice and remaining ingredients. Reduce heat, cover and cook about 30 minutes, or until tender.

YIELD: 6 SERVINGS
APPROX. CAL/SERV.: 220

· · · · · · · · · · · Seasoned Rice Ring

Serve rice in this attractive way. Fill the center with chicken à la king, or another favorite meat dish.

1 TEASPOON SALT
3 CUPS WATER
2⅔ CUPS QUICK-COOKING RICE
2 TABLESPOONS PIMIENTO
2 TABLESPOONS MARGARINE

Put the salt in the water and bring to a boil. Add rice. Cover and remove from heat.

Let rice stand 5 minutes, then fluff with a fork. Stir in margarine and pimiento.

Pack the rice mixture firmly into a well-oiled 9-inch ring mold. Cover and allow to stand several minutes. Then invert onto a serving plate.

YIELD: 6 SERVINGS
APPROX. CAL/SERV.: 125

. . . . **Mexican Fried Rice**

2 TABLESPOONS OIL
1 CUP UNCOOKED RICE
1 CLOVE GARLIC, MINCED
½ CUP FINELY SLICED GREEN ONIONS
⅔ CUP CHOPPED CANNED CALIFORNIA CHILIES
½ CUP DICED FRESH TOMATOES
2 CUPS BOUILLON

Heat oil in a heavy skillet, and sauté the rice, stirring, until golden brown.

Add remaining ingredients. Cover and simmer slowly for 30 minutes.

YIELD: 6 SERVINGS
APPROX. CAL/SERV.: 170

. . . . **Pilaf**

2 CUPS LONG-GRAIN RICE
¼ CUP UNCOOKED VERMICELLI, BROKEN INTO 1- TO 2-INCH PIECES
½ CUP MARGARINE
5 CUPS CHICKEN BROTH
1 TEASPOON SALT
CINNAMON (OPTIONAL)

Brown the broken vermicelli in margarine until it takes on a golden brown color.

Recipe continues…

Add 2 cups of rice to the browned vermicelli and stir lightly until rice is crisp.

Add salt, and pour in the hot chicken broth; cover and steam over low heat for about 30 minutes.

Sprinkle cinnamon over the top before serving, if desired. This gives the pilaf a Middle Eastern flavor.

YIELD: 12 ½-CUP SERVINGS
APPROX. CAL/SERV.: 185

Risotto Milanese

2 TABLESPOONS MARGARINE
1½ CUPS LONG-GRAIN RICE
3 OR 4 GREEN ONIONS, FINELY CHOPPED
¼ CUP DRY WHITE WINE
½ CUP CHOPPED MUSHROOMS
PINCH TURMERIC OR SAFFRON
4 CUPS CHICKEN BOUILLON OR BROTH
1 TABLESPOON GRATED PARMESAN OR SAPSAGO CHEESE

Melt margarine in a heavy saucepan. Add rice and green onions and cook slowly, stirring with a wooden spoon, until rice is milky. Add wine and continue cooking and stirring until it is absorbed. Lower heat and stir in remaining ingredients. Cover and simmer slowly for about 20 minutes.

YIELD: 8 SERVINGS
APPROX. CAL/SERV.: 190

Wild Rice with Mushrooms

1 CUP WILD RICE OR LONG-GRAINED RICE AND WILD RICE COMBINED
⅓ CUP GREEN ONIONS OR SHALLOTS
1 CUP FRESH MUSHROOMS
FRESHLY GROUND PEPPER
2 TABLESPOONS OIL
1 TABLESPOON MARGARINE

Steam the rice or cook according to directions on package.

Sauté fresh mushrooms and green onions in the oil. Stir in margarine and freshly ground pepper. Serve hot.

YIELD: 6 SERVINGS

APPROX. CAL/SERV.: 190

. . . . **Beef Manicotti**

This recipe can be used as a tasty main dish, served with a green salad and zucchini.

. . . . *filling*

1 10-OUNCE PACKAGE FROZEN LEAF SPINACH

1 CLOVE GARLIC, MINCED

1 MEDIUM ONION, CHOPPED

2 TABLESPOONS OIL (1 TABLESPOON OLIVE OIL, 1 TABLESPOON OIL)

1 POUND LEAN GROUND ROUND

½ TEASPOON OREGANO

1 TEASPOON SALT

½ TEASPOON PEPPER

Cook spinach according to package directions. Drain and press water from spinach. Chop into large pieces.

Sauté garlic and onion in 2 tablespoons of oil for a few minutes. Brown the ground meat, breaking it up with a fork. Drain off fat. Add seasonings and spinach. Set aside.

Recipe continues...

· · · · · · · · · · · · · · · · · **sauce**

1 CLOVE GARLIC, MINCED
1 LARGE ONION, CHOPPED
2 TABLESPOONS OIL (1 TABLESPOON OLIVE OIL, 1 TABLESPOON OIL)
½ CUP CHOPPED FRESH PARSLEY
2 16-OUNCE CANS ITALIAN PLUM TOMATOES
1 6-OUNCE CAN TOMATO PASTE
1 6-OUNCE CAN TOMATO SAUCE
½ CUP RED WINE
1 TEASPOON BASIL LEAVES
1 TEASPOON SALT
½ TEASPOON PEPPER

To make the sauce, sauté garlic and onion in 2 tablespoons of the oil until soft but not browned.

Add all other ingredients. Stir, and simmer, uncovered for 20 to 30 minutes, or until thickened.

· · · · · · · · · · · · · · · · **pasta**

12 LARGE MANICOTTI SHELLS
1 CUP LOW-FAT COTTAGE CHEESE OR RICOTTA (MADE FROM PARTIALLY SKIMMED MILK)

Parboil 12 large manicotti shells until soft but not limp. Drain. Stuff with meat and spinach mixture.

Preheat oven to 350 degrees. Oil a shallow casserole dish and pour a little of the sauce in the bottom. Arrange shells in rows in the baking dish, filling spaces between with extra meat sauce. Spread cottage cheese over the top. Pour over the rest of the sauce and bake 20 minutes or until bubbly.

YIELD: 6 SERVINGS
APPROX. CAL/SERV.: 520

Chicken Spinach Manicotti

filling

2 CUPS COOKED CHICKEN MEAT
½ CUP WELL DRAINED, COOKED SPINACH
¼ POUND FRESH MUSHROOMS
⅓ CUP FRESHLY GRATED PARMESAN CHEESE
1 EGG
SALT AND PEPPER TO TASTE

Sauté the mushrooms in a little oil. Chop together with the chicken and spinach until fine. Stir in the Parmesan cheese, the egg, salt and pepper.

pasta

12 MANICOTTI TUBES, COOKED ACCORDING TO PACKAGE INSTRUCTIONS
Fill manicotti tubes and place in an oiled 11 × 7 inch shallow baking dish.

sauce

2 TABLESPOONS MELTED MARGARINE
1½ TABLESPOONS FLOUR
1 13-OUNCE CAN EVAPORATED SKIM MILK
2 TABLESPOONS PARMESAN CHEESE, GRATED
SALT, PEPPER AND NUTMEG TO TASTE

Blend flour and margarine. Cook one minute over moderate heat.
Gradually add the evaporated skim milk, stirring constantly with a whisk. Heat till sauce bubbles, then season with salt, pepper and nutmeg.
Remove from the heat and add the grated Parmesan cheese.
Preheat the oven to 375°F.

Recipe continues...

Pour sauce over manicotti. Sprinkle with ⅓ cup of grated parmesan cheese and bake 10 minutes or until cheese browns.

YIELD: 6 SERVINGS

APPROX. CAL/SERV.: 460

Spaghetti Sauce

1½ POUNDS LEAN GROUND BEEF

2 CUPS CHOPPED ONION

1 CUP CHOPPED GREEN PEPPER

2 CUPS CHOPPED CELERY

1 28-OUNCE CAN ITALIAN PLUM TOMATOES

1 6-OUNCE CAN TOMATO PASTE

2 TEASPOONS SALT

1 TEASPOON EACH BLACK PEPPER, OREGANO, BASIL LEAVES, AND GARLIC SALT

1 TABLESPOON WORCESTERSHIRE SAUCE

2–3 BAY LEAVES

Brown the ground meat in a large pot, stirring frequently. Add onions and when they are slightly brown, add pepper and celery, and cook slightly.

Add all other ingredients. Cover and simmer for 2 hours. Allow to cool, then place in the refrigerator overnight. Skim off the fat that hardens on the surface before reheating.

Cook spaghetti according to package directions. Serve with sauce on top. Sprinkle with Parmesan cheese, if desired.

YIELD: 8 SERVINGS

APPROX. CAL/SERV.: 255

. . . . **Mock Spaghetti**

1 POUND LEAN GROUND BEEF OR VEAL
½ POUND FRESH MUSHROOMS, SLICED
½ CUP CHOPPED ONION
1 8-OUNCE CAN TOMATO SAUCE
1 16-OUNCE CAN ITALIAN PLUM TOMATOES
1 CLOVE GARLIC, PRESSED
1½ TEASPOONS SEASONED SALT
DASH PEPPER
¼ TEASPOON OREGANO
1 TABLESPOON CHOPPED PARSLEY
1 POUND FRESH BEAN SPROUTS, COOKED TENDER-CRISP*

Brown meat in a large skillet. Pour off any fat and add mushrooms and onion. Cook until tender. Add the remaining ingredients except bean sprouts.

Simmer, covered, until sauce thickens. Serve over hot bean sprouts.

YIELD: 6 SERVINGS
APPROX. CAL/SERV.: 225

. . . . **Marinara Sauce**

2 TABLESPOONS OLIVE OIL
2 SMALL WHITE ONIONS, CHOPPED
2 SMALL CARROTS, CHOPPED
1 GARLIC CLOVE, MINCED
FRESHLY GROUND BLACK PEPPER
2 2-POUND 3-OUNCE CANS ITALIAN PLUM TOMATOES
1½ TEASPOONS SALT
3 TABLESPOONS MARGARINE
¼ TEASPOON DRIED HOT RED PEPPER

Sauté the onions, carrots, and garlic in oil until onions are soft. Grind in the black pepper and add the tomatoes. Stir the sauce well, add salt, and cook, uncovered, for 20 minutes.

* Canned bean sprouts may be substituted for fresh.

Recipe continues…

Pass the sauce through a food mill or sieve.

Melt margarine in a pan and add the strained sauce. Cook 15 minutes, stirring often.

YIELD: 1 QUART

APPROX. CAL/SERV.: ½ CUP = 130

· · · · · · · · · · · · · *variation*

WITH MEAT: Brown 1 pound of lean ground beef in a skillet and add to the sauce after sauce has been strained. Simmer 20 or 30 minutes.

APPROX. CAL/SERV.: 255

· · · · · · · · · *Green Sauce for Spaghetti*

  2 CUPS SPINACH LEAVES (WASHED, BUT NOT DRIED, AND PACKED FIRMLY)

  ½ CUP FRESH PARSLEY LEAVES (WASHED, BUT NOT DRIED, AND PACKED FIRMLY)

  2 GARLIC CLOVES

  ½ CUP MARGARINE

  ¼ CUP OLIVE OIL

  ½ CUP PINE NUTS

  ¼ CUP WALNUT MEATS

  ½ CUP FRESHLY GRATED ROMANO CHEESE

  ½ CUP FRESHLY GRATED PARMESAN CHEESE

1½ TEASPOONS SALT

  1 TEASPOON DRIED BASIL

Combine all ingredients in a blender. Blend on high speed until mixture is almost puréed, but still has flecks of spinach and parsley. If too thick, add a small amount of water.

Toss with 1 pound of cooked spaghetti. The heat from the spaghetti warms the sauce.

YIELD: 6 SERVINGS

APPROX. CAL/SERV.: 740

· · · · · · · · ·   *White Clam Sauce*

¼ CUP MARGARINE
1 CLOVE GARLIC, MINCED
2 TABLESPOONS FLOUR
2 CUPS CLAM JUICE
¼ CUP CHOPPED PARSLEY
SALT AND FRESHLY GROUND BLACK PEPPER TO TASTE
1½ TEASPOONS DRIED THYME
2 CUPS MINCED CLAMS, FRESH OR CANNED

In a saucepan, cook the garlic in the margarine for 1 minute over moderate heat. With a wire whisk, stir in the flour and clam juice.

Add the parsley, salt, pepper and thyme; simmer gently for 10 minutes. Add minced clams and heat through. Serve over linguine or spaghetti.

YIELD: 4 SERVINGS
APPROX. CAL/SERV.: 210

Breads

*T*here are several good reasons for making your own bread. Anyone who has ever taken a golden loaf fresh from the oven knows that special joy of eating the first warm slice, and breathing its heady fragrance.

Beyond the earthy pleasures of savoring the flavor, aroma and texture of homemade bread, the best reason for doing your own baking is knowing that the product is thoroughly edible, comprising purely nutritious ingredients with names a child could understand. Children can smell a fresh loaf down the block. If you want company, leave the kitchen door open and a pot of jam on the table.

Bread is a source of vitamins, minerals and protein, particularly when made of whole grain flour.

The saturated fat and cholesterol content of a loaf increases when eggs and milk are ingredients, but each slice will contain only a fraction of the total. The following recipes call for polyunsaturated oils and skim milk. An effort has been made, where possible, to cut down on whole eggs in favor of egg whites. There are recipes for crusty baked breads, quick breads and breads containing fruit, nuts and herbs.

Some tips for perfect bread making: When using active dry yeast, dissolve it in warm (110°F. to 115°F.) liquid; dissolve compressed (moist) yeast in lukewarm (85°F.) liquid. Use enough flour to make a very soft, but not a sticky dough (this requires more flour in humid weather, less in dry weather). Let dough rise in a warm, humid place away from drafts (ideal rising temperature is 80°F. to 85°F.).

When using a glass baking dish, lower the baking temperature by 25 degrees. For example, when a recipe specifies a metal pan with a baking temperature of 350°F., use 325°F. for a glass dish.

If you use whole grain flour, buy it in small quantities and store it tightly covered in the refrigerator or freezer. Enriched flour, less nourishing than whole grain flour despite its name, has a longer shelf life and need not be refrigerated.

In all seasons, bread making is a most satisfying occupation, a form of cookery rooted in the ages and as basic as the land itself, at once an experience to raise the spirit, calm the soul and warm the stomach.

· · · · · · · · · · · · Corn Bread Muffins

1 CUP SIFTED FLOUR
¾ CUP YELLOW CORN MEAL
½ TEASPOON SALT
2½ TEASPOONS BAKING POWDER
2 TABLESPOONS SUGAR
1 EGG
1 CUP SKIM MILK
¼ CUP OIL

Preheat the oven to 425°F.

Sift together the flour, corn meal, salt, baking powder and sugar.

Add the egg, milk and oil stirring quickly and lightly until mixed. Do not beat.

From the bowl, dip the batter into oiled 2¼-inch muffin tins (or an 8 × 8-inch pan or corn-stick pans), filling each cup ⅔ full.

Bake 20 to 30 minutes, or until golden brown.

YIELD: 12 2¼-INCH MUFFINS
APPROX. CAL/SERV.: 130

· · · · · · · · Corn Meal-Whole Wheat Muffins

6 TABLESPOONS OIL
⅓ CUP SUGAR
1¼ CUPS SKIM MILK
1 EGG
1 CUP WHOLE WHEAT FLOUR
½ TEASPOON SALT
4 TEASPOONS BAKING POWDER
1 CUP CORN MEAL

Preheat oven to 425°F. Oil muffin tins.

Mix together the oil and the sugar, then add milk and egg stirring until mixed. In a large mixing bowl, combine flour, salt and baking powder. Add the liquid to the flour mixture, stirring quickly and lightly until mixed. Do not beat. Stir the corn meal into the batter until mixed. From the bowl, dip the batter into oiled muffin tins, filling each cup ⅔ full.

Bake 25 minutes.

YIELD: 12 2½-INCH OR 18 2¼-INCH MUFFINS
APPROX. CAL/SERV.: 1 2½-INCH MUFFIN = 170
 1 2¼-INCH MUFFIN = 115

· · · · · · · · · · · **Banana Bread**

1½ CUPS ALL-PURPOSE FLOUR
 ½ CUP SUGAR
 2 TEASPOONS BAKING POWDER
 1 TEASPOON BAKING SODA
 ½ TEASPOON SALT
 ½ CUP WHEAT GERM
 3 MEDIUM, VERY RIPE BANANAS, MASHED (ABOUT 1 CUP)
 ¼ CUP BUTTERMILK
 ¼ CUP OIL
 4 EGG WHITES

Preheat the oven to 350°F.

Sift together the flour, sugar, baking powder, baking soda and salt. Mix in the wheat germ.

Add all remaining ingredients and beat until well blended.

Place in an oiled 8 × 4-inch loaf pan.

Bake in a moderate oven for about 1 hour, or until done.

YIELD: 1 LOAF (16 SLICES)
APPROX. CAL/SERV.: 1 SLICE = 130

. . . . **Savory Walnut Bread**

2 CUPS SIFTED FLOUR
2 TEASPOONS BAKING POWDER
¼ TEASPOON BAKING SODA
½ TEASPOON SALT
½ CUP LIGHT BROWN SUGAR, FIRMLY PACKED
1 EGG
1 CUP SKIM MILK
¾ CUP GRATED WALNUTS

Preheat the oven to 350°F.

Sift together the flour, baking powder, baking soda, salt, and brown sugar. Beat the egg until thick and lemon-colored. Beat the milk into the egg. Add the sifted dry ingredients and grated walnuts, stirring until the mixture is moist.

Turn into a greased 8 × 4-inch loaf pan. Bake until a cake tester or a wooden toothpick inserted in the center comes out clean, about 40 minutes. Loosen the loaf from sides of pan with spatula. Turn out right side up on a wire rack to cool.

YIELD: 1 LOAF (16 SLICES)
APPROX. CAL/SERV.: 1 SLICE = 125

. . . . **Orange Wheat Bread**

2 CUPS WHITE FLOUR
½ CUP WHOLE WHEAT FLOUR
½ CUP WHEAT GERM
½ CUP SUGAR
1 TABLESPOON BAKING POWDER
½ TEASPOON BAKING SODA
1 CUP ORANGE JUICE
⅓ CUP OIL
1 EGG, BEATEN
½ CUP WALNUTS, CHOPPED AND DUSTED LIGHTLY WITH FLOUR
2 TABLESPOONS GRATED ORANGE RIND

Preheat oven to 350°F.

Measure dry ingredients and mix together in a large bowl. Add remaining ingredients and stir until moist.

Pour into a greased 9 × 5-inch loaf pan.

Bake for 55 minutes, or until a wooden toothpick inserted in the center of the loaf comes out clean.

Remove from pan immediately. To store, wrap securely in foil or plastic.

YIELD: 1 LOAF (16 SLICES)

APPROX. CAL/SERV.: 1 SLICE = 180

Pumpkin-Pecan Bread

This moist, flavorful bread is a winner any time of the day. It makes an especially good snack.

3½ CUPS FLOUR

2 TEASPOONS BAKING SODA

1½ TEASPOONS SALT

1½ TEASPOONS CINNAMON

1 TEASPOON NUTMEG

1 CUP SUGAR

1 CUP OIL

4 EGGS

⅔ CUP WATER

2 CUPS CANNED PUMPKIN

1 CUP CHOPPED PECANS

Preheat the oven to 350°F.

Sift together the flour, soda, salt, cinnamon and nutmeg. Add sugar and stir to mix thoroughly.

Make a well in the center of the dry ingredients and add all at once the oil, eggs, water and pumpkin. Mix well and add the nuts.

Pour batter into four 8 × 4-inch loaf pans, filling each ½ full.

Bake for 1 hour, or until a wooden toothpick inserted in the center of the loaf comes out clean.

YIELD: 4 LOAVES (16 SLICES EACH)

APPROX. CAL/SERV.: 1 SLICE = 85

Applesauce-Nut Bread

¾ CUP GRANULATED SUGAR
1 CUP APPLESAUCE
⅓ CUP OIL
2 EGGS
3 TABLESPOONS SKIM MILK
2 CUPS SIFTED ALL-PURPOSE FLOUR
1 TEASPOON BAKING SODA
½ TEASPOON BAKING POWDER
½ TEASPOON GROUND CINNAMON
¼ TEASPOON SALT
¼ TEASPOON GROUND NUTMEG
¾ CUP CHOPPED PECANS

Preheat oven to 350°F.

In a large mixing bowl, combine sugar, applesauce, oil, eggs and milk. Mix together thoroughly.

Sift together the flour, soda, baking powder, cinnamon, salt and nutmeg. Beat dry ingredients into the applesauce mixture until well combined. Stir in the pecans.

Turn the batter into well-oiled 9 × 5-inch loaf pan.

topping

¼ CUP BROWN SUGAR
½ TEASPOON GROUND CINNAMON
¼ CUP CHOPPED PECANS

Combine the brown sugar, cinnamon and pecans. Sprinkle evenly over the batter, and bake for 1 hour. Cap loosely with foil after the first 30 minutes of baking. When done, remove from the pan and cool on a rack.

YIELD: 1 LOAF (16 SLICES)
APPROX. CAL/SERV.: 215

. . . . *Applesauce-Raisin Bread*

 1 CUP APPLESAUCE
 ½ CUP OIL
 ½ CUP SUGAR
 1¾ CUPS FLOUR, SIFTED
 1 TEASPOON BAKING SODA
 ½ TEASPOON SALT
 1 TEASPOON CINNAMON
 ½ TEASPOON CLOVES
 ½ TEASPOON NUTMEG
 1 EGG, SLIGHTLY BEATEN
 1 CUP RAISINS

Preheat the oven to 325°F.

Mix the applesauce, oil and sugar.

Sift in the flour, baking soda, salt, cinnamon, cloves and nutmeg. Mix well after each addition.

Add the slightly beaten egg and the raisins. Mix, then pour into a greased and floured 8 × 4-inch loaf pan. Bake 1 hour and 20 minutes, or until done.

YIELD: 1 LOAF (16 SLICES)
APPROX. CAL/SERV.: 1 SLICE = 180

. . . . *Whole Wheat Muffins*

 1 CUP WHOLE WHEAT FLOUR
 1 CUP SIFTED ALL-PURPOSE FLOUR
 ½ TEASPOON SALT
 2½ TEASPOONS BAKING POWDER
 3 TABLESPOONS SUGAR
 1 EGG
 1 CUP SKIM MILK
 ½ CUP OIL

Preheat oven to 425°F.

Grease the muffin tins lightly with oil.

Recipe continues...

Sift the two kinds of flour together with the salt, baking powder and sugar.

Add the egg, milk and oil. Stir quickly only until barely blended. Do not beat.

Fill each muffin tin ⅔ full of batter. Bake 20 to 25 minutes.

YIELD: 12 2¼-INCH MUFFINS

APPROX. CAL/SERV.: 175

• • • • • • • • • • • • • • *variation*

WHOLE WHEAT-NUT MUFFINS: Add ½ cup of coarsely chopped walnuts with the egg, milk and oil.

APPROX. CAL/SERV.: 205

• • • • • • • • • • • • • • *Muffins*

2 CUPS SIFTED ALL-PURPOSE FLOUR

3 TEASPOONS BAKING POWDER

2 TABLESPOONS SUGAR

1 TEASPOON SALT

⅓ CUP OIL

1 EGG, WELL BEATEN; OR 2 EGG WHITES, SLIGHTLY BEATEN

1¼ CUPS SKIM MILK

Preheat oven to 425°F.

Sift dry ingredients together. Make a well and put into it all at once the oil, egg and milk. Stir only enough to dampen the flour. Batter should be lumpy.

Fill lightly oiled muffin tins, ⅔ full with the batter. Bake 20 to 25 minutes.

YIELD: 12 2¼-INCH MUFFINS

APPROX. CAL/SERV.: 145

• • • • • • • • • • • • • • *variations*

FRUIT MUFFINS: Add ½ cup of raisins, chopped dates or drained blueberries to the batter.

JELLY MUFFINS: Fill muffin cups ⅓ full and place a small spoonful of jam or jelly in the center of each. Then cover with remaining batter.

NUT MUFFINS: Add ½ cup of coarsely chopped pecans or walnuts to the batter.

APPROX. CAL/SERV.: 1 RAISIN OR DATE MUFFIN = 165

1 BLUEBERRY MUFFIN = 150

1 JELLY OR NUT MUFFIN = 175

. . . . *Boston Brown Bread*

1 15-OUNCE BOX RAISINS
3 CUPS WATER
¾ CUP SUGAR
¼ CUP MARGARINE
2 EGGS
2 TEASPOONS VANILLA
5 CUPS SIFTED FLOUR
4 TEASPOONS BAKING SODA
1 TEASPOON SALT
½ CUP CHOPPED NUTS (OPTIONAL)

Preheat oven to 350°F.

In a saucepan, cover raisins with water and bring to a boil. Set aside to cool.

Cream the margarine and sugar. Beat in the eggs and vanilla.

Sift together the flour, baking soda and salt. Alternately add the raisins and the flour mixture to the liquid.

Mix in the nuts. Oil four 1-pound coffee cans and divide the batter among them. They should each be about ½ full. Bake for 1 hour.

Turn out on a rack to cool.

YIELD: 4 LOAVES (16 SLICES EACH)

APPROX. CAL/SERV.: 1 SLICE = 70   1 SLICE WITH NUTS = 75

· · · · · · · · · · · · · *Hobo Bread*

2 CUPS RAISINS
2 CUPS BOILING WATER
4 TEASPOONS BAKING SODA
4 CUPS FLOUR
1 CUP SUGAR
½ TEASPOON SALT
¼ CUP OIL

Put raisins in a large pot that has a tight-fitting lid. Pour in boiling water to cover. Stir in the baking soda. Cover tightly and let stand overnight.

Preheat oven to 350°F.

Prepare three 1-pound coffee cans by oiling them and coating with flour.

Combine flour, sugar and salt. Add the oil and the flour mixture, 1 cup at a time, to the raisins, stirring well after each addition.

Fill the prepared cans ½ full with the batter. Bake 70 minutes. Remove from the oven and let stand 5 to 10 minutes. Run a knife around the edge of each can to loosen loaf and shake out.

YIELD: 3 LOAVES (16 SLICES EACH)
APPROX. CAL/SERV.: 1 SLICE = 80

· · · · · · · · · · · · *Raisin-Bran Bread*

1 CUP SUGAR
3 CUPS ALL-PURPOSE FLOUR
2 TEASPOONS BAKING SODA
1 TEASPOON SALT
2 CUPS ALL-BRAN CEREAL
1 CUP RAISINS OR CURRANTS
½ CUP CHOPPED NUTS (OPTIONAL)
2 CUPS BUTTERMILK

Preheat the oven to 300°F.

Sift the first 4 ingredients several times to mix thoroughly.

Add the all-bran, then the raisins and nuts. Stir in the buttermilk. Bake in two 8 × 4-inch loaf pans for 1 hour.

YIELD: 2 LOAVES (16 SLICES EACH)
APPROX. CAL/SERV.: 1 SLICE = 95   1 SLICE WITH NUTS = 105

. . . . *Dutch Honey Bread*

A flavorful hint of gingerbread distinguishes this earthy loaf.

2 CUPS UNSIFTED ALL-PURPOSE FLOUR
¼ CUP BROWN SUGAR
1 TABLESPOON BAKING POWDER
1 TEASPOON BAKING SODA
2 TEASPOONS CINNAMON
¼ TEASPOON CLOVES
¼ TEASPOON NUTMEG
¼ TEASPOON SALT
1 CUP BUTTERMILK
1 WELL-BEATEN EGG
¼ CUP HONEY

Preheat oven to 350°F.

Mix all dry ingredients together. Add the buttermilk, egg and honey; blend well.

Pour into an oiled 9 × 5-inch loaf pan and bake 45 to 60 minutes. When done, this bread has a very firm crust.

YIELD: 1 LOAF (16 SLICES)
APPROX. CAL/SERV.: 1 SLICE = 90

. . . . *Cold Oven Popovers*

6 EGG WHITES
3 TABLESPOONS OIL
1 TABLESPOON MELTED MARGARINE
2 CUPS SKIM MILK
2 CUPS SIFTED FLOUR
½ TEASPOON SALT

Recipe continues...

Beat the egg whites lightly with a fork, and combine with the oil, margarine and milk.

Place the flour and salt in a large mixing bowl; add liquids gradually, beating with an electric mixer until well blended. Then mix on high speed for a minute or two.

Thoroughly oil 12 large or 18 medium custard cups. Fill each ½ full of batter and place in a *cold* oven. Turn oven on to 400°F. and leave popovers in for 45 to 60 minutes, or until done.

YIELD: 12 LARGE OR 18 MEDIUM POPOVERS
APPROX. CAL/SERV.: 1 LARGE POPOVER = 130
1 MEDIUM POPOVER = 90

Flaky Biscuits

2 CUPS SIFTED FLOUR
3 TEASPOONS BAKING POWDER
½ TEASPOON SALT
¼ CUP OIL
⅔ CUP SKIM MILK

Preheat the oven to 475°F.

Sift flour, baking powder, and salt together into a mixing bowl.

Pour oil or melted shortening and milk into one measuring cup but do not stir. Add all at once to flour mixture. Stir quickly with a fork until dough clings together.

Knead the dough lightly about 10 times.

Place the dough on a piece of waxed paper 12 inches by 16 inches. Pat dough out to about ½ inch thick. Cut with unfloured medium-sized cookie cutter.

Place biscuits on ungreased cookie sheet and bake for 12–15 minutes.

YIELD: 12 2-INCH BISCUITS
APPROX. CAL/SERV.: 115

. . . . *Drop Biscuits*

2 CUPS FLOUR
1 TABLESPOON BAKING POWDER
1 TEASPOON SALT
⅓ CUP MARGARINE
1 CUP SKIM MILK

[handwritten: 2 C / 4 t BP / 1 stick rm temp butter / mix / add 3/4 c milk]

Preheat the oven to 450°F.

Mix the dry ingredients and cut in the margarine with 2 knives or a pastry blender. Stir in the milk. Drop batter by teaspoonfuls, 1 inch apart, onto a greased cookie sheet.

Bake for 10 to 12 minutes.

YIELD: 12 BISCUITS
APPROX. CAL/SERV.: 120

. . . . *variation*

Add any one of the following to the dry ingredients: dried parsley, basil, tarragon or anise seed.

. . . . *Basic Bread*

1 CAKE YEAST OR 2 ENVELOPES DRY YEAST
¼ CUP LUKEWARM WATER
1¾ CUPS SKIM MILK
2½ TABLESPOONS SUGAR
1 TEASPOON SALT
6 CUPS SIFTED FLOUR
2 TABLESPOONS OIL

Dissolve the yeast in the lukewarm water.

Mix the sugar and milk together and stir into the dissolved yeast. To this mixture, add the salt and 3 cups of flour. Beat until smooth. Add the oil.

Recipe continues…

Gradually mix in the remaining flour until the dough is stiff enough to handle. Knead it until it is smooth and elastic. Place dough in a greased bowl, turning to coat all sides with oil. Cover with a clean cloth and let rise in a warm place (about 85°F.) until double in bulk.

Divide into 2 equal parts. Shape into loaves, and place into two 10 × 5-inch loaf pans. Cover and let rise again until doubled in bulk.

Bake in a preheated oven at 425°F. for 15 minutes. Reduce heat to 375°F. and continue baking 30 minutes longer. Remove bread from pans and place on wire racks to cool.

YIELD: 2 1-POUND LOAVES (16 SLICES EACH)
APPROX. CAL/SERV.: 1 SLICE = 95

· · · · · · · · · · · · · · · *variation*

HERB BREAD: Mix the following herbs into the dough just before kneading: ½ teaspoon of nutmeg, ¼ teaspoon each of thyme and rosemary, 2 teaspoons of caraway seed.

· · · · · · · · · · · . *Cinnamon Bread*

1 RECIPE FOR BASIC BREAD (p. 311)
2 TABLESPOONS MARGARINE, MELTED
½ CUP SUGAR
1 TABLESPOON CINNAMON

Make dough for Basic Bread and let rise the first time.

Roll out dough and spread with ½ of the margarine. Mix the sugar and cinnamon together and sprinkle over the dough, reserving 1 tablespoon for topping.

Roll dough lengthwise like a jelly roll. Shape into a loaf and cut in 2 parts.

Pinch the ends together and tuck under. Place into two oiled 10 × 5-inch loaf pans and spread a little margarine over the top.

Let rise until doubled in bulk. Sprinkle each loaf with the remaining ½ tablespoon of cinnamon and sugar mixture. Bake in a preheated oven at 375°F. for 50 minutes. Remove loaves from pans and cool on a wire rack.

YIELD: 2 1-POUND LOAVES (16 SLICES EACH)
APPROX. CAL/SERV.: 1 SLICE = 115

Fruit Loaf

1 RECIPE FOR BASIC BREAD (p. 311)
½ CUP SEEDLESS RAISINS
½ CUP CHOPPED WALNUTS
¼ CUP CANDIED ORANGE PEEL
¼ CUP CHOPPED CANDIED CHERRIES
¼ CUP CONFECTIONERS' SUGAR
1 TABLESPOON WARM WATER
1–2 DROPS ALMOND OR VANILLA EXTRACT

Make dough for Basic Bread.

Mix together the raisins, walnuts and candied fruit; knead the mixture into the Basic Bread dough. Shape into two 9-inch greased round pans or ring molds. Cover and let rise in a warm place until doubled in bulk. Bake in a preheated oven at 350°F. for 1¼ hours.

To make the frosting, mix together the confectioners' sugar, warm water and extract. Use to frost the bread while loaves are still warm.

YIELD: 2 1-POUND LOAVES (16 SLICES EACH)
APPROX. CAL/SERV.: 1 SLICE = 130

· · · · · · · · · · · · · · *Dilly Bread*

1 PACKAGE DRY YEAST
¼ CUP WARM WATER
1 CUP LOW-FAT COTTAGE CHEESE, HEATED TO LUKEWARM
1 TABLESPOON MARGARINE
2 TABLESPOONS SUGAR
1 TEASPOON SALT
1 TABLESPOON MINCED ONION
2 TEASPOONS DILL SEED
¼ TEASPOON BAKING SODA
2½ CUPS ALL-PURPOSE FLOUR

Soften the yeast in the warm water and combine with the cottage cheese.

Add sugar and all other ingredients except the flour. Gradually mix in the flour to form a stiff dough and beat well. Let rise in a warm place about 60 minutes or until doubled in bulk.

Punch the dough down and put in well-oiled 2-quart round casserole dish or a 9 × 5-inch loaf pan.

Cover and let rise about 40 minutes.

Preheat oven to 350°F.

Bake for 40–50 minutes. Brush with melted margarine while still hot. Cool 5 minutes before removing from pan.

YIELD: 1 9 × 5-INCH LOAF (16 SLICES)
APPROX. CAL/SERV.: 1 SLICE = 90

· · · · · · · · · · · · · *Oatmeal Bread*

1½ CUPS BOILING WATER
1 CUP ROLLED OATS
1 TEASPOON SALT
⅓ CUP LIGHT MOLASSES
1½ TABLESPOONS OIL
1 PACKAGE DRY YEAST
¼ CUP WARM WATER
4–4½ CUPS ALL-PURPOSE FLOUR, SIFTED

Pour the boiling water over the oatmeal. Add the salt, stir, and cool to lukewarm. Dissolve the yeast in the warm water, then add molasses, oil and dissolved yeast to the oatmeal mixture and gradually add the sifted flour until the dough is stiff enough to handle. Knead the dough on a lightly floured board for about 5 minutes or until dough is smooth and elastic.

Place dough in a lighty oiled bowl, turning to coat all sides of the dough with oil. Cover with a clean cloth and let rise in a warm place (about 85°F.) until double in bulk.

Punch down the dough and knead again for a few minutes.

Shape into a loaf and put it in a well-oiled 9 × 5-inch loaf pan. Cover and let rise again (about 1 hour) until doubled in bulk.

Bake in a preheated oven at 375°F. for 50 minutes. Remove bread from pan and place on a wire rack to cool.

YIELD: 1 LOAF (16 SLICES)
APPROX. CAL/SERV.: 1 SLICE = 150

· · · · · · · · · · · · *variation*

A ¼ cup of wheat germ and/or ½ cup of seedless raisins may be added.

APPROX. CAL/SERV.: 1 SLICE = 170

· · · · · · · ***Rapid Mix Cornell Yeast Bread***

1 ENVELOPE DRY YEAST
6 TABLESPOONS SOY FLOUR
2½ TABLESPOONS SUGAR
1 TEASPOON SALT
2 TABLESPOONS WHEAT GERM
6 TABLESPOONS NONFAT DRY MILK
5–6 CUPS ALL-PURPOSE FLOUR
2 TABLESPOONS MARGARINE
2 CUPS SKIM MILK

Mix the yeast with 2 cups of all-purpose flour, sugar, salt, wheat germ, nonfat dry milk and soy flour.

Recipe continues…

Heat milk and margarine over low heat until it reaches 120°–130°F., (use a cooking thermometer to check temperature) then add the mixture to dry ingredients. Beat for 2 minutes with an electric mixer, scraping the sides of the bowl occasionally.

Stir in ½ cup of flour or enough flour to make a thick batter, then keep working in the rest of the flour until the dough is stiff enough to handle.

Turn out onto a floured board; cover and let rest for 10 minutes. Knead the dough until it is blistered and pliable.

Shape dough into a ball. Place in an oiled bowl turning to coat all sides of the dough with oil. Cover with a clean cloth and let rise in a warm place, (about 85°F.) until double in bulk.

Turn onto lightly floured board. Cover and let rest for 10 minutes.

Shape into 3 round loaves or place in three 8 × 4-inch loaf pans. Cover and let rise again until double in bulk.

Bake in a preheated oven at 375°F. for 40 to 50 minutes.

Brush the tops of the hot loaves with margarine.

Remove bread from pans and place on wire racks to cool.

YIELD: 3 LOAVES (16 SLICES EACH)
APPROX. CAL/SERV.: 1 SLICE = 65

· · · · · · *Joan's Cornell Whole Wheat Bread*

   3 CUPS WARM WATER
   2 PACKAGES YEAST, COMPRESSED OR DRY
   2 TABLESPOONS HONEY
   3 CUPS WHOLE WHEAT FLOUR
3½ CUPS UNBLEACHED ALL-PURPOSE FLOUR
1½ TABLESPOONS WHEAT GERM
  ½ CUP SOY FLOUR (STIR BEFORE MEASURING)
  ¾ CUP NONFAT DRY MILK
   4 TEASPOONS SALT
   2 EGGS
   2 TABLESPOONS OIL

In a large bowl dissolve yeast in the warm water, add honey and let stand for 5 minutes. Sift together 3 cups of whole wheat flour, 3½ cups all-purpose flour, wheat germ, soy flour, and nonfat dry milk.

Stir into the yeast mixture, the salt, eggs and ¾ of the flour mixture. Beat with an electric mixer for about 5 minutes. Add the oil and the remainder of the flour mixture. Work the flour in thoroughly. Add additional flour if necessary until the dough is stiff enough to handle.

Turn dough onto a floured board and knead until it is smooth and elastic. Place dough in an oiled bowl, turning to coat all sides with oil. Cover with a clean damp cloth and let rise in a warm place (about 85°F.) until double in bulk. Punch down, fold over the edges and turn upside down in the bowl. Cover and allow to rise for another 20 minutes. Turn dough onto a lightly floured board. Divide into 3 equal portions. Fold each into the center to make a smooth tight ball. Cover with cloth and let rest for 10 more minutes.

Shape into 3 loaves, and place in oiled 8 × 4-inch loaf pans. Or form into rolls. Let rise until double in bulk.

Bake in a preheated oven at 350°F. for 50–60 minutes.

Remove bread from pans, brush with margarine if a softer crust is desired, and place on a wire rack to cool.

YIELD: 3 LOAVES (16 SLICES EACH)
APPROX. CAL/SERV.: 1 SLICE = 75

Anadama Bread

2 CUPS BOILING WATER
½ CUP YELLOW CORN MEAL
1 TEASPOON SALT
¼ POUND MARGARINE
1 PACKAGE DRY YEAST
½ CUP LUKEWARM WATER
¾ CUP MOLASSES
6 TABLESPOONS NONFAT DRY MILK
6 TABLESPOONS SOY FLOUR
2 TABLESPOONS WHEAT GERM
6 TO 7 CUPS UNBLEACHED ALL-PURPOSE FLOUR

Thoroughly mix boiling water, cornmeal, salt and margarine. Let cool to lukewarm. Dissolve the yeast in the lukewarm water, then add it and the molasses to the cornmeal mixture. Stir until well mixed.

Recipe continues...

Combine nonfat dry milk, soy flour and wheat germ with ½ of the all-purpose flour. Add 1 cup at a time to the cornmeal mixture. Beat well after each addition. Add the rest of flour 1 cup at a time until the dough is stiff enough to handle.

Turn out onto a floured board, cover with a clean cloth and let rest 5 minutes. Knead dough until it is smooth and elastic. Place dough in large oiled bowl, turning to coat all sides with oil. Cover with a cloth and let rise in warm place (85°F.) until double in bulk.

Divide into 2 equal parts. Shape into loaves and place in two 8 × 4-inch loaf pans. Lightly oil tops, then cover and let rise again until double in bulk. Bake in a preheated oven at 350°F. for 40–50 minutes.

Remove bread from pans and place on wire rack to cool.

YIELD: 2 LOAVES (16 SLICES EACH)
APPROX. CAL/SERV.: 1 SLICE = 150

· · · · · · **Quick and Easy Refrigerator Rolls**

This dough makes good cinnamon rolls or coffee rings.

2 EGG WHITES, SLIGHTLY BEATEN
½ CUP OIL
½ CUP SUGAR
1 PACKAGE YEAST DISSOLVED IN ¼ CUP WARM WATER
1 TEASPOON SALT
1 CUP LUKEWARM WATER
4 CUPS UNSIFTED ALL-PURPOSE FLOUR

Stir ingredients together in the order given above. Refrigerate dough at least 12 hours. (Dough may be kept in refrigerator several days.)

Roll dough into your favorite shape on a lightly floured board and let rise 2 hours before baking.

Bake in a preheated oven at 375°F. for 10 minutes.

YIELD: 3 DOZEN ROLLS
APPROX. CAL/SERV.: 1 ROLL = 85

. . . . *Southern Raised Biscuits*

2 ½ CUPS ALL-PURPOSE FLOUR
  ½ TEASPOON BAKING SODA
  ½ TEASPOON SALT
  ¼ CUP SUGAR
  5 TABLESPOONS OIL
  1 CAKE YEAST
  1 CUP BUTTERMILK, WARMED

Mix together the dry ingredients. Dissolve the yeast in slightly warmed buttermilk. Combine dry ingredients, oil, yeast and buttermilk, stirring lightly and quickly until mixed.

Turn onto a lightly floured board and knead gently about 20–30 times. Roll out or pat to a ¼-inch thickness. Cut with a floured 1-inch biscuit cutter, then brush each biscuit with oil. Place a biscuit on top of each biscuit on an ungreased baking sheet.

Cover and let rise in a warm place (about 85°F.) for about 2 hours. Bake in a preheated oven at 375°F. for 12–15 minutes.

YIELD: ABOUT 30 1-INCH BISCUITS
APPROX. CAL/SERV.: 65

. . . . *Apple Muffins*

  6 TABLESPOONS OIL
  ⅓ CUP SUGAR
  1 EGG
1 ½ CUPS SKIM MILK
  1 CUP WHOLE WHEAT FLOUR
  1 CUP BUCKWHEAT FLOUR
  ¾ TEASPOON SALT
  4 TEASPOONS BAKING POWDER
  ¾ TEASPOON CINNAMON
  ¼ TEASPOON NUTMEG
  1 LARGE APPLE, CHOPPED

Recipe continues...

Preheat oven to 400°F.

Stir together oil, sugar, egg and milk.

Mix together the dry ingredients.

Add liquid mixture to dry ingredients, stirring only enough to moisten the flour, then add the chopped apple.

Dip the batter into oiled 2½-inch muffin tins, filling each cup ⅔ full. Bake for 20–25 minutes.

YIELD: 18 2½-INCH MUFFINS

APPROX. CAL/SERV.: 115

Judy's Brown Bread

1½ CUPS CURRANTS OR RAISINS
2 TABLESPOONS OIL
2 TEASPOONS BAKING SODA
1 CUP BOILING WATER
⅔ CUP BROWN SUGAR
2 CUPS WHOLE WHEAT FLOUR
1 EGG, WELL BEATEN
¾ CUP CHOPPED NUTS (OPTIONAL)

Preheat the oven to 350°F.

Mix the dried fruit, oil and baking soda with the boiling water.

Let stand until cool.

Beat in the sugar, flour and egg.

Turn into a well-oiled 8 × 4-inch loaf pan and bake 40 to 45 minutes.

YIELD: 1 LOAF (16 SLICES)

APPROX. CAL/SERV.: 1 SLICE = 150   1 SLICE WITH NUTS = 185

Chapati

Try chapati if you want something different when you cook outdoors. Let each person throw his own chapati on the coals. This is strictly an outdoor recipe.

2 CUPS WHOLE WHEAT FLOUR

2 TABLESPOONS RICE FLOUR

Combine and sift the flours. Add enough water to make a stiff dough and set aside for 1 hour.

Knead with a little water until soft, divide into small balls and roll into very thin pancakes 4 to 6 inches in diameter, or use a tortilla press.

Cook on a lightly oiled griddle until half done on one side. Turn and cook the other side until brown spots appear.

Throw over hot coals with the first side down until chapati puffs up.

YIELD: ABOUT 1 DOZEN

APPROX. CAL/SERV.: 70

. . . . ***Whole Wheat-Apricot Bread***

1 CUP CHOPPED DRIED APRICOTS

¼ CUP OIL

½ CUP HONEY

⅔ CUP BOILING WATER

2 CUPS WHOLE WHEAT FLOUR

¼ TEASPOON BAKING SODA

2 TEASPOONS BAKING POWDER

1 CUP PECANS

½ CUP EVAPORATED SKIM MILK

1 EGG, SLIGHTLY BEATEN

Preheat oven to 350°F.

Put the apricots in a bowl with the oil, honey and boiling water. Set aside to cool.

Mix dry ingredients and nuts. Mix the milk and egg and combine with the apricot mixture.

Add liquid mixture to dry ingredients all at once, mixing just until dry ingredients are dampened, then 10 more strokes.

Divide batter into 3 oiled 6 × 3-inch loaf pans. Let stand at room temperature 10 to 20 minutes.

Recipe continues...

Bake 30 to 35 minutes.

Cool thoroughly. Wrap in foil and store overnight before slicing.

YIELD: 3 LOAVES (10 SLICES EACH)

APPROX. CAL/SERV.: 1 SLICE = 105

Garlic Bread

1 LOAF FRENCH BREAD

½ CUP MARGARINE

1 TEASPOON GARLIC SALT; OR 1 CLOVE GARLIC, MINCED

PINCH OREGANO

Preheat oven to 400°F.

Soften margarine and mix with garlic and oregano.

Slice the bread, spread with the herbed margarine, and reassemble the loaf. Wrap in foil and bake about 15 minutes.

YIELD: 1 LOAF (16 SLICES)

APPROX. CAL/SERV.: 1 SLICE = 135

Savory Bread

1 LOAF FRENCH BREAD

½ CUP MARGARINE

½ TEASPOON SALT

½ TEASPOON THYME

½ TEASPOON PAPRIKA

¼ TEASPOON SAVORY

DASH CAYENNE

Preheat oven to 400°F.

Soften the margarine and blend in the herbs.

Spread on sliced French bread. Wrap in foil, and bake on a cookie sheet about 15 minutes.

YIELD: 1 LOAF (16 SLICES)

APPROX. CAL/SERV.: 1 SLICE = 135

· · · · · · · · · · · · **Herb Sticks**

8 HOT DOG BUNS
½ TEASPOON GARLIC SALT
1 TEASPOON CRUSHED DRIED BASIL
¼ TEASPOON PARSLEY FLAKES
½ CUP MARGARINE, SOFTENED

Preheat oven to 300°F.

Split buns in quarters lengthwise.

Combine garlic salt, basil and parsley with the margarine. Spread the cut surfaces of the buns with the mixture, place on cookie sheet and bake until crisp and lightly browned, about 1 hour.

Store in covered container and serve in place of dinner rolls, or in place of crackers with soup or cocktails.

YIELD: 32 STICKS
APPROX. CAL/SERV.: 55

· · · · · · · · · · **Lemon-Parsley Rolls**

8 LARGE FRENCH SOURDOUGH ROLLS
½ CUP SOFTENED MARGARINE
2 TABLESPOONS FINELY CHOPPED FRESH PARSLEY
1 TABLESPOON LEMON JUICE
1½ TABLESPOONS GRATED LEMON RIND

Preheat oven to 350°F.

Mix margarine, parsley, lemon juice and rind.

Cut rolls in half and spread with mixture.

Wrap in aluminum foil and heat in oven for 15 minutes.

YIELD: 8 ROLLS
APPROX. CAL/SERV.: 255

· · · · · · · · **Toasted Honey-Sesame Sticks**

8 SLICES BREAD

2 TABLESPOONS MARGARINE

3 TABLESPOONS HONEY

2 TABLESPOONS TOASTED SESAME SEEDS

Preheat oven to 400°F.

Remove crusts from sliced bread; brush with combined melted margarine and honey; sprinkle with toasted sesame seeds.

Cut each slice of bread into 4 finger-length pieces. Place on baking sheet; toast in oven for 8 to 10 minutes or until crisp and golden brown.

YIELD: 32 STICKS

APPROX. CAL/SERV.: 35

· · · · · · · · · · **Cinnamon Breadsticks**

4 SLICES BREAD

2 TABLESPOONS OIL

1 TABLESPOON SKIM MILK

¼ CUP SUGAR

¾ TEASPOON CINNAMON

Preheat oven to 350°F.

Remove crusts from bread and brush both sides of bread slices with oil and milk.

Cut each slice into 6 equal strips. Roll strips in mixture of sugar and cinnamon.

Toast on cookie sheet in oven for 10 minutes, or until crisp.

YIELD: 24 STRIPS

APPROX. CAL/SERV.: 30

Caramel-Orange Rolls

¼ CUP GRANULATED SUGAR

1 TEASPOON GRATED ORANGE RIND

1½ TABLESPOONS ORANGE JUICE

¼ TEASPOON MACE

1 TABLESPOON MARGARINE

12 BROWN 'N SERVE DINNER ROLLS

Preheat oven to 400°F.

Combine sugar, orange rind, orange juice, mace and margarine. Spread over bottom of ungreased shallow pan.

Place rolls upside down, over sugar mixture. Bake in oven for 15 minutes.

Remove from oven. Let rolls stand in pan until syrup thickens, or about 1 minute. Invert pan and remove rolls so that caramel-orange topping coats rolls.

YIELD: 12 ROLLS

APPROX. CAL/SERV.: 110

Irish Soda Bread

3 CUPS SIFTED ALL-PURPOSE FLOUR

¾ TEASPOON SALT

¼ CUP SUGAR

1 TEASPOON BAKING SODA

½ TEASPOON BAKING POWDER

¼ TEASPOON CREAM OF TARTAR

⅓ CUP MARGARINE

1⅓ CUPS BUTTERMILK

⅓ CUP CURRANTS

Preheat oven to 350°F.

Sift together the first 6 ingredients. Cut in the margarine with a pastry blender until mixture resembles cornmeal.

Recipe continues...

Add buttermilk and stir only until moistened. Mix currants in lightly. Shape into a ball and knead about 15 seconds.

Place on a lightly greased cookie sheet. With the palm of the hand flatten dough into a circle about 7 inches in diameter and 1½ inches thick. With a sharp knife, cut a cross on top, about ¼ inch deep and 5 inches long, to prevent cracking during baking.

Bake 45 to 50 minutes. Cool on a wire rack.

YIELD: 1 ROUND LOAF (20 SLICES)
APPROX. CAL/SERV.: 120

· · · · · · · · · *Irish Brown Soda Bread*

3 CUPS WHOLE WHEAT FLOUR
1½ CUPS SIFTED ALL-PURPOSE FLOUR
1 TEASPOON SALT
1 TEASPOON BAKING SODA
1 TABLESPOON SUGAR
1 TABLESPOON SOFT MARGARINE
1½–1⅔ CUPS BUTTERMILK

Preheat oven to 425°F.

Measure the whole wheat flour into a large mixing bowl. Sift together the all-purpose flour, salt, baking soda and sugar, and mix into the whole wheat flour. Cream in the margarine.

Add buttermilk, a small amount at a time until the dough is soft but not sticky.

Form dough into a ball, and knead in the bowl for 15 to 20 seconds. Place on a lightly greased baking sheet and flatten with the palm of the hand into a circle about 1½ inches thick. Cut a cross on the top to prevent cracking during baking.

Bake at 425°F. for 25 minutes, then reduce heat to 350°F. and bake 15 minutes longer.

Cool on a wire rack, then seal tightly in a plastic bag. To serve, slice about ¼-inch thick. (This bread slices best 24 hours after baking.)

YIELD: 1 ROUND LOAF (20 SLICES)
APPROX. CAL/SERV.: 105

· · · · · · · · · · · · · · · **Bagels**

2 PACKAGES YEAST
4¼–4½ CUPS FLOUR
1½ CUPS LUKEWARM WATER
3 TABLESPOONS SUGAR
1 TABLESPOON SALT

Combine the yeast and 1¾ cups flour, then add water, sugar and salt to the yeast mixture. Beat at a low speed for ½ minute constantly scraping the sides of the bowl, then beat at high speed for 3 minutes.

Stir in enough of the remaining flour to make a moderately stiff dough, then turn out onto a lightly floured board and knead until smooth. Cover and let rest for 15 minutes.

Divide the dough into 12 portions. Shape into smooth balls and punch a hole in the center of each with a floured finger. Pull gently to enlarge hole, keeping uniform shape. Cover and let rise 20 minutes.

Preheat oven to 375°F.

Add 1 teaspoon of sugar to 1 gallon of water and bring to a boil. Reduce to simmer. Cook bagels in the simmering water 4 or 5 at a time for 7 minutes—turning once, then drain on a paper towel. Sprinkle with a topping, if desired.

Place on an ungreased baking sheet in oven. Bake for 30 to 35 minutes.

YIELD: 12 BAGELS
APPROX. CAL/SERV.: 155

· · · · · · · · · · · · · · · *variations*

Before *baking* sprinkle bagels with chopped onion, poppy seeds, sesame seeds, caraway seeds, or kosher salt.

Use ½ whole wheat flour, and ½ all-purpose flour.

. . . . **Currant Bread**

2½ CUPS ALL-PURPOSE FLOUR SIFTED
⅛ TEASPOON SALT
6 TABLESPOONS MARGARINE
½ TEASPOON BAKING POWDER
½ CUP CURRANTS
2 EGGS, WELL BEATEN
¼ CUP SKIM MILK

Cream together flour, salt and margarine. Stir in the baking powder and currants. Add eggs and milk.

Turn into an oiled 8 × 4-inch pan and bake in preheated oven at 350°F. for 45 to 60 minutes.

YIELD: 1 LOAF (16 SLICES)
APPROX. CAL/SERV.: 130

Whole Wheat Pita Bread (Middle Eastern Flat Bread)

A great fun bread. Each flat round forms a pocket while it is baking. Fill the finished bread with falafel, tuna and spinach or other sandwich combinations. Or cut the unfilled round into wedges like a pie and serve with dips as an appetizer.

⅔ CUP SOY FLOUR
3 CUPS WHOLE WHEAT PASTRY FLOUR
2⅓ CUPS UNBLEACHED ALL-PURPOSE FLOUR
1 TABLESPOON SALT
2 TABLESPOONS PLUS 1 TEASPOON SUGAR
1 PACKAGE DRY ACTIVE YEAST
2½–3 CUPS LUKEWARM WATER

Combine the flours, salt and the two tablespoons of sugar in a large bowl. In a small bowl, mix the teaspoon of sugar, with the yeast and ½ cup of the warm water. Set in a warm place for about 10 minutes until the mixture is bubbly.

Stir the yeast mixture and enough of the warm water into the flour to make a soft dough. The dough should be slightly sticky on the outside.

Knead the dough in the bowl until it is smooth and satiny, at least 10 minutes. It loses its stickiness quickly. Grease the top of the dough with oil, cover the bowl and set in a warm place to rise until doubled in bulk, 1¼ hours.

Punch the dough down, knead briefly and divide into 12 equal pieces. Form each into a smooth ball, cover and let stand 10 minutes.

Preheat the oven to 450°F. Roll out the balls of dough into rounds about 5 inches in diameter. If you are using a gas oven, and have a sense of adventure, slide the rounds of dough directly onto the bottom of the oven. Four will fit in the average oven at one time. Bake 8 minutes or until well fluffed and lightly browned. (If you use this method—watch the bread carefully because it may char.)

The other method is to place the rounds on ungreased cookie sheets and bake for 8 to 10 minutes. Cool rounds on a board covered with a towel.

YIELD: 12 ROUNDS
APPROX. CAL/SERV.: 215

NOTE: The rounds puff up in the oven, collapse as they cool, but retain a pocket for filling. Store in plastic bags in the refrigerator or freeze them to hold more than a day or two. This bread loses its freshness quickly.

Desserts

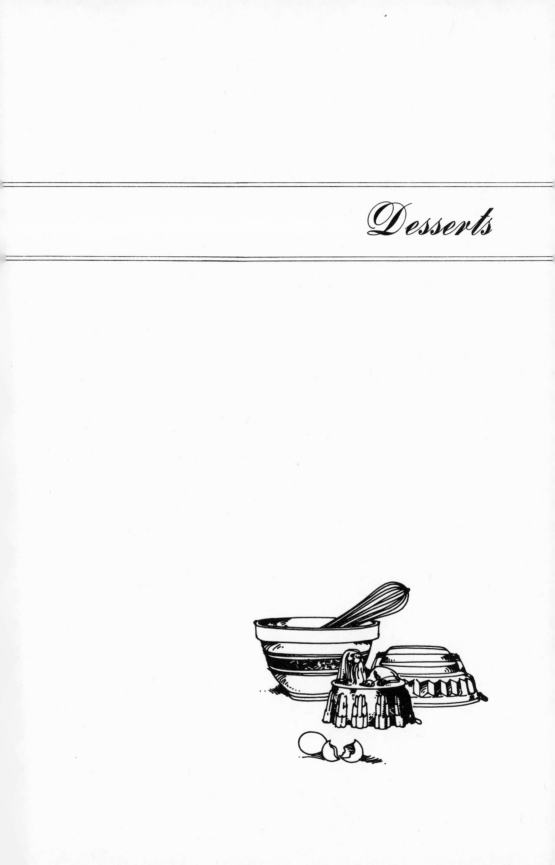

*T*here was once a man who traveled around the world in search of the single most satisfying dessert. At the close of his journey, having tasted all of the great cremes and pastries, he was thankful to end his meal with one juicy apple. The moral: Mother Nature makes great desserts, and not only are they delicious and nutritious, but a load off the mind and frame of the calorie-conscious.

Fresh fruit or cakey concoction, the dessert course can still be tasty and nutritious, yet low in fat. Egg whites, nuts and skim milk contribute protein; fruits and vegetables (pumpkin and rhubarb, for example) provide vitamins and minerals without adding excessive calories.

You do not need to be an expert at reading labels to know that most commercially prepared cakes, cookies and puddings are high in sugar, saturated fats and cholesterol. One exception to this is angel food cake. Hard candies, marshmallows, gumdrops and ices are fat-free but are devoid of nutrients and high in calories. Most pudding mixes are acceptable, including vanilla, chocolate and butterscotch flavors, if they are reconstituted with skim milk.

Be your own baker. Your reward—many more low-calorie, low-fat desserts will find a place on your table. Try the recipes on the following pages, or adapt your own favorites by substituting polyunsaturated oil or margarine where possible and limiting the use of egg yolks. Looking for a dessert topping? Use the whipped cream substitute on p. 386. Complete a super cake by filling the layers with gelatin flavored with liqueurs, nutmeats or fresh fruits.

To those who fear that desserts will never be the same again, do not despair. The taste is unchanged, only the excess fat and sugar have been removed. No one is likely to notice.

. . . . *Nuts*

Nutmeats, good sources of protein, are high in calories (largely monounsaturated fats), but have no cholesterol. The exceptions are coconut and macadamia nuts, both unacceptably high in saturated fats. The following may be used in cooking or eaten as snacks.

ALMONDS

BEECHNUTS

BRAZIL NUTS

CASHEWS

CHESTNUTS

FILBERTS AND HAZELNUTS

HICKORY NUTS AND BUTTERNUTS

PECANS

PINE (INDIAN) NUTS (PIGNOLIA)

PISTACHIO NUTS

PUMPKIN AND SUNFLOWER SEEDS

WALNUTS*

* Walnuts are high in polyunsaturated fats.

APPROX. CAL/SERV.: 1 OUNCE = 200

. . . . *Fruits*

Fresh ripe fruits, the symbols of a bountiful harvest, enhance a simple meal or adorn a banquet table. Here is a partial listing of these natural confections. Serve them chilled or at room temperature, as snacks or as part of a meal.

APPLES   APPROX. CAL/SERV.: 1 MEDIUM = 70

For cooking or eating

BALDWIN

GRAVENSTEIN

GRIMES GOLDEN

JONATHAN

MC INTOSH

RHODE ISLAND GREENING

STAYMAN

WINESAP

YELLOW TRANSPARENT

For dessert

BAKER

DELICIOUS

MC INTOSH

NORTHERN SPY

PIPPIN

ROME BEAUTY

STAYMAN

WINESAP

OTHER   APPROX. CAL/SERV.: 40

APRICOTS—2 MEDIUM

BANANAS—½ SMALL

CHERRIES—10 LARGE

FIGS—2 LARGE

GRAPES—12

GUAVA—½ MEDIUM

MANGOES—½ SMALL

MELONS—¼ CANTALOUPE (6-INCH DIAMETER), ⅛ HONEY-DEW (7-INCH DIAMETER)

PAPAYA—⅓ MEDIUM (*serve chilled, sprinkled with lemon or lime juice*)

PEACHES—1 MEDIUM

PEARS—1 SMALL

PERSIMMONS—½ SMALL

PINEAPPLE—½ CUP

PLUMS—2 MEDIUM

DRIED FRUITS (*Use in cooking or as snacks*)   APPROX. CAL/SERV.: 40

APPLES—¼ CUP

APRICOTS—4 HALVES

CURRANTS—2 TABLESPOONS

DATES—2

FIGS—1 SMALL

PEACHES—2 MEDIUM

PINEAPPLE, DICED—1 TABLESPOON

PRUNES—2 MEDIUM

RAISINS—2 TABLESPOONS

BERRIES   APPROX. CAL/SERV.: 40 (70 WITH SUGAR)

(*Serve with 1 tablespoon confectioners' sugar flavored with a vanilla bean*)

RASPBERRIES—1 CUP

STRAWBERRIES—1 CUP

CITRUS FRUITS   APPROX. CAL/SERV.: 40

CALOMONDIN (*cross between kumquat and tangerine*)—4

GRAPEFRUIT—½ SMALL

KUMQUAT—4

NECTARINE—1 MEDIUM

ORANGES—1 SMALL

TANGERINES—1 LARGE

. . . . *Fudge Brownies*

2 TABLESPOONS COCOA

¾ CUP DARK BROWN SUGAR, FIRMLY PACKED

⅓ CUP MARGARINE, MELTED

1 LARGE EGG, SLIGHTLY BEATEN

½ CUP ALL-PURPOSE UNBLEACHED FLOUR

⅛ TEASPOON SALT

½ CUP COARSELY CHOPPED WALNUTS

½ TEASPOON VANILLA EXTRACT

Preheat oven to 325°F.

In a mixing bowl, combine cocoa and brown sugar. Stir in margarine and egg. Beat with a wooden spoon until thoroughly blended.

Sift together flour and salt. Mix into the batter along with chopped walnuts. Stir in vanilla extract. Pour the batter into a greased 8 × 8 × 2-inch square pan. Bake 25 minutes, or until done.

Remove from oven and cool on a wire rack for about 5 minutes. Cut into squares and let cool further before removing from pan. Store in a covered container.

YIELD: 16 SQUARES
APPROX. CAL/SERV.: 115

Butterscotch Brownies

¼ CUP OIL
1 CUP LIGHT BROWN SUGAR, FIRMLY PACKED
1 EGG, SLIGHTLY BEATEN
¾ CUP SIFTED FLOUR
1 TEASPOON BAKING POWDER
½ TEASPOON SALT
½ TEASPOON VANILLA EXTRACT
½ CUP COARSELY CHOPPED WALNUTS

Preheat oven to 350°F.

Blend oil and sugar. Stir in beaten egg. Sift flour, baking powder and salt together and combine with egg mixture.

Add vanilla and walnuts to the batter, spread in an oiled 8 × 8 × 2-inch pan and bake for 25 minutes. Do not overbake. Cool slightly, and cut into squares.

YIELD: 16 SQUARES
APPROX. CAL/SERV.: 130

Sugar Cookies

½ CUP MARGARINE, SOFTENED
1 CUP SUGAR
1 EGG
2 TABLESPOONS SKIM MILK
1 TEASPOON VANILLA EXTRACT
2 CUPS ALL-PURPOSE FLOUR
½ TEASPOON SALT
2 TEASPOONS BAKING POWDER
GRANULATED SUGAR

Recipe continues...

Preheat oven to 375°F.

Beat the margarine, sugar, egg, milk and vanilla together until light and fluffy. Stir in the flour, salt, and baking powder, mixing well. Chill dough thoroughly.

Roll small portions of dough at a time on a lightly floured board. Using a cookie cutter, cut out shapes, sprinkle with granulated sugar, and place on a lightly greased cookie sheet. Bake about 8 minutes.

Cool and store in tightly covered containers.

YIELD: 4 DOZEN
APPROX. CAL/SERV.: 60

· · · · · · · · · · · · · *variations*

LEMON SUGAR COOKIES: Substitute 2 tablespoons of lemon juice and 1 teaspoon of lemon rind for the milk and vanilla.

CINNAMON SUGAR COOKIES: Follow recipe for sugar cookies, but instead of sprinkling with granulated sugar before baking, brush tops of unbaked cookies with beaten egg white and sprinkle with a mixture of 2 tablespoons of sugar and ½ teaspoon of cinnamon.

· · · · · · · · · *Raisin-Oatmeal Cookies*

    1 CUP FLOUR, SIFTED
    ½ TEASPOON BAKING SODA
    1 TEASPOON SALT
    1½ CUPS QUICK COOKING OATS
    2 EGG WHITES, SLIGHTLY BEATEN
    ¼ TEASPOON CINNAMON
    1 CUP BROWN SUGAR
    ⅓ CUP OIL
    ½ CUP SKIM MILK
    1 TEASPOON VANILLA EXTRACT
    1 CUP SEEDLESS RAISINS

Preheat oven to 375°F.
Sift together flour, baking soda, salt, and cinnamon. Stir in the oats.

Combine egg whites, brown sugar, oil, milk, vanilla, and raisins and add to flour mixture. Mix well.

Drop batter a teaspoon at a time onto an oiled cookie sheet. Bake 12 to 15 minutes, depending on texture desired. Shorter baking time results in a chewy soft cookie, the longer time in a crisp one.

YIELD: 3 DOZEN
APPROX. CAL/SERV.: 70

. . . . *Whiskey or Bourbon Balls*

There is no need to heat up the oven for these well-aged whiskey balls. Make them at least a week ahead.

> 3 CUPS FINELY CRUSHED VANILLA WAFERS
> 1 CUP POWDERED SUGAR
> ½ CUP CHOPPED PECANS
> 3 TABLESPOONS WHITE KARO SYRUP
> 1½ TABLESPOONS COCOA
> 6 TABLESPOONS BOURBON

Mix all ingredients and form into small balls. If balls tend to crumble, add a few extra drops of bourbon to the mixture. Roll each in powdered sugar and store in an airtight container for about 1 week to ripen.

YIELD: 4 DOZEN ½-INCH BALLS
APPROX. CAL/SERV.: 60

. . . . *Ginger Cookies*

> ¾ CUP MARGARINE
> 1 CUP SUGAR
> 1 EGG, SLIGHTLY BEATEN
> ¼ CUP MOLASSES
> 2 CUPS FLOUR
> 2 TEASPOONS BAKING SODA
> ¼ TEASPOON SALT
> 1 TEASPOON CINNAMON
> 1 TEASPOON GINGER
> 1 TEASPOON SUGAR

Recipe continues...

Preheat oven to 350°F.

Cream the margarine and cup of sugar. Beat in the egg and molasses. Sift the flour with soda, salt, and spices, and mix with the wet ingredients. Chill the dough. Shape into balls about 1 inch in diameter, roll in sugar and place 3 inches apart on an oiled baking sheet. Bake about 15 minutes.

YIELD: 24 2-INCH COOKIES

APPROX. CAL/SERV.: 130

• • • • • • • • • • • • • • • *variation*

GINGERBREAD MEN: Follow above recipe for Ginger Cookies, but add ½ cup more flour to make 2½ cups. When dough is chilled, on a lightly floured board, roll dough to ⅛-inch thickness. Cut out gingerbread men shapes with a 6-by-3½-inch cookie cutter. Bake 8 to 10 minutes at 350°F. Decorate with Confectioners' Glaze (p. 389).

YIELD: 2–3 DOZEN GINGERBREAD MEN DEPENDING ON THE SIZE OF YOUR COOKIE CUTTER.

• • • • • • • • • • • • *Spice Cookies*

½ CUP MOLASSES
¼ CUP LIGHT BROWN SUGAR
½ CUP MARGARINE
1½ CUPS FLOUR
½ CUP TOASTED WHEAT GERM
⅛ TEASPOON SALT
1 TABLESPOON BREWERS' YEAST
1½ TEASPOONS GINGER
½ TEASPOON CINNAMON
1½ TEASPOONS BAKING SODA

Preheat oven to 350°F.

Heat molasses to the boiling point, add sugar and margarine.

Mix all dry ingredients together. Stir into molasses mixture.

Drop by teaspoonsful on cookie sheets ½ inch apart. Bake 8 to 10 minutes, until firm.

YIELD: ABOUT 4 DOZEN
APPROX. CAL/SERV.: 50

Refrigerator Cookies

½ CUP MARGARINE
¾ CUP SUGAR
1 EGG
¼ CUP DUTCH PROCESS COCOA
¾ CUP GROUND NUTS
1¾ CUPS SIFTED FLOUR
½ TEASPOON BAKING POWDER
½ TEASPOON CINNAMON
¼ TEASPOON CLOVES
1 TABLESPOON EVAPORATED SKIM MILK
THIN CONFECTIONERS' GLAZE (p. 389)
TINY MULTI-COLORED CANDIES

Cream the margarine and sugar until light and fluffy. Beat in the egg and cocoa. Add the nuts.

Sift together the flour, baking powder, cinnamon and cloves, and combine with the cocoa mixture alternately with the milk, stirring until blended. Shape into a roll about 1 to 1½ inches in diameter, wrap in wax paper and chill overnight.

Preheat oven to 350°F.

Cut roll into thin slices. Bake about 10 minutes. Cool and frost with the glaze. Sprinkle with candies.

YIELD: 2½ DOZEN
APPROX. CAL/SERV.: 105

. . . . *Sherry Thins*

¾ CUP MARGARINE

1 CUP SUGAR

1 EGG

3 CUPS SIFTED FLOUR

2 TEASPOONS BAKING POWDER

½ TEASPOON NUTMEG

½ TEASPOON SALT

½ CUP CREAM SHERRY

GRATED ALMONDS OR TINY CANDIES

Cream margarine and sugar until light and fluffy. Beat in egg. Add sifted dry ingredients alternately with the sherry, beating until smooth. Wrap dough in foil and chill several hours, or overnight.

Preheat oven to 400°F.

Roll dough out thin on floured board or pastry cloth and cut out shapes with small cookie cutters. Put on a cookie sheet, sprinkle with almonds or candies, and bake for 8 to 10 minutes.

YIELD: 6–7 DOZEN

APPROX. CAL/SERV.: 40

. . . . *Peanut Butter Cookies*

½ CUP MARGARINE

½ CUP PEANUT BUTTER

½ CUP GRANULATED SUGAR

½ CUP BROWN SUGAR

1 EGG

½ TEASPOON VANILLA EXTRACT

½ TEASPOON SALT

½ TEASPOON BAKING SODA

1 CUP FLOUR

Preheat oven to 350°F.

Cream together the margarine and peanut butter. Add white and brown sugar. Stir in egg, vanilla, salt, flour and baking soda. Place dough, a teaspoon at a time, onto a cookie sheet, pressing each dab flat with a floured fork. Bake for 10 minutes. Cool a minute or two before removing from cookie sheet.

YIELD: 5 DOZEN
APPROX. CAL/SERV.: 50

Carob Nut Roll

½ CUP SOFT MARGARINE
6 TABLESPOONS HONEY
2 TABLESPOONS MOLASSES
½ CUP CAROB POWDER
¾–1 CUP NONFAT DRY MILK
½ CUP CHOPPED ENGLISH WALNUTS
¼ CUP GROUND ENGLISH WALNUTS

Cream the margarine with the honey and molasses. Beat in the carob powder. Gradually beat in the dry milk until the mixture is stiff enough to hold a shape. Add chopped walnuts and form into an 8-inch roll, 1½ inch in diameter. Coat with the ground walnuts.

Chill for 2 hours. Slice and serve as cookies.

YIELD: 1 ROLL (16 ½-INCH SLICES)
APPROX. CAL/SERV.: 1 SLICE = 140

Lemon Fluff Pudding

1 TABLESPOON UNFLAVORED GELATIN
1 TABLESPOON COLD WATER
½ CUP SUGAR
1 CUP BOILING WATER
½ CUP COLD WATER
¼ CUP LEMON JUICE
½ CUP NONFAT DRY MILK
½ CUP ICE WATER
1 TEASPOON GRATED LEMON RIND

Recipe continues...

Soften gelatin in the 1 tablespoon of cold water, and combine with boiling water to dissolve. Add sugar, the ½ cup of cold water, and lemon juice and rind. Chill until nearly firm.

Chill a deep mixing bowl and beaters. In the bowl, mix the powdered nonfat dry milk with the ice water. Beat until fluffy. Chill.

Break up the frozen lemon mixture with a fork and add to the whipped milk mixture. Beat well with an electric mixer until the pudding is fluffy, but not too soft.

Chill again until firm.

YIELD: 6 SERVINGS
APPROX. CAL/SERV.: 90

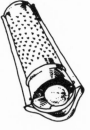

· · · · · · · · · · · · · *Gelatin Crème*

1 PACKAGE FLAVORED GELATIN DESSERT
1 CUP BOILING WATER
½ CUP COLD WATER
½ CUP NONFAT DRY MILK, MIXED WITH ½ CUP ICE WATER
2 TABLESPOONS SUGAR
FLAVORING IF DESIRED

Dissolve the gelatin dessert in 1 cup of boiling water. Add ½ cup of cold water. Chill until nearly firm.

Beat the nonfat dry milk with the cold water until fluffy. Add sugar and chill.

Break up the chilled gelatin mixture with a fork and add it to the whipped milk mixture. Beat with an electric mixer until fluffy.

Chill until set. If desired, ¼ teaspoon of almond flavoring may be added or fruit may be folded in.

Serve within 4 hours, or crème may separate.

YIELD: 4 SERVINGS
APPROX. CAL/SERV.: 130

. . . . *Fruit Bavarian*

1 16-OUNCE CAN CRUSHED PINEAPPLE; OR 1 10-OUNCE PACKAGE
  FROZEN STRAWBERRIES; OR 1 10-OUNCE PACKAGE FROZEN
  RASPBERRIES
1 ENVELOPE PLAIN GELATIN
1 CUP LOW-FAT YOGURT (PINEAPPLE, STRAWBERRY OR RASPBERRY
  FLAVORED)
1 EGG WHITE

Soak the gelatin in ¼ cup of cold water.

Drain the fruit well. Reserve ¾ cup of the juice, adding water if
necessary. Heat. Stir in the gelatin until dissolved, then add the fruit.
Chill.

Whip the egg white until peaks form. When the gelatin mix begins
to thicken, fold in the yogurt and egg white. Pile into parfait glasses, or
spoon into a baked Pie Pastry (p. 369), Crumb Pie Crust (p. 371) or
Meringue Shell (p. 367)

This also makes an excellent filling for angel cake. Split the cake
horizontally in thirds and fill with Fruit Bavarian.

YIELD: 8 SERVINGS
APPROX. CAL/SERV.: PINEAPPLE = 85   STRAWBERRY = 75   RASP-
  BERRY = 70

. . . . *Yogurt and Gelatin Delight*

1 PACKAGE FRUIT-FLAVORED GELATIN
1 CUP LOW-FAT YOGURT THE SAME FLAVOR AS THE GELATIN

Prepare the fruit gelatin according to package directions. Chill until
it begins to set.

Stir the yogurt in until thoroughly combined with the gelatin. Return to the refrigerator until set.

YIELD: 6 SERVINGS
APPROX. CAL/SERV.: 95

Recipe continues…

• • • • • • • • • • • • • • *variation*

FLUFFY YOGURT-GELATIN DELIGHT: When gelatin has started to set, whip with an electric beater until light and fluffy. Fold in the yogurt and place in refrigerator to set.

✓ • • • • • • • • • • • • **Rice Pudding**

2 CUPS SKIM MILK
3 TABLESPOONS RAW LONG-GRAIN RICE
3 TABLESPOONS SUGAR
¼ TEASPOON SALT
½ TEASPOON VANILLA EXTRACT
⅛ TEASPOON NUTMEG
⅛ TEASPOON CINNAMON
¼ CUP LIGHT OR DARK SEEDLESS RAISINS

Preheat oven to 325°F.

Mix all ingredients together and place in a 1-quart ovenproof casserole.

Bake uncovered for 2 to 2¼ hours or until rice is tender, occasionally stirring the surface skin into the pudding as it forms.

Served warm or cold. If served cold, stir in enough skim milk to thin the pudding to desired consistency.

YIELD: 6 SERVINGS
APPROX. CAL/SERV.: 90

Lemon Rice Pudding

½ CUP RAW RICE
1½ CUPS WATER
4 TABLESPOONS RAISINS
DASH NUTMEG
½ TEASPOON SALT
1 CUP SKIM MILK
¼ CUP SUGAR
1 TEASPOON GRATED LEMON RIND
1 TEASPOON LEMON JUICE
½ TEASPOON VANILLA EXTRACT

Place the water, rice, raisins, nutmeg and salt in the top of a double boiler. Mix thoroughly, cover and cook over boiling water for 20 minutes.

Stir in the milk and cook uncovered until it is absorbed, about 10 minutes. Stir in the sugar. Cool.

Add the lemon rind, juice and vanilla. Chill until ready to serve.

YIELD: 6 SERVINGS
APPROX. CAL/SERV.: 120

Fudge Wonder Pudding

1 CUP FLOUR
2 TEASPOONS BAKING POWDER
¼ TEASPOON SALT
¾ CUP SUGAR
2 TABLESPOONS COCOA
½ CUP SKIM MILK
2 TABLESPOONS MARGARINE, MELTED
1 TEASPOON VANILLA EXTRACT
½ CUP CHOPPED NUTS
¾ CUP BROWN SUGAR, FIRMLY PACKED
¼ CUP COCOA
1¾ CUPS HOT WATER

Recipe continues...

Preheat oven to 350°F.

Sift the first 5 ingredients together into a mixing bowl. Stir in the milk, margarine, vanilla extract and nuts. Turn into a 9-inch square pan. Mix the brown sugar and cocoa, sprinkle over the top and carefully pour hot water over the entire batter.

Bake 45 minutes. During baking, the cake will rise to the top of the pan while the chocolate sauce settles to the bottom. Remove from the oven, cool slightly and invert onto a deep serving plate. Serve pudding while it is still warm.

YIELD: 9 SERVINGS
APPROX. CAL/SERV.: 260

· · · · · · · · · · · · *Indian Pudding*

¼ CUP CORN MEAL
2 CUPS HOT SKIM MILK
¼ CUP SUGAR
⅛ TEASPOON BAKING SODA
½ TEASPOON SALT
½ TEASPOON GROUND GINGER
½ TEASPOON GROUND CINNAMON
¼ CUP MOLASSES
1 CUP COLD SKIM MILK
NUTMEG

Preheat oven to 275°F.

Stir the corn meal, a little at a time, into the hot milk and cook over low heat, or in a double boiler, stirring constantly, for 15 minutes, or until thick. Remove from the heat.

Mix together the sugar, soda salt and spices and stir into the corn meal mixture. Thoroughly mix in the molasses and cold milk. Pour into a 1-quart casserole and bake 2 hours.

Serve warm with a light sprinkling of nutmeg.

YIELD: 8 SERVINGS
APPROX. CAL/SERV.: 95

. . . . . . **Mandarin Orange Pudding** *(Tanjulin)*

A good "pantry-shelf" special to make for unexpected company.

1 PACKAGE VANILLA PUDDING MIX
2 CUPS SKIM MILK
1 11-OUNCE CAN MANDARIN ORANGES, WELL DRAINED
DASH SUGAR
1 TABLESPOON SHERRY
TOASTED ALMONDS, SLIVERED

Prepare vanilla pudding according to directions on the package; or, make your own pudding using skim milk. Cool.

Before serving, fold in the drained mandarin oranges and the sherry. Serve in individual glass dishes garnished with the toasted slivered nuts.

YIELD: 6 SERVINGS
APPROX. CAL/SERV.: 135

. . . . **Apple Cobbler**

5 COOKING APPLES
¾ CUP SUGAR
½ TEASPOON CINNAMON
2 TEASPOONS LEMON JUICE
1 CUP CAKE FLOUR
1 TEASPOON BAKING POWDER
3 TABLESPOONS MARGARINE
¼ CUP SKIM MILK
¼ CUP SUGAR
¼ CUP WATER

Preheat oven to 350°F.

Peel, core and slice the apples. Place in a 9-inch baking dish. Combine the sugar, cinnamon and lemon juice. Sprinkle over the apple slices, and bake for 30 minutes.

Meanwhile, sift the flour and the baking powder. Using a pastry blender, cut in the margarine. Sprinkle in the milk and press the dough

Recipe continues…

into a ball. Turn the dough onto a floured board and pat to ⅓-inch thickness. When the apples have cooked for 30 minutes, remove from the oven, place dough on top of apples and cut slits for steam. Raise oven heat to 450°F. and bake cobbler 20 minutes more. Boil together the ¼ cup of sugar and the ¼ cup of water. Pour this over the cobbler and continue baking 10 minutes longer.

YIELD: 9 SERVINGS
APPROX. CAL/SERV.: 205

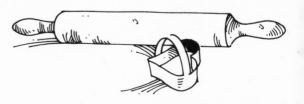

Cherry Crisp

⅓ CUP FLOUR
¾ CUP ROLLED OATS
⅓ CUP MARGARINE
⅔ CUP SUGAR
1 16-OUNCE CAN PITTED SOUR CHERRIES
1½ TABLESPOONS CORNSTARCH
⅛ TEASPOON CINNAMON
⅛ TEASPOON NUTMEG
1 TABLESPOON LEMON JUICE

Preheat oven to 375°F.

Combine the flour and rolled oats. Cut in the margarine until the mixture is crumbly; mix in ⅓ cup of the sugar. Set aside for topping.

Drain the cherries reserving the juice. Combine the remaining sugar with the cornstarch, spices and lemon juice; slowly blend in the cherry juice. Cook over low heat stirring constantly, until the sauce is thick and clear. Add the cherries. Pour into a greased 8-inch square baking pan. Sprinkle with the topping.

Bake 30 minutes.

YIELD: 9 SERVINGS
APPROX. CAL/SERV.: 185

· · · · · · · · · · · *Apple Dumplings*

In Pennsylvania Dutch country this dish is served as a complete meal—usually with skim milk.

1 RECIPE FOR PIE PASTRY (p. 369)
4 MEDIUM-SIZE BAKING APPLES, WHOLE BUT PEELED AND CORED
½ CUP BROWN SUGAR
¼ TEASPOON SALT
½ TEASPOON CINNAMON
½ TEASPOON GRATED LEMON RIND
2 TEASPOONS MARGARINE

Preheat oven to 350°F.

Roll the pastry in a large square and cut it into 4 smaller squares each large enough to enclose an apple. Combine the sugar, salt, cinnamon and lemon rind. Place an apple on each square of dough and fill the cavity with the sugar mixture. Dot with margarine. Gently bring up opposite corners of the square to enclose the apple. Pinch together, using a little water. Tuck edges in as though wrapping a package; bring remaining two corners of dough together at the top of the apple; press together to seal.

Place dumplings in a shallow baking pan and bake about 30 minutes.

YIELD: 4 SERVINGS
APPROX. CAL/SERV.: 760

· · · · · · · · · · · *Deep Dish Fruit Pie*

3 CUPS RAW FRUIT (APPLES, RHUBARB, CHERRIES, PEACHES, OR APRICOTS)
1 TABLESPOON LEMON JUICE
¼–½ CUP SUGAR, DEPENDING ON THE TARTNESS OF THE FRUIT
½ CUP FLOUR
½ CUP BROWN SUGAR
1 TABLESPOON OIL
½ TEASPOON CINNAMON

Recipe continues…

Preheat oven to 375°F.

Pit, peel and slice the fruit as though for a pie. Mix together and place in a deep 8-inch baking dish with the white sugar and lemon juice. Bake until fruit is tender(about 45 minutes for apples).

With a pastry blender, mix together the flour, brown sugar, oil and cinnamon until it is crumbly. Place atop the cooked fruit and continue to bake until brown and bubbly. Top each serving with ice milk or sherbet.

YIELD: 6 SERVINGS

APPROX. CAL/SERV.: 200

· · · · · · · · · · · · *Champagne Ice*

A truly elegant dessert.

¾ CUP SUGAR

1½ CUPS WATER

3 TABLESPOONS ORANGE LIQUEUR

1 LEMON

2 ORANGES

3 CUPS CHAMPAGNE

2 CUPS HALVED STRAWBERRIES

In a saucepan, combine the sugar and water. Bring to a boil and cook for 5 minutes; let cool. Squeeze the juice from 2 oranges and 1 lemon and reserve the juice. Peel the lemon and one of the oranges. To the cooled syrup, add the liqueur and the lemon and orange peels. Chill the syrup for 2 hours, then remove and discard the peels.

Stir in 2 cups of the champagne and all of the reserved fruit juice. Freeze until it begins to turn mushy. Beat with a rotary beater until smooth. Then place in a freezing tray in the freezer. Let sit for several hours, stirring occasionally.

Meanwhile, sprinkle the halved strawberries with a little sugar, and pour the remaining cup of champagne over them. Let stand in the refrigerator for 4 hours.

At serving time, place strawberries in crystal goblets, and fill with champagne ice.

YIELD: 6 SERVINGS

APPROX. CAL/SERV.: 230

. . . . *Fresh Fruit Ice*

1 ENVELOPE UNFLAVORED GELATIN
½ CUP COLD WATER
1 CUP ORANGE JUICE
6 TABLESPOONS LEMON JUICE
4 TABLESPOONS SUGAR
1 CUP STRAWBERRIES, PEACHES OR OTHER FRESH FRUIT
3 BANANAS, MASHED

Soften the gelatin in the water. Stir over low heat until dissolved. Mix in the juices, sugar and sliced fruit, and place in the freezer until almost set. Beat with an electric mixer on high speed until creamy, but fluffy.

Cover and return to the freezer. If fruit ice is made some time before serving, it must be rebeaten and then returned to the freezer for a brief period.

YIELD: 8 SERVINGS
APPROX. CAL/SERV.: 90

. . . . *Lemon Sherbet*

1 ENVELOPE UNFLAVORED GELATIN
½ CUP SKIM MILK
1½ CUPS EVAPORATED SKIM MILK
1 CUP SUGAR
⅛ TEASPOON SALT
1 TEASPOON GRATED LEMON PEEL
½ CUP FRESH LEMON JUICE
2 EGG WHITES, STIFFLY BEATEN

Soften the gelatin in the ½ cup of skim milk. Heat the evaporated milk with the sugar and salt. Add the softened gelatin and stir until dissolved. Cool.

Slowly add the lemon peel and juice to the cooled gelatin mixture, stirring constantly. Pour into ice cube trays and place in the freezer. When the mixture is mushy, remove from the freezer and fold in the stiffly beaten

Recipe continues...

egg whites. Return to the freezer until firm, then remove, put in a chilled bowl and beat until fluffy.

Refreeze and serve.

YIELD: 8 SERVINGS
APPROX. CAL/SERV.: 150

Ginger Ale Sherbet

½ CUP WATER
1½ CUPS SUGAR
4 EGG WHITES, STIFFLY BEATEN
1 CUP ORANGE JUICE
½ CUP LEMON JUICE
½ CUP PINEAPPLE JUICE
3 CUPS GINGER ALE

In a saucepan, heat the water and 1 cup of the sugar to the boiling point and cook until the syrup reaches the soft-ball stage—234°F. to 238°F.

Beat the egg whites until stiff. Continue beating while gradually adding ½ cup of the sugar. Slowly pour the hot syrup into the egg whites, beating constantly until mixture has cooled. Then gradually beat in the ginger ale and fruit juices.

Place in the freezer until partially frozen, then remove and whip quickly. Pour into freezing trays, cover and return to the freezer. The texture should resemble that of an Italian ice.

YIELD: 8 SERVINGS
APPROX. CAL/SERV.: 210

Tequila-Lime Sherbet

1 TABLESPOON GELATIN
1 TABLESPOON COLD WATER
1½ CUPS SUGAR
1 CUP WATER
⅓ CUP TEQUILA
⅓ CUP LEMON OR LIME JUICE
1 TABLESPOON GRATED LEMON RIND
1 CUP EVAPORATED SKIM MILK

Soften the gelatin in the cold water. Boil the other cup of water and the sugar for 5 minutes. Remove from the heat and stir in softened gelatin until dissolved. Stir in the tequila, lemon or lime juice, and rind. Freeze until mushy.

Chill the evaporated skim milk in the freezer until crystals start to form. Whip until thick, and beat with the frozen lime mixture until smooth. Freeze again, beating every half hour or at least once every hour until creamy and thoroughly frozen.

YIELD: 8 SERVINGS
APPROX. CAL/SERV.: 200

Spiced Nuts

Here are two crunchy nut sweets that will quickly become favorites of family or guests.

½ CUP SUGAR
¼ CUP CORNSTARCH
½ TEASPOON SALT
1½ TEASPOONS CINNAMON
½ TEASPOON ALLSPICE
½ TEASPOON GINGER
½ TEASPOON NUTMEG
1 EGG WHITE
2 TABLESPOONS WATER
2 CUPS NUTS

Recipe continues...

Preheat oven to 250°F.

Sift dry ingredients together into a small bowl. Combine egg white and water and beat slightly.

Dip the nutmeats first in the egg white mixture. Roll them about in the dry ingredients lightly, keeping them separated. Place on an oiled cookie sheet and bake about 1½ hours. Cool on the cookie sheet. Store in a tightly covered container.

YIELD: ABOUT 2 CUPS

APPROX. CAL/SERV.: ¼ CUP = 260

Cinnamon Nuts

1 CUP SUGAR
½ TEASPOON CINNAMON
⅛ TEASPOON CREAM OF TARTAR
¼ CUP BOILING WATER
1½ CUPS WALNUTS OR OTHER NUTMEATS

Combine the sugar, cinnamon, cream of tartar and boiling water. Continue to boil until a candy thermometer registers 246°F. Add the nuts and cool, stirring until the syrup sugars on the nuts.

Turn out onto a flat surface. Separate the nuts and cool until dry. Store in a lightly covered container.

YIELD: ABOUT 1½ CUPS

APPROX. CAL/SERV.: ¼ CUP = 325

Wacky Cake

1½ CUPS FLOUR
1 CUP SUGAR
1 TEASPOON BAKING SODA
¼ CUP COCOA
1 TEASPOON VANILLA EXTRACT
1 TEASPOON VINEGAR
6 TABLESPOONS MARGARINE, MELTED
1 CUP WATER

Preheat the oven to 350°F.

Use an ungreased 8-inch cake pan. In the pan, sift and mix together the flour, sugar, soda and cocoa.

Make 3 wells in the flour mixture. Put 1 teaspoon of vanilla in the first, 1 teaspoon of vinegar in the second, and 6 tablespoons of melted margarine in the third.

Pour 1 cup of water over all and mix with a fork until ingredients are entirely moist. Bake 30 minutes, or until done.

YIELD: 9 SERVINGS
APPROX. CAL/SERV.: 230

. . . . **Black Devil's Food Cake**

      2 CUPS FLOUR
  1 ¾ CUPS SUGAR
      ½ CUP COCOA
      ½ TEASPOON SALT
      1 TABLESPOON BAKING SODA
      ⅔ CUP OIL
      1 CUP BUTTERMILK
      1 CUP STRONG COFFEE (INSTANT COFFEE MAY BE USED)

Preheat oven to 350°F.

Sift together the flour, sugar, cocoa, salt and baking soda. Add the oil and buttermilk. Stir until well blended. Bring the coffee to a boil and stir it gently into the batter. Mixture will be soupy. Bake in a greased and floured 9 × 13-inch pan, for 35 to 40 minutes.

Decorate with Minute Fudge Frosting (p. 358).

YIELD: 1 PAN (20 SERVINGS)
APPROX. CAL/SERV.: 185

· · · · · · · · · · *Minute Fudge Frosting*

    3 TABLESPOONS COCOA
    1 CUP SUGAR
    ⅓ CUP EVAPORATED SKIM MILK
    ¼ CUP MARGARINE
    ¼ TEASPOON SALT
    1 TEASPOON VANILLA EXTRACT

Mix all ingredients except vanilla. Bring to a boil and simmer one minute. Remove from the heat, add vanilla and beat until thick enough to spread.

YIELD: 20 SERVINGS
APPROX. CAL/SERV.: 250

· · · · · *Spice Cake with Meringue-Nut Topping*

Use meringue topping immediately. It tends to toughen if it stands overnight, or for a longer period.

    1 EGG, SEPARATED
    ¼ CUP SUGAR
    1 CUP SIFTED CAKE FLOUR
1 ½ TEASPOONS BAKING POWDER
    ½ TEASPOON SALT
    ½ TEASPOON CINNAMON
    ½ TEASPOON NUTMEG
    ¼ TEASPOON GROUND CLOVES
    ½ TEASPOON ALLSPICE
    ½ CUP DARK BROWN SUGAR, FIRMLY PACKED
    3 TABLESPOONS OIL
    ½ CUP SKIM MILK

Preheat oven to 350°F.
Beat the egg white until frothy. Gradually beat in the sugar until stiff and glossy.
In another bowl, sift together the flour, baking powder, salt and

spices. Mix in the brown sugar. Blend in the oil and ⅔ of the milk. Beat 1 minute. Add remaining milk and egg yolk and beat 1 minute longer.

Fold in the stiffly beaten egg white. Pour batter into a lightly oiled 8 × 8 ×2-inch pan. Bake 30 minutes, or until done.

This cake may be sprinkled with chopped nuts before baking or topped after baking with the following meringue.

YIELD: 1 PAN (9 SERVINGS)
APPROX. CAL/SERV.: 160

Meringue-Nut Topping

1 EGG WHITE
⅓ CUP DARK BROWN SUGAR, FIRMLY PACKED
¼ CUP CHOPPED PECANS

Beat egg white until frothy. Gradually add sugar, beating until meringue is stiff. When cake is done, spread meringue over top, and broil just until golden. Watch carefully, meringue will brown very quickly. Decorate top with chopped pecans.

APPROX. CAL/SERV.: 215

Gingerbread

1 CUP NEW ORLEANS MOLASSES (DARK)
½ CUP BROWN SUGAR
½ CUP OIL
½ TEASPOON CINNAMON
½ TEASPOON CLOVES
½ TEASPOON NUTMEG
1 TEASPOON GINGER
1 CUP BOILING WATER
2½ CUPS FLOUR, UNSIFTED
1 TEASPOON BAKING SODA

Preheat oven to 350°F.
Blend together the first 7 ingredients and stir in the boiling water.

Recipe continues...

Mix in the unsifted flour. Dissolve the baking soda in 2 tablespoons of hot water; add to batter. Pour into a greased 8 × 8 × 2-inch cake pan. Bake 30 minutes.

YIELD: 1 PAN (9 SERVINGS)
APPROX. CAL/SERV.: 350

············· *Refrigerator Pineapple Cheese Cake*

    1 CUP GRAHAM CRACKER CRUMBS
    2 TABLESPOONS MARGARINE, MELTED
    1 TABLESPOON OIL
    1 3-OUNCE PACKAGE PINEAPPLE-FLAVORED GELATIN
    1 CUP BOILING WATER
 1½ POUNDS LOW-FAT COTTAGE CHEESE
    ¼ CUP SUGAR
    ½ TEASPOON SALT
    1 8½-OUNCE CAN CRUSHED PINEAPPLE IN JUICE, UNDRAINED
    1 TABLESPOON WATER
    2 TEASPOONS CORNSTARCH

Combine the first 3 ingredients. Press onto the bottom of an 8-inch spring form pan. Chill.

Dissolve the gelatin in the boiling water and cool to lukewarm.

In a blender, thoroughly mix the cheese, sugar and salt. Slowly add the gelatin and blend well.

Pour mixture into the chilled crust, and refrigerate until firm.

In a saucepan, bring the crushed pineapple and juice, the water and the cornstarch to a boil, stirring constantly. Cool 15 minutes and spread over the top of the cheese cake. Chill at least 1 hour.

YIELD: 16 SERVINGS

APPROX. CAL/SERV.: 125

· · · · · · · · · · · · **Baked Cheese Pie**

Crust:

 1 CUP GRAHAM CRACKER CRUMBS
 ¼ CUP MELTED MARGARINE

Filling:

 2 CUPS LOW-FAT COTTAGE CHEESE
 2 TABLESPOONS MELTED MARGARINE
 2 MEDIUM EGGS
 ½ CUP SUGAR
 ½ CUP SKIM MILK
 ¼ CUP FLOUR
 ½ TEASPOON SALT
 ¼ CUP LEMON JUICE
 1 TABLESPOON GRATED LEMON RIND

Preheat oven to 300°F.

Mix the graham cracker crumbs with the margarine, and press ¾ of the mixture into bottom and to sides of a 9-inch pie plate. Save remaining crumbs to sprinkle on top of the pie, if a fruit topping is not used.

To make the filling, in a blender or a mixing bowl, beat cottage cheese until creamy. Mix in the melted margarine.

Add eggs, 1 at a time, then the sugar and skim milk beating well after each addition. Add the remaining ingredients, beating until smooth. Pour the cheese mixture into the prepared graham cracker crust and sprinkle remaining crumbs on top. Bake 1½ hours or until set. Cool for several hours before cutting.

YIELD: 10 SERVINGS

APPROX. CAL/SERV.: 205 (OR 225 WITH FRUIT TOPPING)

Recipe continues…

· · · · · · · · · · · · · · · · *variation*

If a fruit topping is desired, omit the crumb topping and, after baking, spread on any thickened fruit mixture such as the one for Refrigerator Pineapple Cheese Cake (p. 360). Strawberries, cherries or blueberries are also excellent fruits to use.

· · · · · · · · · · · *Easy Apple Cake*

It is very good just as it is, when served soon after baking. Any left-over cake would be delicious served with a lemon sauce.

  2 CUPS DICED APPLES
  1 CUP SUGAR
  ⅓ CUP OIL
  ½ TEASPOON VANILLA EXTRACT
  1 EGG, BEATEN
1½ CUPS UNSIFTED FLOUR
  1 TEASPOON BAKING POWDER
  1 TEASPOON BAKING SODA
  1 TEASPOON CINNAMON
  ½ TEASPOON SALT
  ½ CUP RAISINS

Preheat oven to 350°F.

Combine apples and sugar in a mixing bowl and let stand 10 minutes. Blend oil, vanilla and egg with the apples. Then combine the dry ingredients and mix in well. Stir in the raisins.

Pour into greased 8-inch square cake pan. Bake 35 to 40 minutes.

YIELD: 9 SERVINGS
APPROX. CAL/SERV.: 290

· · · · *Whole Wheat Applesauce Cake or Cupcakes*

½ CUP OIL
¾ CUP GRANULATED BROWN SUGAR
1 CUP APPLESAUCE
1½ CUPS UNSIFTED WHOLE WHEAT FLOUR
1 TEASPOON BAKING SODA
1 TEASPOON CINNAMON

Preheat oven to 375°F. Oil and flour an 8-inch round or square baking pan, or muffin tins.

Cream the oil and sugar together and mix in the applesauce and baking soda. Add flour and cinnamon, blending thoroughly.

Pour the batter into pan, or make individual cakes in muffin tins. Bake 30 minutes for an 8-inch cake, about 20 minutes for cupcakes.

YIELD: 12 CUPCAKES OR 1 8-INCH PAN (9 SERVINGS)
APPROX. CAL/SERV.: 1 CUPCAKE = 200   1 SQUARE = 265

· · · · · · · *Williamsburg Orange-Wine Cake*

The wine is in the frosting. A delicious tasting cake.

½ CUP MARGARINE
1 CUP SUGAR
4 EGG WHITES, UNBEATEN
2 TEASPOONS GRATED ORANGE RIND
1 TEASPOON VANILLA EXTRACT
1 CUP SEEDLESS GOLDEN RAISINS
½ CUP CHOPPED WALNUTS
2 CUPS SIFTED CAKE FLOUR
1 TEASPOON BAKING SODA
½ TEASPOON SALT
1 CUP BUTTERMILK

Preheat oven to 350°F.
Cream the margarine and sugar until fluffy. Thoroughly blend in

Recipe continues...

the unbeaten egg whites, orange rind, vanilla, raisins and walnuts. Sift the flour with the baking soda and salt and add to the batter alternately with the buttermilk, beginning and ending with the flour mixture.

Pour into a 9 × 9-inch oiled and floured square cake pan. Bake 30 to 40 minutes.

YIELD: 12 SERVINGS
APPROX. CAL/SERV.: 275 (OR 425 WITH FROSTING)

· · · · · · · · · · · · · *frosting*

½ CUP SOFT MARGARINE
2 CUPS CONFECTIONERS' SUGAR
2 TABLESPOONS SHERRY

Cream together margarine, confectioners' sugar and sherry until fluffy. Use to frost cooled cake.

· · · · · *Quick Pineapple Upside-Down Cake*

¼ CUP MELTED MARGARINE
½ CUP FIRMLY PACKED BROWN SUGAR
1½ CUPS CRUSHED PINEAPPLE
1 CUP SIFTED CAKE FLOUR
½ TEASPOON SALT
¾ CUP SUGAR
¼ CUP OIL
½ CUP SKIM MILK
1½ TEASPOONS BAKING POWDER
2 EGG WHITES, UNBEATEN
½ TEASPOON VANILLA EXTRACT

Preheat oven to 350°F.

Pour the melted margarine into an 8-inch square pan. Sprinkle with brown sugar and line bottom of pan with crushed pineapple.

In a mixing bowl, sift together the flour, salt and white sugar. Add the oil and ¼ cup of the milk. Stir until the flour is dampened, then beat 1 minute. Stir in the baking powder and the remaining milk, the un-beaten egg whites and the vanilla. Beat for 2 minutes. Pour batter over the crushed pineapple in the cake pan and bake 35 to 40 minutes, or until a toothpick inserted in the cake comes out clean. Remove from the oven, cool slightly and invert onto a serving plate.

YIELD: 1 PAN (9 SERVINGS)

APPROX. CAL/SERV.: 290

· · · · · · · · · · · · *White Layer Cake*

½ CUP (1 STICK) MARGARINE, SOFTENED
1 TEASPOON VANILLA EXTRACT
½ TEASPOON ALMOND EXTRACT
1½ CUPS SUGAR
2½ CUPS SIFTED CAKE FLOUR
1½ TEASPOONS BAKING POWDER
½ TEASPOON SALT
1⅓ CUPS BUTTERMILK
4 EGG WHITES, AT ROOM TEMPERATURE
1 RECIPE FOR 7-MINUTE FROSTING, FLAVORED (p. 366)

Preheat oven to 350°F.

Cream together the margarine, vanilla extract, almond extract and all but ¼ cup of the sugar. Sift together the flour, baking powder and salt, and add the creamed mixture alternately with the buttermilk, start-ing and ending with the dry ingredients.

Beat the egg whites until foamy. Gradually add the remaining ¼ cup of sugar and beat to stiff peaks. Fold into batter and pour into 2 9-inch layer cake pans lined with wax paper.

Bake at 350°F. for about 30 minutes. Cool 10 minutes and remove from pans. When cake is thoroughly cool, frost with a flavored 7-Minute Frosting (p. 366).

YIELD: 16 SERVINGS

APPROX. CAL/SERV.: 190 (OR 265 WITH FROSTING)

Recipe continues...

. . . . *variations*

Fill layers with jam or an acceptable pudding mix, which may be combined with fruit. Example: Put lemon pudding between layers and ice with Lemon Flavored 7-minute Frosting.

Fill layers with fruits or pudding and dribble flavored Confectioners' Glaze (p. 389) over the top and sides of the cake.

APPROX. CAL/SERV.: 410

. . . . *Nell's Irish Boiled Cake*

½ CUP BROWN SUGAR
¼ POUND MARGARINE
½ CUP DARK RAISINS
½ CUP CURRANTS
½ CUP WHITE RAISINS
1 CUP WATER
2 CUPS WHOLE WHEAT FLOUR
1½ TEASPOONS BAKING POWDER
⅛ TEASPOON SALT

Preheat oven to 350°F.
Combine sugar, margarine, fruits and water. Boil 20 minutes. Cool.
Add remaining ingredients and mix well.
Pour into a 4 × 8-inch loaf pan.
Bake 45 minutes at 350°F.; lower heat to 325°F. and bake 15 minutes or until done.

YIELD: 1 LOAF (16 SLICES)
APPROX. CAL/SERV.: 170

. . . . *7-Minute Frosting*

2 EGG WHITES (ABOUT ¼ CUP)
1½ CUPS SUGAR
¼ TEASPOON CREAM OF TARTAR; OR 1 TABLESPOON LIGHT CORN SYRUP
⅓ CUP WATER
1 TEASPOON VANILLA EXTRACT

Combine egg whites, sugar, cream of tartar and water in the top of a double boiler. With an electric mixer beat on high speed 1 minute, then place over boiling water and beat on high speed 7 minutes. Remove top of double boiler from the heat; add vanilla. Then, beat 2 minutes longer on high speed.

YIELD: SUFFICIENT TO FROST 1 2-LAYER CAKE (16 SERVINGS)
APPROX. CAL/SERV.: 75

· · · · · · · · · · · · · · *variations*

LEMON FLAVORED: Substitute 1 tablespoon of lemon juice for the vanilla extract and add ¼ teaspoon grated lemon peel during the last minute of beating.

FRUITS: Add crushed fruits to the frosting or substitute fruit flavorings for the vanilla extract.

RUM: Substitute rum or sherry flavoring for the vanilla extract.

· · · · · · · · · · · · *Meringue Shells*

3 EGG WHITES
DASH SALT
¼ TEASPOON CREAM OF TARTAR
¼ TEASPOON VANILLA EXTRACT
⅔ CUP SUGAR

Preheat oven to 275°F.

For a single large shell, lightly oil a 9-inch pie pan. For small individual meringues, place unglazed brown paper on a cookie sheet.

Beat the egg whites, salt and cream of tartar until foamy. Add sugar gradually, beating until stiff glossy peaks form and sugar is completely dissolved. Add vanilla and beat 1 minute more.

Spread the meringue in a pie pan, building up the sides to be thicker than the bottom, or shape into 12 4-inch diameter shells making a depression in each with the back of a spoon.

Bake 1 hour and 15 minutes (until dry and a light creamy color).

Recipe continues...

Let cool, and remove carefully from the pan or sheet. Meringues may be stored in an airtight container until ready for filling.

YIELD: 1 9-INCH SHELL OR 12 INDIVIDUAL MERINGUES
APPROX. CAL/SERV.: 1 SHELL = 60   1 MERINGUE = 45

. . . . **Ginger-Berry Filling**

1 10-OUNCE PACKAGE FROZEN BERRIES
1 TABLESPOON SUGAR
1½ TEASPOONS CORNSTARCH
1 TABLESPOON LEMON JUICE
¼ TEASPOON POWDERED GINGER
4 INDIVIDUAL MERINGUE SHELLS

Thaw the berries and drain them, reserving ½ cup of syrup. Combine the syrup with the sugar and cornstarch; cook, stirring until thickened. Stir in the berries, lemon juice and ginger.

Spoon the berry mixture into the meringue shells. Chill until filling becomes firm.

YIELD: 4 SERVINGS
APPROX. CAL/SERV.: 130

. . . . **Strawberry Frozen Dessert**

1 10-OUNCE PACKAGE FROZEN STRAWBERRIES
3 TABLESPOONS FROZEN LEMONADE CONCENTRATE
6 TABLESPOONS SUGAR
1½ CUPS EVAPORATED SKIM MILK
1 EGG WHITE
1 9-INCH MERINGUE SHELL (OPTIONAL)

Combine the strawberries with the lemonade concentrate. Pour the evaporated skim milk into a freezing tray and freeze until mushy around the edges.

Put into a chilled bowl and beat to the consistency of whipped cream.

Beat 1 egg white until frothy. Add the sugar slowly, beating well after each addition. Fold in the whipped milk and the strawberry mixture. Pour into 3 freezing trays and freeze partially.

Place in a chilled bowl and beat again. Return to the freezer for 8 hours, or overnight.

Beat again until the dessert is the consistency of ice cream. Freeze until set. Serve plain or in a meringue shell.

YIELD: 9 SERVINGS

APPROX. CAL/SERV.: 110 (OR 170 WITH MERINGUE)

Meringue "Egg" Baskets

2 CUPS FRUIT-FLAVORED ICE (ORANGE, LEMON, RASPBERRY)*
4 INDIVIDUAL MERINGUE SHELLS

For each serving, place 1 tablespoon each of orange, lemon and raspberry ice into an individual meringue shell. To complete the egg basket, pipe cleaner handles may be inserted through the edges of the meringues.

YIELD: 4 SERVINGS

APPROX. CAL/SERV.: 125

Pie Pastry

Pie pastries made with oil are tender though not as flaky as pastries made with harder fats. They are, nonetheless, pleasing as well as simple and quick to make.

2 CUPS ALL-PURPOSE FLOUR
1¼ TEASPOONS SALT
⅓ CUP OIL
3 TABLESPOONS COLD SKIM MILK

Preheat oven to 425°F.

Sift flour and salt together into a mixing bowl. Mix the oil with the

---

* *Meringues may also be filled with other ices or sherbets, ice milk, fresh fruit or Bavarian cream.*

Recipe continues...

cold milk, and pour all at once into the flour. Stir lightly with a fork until blended, adding more liquid if necessary to make dough hold together. Divide into 2 portions. Refrigerate for a few minutes to make dough easier to work. Flatten one ball of dough slightly and place on a sheet of wax paper or cellophane wrap. Put another sheet over top, and roll out quickly. Do not roll too thin. Remove top sheet of paper and turn over dough onto pie plate. Remove second sheet, and lift crust around the edges so it settles into the plate. Trim and flute the edges with a fork or your fingers. Crust may be refrigerated before filling, or frozen if not needed for several days. Bake according to pie recipe.

YIELD: PASTRY FOR A 9-INCH 2-CRUST PIE

APPROX. CAL/SERV.: 735

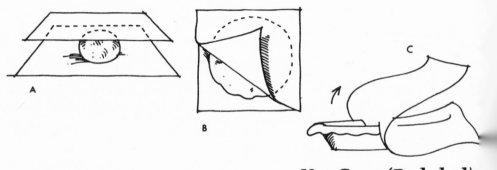

Nut Crust (Prebaked)

This prebaked crust makes an excellent base for many single crust pies, and goes well with chiffon filling. It resembles cookie dough.

1 CUP ALL-PURPOSE FLOUR

⅓ CUP MARGARINE, SOFTENED

¼ CUP FINELY CHOPPED PECANS

¼ CUP CONFECTIONERS' SUGAR

Preheat oven to 400°F.

Mix all ingredients to a soft dough. Press firmly and evenly against the bottom and sides (not the rim) of a 9-inch pie pan.

Bake 12 to 15 minutes, or until lightly browned. Cool and fill.

YIELD: 1 9-INCH CRUST (8 SERVINGS)

APPROX. CAL/SERV.: 130

· · · · · · · · · · · · **Crumb Pie Crust**

Another excellent prebaked crust for cooked fillings.

1 CUP DRY CRUMBS, MADE FROM MELBA TOAST, GRAHAM CRACKERS,
CORNFLAKES OR OTHER CRISP CEREAL
¼ CUP SUGAR
2 TABLESPOONS OIL
¼ TEASPOON CINNAMON

Preheat oven to 375°F.
Toss ingredients until crumbs are well moistened with the oil. Press
carefully into a pie pan, covering bottom and sides. Bake 10 minutes.

YIELD: 1 9-INCH CRUST (8 SERVINGS)
APPROX. CAL/SERV.: 105

· · · · · · · · · · · **Fresh Strawberry Pie**

An attractive, tasty dessert, especially good served with whipped
cottage cheese lightly dusted with cinnamon.

1 9-INCH BAKED PIE SHELL
¾ CUP SUGAR
2 TABLESPOONS CORNSTARCH
2 TABLESPOONS WHITE CORN SYRUP
1 CUP WATER
2 TABLESPOONS STRAWBERRY GELATIN POWDER
1 QUART FRESH WHOLE STRAWBERRIES, TRIMMED AND WASHED

Recipe continues...

Mix the sugar, cornstarch, syrup and water together. Bring to a boil and cook until thick and clear. Add the gelatin powder, stirring until dissolved. Cool.

Arrange the whole strawberries to cover the bottom of the baked pie shell. Pour the gelatin mixture over the strawberries and chill until set.

YIELD: 8 SERVINGS

APPROX. CAL/SERV.: 230 (OR 185 IN 10 SERVINGS)

Apple Pie

PIE PASTRY FOR 9-INCH 2-CRUST PIE, UNBAKED

  4 CUPS APPLES, SLICED

  1 CUP SUGAR

  ½ TEASPOON CINNAMON

  ½ TEASPOON VANILLA EXTRACT

GRATED RIND FROM HALF A LEMON

  1 TABLESPOON LEMON JUICE

  1 TABLESPOON MARGARINE

Preheat oven to 450°F.

Line a 9-inch pan with half the pastry and place in refrigerator to chill.

In a bowl, mix the sliced apples with the sugar, cinnamon, vanilla. lemon rind and juice.

Put into the unbaked pie shell, cover with the remaining crust, and cut steam holes. Bake 10 minutes at 450°F., then reduce oven heat to 350°F. and bake 30 to 35 minutes more. Sprinkle with granulated sugar.

YIELD: 8 SERVINGS

APPROX. CAL/SERV.: 345 (OR 270 IN 10 SERVINGS)

Walnut-Crumb Apple Pie

· · · · · · · · ·

1 9-INCH PIE SHELL, UNBAKED
¾ CUP FLOUR
½ CUP LIGHT BROWN SUGAR, PACKED
½ TEASPOON NUTMEG
½ TEASPOON CINNAMON
¼ CUP MARGARINE
½ CUP CHOPPED WALNUTS
½ TEASPOON BAKING SODA
⅓ CUP BOILING WATER
¼ CUP LIGHT MOLASSES
1 20-OUNCE CAN SLICED APPLES, DRAINED

Preheat oven to 400°F.

Combine flour, sugar and spices.

Cut in the margarine until mixture has a crumbly consistency. Mix in the nuts. Turn half of the mixture into the unbaked pie shell.

In a large bowl, dissolve baking soda in the boiling water. Add molasses and apples. Pour apples on top of flour mixture in the pie shell. Cover with remaining flour mixture. Place in the oven *on a cookie sheet* and bake 40 minutes.

YIELD: 8 SERVINGS
APPROX. CAL/SERV.: 340 (OR 275 IN 10 SERVINGS)

Norwegian Apple Pie

· · · · · · · · ·

1 EGG
¾ CUP SUGAR
1 TEASPOON VANILLA EXTRACT
¼ TEASPOON SALT
1 TEASPOON BAKING POWDER
½ CUP FLOUR
½ CUP CHOPPED WALNUTS
1 CUP DICED APPLES

Recipe continues...

Preheat oven to 350°F.

Beat egg, sugar, vanilla extract, salt and baking powder together until smooth and fluffy. Beat in the flour until smooth and well blended.

Stir in walnuts and apples. Turn into a lightly greased 8-inch pie plate and bake 30 minutes. Pie will puff up as it cooks, then collapse as it cools.

Serve warm, topped with a scoop of ice milk.

YIELD: 8 SERVINGS
APPROX. CAL/SERV.: 170 (OR 270 WITH ICE MILK)

Pink Lemonade Pie

A simple pie but just delicious. Great for a hot summer day!

1 9-INCH PIE SHELL, BAKED
1 CUP EVAPORATED SKIM MILK
1 ENVELOPE UNFLAVORED GELATIN
¼ CUP COLD WATER
1 6-OUNCE CAN FROZEN PINK LEMONADE CONCENTRATE, THAWED
¾ CUP SUGAR

Chill the evaporated milk in the freezer until ice crystals begin to form around the edges.

Soften the gelatin in water. Add lemonade and stir over low heat until the gelatin dissolves. Add the sugar, stirring until dissolved, but not thickened.

Transfer the evaporated milk to a chilled bowl and beat at high speed until stiff. Fold in the cooled gelatin mixture. Pour into the baked pie shell and chill until firm, 3 or 4 hours.

YIELD: 8 SERVINGS
APPROX. CAL/SERV.: 245 (OR 195 IN 10 SERVINGS)

. . . . **Lime Chiffon Pie** ✓

1 9-INCH PASTRY SHELL, BAKED AND COOLED
1 3-OUNCE PACKAGE LIME-FLAVORED GELATIN
¾ CUP BOILING WATER
1 TEASPOON GRATED LEMON RIND
½ CUP SUGAR
½ CUP NONFAT DRY MILK
½ CUP ICE WATER
2 TABLESPOONS LEMON JUICE

Dissolve the gelatin in boiling water. Add grated lemon rind and ¼ cup of the sugar. Stir well. Cool until the mixture is the consistency of unbeaten egg white (about 20 minutes).

Place the nonfat dry milk and ice water in a mixing bowl. With an electric mixer, beat on high speed 3 to 4 minutes until soft peaks form. Add lemon juice and continue beating. Add the remaining ¼ cup of sugar gradually, and continue beating until stiff peaks form. Fold into gelatin mixture and combine thoroughly.

Pour into the cool pastry shell. Chill until firm (about 3 hours).

YIELD: 8 SERVINGS
APPROX. CAL/SERV.: 210 (OR 160 IN 10 SERVINGS)

. . . . **Baked Pumpkin Pie**

1 9-INCH PIE SHELL, UNBAKED
⅔ CUP GRANULATED SUGAR
½ TEASPOON SALT
½ TEASPOON CINNAMON
½ TEASPOON GINGER
½ TEASPOON NUTMEG
PINCH OF GROUND CLOVES
1½ CUPS CANNED PUMPKIN
1 TEASPOON VANILLA EXTRACT
1½ CUPS EVAPORATED SKIM MILK
½ TEASPOON ORANGE RIND
3 EGG WHITES, SLIGHTLY BEATEN

Recipe continues...

Preheat oven to 450°F.

Combine the sugar, salt, cinnamon, ginger, nutmeg and cloves. Stir in the pumpkin. Add the vanilla, evaporated milk, orange rind and egg whites. Beat with an electric mixer until smooth.

Pour into the unbaked pie shell and bake 10 minutes at 450°F. Reduce the heat to 325°F. and bake until a knife inserted in the filling comes out clean, about 45 minutes.

YIELD: 8 SERVINGS

APPROX. CAL/SERV.: 210 (OR 165 IN 10 SERVINGS)

· · · · · · · · · · *Pumpkin Chiffon Pie*

1 9-INCH PIE SHELL, BAKED
1 ENVELOPE UNFLAVORED GELATIN
¼ CUP COLD WATER
1 CUP SUGAR
3 TABLESPOONS CORNSTARCH
½ TEASPOON SALT
½ TEASPOON GINGER
¼ TEASPOON NUTMEG
1 TEASPOON CINNAMON
1 CUP CANNED PUMPKIN
1 CUP EVAPORATED SKIM MILK
2 TABLESPOONS MARGARINE
4 EGG WHITES
¼ CUP CRUSHED PECANS

Soften the gelatin in the cold water.

Combine ½ cup of the sugar, with the cornstarch, salt, ginger, nutmeg and cinnamon. Add pumpkin and milk. Mix well. Cook over medium heat until thickened, stirring constantly. Add the gelatin mixture and the margarine, stirring until dissolved. Cool until partially set.

Beat the egg whites until soft peaks form, and gradually beat in the remaining ½ cup of sugar. Continue beating until stiff, and fold into pumpkin mixture. Place in the pastry shell. Garnish with crushed pecans.

Serve chilled.

YIELD: 8 SERVINGS

APPROX. CAL/SERV.: 285 (OR 225 IN 10 SERVINGS)

Aunt Emma's Shoo-Fly Pie

A Pennsylvania Dutch delight!

PIE PASTRY FOR A 9-INCH ONE-CRUST PIE
1½ CUPS FLOUR
 ½ CUP FIRMLY PACKED LIGHT BROWN SUGAR
 ⅛ TEASPOON SALT
 ¼ CUP MARGARINE
 1 TEASPOON BAKING SODA
 ¾ CUP BOILING WATER
 ¾ CUP DARK CORN SYRUP
 ¼ TEASPOON NUTMEG
 ¼ TEASPOON CINNAMON
 ¼ TEASPOON CLOVE

Preheat oven to 375°F.

Line a 9-inch pie pan with pie pastry. Combine flour with brown sugar and salt. Cut in the margarine until the mixture resembles corn meal. Pour ⅓ of the crumbs into the pie shell.

Add baking soda to the hot water, stir in the dark corn syrup and spices and pour ⅓ of the mixture over the crumbs in the pie shell. Continue alternating layers, ending with crumbs on top, and bake 35 minutes. Serve warm or cold.

YIELD: 8 SERVINGS
APPROX. CAL/SERV.: 395 (OR 315 IN 10 SERVINGS)

Nutty Cranberry Pie

PASTRY FOR 1 9-INCH TWO-CRUST PIE, UNBAKED
 1 CUP SUGAR
1½ TABLESPOONS CORNSTARCH
 ⅓ CUP LIGHT CORN SYRUP
 ¾ CUP WATER
 1 TEASPOON GRATED ORANGE OR LEMON RIND
 3 CUPS FRESH CRANBERRIES
 ½ CUP SEEDLESS RAISINS
 ¾ CUP WALNUTS (FINELY CHOPPED)
 2 TABLESPOONS OIL

Recipe continues...

Preheat oven to 425°F.

Combine the sugar and cornstarch. Mix the corn syrup and lemon peel with the water and add to the sugar and cornstarch.

Bring to a boil, then stir in the cranberries and raisins. Boil until the cranberries pop, then remove from the heat and add the nuts and the oil. Cool until mixture is lukewarm.

Pour cranberry mixture into an unbaked 9-inch pie shell. Top with lattice or regular crust. Bake at 425°F. for 20 minutes, then reduce the heat to 375°F. and bake for 20 minutes.

This pie may be served either hot or cold.

YIELD: 8 SERVINGS

APPROX. CAL/SERV.: 480 (OR 380 IN 10 SERVINGS)

. . . . ***Raspberry Chiffon Pie***

1 9-INCH PIE SHELL, BAKED

1¼ CUPS (10-OUNCE PACKAGE) FROZEN RASPBERRIES, SWEETENED

1 TABLESPOON UNFLAVORED GELATIN

½ CUP WATER, AT ROOM TEMPERATURE

¼ CUP PLUS 2 TABLESPOONS SUGAR

1 TABLESPOON ALL-PURPOSE FLOUR

¼ TEASPOON SALT

2 TABLESPOONS LEMON JUICE

⅓ CUP ICE WATER

⅓ CUP NONFAT DRY MILK

1 TABLESPOON LEMON JUICE

2 TABLESPOONS GRANULATED SUGAR

Thaw the raspberries and drain, reserving the juice and saving 6 firm berries for garnish.

Soften the gelatin powder in the water. Combine ¼ cup of the sugar, with the flour and salt in a saucepan. Add the raspberry juice and softened gelatin. Stir and heat slowly until sugar is dissolved. Remove from heat and add 2 tablespoons of the lemon juice and the berries. Cool until thick and syrupy, but not set.

Chill the beaters of the electric mixer. In a chilled bowl, combine ice water and nonfat dry milk. Beat until soft peaks are formed (about 3 or 4 minutes). Add the remaining tablespoon of lemon juice and beat another 3 or 4 minutes, until stiff. Fold in the 2 tablespoons of sugar, blending well on low speed. Whip this into the raspberry-gelatin mixture.

Pour into baked pastry shell, and chill until firm.

YIELD: 8 SERVINGS
APPROX. CAL/SERV.: 180 (OR 145 IN 10 SERVINGS)

Baked Ginger Pears

8 CANNED PEAR HALVES, WITH JUICE
½ CUP BROWN SUGAR
1 TEASPOON LEMON JUICE
½ TEASPOON GROUND GINGER; OR CHOPPED CRYSTALLIZED GINGER TO TASTE
¼ CUP CHOPPED PECANS
CRYSTALLIZED GINGER FOR GARNISH

Preheat oven to 350°F.

Drain the pears, reserving the juice. Mix brown sugar, lemon juice, ginger and pecans. Stuff pears with this mixture and sprinkle lightly with ginger. Place close together in a baking dish and pour in the reserved pear juice to cover the bottom of the dish.

Bake 15 to 20 minutes.

Serve warm or chilled, garnished with bits of the crystallized ginger.

YIELD: 8 SERVINGS
APPROX. CAL/SERV.: 135

Lime Melon Balls

1 CUP WATER
2 TABLESPOONS SUGAR
2 TABLESPOONS LIME JUICE
2 CUPS ASSORTED MELON BALLS
POMEGRANATE SEEDS, MINT SPRIGS OR THIN LIME SLICES

Recipe continues...

Boil together the water and sugar. Cool to room temperature and add lime juice.

Pour over melon balls in sherbet glasses. Garnish with pomegranate seeds, a sprig of mint, or a thin slice of lime.

YIELD: 4 SERVINGS
APPROX. CAL/SERV.: 55

. . . . *Baked Apples*

4 BAKING APPLES
¼ CUP HONEY
½ CUP WATER
1 TEASPOON GRATED LEMON OR ORANGE RIND

Preheat oven to 375°F.
Wash and core apples, and place in baking dish.
Combine the honey with the water and grated rind. Pour over the apples and bake, covered, for 30 minutes, basting two or three times.
Uncover, baste again and bake 15 minutes longer, or until tender.

YIELD: 4 SERVINGS
APPROX. CAL/SERV.: 135

. . . . *Minted Grapefruit*

2 FRESH GRAPEFRUIT OR CANNED OR FROZEN GRAPEFRUIT SECTIONS
1½ OUNCES CRÈME DE MENTHE
MINT SPRIGS

If fresh grapefruit is used, cut in halves and loosen sections with a grapefruit knife, leaving them in the shells. Or if canned or frozen grapefruit is used, pile pieces into dessert dishes.

Pour crème de menthe over top, garnish with mint sprigs.

YIELD: 4 SERVINGS
APPROX. CAL/SERV.: 80

Bananas Flambé

4 RIPE PEELED BANANAS
1 TABLESPOON LEMON JUICE
1 TABLESPOON SUGAR
4 SUGAR CUBES SOAKED IN LEMON EXTRACT

Preheat oven to 400°F.

Sprinkle lemon juice and sugar over the peeled whole bananas and place on a lightly oiled pie plate. Bake 20 minutes or until slightly brown.

Flame the bananas by placing on each a sugar cube soaked in lemon extract. Light the cubes at the table.

YIELD: 4 SERVINGS
APPROX. CAL/SERV.: 120

Baked Prune Whip

2 CUPS COOKED PRUNES
4 TABLESPOONS SUGAR
2 TABLESPOONS ORANGE JUICE
1 TEASPOON GRATED ORANGE PEEL
½ TEASPOON CINNAMON
4 EGG WHITES

Preheat oven to 350°F.

Remove pits from the prunes and purée in a blender. Add 2 tablespoons of the sugar, and the orange juice, orange peel and cinnamon. Blend well.

Beat the egg whites with the remaining 2 tablespoons of sugar until stiff. Fold the puréed fruit into the egg whites, and pile lightly in a greased 1½-quart casserole dish. Bake uncovered 20 to 30 minutes, until lightly browned and puffed up like a soufflé. If desired, serve with Orange Sauce (p. 389).

YIELD: 8 SERVINGS
APPROX. CAL/SERV.: 105

· · · · · · · · · · · *Claret Spiced Oranges*

4 ORANGES, PEELED AND SECTIONED
5 TABLESPOONS SUGAR
½ CUP WATER
¾ CUP CLARET WINE
2 WHOLE CLOVES
1 3-INCH STICK CINNAMON
1 TABLESPOON LEMON JUICE

Place orange sections in a bowl.

In a saucepan, combine the remaining ingredients, bring to a boil and simmer 5 minutes. Pour hot syrup over the oranges. Let cool and refrigerate about 4 hours or overnight. Remove whole spices and serve cold.

YIELD: 6 SERVINGS
APPROX. CAL/SERV.: 120

· · · · · · · · · · · · · *Cherries Jubilee*

2 CUPS PITTED BING CHERRIES, WITH JUICE
½ CUP CURRANT JELLY
1 TABLESPOON CORNSTARCH
1 TABLESPOON GRATED ORANGE RIND
2 TABLESPOONS HEATED BRANDY

Pour juice from cherries into a saucepan with the currant jelly, cornstarch and orange rind. Cook over low heat until the jelly melts. Stir in the cherries. Cover and simmer 10 minutes.

At the table, pour the warm brandy over the cherries in the serving pan and flame. Spoon into meringue shells or over ice milk while cherries are still flaming.

YIELD: 8 SERVINGS
APPROX. CAL/SERV.: 115

· · · · · · *Fresh Fruit Compote with Wine*

Buy fresh seasonal fruits; wash and prepare them by separating into sections, cubing or slicing, or leaving them whole. You may use pineapple, oranges or peaches, whichever combination seems best. Combine in a bowl and pour white or rosé wine to cover. Marinate several hours in the refrigerator. Heap into long-stemmed crystal compotes and garnish with fresh pomegranate seeds.

APPROX. CAL/SERV.: ½ CUP = 80

· · · · · · · · · *Mint Julep Fruit Cup*

Combine fresh fruit and spoon into compotes. Sprinkle with crème de menthe or mint extract. Garnish with a small scoop of lime sherbet and a fresh mint leaf or with crystallized mint leaves.

APPROX. CAL/SERV.: ½ CUP = 155

· · · · · · *Fresh Fruit Compote with Kirsch*

Cut up apples, pears and persimmons. Mix with frozen drained raspberries. Pour orange juice and kirsch, if desired, over all. Chill and serve.

APPROX. CAL/SERV.: ½ CUP = 110

· · · · · · · · · · *Pineapple Boats*

Select a medium-size pineapple. Split it lengthwise into quarters, leaving plume attached to each quarter. With a sharp knife, separate flesh from the shell in one piece. Trim away the core. Return the long

Recipe continues...

section of flesh to its shell, and cut it vertically into ½-inch wedges. Stick a toothpick in each, and arrange pineapple quarters in a circle on a round, flat serving tray. Place small bunches of grapes between them.

Some other fruits also make excellent boats. Cut cantaloupe or honeydew into eighth's, separate flesh in a single piece from each section, then slice vertically into small wedges. Stick a toothpick in each. Set boats on a tray garnished with rhododendron or lemon leaves.

APPROX. CAL/SERV.: 1 PINEAPPLE WEDGE PLUS 6 GRAPES = 30

2 MELON WEDGES = 20

· · · · · · · · · · · *Watermelon Basket*

This is not only a delicious dessert, it is also beautiful.

1 WATERMELON

FRUITS OF YOUR CHOICE; CANTALOUPE, HONEYDEW, BANANA, ORANGE, GRAPEFRUIT, FRESH PINEAPPLE, PEACHES, BLUEBERRIES, STRAW-BERRIES, CHERRIES, SEEDLESS GRAPES, APPLES, WHATEVER IS AVAIL-ABLE

Select a watermelon that is a good green color and is not too big to fit on a serving tray. If the bottom side is not flat enough to keep it stable, carefully cut off a very thin slice of the green outer covering to form a flat bottom.

Outline with a shallow cut in the rind, a handle 2 to 3 inches wide across the top of the melon. When you are sure you have it well placed, deepen the cuts with a sharp knife and remove the sections.

It will then look like this:

Hollow out portions of melon under the handle which should remain about ½ inch thick.

Hollow out the meat of the melon, making as many melon balls as possible with a melon scoop, making certain to leave a sufficiently heavy rind to hold its shape. Drain the juice.

Outline the rim of the "basket" with a sawtooth pattern and fill it with the melon balls and other fruits of your choice. Decorate it with mint or other greens.

APPROX. CAL/SERV.: ½ CUP = 40

• • • • • • • • • • • • • • • • *Crêpes* ✓

This recipe makes 18 to 24 crêpes but uses only 2 eggs. Result: Only a fraction of an egg per serving and no need to worry about the fat content, if each person eats only 2.

2 EGGS
1 CUP SKIM MILK
½ TEASPOON SALT
1 CUP FLOUR

Beat the eggs, and blend with all other ingredients until batter is smooth and just thick enough to coat a spoon. If batter is too thick, add a little more milk. Cover and let stand *at least* ½ hour.

Heat a 5- or 6-inch frying pan or crêpe pan. Oil lightly. Pour in just enough batter to form a very thin layer, tilting pan so batter spreads evenly. Cook on one side, turn and brown on the other side.

Repeat until all batter is used. As crêpes are finished, stack them with a layer of wax paper or foil between each. Keep warm if you are serving them immediately, or set them aside and reheat later.

Crêpes are an excellent low-fat dessert when filled with whipped low-fat cottage cheese (flavored with vanilla or grated lemon rind, sugar to taste if desired) and topped with fresh strawberries. Other fruits such as fresh raspberries or blueberries, may be used. Crêpes may also be rolled up with fruit inside—for example applesauce and topped with cinnamon flavored whipped cottage cheese).

For an elegant occasion, serve strawberries flambé over cottage-cheese-filled crêpes.

YIELD: 18–24 CRÊPES

APPROX. CAL/SERV.: 18 CRÊPES = 35   25 CRÊPES = 25

√ . . . . *Poly Whipped Topping*

This polyunsaturated substitute has a taste and consistency closely
resembling whipped cream, but it has no saturated fat.

1 TEASPOON GELATIN

2 TEASPOONS COLD WATER

3 TABLESPOONS BOILING WATER

½ CUP ICE WATER

½ CUP NONFAT DRY MILK

3 TABLESPOONS SUGAR

3 TABLESPOONS OIL

Chill a small mixing bowl. Soften gelatin with 2 teaspoons of cold
water, then add the boiling water, stirring, until gelatin is completely
dissolved. Cool until tepid. Place ice water and nonfat dry milk in the
chilled mixing bowl. Beat at high speed until the mixture forms stiff peaks.
Add the sugar, still beating, then the oil and the gelatin. Place in freezer
for about 15 minutes, then transfer to the refrigerator until ready for use.
Stir before using to retain a creamy texture.

YIELD: 2 CUPS

APPROX. CAL/SERV.: 1 CUP = 320   1 TABLESPOON = 20

. . . . *Hong Kong Sundae Topping*

1 11-OUNCE CAN MANDARIN ORANGES

1 TABLESPOON CORNSTARCH

1 8½-OUNCE CAN CRUSHED PINEAPPLE AND LIQUID

½ CUP ORANGE MARMALADE

½ TEASPOON GROUND GINGER

½ CUP SLICED, PRESERVED KUMQUATS

Drain oranges, reserving ¼ cup of syrup. Combine the syrup with
cornstarch in a saucepan. Stir in the pineapple with its liquid, the marmalade and the ginger. Cook, stirring, over medium heat until mixture
thickens and bubbles.

Stir in the oranges and kumquats.

To make a Hong Kong Sundae, pour a little of the sauce, warm or cold, over ice milk.

YIELD: 2½ CUPS

APPROX. CAL/SERV.: 1 CUP = 330   1 TABLESPOON = 20

Fresh Fruit Sauce

½ CUP SUGAR

2 TABLESPOONS CORNSTARCH

½ CUP WATER

2 CUPS FRESH FRUIT (STRAWBERRIES, RASPBERRIES, PEACHES OR OTHER FRUITS)

If large fruits are used, chop them roughly. Bring cornstarch, sugar and water to a boil.

Put in 1 cup of fresh fruit. Bring to a boil again, then remove immediately from the heat and add the remaining cup of fruit. Do not cook further. Last addition of fruit should remain uncooked.

Spoon over ice milk or over cake.

YIELD: 2½ CUPS

APPROX. CAL/SERV.: 1 CUP = 240   1 TABLESPOON = 15

Instant Jubilee Sauce

Make an elegant ice milk sundae instantly with only three ingredients.

1 16-OUNCE JAR DARK CHERRY PRESERVES

¼ CUP PORT WINE

½ TEASPOON ALMOND EXTRACT

Stir both the port wine and almond extract into the cherry preserves. Chill. Serve over ice milk.

YIELD: 1⅔ CUPS (26 TABLESPOONS)

APPROX. CAL/SERV.: 1 TABLESPOON = 50

. . . . *Cardinal Sundae Sauce*

A special sauce for lime sherbet.

½ CUP FROZEN STRAWBERRY HALVES, THAWED
½ CUP FROZEN RASPBERRIES, THAWED
 1 TEASPOON CORNSTARCH
¼ TEASPOON LEMON JUICE
 1 TABLESPOON CURRANT JELLY

Drain the strawberries and raspberries, reserving the juice. Set the berries aside.

In a saucepan, combine the cornstarch and lemon juice with the berry liquid. Bring to a boil and cook gently for 1 minute. Stir in the jelly until it melts. Remove from the heat and stir in the berries. Chill.

For each serving, spoon some sauce over a scoop of lime sherbet.

YIELD: 1 CUP
APPROX. CAL/SERV.: ½ CUP = 140   1 TABLESPOON = 20

. . . . *Chocolate Ice Milk Sauce*

2 TABLESPOONS MARGARINE
2 TABLESPOONS COCOA
2 TABLESPOONS WHITE CORN SYRUP
½ CUP SUGAR
DASH SALT
¼ CUP EVAPORATED SKIM MILK
1 TEASPOON VANILLA

In a saucepan, melt the margarine and add the cocoa, sugar, salt and syrup. Add the milk, bring to a boil and stir until smooth.

Remove from the heat and stir in the vanilla.

Serve warm or cold over ice milk.

YIELD: 1 CUP
APPROX. CAL/SERV.: 1 TABLESPOON = 50

Orange Sauce

½ CUP SUGAR

1 TABLESPOON CORNSTARCH

DASH SALT

DASH CINNAMON

¾ CUP BOILING WATER

1 TABLESPOON OIL

¼ CUP ORANGE JUICE

1 TEASPOON GRATED ORANGE RIND

2 TEASPOONS LEMON JUICE

In a saucepan, mix together the sugar, cornstarch, salt and cinnamon. Gradually add the water, bring to a boil over medium heat and cook, stirring, for 5 minutes. Remove from heat. Add oil, orange and lemon juices, and the rind.

Serve over rice pudding, plain cake or gingerbread.

YIELD: 1 CUP

APPROX. CAL/SERV.: 1 TABLESPOON = 35

Hard Sauce

½ CUP MARGARINE

2 CUPS SIFTED CONFECTIONERS' SUGAR

1 TABLESPOON SHERRY, BRANDY OR FRUIT JUICE

Cream the margarine with the sugar until fluffy. Beat in the liquid. Store in a covered container in the refrigerator. Use as needed.

YIELD: 1½ CUPS

APPROX. CAL/SERV.: 1 TABLESPOON = 70

Confectioners' Glaze

¼ CUP SKIM MILK

1 CUP CONFECTIONERS' SUGAR

½ TEASPOON VANILLA OR RUM EXTRACT

Recipe continues...

In a small bowl, stir confectioners' sugar and extract into the milk until mixture is thick enough to spread.

YIELD: ABOUT 1 CUP
APPROX. CAL/SERV.: 1 TABLESPOON = 30

· · · · · · · · · · · · · · *variations*

LEMON OR ORANGE CONFECTIONERS' GLAZE: Use lemon or orange juice in place of milk.

CHOCOLATE CONFECTIONERS' GLAZE: Add 2 tablespoons of cocoa to the sugar and follow directions for confectioners' glaze.

· · · · · · · · · · · · *Asiatic Bean Pie*

1 CUP UNCOOKED NAVY BEANS
¼ CUP MARGARINE
½ CUP SUGAR
1 WHOLE EGG AND 3 EGG WHITES
¼ TEASPOON CINNAMON
1 TEASPOON VANILLA
⅔ CUP EVAPORATED SKIM MILK

Soak beans.
Preheat oven to 350°F.
Cook beans until tender, then drain.
Mash beans using a food mill or potato masher.
Cream margarine and sugar.
Mix the eggs with the creamed margarine and sugar, then add the beans, nutmeg, cinnamon, and vanilla and mix well.
Add the milk and beat.
Pour the mixture into a 9-inch oil-pastry shell. (See Pie Pastry, p. 369.)
Bake at 350° until brown on top.

YIELD: 10 SERVINGS
APPROX. CAL/SERV.: 250

. . . . *Melon Rings with Strawberries*

1 MEDIUM CANTALOUPE OR HONEYDEW MELON
1 PINT STRAWBERRIES

Cut melon crosswise into rings 1 inch thick. Remove seeds.

Place slices on individual plates, and with a knife carefully loosen pulp by cutting around the slice ¼ inch from the rind. Do not remove rind. Slice pulp to make bite-sized pieces, leaving rind intact.

Rinse strawberries, but do not hull.

Arrange 5 or 6 strawberries in the center of each melon slice.

YIELD: 5 SERVINGS
APPROX. CAL/SERV.: 45

. . . . *Duq*

2 CUPS WATER
1 CUP LEMON LOW-FAT YOGURT

Blend water and yogurt.
Chill thoroughly and serve in a frosty pitcher.

YIELD: 3 CUPS
APPROX. CAL/SERV.: 85

. . . . *Fruit Drinks for Desserts*

1 CUP STRAWBERRIES
1 CUP ORANGE JUICE
1 BANANA

YIELD: 2 SERVINGS
APPROX. CAL/SERV.: 130

. . . . *variation*

1 CUP RASPBERRIES
1 CUP ORANGE JUICE
1 BANANA

Recipe continues...

Blend fruits and juices until smooth in an electric blender. If your blender can crush ice, add ice to make a sherbetlike dessert.

YIELD: 2 SERVINGS
APPROX. CAL/SERV.: 140

Breakfast

*M*ore people disagree about breakfast than about any other meal, whether to have one at all, or what to eat and how much. No doubt, one's attitude toward breakfast is relative to one's view of life as the day begins and to the chores that lie ahead.

In earlier times down on the farm, breakfast was an elaborate meal set out after the day's labor had started and all hands had literally worked up an appetite.

For the less active, the continental breakfast of rolls and coffee seemed quite enough.

The experts suggest that one-fourth of the day's calories be consumed at breakfast. They do not suggest that these calories be composed largely of saturated fat. Nevertheless, many breakfasts do contain far more saturated fat than one person should consume in an entire day. And of course, the more fat a meal contains, the less protein, vitamins and minerals it provides.

Pancakes or kippers, crunchy cereals or cottage cheese, be sure you are getting solid nutriment in your morning meal.

. . . . *French Toast I*

    1 EGG PLUS 1 EGG WHITE, BEATEN TOGETHER
    ¼ CUP SKIM MILK
    ¼ TEASPOON VANILLA EXTRACT
    NUTMEG
    6 SLICES BREAD, CRUSTS REMOVED

Mix egg, milk and vanilla extract. Soak bread in mixture for 5 minutes. Brown the bread slices on a greased griddle. Sprinkle each slice with nutmeg, and serve with honey, jelly or pure maple syrup.

    YIELD: 6 SERVINGS
    APPROX. CAL/SERV.: 85   1 TABLESPOON HONEY = 65
                              1 TABLESPOON JELLY = 50
                              1 TABLESPOON SYRUP = 60

. . . . *French Toast II*

This French toast made with egg whites has a smooth glazed coating.

    2 SLICES DAY-OLD WHOLE WHEAT OR ENRICHED WHITE BREAD
    2 EGG WHITES
    2 TABLESPOONS SKIM MILK
    ¼ TEASPOON VANILLA EXTRACT
    ⅛ TEASPOON CINNAMON
    DASH SALT
    ½ TABLESPOON OIL

In a mixing bowl, combine the egg whites, milk, vanilla, cinnamon and salt. Beat lightly. Heat a griddle or heavy frying pan until hot, and grease it well with oil.

Dip bread slices in the egg white mixture, and fry on both sides until golden brown and crisp. Serve with jelly.

    YIELD: 2 SERVINGS
    APPROX. CAL/SERV.: 115

. . . . *Wheat Germ Pancakes*

These pancakes deserve the raves they get, both for taste and for nutrition.

1 CUP WHITE FLOUR
2 ½ TEASPOONS BAKING POWDER
½ TEASPOON SALT
1 TABLESPOON SUGAR
½ CUP WHEAT GERM, TOASTED WITH HONEY
1 ¼ CUPS SKIM MILK
2 TABLESPOONS OIL
½ CUP LOW-FAT COTTAGE CHEESE

Sift together flour, baking powder, salt and sugar. Add wheat germ. Combine the milk and oil and stir into the dry ingredients until just moistened. Stir in cottage cheese only until mixture is slightly lumpy. (If a smooth batter is desired, you may whip the cottage cheese with the liquid ingredients in a blender.) Drop batter by spoonfuls onto a greased pan. Cook until bubbles appear on upper surface, then turn and brown on the other side. Turn only once. Continue until all batter is used. Serve with maple syrup.

YIELD: 10 4-INCH PANCAKES
APPROX. CAL/SERV.: 1 PANCAKE = 115

. . . . . . *Cottage Cheese and Cinnamon Toasties*

For each serving, spread a piece of toast with ¼ cup of low-fat cottage cheese and sprinkle with ½ teaspoon of sugar mixed with cinnamon. Put under the broiler or in a toaster-oven until sugar-cinnamon mixture bubbles. Serve at once.

APPROX. CAL/SERV.: 115

. . . . *variation*

WITH PEACH SLICES: Omit sugar. Spread toast with cottage cheese, top

Recipe continues...

with a fresh peach slice and sprinkle with cinnamon. Place in broiler until heated through. Serve immediately.

Applesauce Toast

1 TABLESPOON MARGARINE
1½ TABLESPOONS SUGAR
1 CUP APPLESAUCE
CINNAMON AND NUTMEG TO TASTE
4 SLICES BREAD (WHOLE WHEAT OR SPROUTED WHEAT BREADS ARE BEST)*

Melt margarine and combine with sugar, applesauce, cinnamon and nutmeg. Spread some of mixture on each bread slice and toast in the oven or under the broiler.

YIELD: 4 SERVINGS
APPROX. CAL/SERV.: 160

Cinnamon-Cheese Spread

Stir 1 teaspoon of cinnamon and 2 tablespoons of sugar into 1 cup of Basic Cheese Sauce (p. 11). Chill and use as a spread on toast or as a cold topping for waffles or French toast.

YIELD: 1 CUP
APPROX. CAL/SERV.: 1 TABLESPOON = 15

Fried Cornmeal Cakes

Cook cornmeal or hominy grits as for cereal. Pour into a loaf pan and chill. Turn out and slice as you would for bread. Dip in flour and sauté slowly in margarine. Serve with syrup or jam.

APPROX. CAL/SERV.: 1 SLICE = 140

*If a soft white bread is used, toast on one side before spreading mixture on the other side.

. . . . *Crunchy Cereal I*

2½ CUPS REGULAR ROLLED OATS (NOT QUICK-COOKING)
½ CUP COARSELY CHOPPED PEANUTS
½ CUP SESAME SEEDS
½ CUP SUNFLOWER SEEDS
½ CUP NONFAT DRY MILK
½ CUP WHEAT GERM
¼ CUP BROWN SUGAR, PACKED
¼ CUP OIL
2 TEASPOONS GROUND CINNAMON
2 TEASPOONS VANILLA EXTRACT

In a large bowl, mix together the oats, nuts, seeds, milk and wheat germ.

Combine brown sugar, cinnamon and oil, stirring until smooth. Mix with dry ingredients and spread mixture on a cookie sheet. Cook at 300°F. for 1 hour, stirring every 10 minutes.

Remove from oven, sprinkle with vanilla and allow to cool.

Mixture keeps well if stored in an airtight container.

YIELD: 16 SERVINGS
APPROX. CAL/SERV.: ⅓ CUP = 210

. . . . *Crunchy Cereal II*

6 CUPS ROLLED OATS (NOT QUICK-COOKING)
1 CUP WHEAT GERM (UNTOASTED)
1 CUP SESAME SEEDS (OPTIONAL)
1 CUP SLICED ALMONDS
½ CUP HONEY
½ CUP OIL
⅛ TEASPOON SALT

Combine rolled oats, wheat germ, sesame seeds and almonds; spread evenly, to a depth of ½ to 1 inch, in the bottom of a large baking pan (a jelly roll pan is good).

Mix the honey, oil and salt. (Heat gently if necessary to dissolve honey.)

Recipe continues...

Pour the syrup over the dry mixture. Combine thoroughly and place in oven at 225°F. for approximately 2 hours, lifting the mixture with a spatula about every 20 minutes.

Serve alone, or with fresh fruit and skim milk. Cereal keeps well in the refrigerator.

YIELD: 36 SERVINGS.
APPROX. CAL/SERV.: 180

Mock Sausage Patties

A good idea for those who like a meaty breakfast.

1   POUND LEAN BEEF, GROUND TWICE
1   TABLESPOON LEMON JUICE
RIND OF MEDIUM LEMON, GRATED
¼   CUP FINE DRY BREAD CRUMBS
1   TEASPOON SALT
¼   TEASPOON SAGE
¼   TEASPOON GINGER
1   BOUILLON CUBE DISSOLVED IN ½ CUP BOILING WATER

Mix together beef, lemon juice and rind, bread crumbs, salt, sage, ginger, and bouillon. Let stand 15 minutes.
Form into 8 patties about ¾-inch thick.

Brush a heavy skillet with oil, and set over heat for 1 or 2 minutes. Put in the sausage patties and cook 7 or 8 minutes on each side. Serve hot.

YIELD: 8 PATTIES
APPROX. CAL/SERV.: 140

· · · · · · · · · · *Cinnamon Coffee Cake*

1½ CUPS SIFTED FLOUR
2½ TEASPOONS BAKING POWDER
½ TEASPOON SALT
½ CUP SUGAR
1 EGG WHITE
¼ CUP OIL
¾ CUP SKIM MILK

Preheat oven to 375°F. Sift together flour, baking powder, salt and sugar. Blend in egg white, oil and milk. Stir until flour is moistened.

· · · · · · · · · · · · · · *topping*

½ CUP BROWN SUGAR
½ CUP CHOPPED PECANS
2 TABLESPOONS FLOUR
2 TABLESPOONS OIL
2 TEASPOONS CINNAMON

Make the topping by mixing together brown sugar, pecans, flour, oil and cinnamon.

Spread half of the batter in an oiled 8-inch square pan. Sprinkle with half of the topping. Add the remaining batter, and sprinkle with the rest of the topping.

Bake 30 minutes, or until done.

YIELD: 9 SERVINGS
APPROX. CAL/SERV.: 295

Quick Orange Streusel Cake

2 CUPS SIFTED FLOUR
½ CUP SUGAR
2 TEASPOONS BAKING POWDER
1 TEASPOON SALT
1 TABLESPOON GRATED ORANGE RIND
1 EGG, SLIGHTLY BEATEN
½ CUP SKIM MILK
½ CUP ORANGE JUICE
⅓ CUP OIL

Preheat oven to 375°F.

Sift together the flour, sugar, baking powder and salt. Add the orange rind.

Make a well in the dry ingredients and add the beaten egg, the milk, orange juice and oil. Stir until mixture is dampened but still somewhat lumpy. Turn into an oiled 10-inch pie pan or 8 × 8 × 2-inch cake pan.

topping

¼ CUP FLOUR
½ CUP SUGAR
2 TABLESPOONS MARGARINE

Mix the flour and sugar together, then cut in the margarine to the consistency of cornmeal.

Sprinkle over the cake batter and bake 35 minutes, or until browned.

YIELD: 9 SERVINGS
APPROX. CAL/SERV.: 305

· · · · · · · · *Whole Wheat and Soy Waffles*

1 CUP WHOLE WHEAT FLOUR
¼ CUP SOY FLOUR
1 TEASPOON SALT
2 TEASPOONS BAKING POWDER
2 EGGS, SEPARATED
1½ CUPS SKIM MILK
3 TABLESPOONS OIL
2 TABLESPOONS HONEY

Preheat waffle iron.

Stir together the two kinds of flour and the salt and baking powder. Beat egg yolks until they are light yellow; add milk, oil and honey. Blend well and stir into the dry ingredients. Beat egg whites until stiff, and fold into batter. Pour batter onto the hot waffle iron.

YIELD: ABOUT 10 WAFFLES
APPROX. CAL/SERV.: 130

· · · · · · · · · · · · · *variation*

WITH NUTS: Fold ½ cup of chopped nuts into the beaten egg whites before adding them to the batter.

APPROX. CAL/SERV.: 170

· · · · · · · · · · · · *Omelet*

Don't forsake the omelet just because it is made with eggs. Make a two-egg omelet with three whites and one yolk, or use a commercially produced egg substitute. Add a filling. The results: Less rich, but scarcely less delicious.

2 EGG WHITES
1 WHOLE EGG
1 TABLESPOON COLD WATER
DASH SALT
DASH TABASCO SAUCE
1 TABLESPOON MARGARINE

Recipe continues...

Beat eggs, water and seasonings with a fork until light and foamy. Place omelet pan over medium heat. Add margarine and swirl around in the pan until melted.

Pour egg mixture in quickly. With one hand move the pan back and forth while stirring eggs in a circular motion with a fork held in other hand. Do not scrape the bottom of the pan.

When the omelet is almost cooked, add a filling, if desired, then fold the omelet over by elevating pan to a 45-degree angle. Roll omelet out onto a plate.

You may add any of these fillings to the omelet just before fol ing.

SAUTÉED MUSHROOMS—2 TABLESPOONS = 50 CALORIES
TOMATO SAUCE, HEATED—¼ CUP = 30
CRÉOLE SAUCE (p. 244)—¼ CUP = 45
GRATED MOZZARELLA CHEESE (MADE FROM PARTIALLY SKIMMED MILK)
  —1 OUNCE = 70
CREAMED CHICKEN—¼ CUP = 50
ANY GREEN VEGETABLE—NEGLIGIBLE CALORIES
LEAN COOKED HAM OR CANADIAN BACON, CUT INTO SMALL PIECES—
  1 OUNCE = 70

YIELD: 1 SERVING
APPROX. CAL/SERV.: 210

· · · · · · · · · · · · · · *variation*

For an herb omelet, mix finely chopped parsley, chives, and chervil into egg mixture before cooking.

· · · · · · · · *Fluffy Cottage Cheese Blintzes*

1 EGG YOLK
½ CUP LOW-FAT COTTAGE CHEESE
⅓ CUP SKIM MILK
¼ CUP FLOUR
¼ TEASPOON SALT
3 EGG WHITES

In a mixing bowl beat egg yolk until thick and lemon colored.

Add cottage cheese; beat until almost smooth.

Blend in skim milk, flour, and salt.

Beat egg whites until peaks fold over. Fold into batter.

Let batter stand 5 minutes.

Pour ¼ cup of batter onto a preheated griddle which has been brushed lightly with oil. Bake until the top is bubbly and edges are baked. Turn and bake the other side.

Serve at once with mock sour cream or fruit.

YIELD: 6 SMALL BLINTZES

APPROX. CAL/SERV.: 55

Menus for Holidays and Special Occasions

*H*oliday celebrations need not mean rich food—overeating—and all the usual consequences.

No need to resist the temptation to sample "just a little" of everything on the table when your menu is made up of tempting recipes from this cookbook.

The following menus are suggested to you to trigger ideas of your own—mix and match the menus to suit your own taste and the occasion.

You will enjoy planning interesting meals. Be sure to consider attractive colors that go well together, flavors that blend, and textures that form an appealing contrast. All the while, keep your food budget in mind. The kudos of your family and guests will be your reward.

Holiday Dinner

CHRISTMAS TREE RELISH TRAY

WHIPPED COTTAGE CHEESE DIPS

*

ROAST TURKEY WITH APPLE DRESSING

*

WHIPPED POTATOES

BROCCOLI WITH MUSTARD-DILL SAUCE

CREAMED ONIONS

*

CRANBERRY-ORANGE MOLD

*

CORN BREAD MUFFINS   WATERMELON PICKLES

*

PUMPKIN CHIFFON PIE

A Very Special Dinner

MARINATED MUSHROOMS

*

ROAST STUFFED CORNISH HENS WITH WILD RICE DRESSING

*

ASPARAGUS PAR EXCELLENCE

*

SPINACH-AVOCADO-ORANGE TOSS

*

CHERRIES JUBILEE ON ICE MILK

Just Good Eating

APRICOT HAM STEAK

*

SCALLOPED POTATOES

*

DILLED GREEN BEANS

*

WALDORF SALAD
*

LEMON RICE PUDDING

. . . . *For Fish Lovers
and Those Who Didn't Know They Were!*

PLAKI
(GREEK BAKED FISH ON A BED OF TOMATOES AND ONIONS, HIGHLY SEA-
    SONED, SURROUNDED WITH GREEN SPINACH)
*

TINY NEW POTATOES
*

FRESH VEGETABLE SALAD
*

FRUIT BAVARIAN

. . . . *For a Hot Summer Day*

GAZPACHO SOUP
*

CHICKEN CASSEROLE
(A LIGHT, BUT *hot* SALAD-TYPE DISH)
OR—IF YOU PREFER IT ALL COLD—
CHICKEN-FRUIT SALAD
*

CORN BREAD-WHOLE WHEAT MUFFINS

. . . . *Football Season
"After the Game" Supper*

MUGS OF STEAMING PUMPKIN SOUP
*

HAMBURGER CORN-PONE PIE
*

RELISH TRAY OF APPETIZER VEGETABLES (FINGER FOODS)
*

JUICY RED APPLES

· · · · · · *Morning Coffee for a Festive Occasion*

FRESH PINEAPPLE FRUIT PLATTER
*

SPICED NUTS AND CINNAMON NUTS
*

PUMPKIN PECAN BREAD
WHOLE WHEAT-APRICOT BREAD
TOASTED HONEY-SESAME STICKS
ORANGE STREUSEL COFFEE CAKE
*

COFFEE

All these "finger foods" are a pleasant change from the usual table filled
with an assortment of coffee cakes that are loaded with calories and light
in nourishment.

· · · · · · · · *A Family Affair for a Busy Day*

TUNA CHOP SUEY OVER RICE
*

GRAPEFRUIT AND ORANGE SALAD
*

RAISIN OATMEAL COOKIES

· · · · · · · · · *A Summer Luncheon*

SALMON MOUSSE
*

TOMATOES ROCKEFELLER
*

COLD OVEN POPOVERS
*

CHAMPAGNE ICE
*

CINNAMON WALNUTS

. . . . *Spring Is Here*

ROAST LEG OF LAMB
ARTICHOKE HEARTS RIVIERA
BAKED GRATED CARROTS
BAKED POTATO——MOCK SOUR CREAM
REFRIGERATOR ROLLS
TOSSED GREEN SALAD
*

MERINGUE "EGG" BASKETS FILLED WITH SHERBET
    OR ORANGE-WINE CAKE

Leftovers make two delightfully different family meals:

LAMB CURRY
*

LAMB STUFFED CABBAGE
(WHOLE CABBAGE STUFFED WITH GROUND LAMB, AND BAKED IN TOMATO
    SAUCE)

. . . . . *Dinner with a Pennsylvania Dutch Accent*

GOOD AND EASY SAUERBRATEN
*

PARSLEYED POTATOES
*

SPICED RED CABBAGE
*

AUNT EMMA'S SHOO-FLY PIE

Party Buffet

CURRIED TURKEY WITH WATER CHESTNUTS
*

CRANBERRY CHUTNEY
*

TART ASPARAGUS MOLD
*

LEMON-PARSLEY ROLLS
*

FRESH FRUIT PLATTER
SHERRY THINS

Backyard Barbeque

MARINATED LONDON BROIL OR FLANK STEAK
*

HOBO VEGETABLES
*

SALAD OF TOSSED CRISP GREENS WITH BLUE CHEESE DRESSING
*

CHAPATI
*

FRESH FRUIT

Summertime Picnic

CRISPY BAKED CHICKEN
*

PARSLEY POTATO SALAD
*

FRESH VEGETABLE RELISH TRAY
*

HOME-BAKED ROLLS (REFRIGERATOR ROLLS)
*

WATERMELON BOAT
*

PEANUT BUTTER COOKIES

A Healthy Way to Start the Day!!!

MELON (IN SEASON) OR MINTED GRAPEFRUIT
*

WHOLE WHEAT-SOY WAFFLES WITH SYRUP OR BLENDED FRESH FRUIT
*

COFFEE, TEA OR LOW-FAT MILK

Buffet Supper

BRAISED SIRLOIN TIPS OVER RICE
*

PLATTER OF VEGETABLES À LA GRECQUE
*

SOUTHERN RAISED BISCUITS
*

TOSSED GREEN SALAD
*

REFRIGERATOR PINEAPPLE CHEESE CAKE

Brunch—for Two—or Just a Few

LIME MELON BALLS
*

FRESH MUSHROOM OMELET
CANADIAN BACON
WHOLE WHEAT TOAST
*

CINNAMON COFFEE CAKE

· · · · · · · · · · *Company for Lunch?*

SALAD NIÇOISE
*

HOT BISCUITS
*

FRESH FRUIT COMPOTE WITH KIRSCH

· · · · · · · · *South of the Border Luncheon*

MEXICAN CHICKEN SOUP
*

GREEN PEPPER TOSTADAS
FRIJOLES REFRITOS TOSTADAS
*

TEQUILA-LIME SHERBET

Or—to make it a dinner—just add—Enchilada Casserole

· · · · · · *Chicken Dinner—with a New Flavor*

LEMON BAKED CHICKEN
RISOTTO MILANESE
*

BAKED CURRIED FRUIT
*

FRESH VEGETABLE SALAD BOWL
*

DUQ

In a Festive Mood—Entertain Your Friends at Brunch with

BEEF MANICOTTI
*

HERBED ZUCCHINI
*

SESAME STICKS
*

A BOWL OF FRESH FRUIT
*

COFFEE

· · · · · · · · · · · · · · · *Elegance*

JULEP LAMB CHOPS, FLAMBÉ
*

TRIPLE VEGETABLE BAKE
*

CRISP TOSSED GREEN SALAD WITH GREEN GODDESS DRESSING
*

WHOLE WHEAT MUFFINS
*

FRESH STRAWBERRY PIE

· · · · · · · · · *A Vegetarian Delight*

NUTTY NOODLE CASSEROLE
*

BROCCOLI WITH LEMON
*

HERBED BAKED TOMATOES
*

MINTED GRAPEFRUIT

How to Adapt Your Own Recipes

To reduce the fat, cholesterol and caloric content of your own recipes, try these substitutions.

WHEN YOUR RECIPE CALLS FOR: USE

Sour Cream — Mock Sour Cream (see recipe on page 175), or low-fat cottage cheese blended until smooth or cottage cheese plus low-fat yogurt for flavor, or ricotta cheese made from partially skimmed milk (thinned with yogurt or buttermilk, if desired).

One can of chilled evaporated skim milk whipped with 1 teaspoon of lemon juice. Low-fat buttermilk or low-fat yogurt.

Whipped Cream — Poly Whipped Topping (recipe, page 386).

Chocolate

Cocoa blended with polyunsaturated oil or margarine (1 1-oz. square of chocolate = 3 tablespoons of cocoa + 1 tablespoon polyunsaturated oil or margarine).

Butter

[handwritten: y crisco = 3/4 c oil]
[handwritten: 1c crisco = 3/4 c oil]

Polyunsaturated margine or oil. One tablespoon butter = 1 tablespoon margarine or ¾ tablespoon oil. If you wish to substitute margarine for oil, use 1¼ cups of margarine for 1 cup of oil. Use 1¼ tablespoons of margarine for 1 tablespoon of oil.

Eggs

Use commercially produced cholesterol-free egg substitutes according to package directions. Or use 1 egg white plus 3 teaspoons of polyunsaturated oil.

Milk

Use 1 cup of skim or nonfat dry milk plus 2 tablespoons of polyunsaturated oil as a substitute for 1 cup of whole milk.

Buttermilk

One cup lukewarm nonfat milk plus 1 tablespoon of lemon juice = 1 cup buttermilk. Let the mixture stand for five minutes and beat briskly.

Cornstarch

Use 1 tablespoon flour for 1½ teaspoons cornstarch, or 2 tablespoons flour or 1 tablespoon arrowroot for 1 tablespoon cornstarch.

Cream Cheese

Blend 4 tablespoons of margarine with 1 cup dry low-fat cottage cheese. Add salt to taste and a small amount of skim milk if needed in blending mixture. Vegetables such as chopped chives or pimiento and herbs and seasonings may be added for variety.

Definitions

CHOLESTEROL is a waxy material used in many of the body's chemical processes. Everyone requires it in correct amounts for good health, but too much cholesterol in the blood encourages the development of heart and blood vessel diseases.

We get cholesterol in two ways: It is manufactured by the body; and we absorb it directly from foods of animal origin.

Egg yolks and organ meats are very high in cholesterol, and shrimp is moderately high in this substance. Such foods are restricted in these recipes. There is no cholesterol in foods of plant origin, such as fruits, vegetables, grains, cereals and nuts, and these foods are recommended.

SATURATED FATS tend to raise the level of cholesterol in the blood and are therefore restricted in these recipes. These are fats that harden at room temperature, and they are found in most animal products and some hydrogenated vegetable products:

SATURATED ANIMAL FATS are found in beef, lamb, pork and ham; in butter, cream and whole milk; and in cheeses made from cream and whole milk.

SATURATED VEGETABLE FATS are found in many solid and hydrogenated shortenings; and in coconut oil, cocoa butter and palm oil (used in commercially prepared cookies, pie fillings and nondairy milk and cream substitutes).

POLYUNSATURATED FATS, which are recommended in this meal plan, are usually liquid oils of vegetable origin. Oils such as corn, cottonseed, safflower, sesame seed, soybean and sunflower seed are high in polyunsaturated fat. They tend to lower the level of cholesterol in the blood.

Your daily use of salad dressing, cooking fats and margarines should emphasize the recommended polyunsaturated vegetable oils for their cholesterol-lowering effect.

MONOUNSATURATED FATS: Fats that neither contribute to atherosclerosis nor help to prevent it. These are fats such as those found in olive oil. You may want to use it for flavor occasionally, but it should not take the place of polyunsaturated vegetable oils.

A fat is never completely saturated, polyunsaturated or monounsaturated. For practical purposes, however, it is called one or the other. The distinction depends on the chemical make-up of the particular fat. If it is largely composed of polyunsaturated fatty acids it is called a polyunsaturated fat.

HYDROGENATION changes liquid fats to solid fats. Completely hydrogenated (hardened) oils resemble saturated fats and should be avoided or used in moderation.

FAT CONTROLLED DIET: A cholesterol-lowering diet, such as the one recommended in this cookbook, in which polyunsaturated fat intake is increased to equal that of saturated fats and total fat and cholesterol are moderately reduced.

ATHEROSCLEROSIS: A disease in which there is a thickening and narrowing of the arteries (major blood vessels). The mushy deposit of fat, cholesterol and other materials in the inner layer of the arterial wall interferes with the normal blood flow and the nourishment of the tissues. Atherosclerosis is often called "hardening of the arteries" and is the basic cause of most heart attacks and strokes.

CORONARY HEART DISEASE: The most common form of adult heart disease in which the main arteries of the heart (the coronary arteries) have atherosclerotic deposits (see atherosclerosis) and the normal blood flow of the heart is impaired.

TRIGLYCERIDES: Fatty substances found in foods and also manufactured by the body from excess sugar and/or alcohol.

When You Eat Out

Americans on the go! For some, travel is an integral part of work; for many others, it is solely a time of pleasure. Regardless, the nation's restaurant operators are hard at work to make mealtime more enjoyable for Americans on the go. Various types of food services and food to suit the convenience and tastes of every traveler have been provided—from fast-food service offering simple fare, to leisurely dining on exotic foods in attractive surroundings. The choice belongs to the consumer.

By careful selection, it is possible to eat out and still enjoy healthful, delicious meals not excessive in calories or fat. Here are a few general suggestions.

IN THE MORNING

Breakfast need not be dull. Fish, chicken or lean Canadian bacon can provide a welcome change of pace. The variety of hot or cold cereals available is almost endless. Request low-fat milk instead of cream to use in coffee and cereal. Instead of an egg every day, limit eggs to two or three a week. Cut calories by asking for a poached or soft-cooked egg, thus avoiding the fat used in frying or scrambling. Skip the Danishes and doughnuts in favor of English, corn or bran muffins or slices of whole wheat, rye and raisin bread. Try a bagel with lox or protein-rich peanut butter. Request firmly that bread or bagels not be buttered, and ask that margarine be served at the table. A small amount of jam or jelly may be used as a spread. Fruit or juice of any variety is a delightful introduction or conclusion to the first meal of the day.

AT NOONTIME

For lunch, travelers frequently prefer a light meal such as a sandwich or salad. Try turkey, chicken, fish, large fruit or vegetable salads. For sandwiches, order lean meat, chicken, turkey or peanut butter. Avoid cold cuts and cheese. Smoked salmon is an ideal selection. Eat it with cottage cheese rather than cream cheese. If you must choose among a grilled hamburger, hot dog or grilled cheese, select the hamburger, but blot the meat with a paper napkin to remove as much fat as possible.

Coleslaw and potato salad are acceptable, since mayonnaise is largely vegetable oil. Salad dressings such as French or Italian are recommended. All salad dressings, however, are rich in calories. Try sliced tomato without dressing if calories are a concern.

IN THE EVENING

The dinner hour is usually the most leisurely in the traveler's schedule. A delicious meal served with style and grace can be the highlight of the day.

It should be noted here that alcohol adds nothing but calories to the diet—about 90 calories per ounce of liquor. However, for those who do have a before-dinner cocktail, liquor mixed with water adds far fewer calories than a sweetened mixed drink such as a Manhattan or whiskey sour. Better still is a glass of dry white or red wine. Ask servers to omit snacks such as peanuts or potato chips. But if the snacks are crispy raw vegetables, enjoy them.

Study the menu thoughtfully before ordering. Select food for quality, not quantity. An appetizer of melon, fish, tomato juice or fresh vegetable plate is a wise choice. Ignore the liver paté, egg dishes and items prepared in cream sauces.

Thin broths and consommés are the best bets in the soup category. Most other soups are made with a base of fatty meat stock or have a cream sauce base. For the entrée, broiled, baked or roasted meat, fish or poultry should take precedence over fried, grilled or sautéed versions of the same. Duck and goose are taboo since they are too fatty. If fried or breaded foods are unavoidable, remove the outer crust and eat only the inside. On request, chefs are usually willing to serve entrées without fatty sauces or gravies. It is a good idea to order your meat broiled specifically without butter. Many fine restaurants make a practice of heaping a generous pat of butter on meats before broiling.

You should not expect the chef to trim off every bit of visible fat, but you can do it yourself easily enough. If chicken or turkey is served intact, remove the skin before eating because most of the fat in fowl is under the skin. As a general rule, dishes prepared in wine are acceptable as opposed to those prepared in thick sauces and gravies such as stews. Oriental cuisine offers a great variety of low-fat dishes.

Vegetables pose little problem unless they are swimming in butter. Instruct the server accordingly. Enjoy the natural goodness of a baked potato, but avoid the sour cream. For a new taste, try a dash of Worcestershire sauce or sprinkle a tablespoon of grated Parmesan cheese on the potato.

Mix your own delectable salad dressing at the table with oil and vinegar. Most salad dressings, with the exception of those made with cheese, are acceptable.

Ask that bread or rolls be served with the meal, not before. This not only prevents your filling up on bread, but cuts down on your use of butter or margarine. Remember, margarine, like butter, also adds calories.

The best choices for dessert are fruits, fruit ice, sherbet, gelatin and angel food cake without icing. Whipped cream, whipped toppings and custard sauces should not grace desserts.

An exotic finish to a gourmet meal is espresso or demitasse coffee, black with a twist of lemon. Some may prefer to forgo dessert in favor of a brandy or cordial or even add a splash of anisette to demitasse.

THE COFFEE BREAK

Coffee breaks can be culprits as far as excessive calories are concerned. Instead of cream, try milk in coffee, or better still take a fruit juice break. To alleviate hunger pangs, have a piece of fruit and leave the candy at the counter.

Lunch Box

Foods purchased away from home in vending machines or coffee shops may represent a significant stumbling block in following your master plan for low-fat, calorically controlled eating. It is to everyone's advantage, whenever possible, to get into the habit of bringing his or her own lunch, snacks, or portions thereof—to be sure of getting the proper ingredients.

A vacuum bottle for carrying hot drinks and soups is a good investment; and it can be used to carry hot dishes such as stew, chili, a casserole, or a salad to add variety. If you do not wish to bring all of your food from home, bring a portion and perhaps add a hot item from a cafeteria.

Packed lunches need not be cold or unappetizing. With a little imagination you can bring mid-day meals that offer variety and taste appeal.

Start your lunch with a refreshing salad.

. . . . *Salads*

BEAN SALAD*

FRESH VEGETABLE SALAD*

CARROT RAISIN SALAD*

* *Recipes included in this book.*

CELERY SEED COLE SLAW*
CHEF'S SALAD*
CUCUMBERS IN SOUR CREAM*
PARSLEY POTATO SALAD*
LOW-FAT COTTAGE CHEESE WITH FRUIT
CHICKEN-FRUIT SALAD*
CRISPY VEGETABLES

. . . . *Sandwiches*

Sandwiches can be interesting, too. Use breads such as whole wheat, rye, pumpernickel or Italian. Select from these spreads.

TUNA SALAD
SALMON SALAD
SLICED TURKEY OR CHICKEN
LEAN HAM OR ROAST BEEF
MEAT LOAF*
PEANUT BUTTER WITH BANANAS OR CUCUMBERS
TOMATO AND LOW-FAT CHEESE
VEGETABLE COTTAGE CHEESE*

Hot vegetable soup, baked beans or Spanish rice in a vacuum jar are appetizing alternatives to sandwiches and will add both variety and spice. Fresh fruit, such as oranges, bananas or apples, or homemade cookies will make the most nutritious away-from-home dessert. Round out your luncheon menu with low-fat yogurt or fortified skim or low-fat milk.

* *Recipes included in this book.*

$\mathscr{Fat\text{-}Cholesterol\ Chart}$

Foods which provide the major sources of fat in the diet are divided into three classifications:

DAIRY AND RELATED PRODUCTS

MEAT, POULTRY, FISH AND RELATED PRODUCTS

FATS AND OILS

This chart, based on available data, will help you become familiar with the approximate fat and cholesterol content of some foods. More research in food composition is necessary to provide data about the fatty acid and cholesterol composition of all foods.

In using this chart you may find a difference between the total fat in a food and the sum of the values listed for the fatty acids. This is because some highly polyunsaturated, long-chain fatty acids are not included in the reference material from which this chart was primarily developed (U.S.D.A.).* Computations and interpretations were prepared by the nutritionists of the American Heart Association with the assistance of the Medical Director and members of the Nutrition Committee.

* Watt, B. L. and Merrill, A. L. Composition of Foods, raw, processed, prepared. Agriculture Handbook No. 8 ARS, Washington, D.C., revised December 1963. U.S. Department of Agriculture.

Approximate food values are rounded to the nearest one-tenth for fatty acids, to the nearest calorie and to the nearest milligram of cholesterol. The household measure shown for each food is in cups, tablespoons, teaspoons, ounces, or other well-known units. This information will help you modify your favorite recipes as well as understand the fat and cholesterol content of average portions of food.

· · · · · · · · · · · · · *bibliography*

FEELEY, R. M., P. E. CRINER and B. K. WATT. Cholesterol content of foods. *J. Am. Diet. Assn.* 61 (1972): 134–148.

GRUGER, E. H., R. W. NELSON, and M. E. STANSBY. Fatty acid composition of oils from 21 species of marine fish, fresh water fish and shell fish. *J. of Am. Oil Chemists Society* 41 (1964): 662–667.

KRZECZKOWFKI, R. A. Fatty acids in raw and processed Alaska pink shrimp. *J. of Am. Oil Chemists Society* 47 (1971): 451–452.

UNITED STATES DEPARTMENT OF AGRICULTURE CONSUMER AND FOOD ECONOMICS RESEARCH DIVISION. Nutritive value of foods (Revised). *Home and Garden* Bulletin No. 72, 1971.

UNITED STATES DEPARTMENT OF AGRICULTURE. Fats in food and diet. Agriculture Information Bulletin, No. 361, revised November 1974.

WATT, B. L. and A. L. MERRILL. Composition of foods, raw, processed, prepared. Agriculture Handbook No. 8 ARS, U.S. Department of Agriculture. Washington, D.C., revised December 1963.

ZUKEL, M. C. Background information on fat controlled diets (Revised). December 1967 (Unpublished).

DAIRY PRODUCTS AND RELATED PRODUCTS

	SIZE SERVING	TOTAL FAT (GRAMS)	SATURATED FATTY ACIDS (GRAMS)	MONOUN-SATURATED FATTY ACIDS (GRAMS)	POLYUN-SATURATED FATTY ACIDS (GRAMS)	CHOLES-TEROL (MILLI-GRAMS)	FOOD ENERGY (CAL-ORIES)
Milk:							
Fluid Whole	1 cup	9.0	5.0	3.0	Trace	34	165
2% (nonfat milk solids added)	1 cup	5.0	3.0	2.0	Trace	22	145
1%	1 cup	2.5	1.6	.8	Trace	14	103
Skim	1 cup	Trace	No Data	No Data	No Data	5	90
Buttermilk (Skim)	1 cup	Trace	No Data	No Data	No Data	5	90
Cheese:							
American	1 oz.	9.0	5.0	3.0	Trace	25	105
Blue or Roquefort	1 oz.	9.0	5.0	3.0	Trace	24	105
Camembert	1⅓ oz.	9.0	5.0	3.0	Trace	35	115
Cheddar	1 oz.	9.0	5.0	3.0	Trace	28	115
Cottage–Creamed (4% fat)	1 cup	10.0	6.0	3.0	Trace	48	260
Cottage–Uncreamed	1 cup	1.0	Trace	Trace	Trace	13	170
Cream	1 Tbsp.	6.0	3.0	2.0	Trace	16	60
Feta	1 oz.	5.3	3.3	1.9	Trace	16	84
Mozzarella (made from partially skimmed milk)	1 oz.	4.7	2.3	2.3	Trace	18	70
Muenster	1 oz.	8.5	4.2	4.2	Trace	25	105
Parmesan	1 Tbsp.	1.8	1.0	.6	Trace	5	26

	SIZE SERVING	TOTAL FAT (GRAMS)	SATURATED FATTY ACIDS (GRAMS)	MONOUN- SATURATED FATTY ACIDS (GRAMS)	POLYUN- SATURATED FATTY ACIDS (GRAMS)	CHOLES- TEROL (MILLI- GRAMS)	FOOD ENERGY (CAL- ORIES)
Port du Salut	1 oz.	7.7	4.8	2.6	Trace	23	105
Ricotta (part skim)	1 oz.	2.3	1.2	1.1	Trace	9	50
Swiss	1 oz.	8.0	4.0	3.0	Trace	28	105
Tilsit	1 oz.	7.6	4.7	2.6	Trace	23	104
Cream: Light	1 Tbsp.	3.0	2.0	1.0	Trace	10	30
Heavy Whipping (unwhipped)	1 Tbsp.	6.0	3.0	2.0	Trace	20	55
Sour	1 Tbsp.	2.0	1.0	1.0	Trace	8	25
Imitation Cream products made with vegetable fat: Liquid	1 Tbsp.	2.0	1.0	Trace	0	0	20
Powdered	1 Tbsp.	1.0	Trace	Trace	0	0	10
Related Products: Ice Milk	1 cup	7.0	4.0	2.0	Trace	26	200
Ice Cream– Regular (approx. 10% fat)	1 cup	14.0	8.0	5.0	Trace	53	255
Yogurt– Plain made from partially skimmed milk	8 oz. 1 cup	4.0	2.0	1.0	Trace	17	125

COOKED MEAT, POULTRY, FISH AND RELATED PRODUCTS

	SIZE SERVING	TOTAL FAT (GRAMS)	SATURATED FATTY ACIDS (GRAMS)	MONOUN-SATURATED FATTY ACIDS (GRAMS)	POLYUN-SATURATED FATTY ACIDS (GRAMS)	CHOLES-TEROL (MILLI-GRAMS)	FOOD ENERGY (CAL-ORIES)
Lean Beef, Lamb, Pork & Ham	3 oz.	8.4	3.9	3.5	Trace	77	189
Lean Veal	3 oz.	4.8	2.4	2.3	Trace	84	177
Poultry	3 oz.	5.1	1.5	2.6	1.0	74	150
Fish[1]	3 oz.	4.5	.9	No Data	.3	63	126
Shellfish: Crab	½ cup	2.0	.5	.7	.8	62	85
Clams	6 large	1.0	.3	.3	.4	36	65
Lobster	½ cup	1.0	No Data	No Data	No Data	62	68
Oysters	3 oz. (6 oysters)	1.5	.5	.2	.8	45	53
Scallops	3 oz.	1.3	.4	.1	.8	45	90
Shrimp	½ cup (11 large)	1.0	.2	.3	.5	96	100
Canned Fish: Sardines canned in oil; drained solids	3¼ oz. (1 can)	9.0	No Data	No Data	No Data	129	175
Salmon, pink canned[1]	3 oz.	5.0	2.0	1.0	Trace	32	120
Tuna packed in oil; drained solids[1]	3 oz.	8.2	3.0	No Data	2.0	65	197

[1] *Does not account for all of the highly polyunsaturated fatty acids present in fish.*

	SIZE SERVING	TOTAL FAT (GRAMS)	SATURATED FATTY ACIDS (GRAMS)	MONOUN- SATURATED FATTY ACIDS (GRAMS)	POLYUN- SATURATED FATTY ACIDS (GRAMS)	CHOLES- TEROL (MILLI- GRAMS)	FOOD ENERGY (CAL- ORIES)
Related Products: Liver (Beef)	3 oz.	3.4	No Data	No Data	No Data	372	136
Sweet Breads, calf	3 oz.	1.8	No Data	No Data	No Data	396	82
Frankfurters (all beef– 30% fat)	8/lb.	17.0	7.1	6.7	Trace	34	185
Eggs, chicken, whole	1 large	6.0	2.0	3.0	Trace	250[2]	80

[2] *Cholesterol is found only in egg yolks.*

FATS AND OILS

	SIZE SERVING	TOTAL FAT (GRAMS)	SATURATED FATTY ACIDS (GRAMS)	MONOUN-SATURATED FATTY ACIDS (GRAMS)	POLYUN-SATURATED FATTY ACIDS (GRAMS)	CHOLES-TEROL (MILLI-GRAMS)	FOOD ENERGY (CAL-ORIES)
Peanut Butter	2 Tbsp.	16.0	3.2	8.0	4.5	0	190
Bacon, cooked crisp	2 slices	8.0	3.0	4.0	1.0	14	90
Bacon, Canadian (unheated)	3¼ oz.	14.4	5.0	6.0	1.0	75	216
Butter	1 Tbsp.	12.0	6.0	4.0	Trace	35	100
Lard	1 Tbsp.	13.0	5.0	6.0	1.0	13	115
Tub Margarines: Safflower oil, liquid[1,2]	1 Tbsp.	11.2	1.5	2.5	6.7	0	100
Corn oil, liquid[1,2]	1 Tbsp.	11.2	2.0	3.6	5.3	0	100
Stick Margarines Corn oil, liquid[1,2]	1 Tbsp.	11.2	2.1	4.6	4.1	0	100
Stick or Tub Margarines Partially hydrogenated or hardened fat[1,2]	1 Tbsp.	11.2	2.4	6.2	2.0	0	100
Imitation Margarine (Diet)[2]	1 Tbsp.	5.5	1.0	1.8	2.5	0	50
Mayonnaise	1 Tbsp.	11.0	2.0	2.0	6.0	8	100

First ingredient as listed on label.

Summary of available data. Composition of margarine changes periodically. Follow guidelines in section on Shopping Tips when purchasing margarine.

	SIZE SERVING	TOTAL FAT (GRAMS)	SATURATED FATTY ACIDS (GRAMS)	MONOUN-SATURATED FATTY ACIDS (GRAMS)	POLYUN-SATURATED FATTY ACIDS (GRAMS)	CHOLES-TEROL (MILLI-GRAMS)	FOOD ENERGY (CAL-ORIES)
Vegetable Shortening (hydrogenated)	1 Tbsp.	13.0	3.0	6.0	3.0	0	110
Poly-unsaturated Oils: Corn Oil	1 Tbsp.	14.0	2.0	4.0	8.0	0	125
Cottonseed Oil	1 Tbsp.	14.0	4.0	3.5	6.5	0	125
Safflower Oil	1 Tbsp.	14.0	1.5	2.0	10.5	0	125
Sesame Oil	1 Tbsp.	14.0	2.0	6.0	6.0	0	125
Soybean Oil	1 Tbsp.	14.0	2.0	3.5	8.5	0	125
Soybean Oil (lightly hydrogenated)	1 Tbsp.	14.0	2.0	7.0	4.8	0	125
Sunflower Oil	1 Tbsp.	14.0	1.6	3.9	8.5	0	125
Mono-unsaturated Oils: Olive Oil	1 Tbsp.	14.0	2.8	7.0	3.9	0	125
Peanut Oil	1 Tbsp.	14.0	2.0	10.0	2.0	0	125
Saturated Oil Coconut Oil	1 Tbsp.	14.0	13.0	1.0	Trace	0	125

Index